FOREIGN POLICY IN A CONSTRUCTED WORLD

International Relations in a Constructed World

International Relations in a Constructed World
Vendulka Kubálková, Nicholas Onuf, and Paul Kowert, editors

Commonsense Constructivism, or The Making of World Affairs
Ralph Pettman

Constructing International Relations: The Next Generation
Karin M. Fierke and Knud Erik Jørgensen, editors

Foreign Policy in a Constructed World
Vendulka Kubálková, editor

FOREIGN POLICY IN A CONSTRUCTED WORLD

VENDULKA KUBÁLKOVÁ

EDITOR

M.E.Sharpe
Armonk, New York
London, England

Library of Congress Cataloging-in-Publication Data

Foreign policy in a constructed world / by Vendulka Kubálková, editor.
    p. cm. — (International relations in a constructed world)
    Includes bibliographical references and index.
    ISBN 0-7656-0787-5 (cloth: alk. paper) — ISBN 0-7656-0788-3 (pbk.: alk. paper)
    1. International relations—Philosophy. 2. Constructivism (Philosophy) I. Kubálková,
V. II. Series.

JZ1242 .F675 2001   2001034490
327.1′01—dc21   CIP

Printed in the United States of America

The paper used in this publication meets the minimum requirements of
American National Standard for Information Sciences
Permanence of Paper for Printed Library Materials,
ANSI Z 39.48-1984.

BM (c)   10   9   8   7   6   5   4   3   2   1
BM (p)   10   9   8   7   6   5   4   3   2   1

For Nicholas Onuf

Contents

List of Tables and Figures

Tables

Figures

Boxes

FOREIGN POLICY IN A CONSTRUCTED WORLD

Introduction

Vendulka Kubálková

I first came into contact with *constructivism* in 1995 when faculty and graduate students at Florida International University and University of Miami formed a continuing seminar called the Miami International Relations Group. Among the group's founding members was Nicholas Onuf, whose *World of Our Making* (1989) helped to bring into focus the processes of social construction in the field of International Relations (IR).[1]

When we established the Miami IR Group, constructivism was still very much on the margins of the field. It was misunderstood and frequently confused with the poststructuralist/postmodern preoccupation with textual deconstruction. Since then, constructivism has gained considerable popularity in IR and in other fields, in the United States and other countries. Constructivism is now literally everywhere: in literary theory, sociology, communications, anthropology, and feminist studies to name but a few fields. In Britain, constructivism—or constitutivism, as it is sometimes called there— has also excited a great deal of attention (Smith 1996, 26–27). British scholars are rediscovering in E.H. Carr and Hedley Bull an emphasis on international society that they identify as constructivist in character. Constructivist scholarship in European countries is also sharply on the increase (cf. Fierke and Jørgensen 2001).

The meteoric rise has culminated in the sudden recognition of constructivism by mainstream IR scholars. In journals surveying the state of the art in the field in the late 1990s, constructivism is prominently mentioned (e.g., Katzenstein, Keohane, and Krasner, 1998). In one such survey article, there is even a picture drawn of three Doric pillars on which the study of IR allegedly rests (Figure I.1). Constructivism is one of these three pillars, along with realism and liberalism. Why this sudden fame? After all, IR constructivism is only into its second decade, merely in its teens, a mere

Figure I.1   **Three Approaches to IR** (based on Walt 1998, 38)

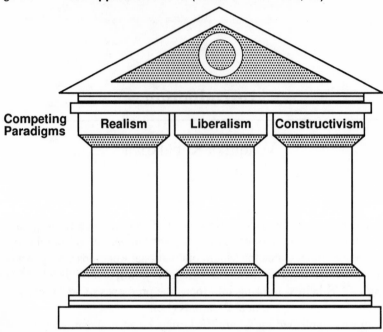

moment compared to the two millennia that, by pointing to Thucydides, realism, the main approach to IR, claims for its genealogy. Furthermore, as the
third approach to IR, constructivism is portrayed as a successor to the "radical," that is, the mainly Marxist-derived traditions (Walt 1998) with equally
distinguished genealogy.

Despite the increasing interest in constructivism and a growing body of literature on the subject, my graduate students keep asking the same questions:

- "How can I use constructivism in my research?"
- "How do I write a constructivist dissertation?"
- "If I am interested in identity, culture, religion, or other 'ideational'
  aspects of international relations, does it mean that I am—or I have to
  be—a constructivist?"
- "How else, without necessarily focusing on identity and culture, do I be-
  come a constructivist?"
- "How do I know a constructivist when I see one?"
- "What *is* constructivism and why is it suddenly so important?"

Onuf's *World of Our Making* is difficult to read; so, for that matter, is Friedrich
Kratochwil's *Rules, Norms and Decisions* (1989), which is also a key text for

constructivism, and Alexander Wendt's *Social Theory of International Politics* (1999), which is the latest general treatment of the subject. Why is it that constructivism is apparently so difficult? On closer scrutiny some forms of constructivism are quite simple, despite the technically difficult idiom characteristic of all constructivists. Some are more difficult to grasp. Some, despite their difficult idiom, propose only cosmetic changes to well-established approaches. Some, particularly the form of constructivism on which this book focuses, the "rule-oriented" constructivism that Onuf introduced in 1989 and then refined as a Miami IR Group member,[2] requires a rethinking of how social scientists see and understand the world. However, if students are first exposed to this form of constructivism without prior training in positivist social science, they do not find it very difficult. In fact, in many regards, constructivism is closer to common sense than the mainstream approaches.

About This Book

This book is part of a series entitled "International Relations in a Constructed World," inspired by the book of the same name (Kubalkova, Onuf, and Kowert 1998) and reflecting the work of the Miami IR Group over the first two years of its existence. It is meant to build on its predecessor while taking into account the critical comments made by readers and reviewers. We have tried to strengthen three important aspects of the book: first, its pedagogical purpose and accessibility to students and lay audience; second, the discussion of more than one form of constructivism; and, third, attention to empirical case studies.

The Pedagogical Purpose of This Volume

First of all, there still does not exist a constructivist primer written specifically with upper-division undergraduate and new graduate students in mind, although our 1998 book has gone some way to filling that gap. The rationale of this volume is primarily pedagogical. I stress this point as a justification for the inevitable simplifications that certainly characterize my contribution to this volume, chapters 1, 3, and 5. These three chapters are closely interconnected, each providing a framework for the other. I pack into chapter 1 a summary of an enormous amount of scholarly writing regarding evolution of the split between Foreign Policy Analysis and International Relations studied as a system. In 1961, David Singer formulated this split as the "levels of analysis" problem. Each of these two levels—the behavioral and the systemic—starts from different premises, calls on different methods of analysis, and yields propositions altogether different in scale. Scholars working at the behavioral level typically focus on foreign policy decision makers, and their work is readily identified as Foreign Policy Analysis (FPA). Scholars working at the systemic level focus on the relation between states as a political system, but no single label has stuck to their work. For convenience, I have called them International Politics (IP). There are literally hundreds of volumes, entire libraries, devoted to FPA and just as many devoted to IP (or to IR where this is presumed to consist wholly of IP). The purpose of my chapter is not to replace the massive literature on these subjects, but to set the stage for one of the main constructivist claims of this book—namely, that the distinction between foreign policy analysis and IR studied as a system is artificial, that it can and should be eliminated, and that one of the important roles of constructivism is its assistance in this elimination process.

Chapter 1 is so thickly packed with definitions that if they were in alphabetic order, the chapter could pass for a glossary. Because it covers so much material, it might require some background or, as my students confirmed, repeated reading. In contrast to chapter 1, chapter 3 certainly does not need much of a background. Entitled "A Constructivist Primer," it takes nothing for granted, using metaphors, stories, and a multitude of tables to explain constructivism and how to go about using it for research. Chapter 5, the third of the three pedagogically motivated chapters, is a case study for both chapters 1 and 3. I have concluded that in a book written for students it is incumbent upon me not only to outline the various frameworks, but also to show in practical examples how they work. I take one particular case, Gorbachev's "new thinking," and using the frameworks I set out in chapters 1 and 3, I subject "new thinking" to a number of different approaches, both constructivist and nonconstructivist.

Throughout this part of the text I draw on insights gained from teaching constructivism, from the countless useful comments students made on early drafts of these chapters, from the work of my colleagues in the Miami IR Group, and from its student members—who have used constructivism in their empirical work, in this volume, and elsewhere. However, I alone take the responsibility for the simplifications to which some of my colleagues might object. I am happy to accept the blame, since I am convinced of constructivism's tremendous potential for IR studies and think it is important that it becomes accessible to more than an exclusive group of academic cognoscenti.

Different Forms of Constructivism

The second lesson we have learned from the reception of the 1998 book was that, for example, according to a review in *American Political Science Review*,[3] we have apparently not paid enough attention to distinctions among the various forms of constructivism and particularly their relation to the main-stream form of constructivism. When we worked on our first volume, interest in constructivism had only just started to pick up. It was by no means clear at that time that mainstream scholars would undergo a change of heart in this regard, and that constructivism would become one of the main IR approaches. Now that constructivism has caught on, we have tried to correct the problem identified above.

There are chapters at the beginning (e.g., chapter 2) and at the end (e.g., chapter 11) that deal with the constructivism of its most visible contemporary proponent, Alexander Wendt. Throughout the volume, particularly in chapters 1 and 5, there are references to other forms of constructivism, as well.

Case Studies

Third, case studies in our first volume, some critics averred, were not always found convincing in demonstrating constructivist precepts and strengths. I have already explained that chapter 3, "A Constructivist Primer," has been written specifically for the student who is choosing a research topic and looking for a framework to use. Chapter 3 assumes no prior knowledge of constructivism. It seeks to facilitate students' first encounters with constructivism and to show even the least theoretically inclined of them the empirical possibilities of "rule-oriented" constructivism. The four steps that I use to structure the chapter make clear the points of difference among constructivists, thus enabling students to make their choices more readily.

Not all chapters, however, have been written with students in mind. The book is divided into three parts. Moving from Part I, "Frameworks," which prepares the reader for the empirical work, to Part II, "Constructivists at Work," the balance of theory and practice shifts in the direction of the latter. We can also see how constructivist premises inform different types of research. In the process, not only do we come to see how constructivism sheds light on specific "cases" or disciplines, but also how constructivism is itself expanded beyond its original premises as a result of the healthy interaction with other disciplines. This is possible because constructivists do not generally feel that they need to remain within the boundaries of any given discipline. As these boundaries become porous, new areas of inquiry are exposed.

Chapter 2 has been specially commissioned for this book by a leading British IR theorist, Steve Smith. In his characteristically lucid way, Professor Smith explains some key terms and issues, complementing the introductory chapter 1. He discusses the difference between rationalist and reflectivist approaches, for example, and between explaining and understanding and relevant terms of philosophy of science. He also deals with the question of the relationship between constructivism and more mainstream IR approaches, and the relationship between the different constructivisms. He singles out for special attention the mainstream constructivist Alexander Wendt and the Miami IR Group, of which most, but not all, contributors to this volume are members. The title of Smith's chapter paraphrases Wendt's famous claim that "anarchy is what states make of it." Smith uses the paraphrase "foreign policy is what states make of it" to make two important points: first, that mainstream constructivism, certainly in the form that Wendt presents it, can make only a limited contribution to the study of foreign policy. The second important point Smith makes goes to the heart of how we study IR, arguing that the split between IP and FPA is an artificial and distorting one, and that it ought to be overcome.

Chapter 4, Onuf's "Speaking of Policy," is theoretically the most demanding of the entire volume and will no doubt be added to the collection of key theoretical pieces elucidating and extending his initial constructivist statement (1989). Despite its technical difficulty, its inclusion in this volume is crucial in at least three respects. First, FPA is centered on the study of policy, and yet the term "policy," argues Onuf, has been used very sloppily. Second, Onuf uses speech act theory to show how agents interact strategically by making policy statements. No rule-oriented constructivist could engage in the study of FPA without this understanding. Finally, Onuf demonstrates the point made in chapters 1 and 3, that is, the virtue of rule-oriented constructivism and its compatibility with a great deal of work produced by scholars in other fields. Onuf disagrees with constructivists such as Martha Finnemore who point out that with the realization that interests of states are not given (and identical), the validity and utility of strategic interaction and rational choice theory, the main model for understanding of FPA, is undermined and can no longer be used (Finnemore 1996, ix). Onuf disagrees and, on the contrary, gives both the game theory and the rational choice theory a new lease on life by giving a constructivist spin to the key contributions made by Thomas Schelling on the game theory and Jon Elster on the theory of rational choice.

The collection of case studies of Part II is a sampler of applications of a constructivist approach to a range of topics. Each of the contributors selects (defines and develops) his/her own approach. Nizar Messari's chapter analyzing U.S. foreign policy toward Islamic countries, for example, draws on postmodernist ideas of "the Other" and the work of David Campbell. Michael W. Collier's study of corruption in the foreign policy of Latin American countries will appeal to the student unwilling to give up some aspects of positivism and causality, while making the four steps that rule-oriented constructivism depends upon nonetheless. Government corruption is fast becoming one of the key problems of our times, and Collier uses constructivism to show how to combine within constructivist framework insights of several disciplines/approaches into a more comprehensive social theory of corruption. Gonzalo Porcel Quero focuses on the study of Spanish foreign policy during Franco's time to show how rule-oriented constructivism can shed light on the important links among the makings of history, what he calls the politics of memory, and the formulation of foreign policy. In doing so, he describes how domestic politics can be a source for and a context from which foreign policy emanates. The opposite also holds true; that is, foreign policy often becomes a tool for the legitimation of domestic politics. Thus, the careful study of Franco's regime casts much doubt on the separation between domestic and foreign policy. It also calls into question the legitimation discourse of the regime itself. His work, therefore, has important implications for a number of fields. It highlights the importance of historical analysis for FPA. It also underscores how one might go about classifying different types of regimes according to the rule-type that is most prevalent in them. By doing all of this, and perhaps more importantly, he shows us how one can move freely and productively from the field of IR into comparative politics, social theory, or linguistics, and vice versa. Chapter 8 by Shiping Zheng is an example of a nonmember of the Miami IR Group picking up Onuf's framework to elucidate two points in the relation of the People's Republic of China and the Republic of China (Taiwan), the importance of "words" in constructing what is China and the relationship between the two claimants of that mantle and the flexibility afforded by constructivism in integrating in his theoretical framework "agents" other than the two states.

As already mentioned, chapter 5 uses one case to show the range of different narratives produced by different approaches, constructivist and mainstream, in making sense of Gorbachev's "new thinking." The number of case studies is small, but it represents different degrees of uses of constructivism. The choice of the topics is also not without significance. They include the discussion of the end of the Cold War, China, and Islam in U.S. foreign policy, international corruption, and an example of what Porcel Quero calls "historical constructivism."

Part III, "Reflections," contains a critical evaluation of the volume and of constructivism from positions close to the two perspectives in the middle of which constructivism is believed to stand (Adler 1997), namely, postmodernism (chapter 10 by Ralph Pettman) and positivism (chapter 11 by Paul Kowert).

Both Parts I and II amply demonstrate a point that might be found surprising, namely, that the relationship between constructivism and FPA is one of mutual benefit. Constructivism has already established its relevance to IP.

Cumulatively, the constructivist study of IR will help to integrate these two issue areas once again and return foreign policy to its place in the context of international system. Conversely, FPA is highly relevant to constructivism as a source of conceptual enrichment because it anticipates many constructivist concerns, although to a constructivist's eye, in a somewhat truncated way. Thus, although this book is about foreign policy, it is at the same time a primer for the constructivist study of international relations in general.

Notes

My thanks go not only to the Miami IR Group members, but to countless graduate students on whom I practiced my explanations of constructivism. They made valuable comments on how to improve particularly chapters 1, 3, and 4. Nick Onuf and Ralph Pettman as usual helped me with the different drafts, Ralph Pettman in particular "anglicizing" my prose.

1. Here I follow convention. If "international relations" is capitalized, I and other contributors are referring to an academic field of study. If the term is not capitalized, then it refers to the subject matter of that field of study.

2. The term "rule-oriented constructivism" is Kurt Burch's, who distinguishes it from structure-oriented constructivism and norm-oriented constructivism. See 2001. The term "rule based" has been used by Emmanuel Adler (1997).

3. See Mark Peceny's book review of Kubálková et al., 1998, in *American Political Science Review*.

References

Adler, Emmanuel. 1997. "Seizing the Middle Ground: Constructivism in World Politics." *European Journal of International Relations* 3: 319–363.

Burch, Kurt. Forthcoming. "Toward a Constructivist Comparative Politics." In Daniel Green, ed. *Constructivist Comparative Politics: Theoretical Issues and Case Studies.* Armonk, NY: M.E. Sharpe.

Fierke, K.M., and Jørgensen, K.E., eds. 2001. *Constructing International Relations: The Next Generation.* Armonk, NY: M.E. Sharpe.

Finnemore, Martha. 1996. *National Interests in International Society.* Ithaca, NY: Cornell University Press.

Katzenstein, Peter J., Keohane, Robert O., and Krasner, Stephen D. 1998. "International Organization and the Study of World Politics." *International Organization* 52(4): 645–685.

Kratochwil, Friedrich V. 1989. *Rules, Norms, and Decisions: On the Contradictions of Practical and Legal Reasoning in International Relations and Domestic Affairs.* Cambridge, UK: Cambridge University Press.

Kubálková, Vendulka, Onuf, Nicholas, and Kowert, Paul, eds. 1998. *International Relations in a Constructed World.* Armonk, NY: M.E. Sharpe.

Onuf, Nicholas Greenwood. 1989. *World of Our Making. Rules and Rule in Social Theory and International Relations.* Columbia: University of South Carolina Press.

Peceny, Mark. 1999. Book Review. *American Political Science Review* 94(1): 243.

Singer, J. David. 1961. "The Level of Analysis Problem in International Relations." In K.

Knorr and S. Verba, eds. *The International System: Theoretical Essays*, pp. 85–90. Princeton, NJ: Princeton University Press.

Smith, Steve. 1996. "The Self-Images of a Discipline: A Genealogy of International Relations Theory." In Ken Booth and Steve Smith, eds. *International Theory Today*, pp. 1–37. University Park: Pennsylvania State University Press.

Walt, Stephen. 1998. "International Relations: One World, Many Theories." *Foreign Policy* 110: 29–46.

Wendt, Alexander. 1999. *Social Theory of International Politics*. Cambridge, UK: Cambridge University Press.

I
Frameworks

1

Foreign Policy, International Politics, and Constructivism

Vendulka Kubálková

The field of International Relations (IR) split in the 1950s into two parts: Foreign Policy Analysis (FPA) and the study of International Politics (IP) as seen from a systemic point of view.[1] At the core of this split was the opening up of the state, previously regarded in IR as a black box whose contents were of interest only to Political Scientists. Foreign policy analysts opened up the box in order to explain state behavior. In a nutshell, FPA directs attention to the attributes of states as units in order to reach conclusions about their relations. In contrast, IP focuses its attention on the relations of states, as a system, in order to learn about the system's attributes. One proceeds from the parts to the whole, the other from the whole to the parts. Once FPA had "moved inside the box" (Figure 1.1), scholars on each side saw little need for each other, and the two subfields began to grow apart.

The purpose of this chapter is to set the scene for the entire volume, to introduce and explain most of the terms (referring to those handled in chapter 2) and include enough information about each of them to enable the reader to follow the main theme of the book, which is the relevance of constructivism in IR to both FPA and IP subfields. Indeed, most constructivists believe that the FPA/IP split need not have occurred and that constructivism provides the tools for putting the two fields back together.

I divide this chapter into two parts so that I can go twice over the same ground, each time from a different angle. The first time around, I introduce the main elements of my argument by defining FPA and IP, and then by showing how they differ from each other and from other cognate fields and why they developed the way they did. I take this story to the point at which constructivism makes an entry into IR and discuss briefly how it has made its presence felt. The second part goes over the same ground and both sim-

Figure 1.1   **Foreign Policy and International Politics**

Foreign Policy
multilayered process,
associated with official
contacts with
foreign countries,
including,
decision making,
models of bargaining and
rational choice strategies,
objectives, and means,
**internal environment or
domestic sources of fp**,
fp apparatus of agencies,
relations, hierarchies,
communications within, the
nature of domestic politics,
psychological factors
perceptions, and
misperceptions, ideologies,
psychology of individuals
and groups, images
of other countries,
**external environment
(also called middle
range theories)**, i.e.,
geopolitics, technology,
geography, development
"lateral expansion", agent
structure debate.

International Politics
relations of interconnected parts
"black boxes"

State D

State A

State B

State C

State E

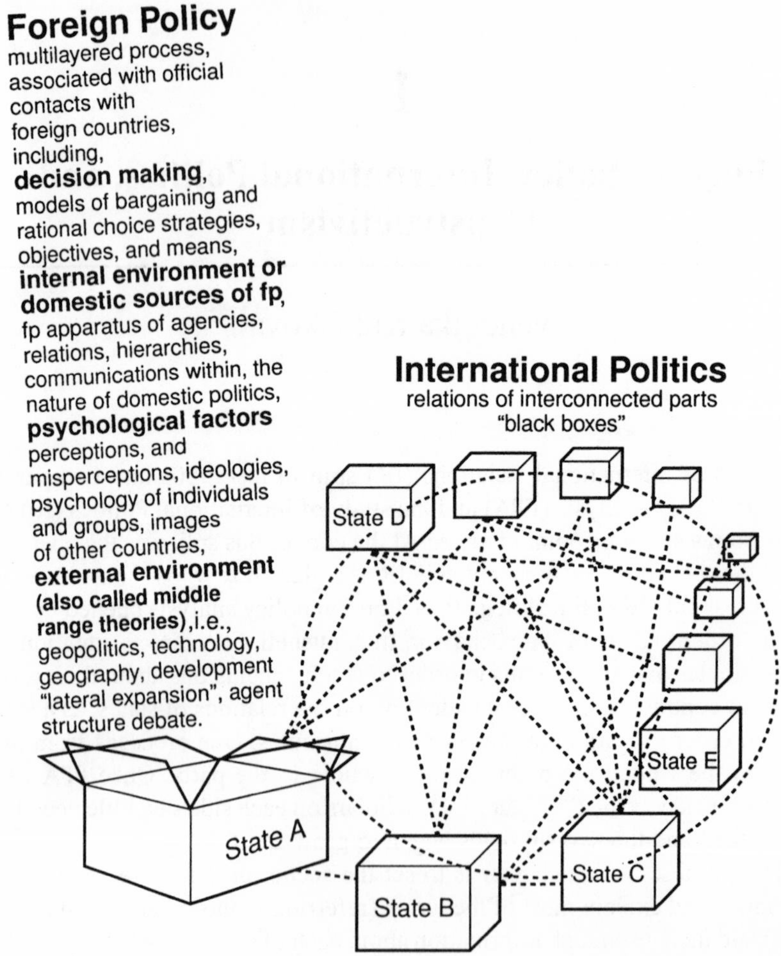

plifies and complicates the argument at the same time. I distill the main question that each of these approaches has tried to answer. This enables me to
show in a much more practical way the differences among the different approaches, while at the same time adding more detail of the individual approaches and introducing such important concepts as rationality, identity,
intersubjectivity, decision making, structure, and institutions. There are four
tables in this chapter and I refer to them many times throughout the entire
chapter. In fact, each follows from the one before, zooming in on a particular
part of it. There are entire libraries devoted to FPA and to IP, and the

constructivist literature is also growing rapidly. It is important for me to stress that the purpose of my brief walk through FPA and IP is not to make a contribution to their respective literatures or to suggest they ought to be skipped. On the contrary, the chapter and the volume are supposed to encourage the reader to go back to the IR literature, and to FPA in particular, to look at it with constructivist eyes.

FPA and IP, Agent and Structure

To this day, FPA and IP continue to be separated,[2] intellectually disconnected, and even in some respects contradicting each other's assumptions and conclusions (Light 1994, 93). Their separation originally coincided with the "scientific" or "behavioralist" revolution in the social sciences, its controversial impact on IR studies having been played out in the course of what has been known as the Second Debate. Scholars on both sides of the FPA/IP divide stood together in this debate, since their common intention was to make IR more scientific. To do so, scholars on both sides agreed that they had to leave a great deal out of the picture. They were diametrically opposed, however, in what need not be studied. In effect, each ceded what it did not study to the other. Both claimed mutual complementarity of focus, and a primary connection to realism, the main source of wisdom in IR that had emerged victorious over "idealism" in what is referred to in IR studies as the First Debate. Realism proved an ever more tenuous bond between FPA and IP, however. For half a century now scholars on each side of the divide have followed their own paths. They have drawn on different intellectual sources, they have developed separate journals and subsections of professional organizations, and they have offered different university courses and, in many cases, different fields for the examination of graduate students.

Before the split, the study of FPA and IP differed from each other largely in emphasis. IR scholars were engaged in the description and evaluation of dramatic events and self-dramatizing individuals. What became later two separate—FPA and IP—perspectives were still combined, with one the backdrop to the other. FPA lifted foreign policy out of its broader context. There was still a lot left. According to most definitions, FPA refers to a complex, multilayered process, consisting of the objectives that governments pursue in their relations with other governments and their choice of means to attain these objectives. Governments rely in this regard on professional staffs, including diplomats, trade negotiators, and military officials, but they draw on other resources as well. Thus foreign policy encompasses the complicated communications within governments and amongst its diverse agents, plus the perceptions and misperceptions, the images of other countries, and the ideologies and personal dispositions of everyone involved. An important part of the study of foreign policy has been the nature and impact of domestic politics.[3]

During the formative first twenty years of FPA, a multitude of systematic (but not systemic) frameworks was developed for what became known as the comparative study of foreign policy making, for a long time one of the main approaches to FPA. Comparative studies of foreign policy were thought to increase the generalizing power of the sorts of explanations that lent themselves to scientific treatment. If the point was to develop theory that would substitute for IR theory, many scholars thought that such an undertaking sacrificed the descriptive richness that followed from concentrating analytic attention on particular governments, important decisions, and the complexities of domestic politics. FPA scholars either were guided by more modest or "middle-range" theories, or they took a single state as a frame of reference, focusing on what was styled as the "internal setting of foreign policy" or the study of "domestic sources of FP." "Comparative studies of foreign policy," "middle-range theories," and "domestic sources of FP" were for a long time the three main approaches to FPA.

As we shall discuss later, IR scholars had always treated states as "actors" analogous to human individuals. FPA turned away from states as quasi-persons to the actual people who constitute governments and act on behalf of states. As the term "behavioralism" suggests, the focus on people's "behavior," and not their motives or mental processes, was seen as the key to making IR scientific. Behavior, it was argued, provided direct factual evidence that could be objectively measured and used to evaluate theoretically derived hypotheses. The goal of FPA as a science—namely, the search for regularities in the behavior across decision makers in different states, but also in distinct groups of states, categorizing and comparing them either by region, size, political system, or degree of development—was consistent with the positivist goals of the social sciences discussed in greater detail in chapter 2.

In the 1980s and 1990s, Comparative Foreign Policy practically vanished, at least in part because the enthusiasm for science waned in IR, and perhaps also because of new developments on the other side of the intellectual divide. In the years when FPA flourished in the name of behavioral science, IP had failed to provide a scientific account of the system. The turning point did not come until 1979 when Kenneth Waltz published his seminal work, *Theory of International Politics*. By this time the fortunes of FPA and realism, the doctrine underpinning both FPA and IP, had been flagging. The account of the system provided by Waltz, referred to as structural realism or neorealism, could claim to be scientific because it found a place for people—highly abstracted people—who behave, as rational maximizers, very much the way economists claim that people do in a market. Markets in economics are structures, and Waltz borrowed the idea. Waltz's systematic effort to formulate a general realist theory of international politics was based on the use of the concept of structure, which gave this form of realism the adjective "structural." Waltz used the concept of structure both to prop up the concept of system and to exclude all else from consideration. Waltz's elegantly simple reformulation of realism abstracted from the picture everything internal to states: subjective influences, ideas, unique events—all of which affect actual foreign policies. Once the mantle of science had passed from FPA to IP, however, most foreign policy analysts have been content to describe, although with a high degree of sophistication and subtlety, the problems foreign-policy makers face and the ways they respond to those problems.

Constructivism into the Breach

Since the late 1980s and the early 1990s, when constructivism as a new approach was introduced to IR, constructivists found in the split between foreign policy and international politics an important point of departure. Superficially at least, the FPA/IP split appears to be a variation of a distinction extremely important to constructivists, namely, between the foreign-policy maker as agent on the one hand and the structure of the international system on the other.

The arrival of constructivism complicates a feature characteristic of approaches to IR, namely, that they borrow from other fields. As Figure 1.2 illustrates, FPA and IP have drawn on different ideas from different disciplines. The arrival of constructivism has coincided with what has been known as the Third Debate in IR, a debate over the positivist assumptions of science and their relevance to social phenomena. Thanks to this debate, the range of intellectual influences has been significantly enlarged, as Steve Smith shows in the next chapter. The FPA/IP split literally begs to be explored through the concepts of agent and structure, as developed in sociology and adopted by constructivists. Constructivists applaud the tendency of FPA to look for the agent—the foreign-policy decision maker—wherever he/she might be found. The active mode of foreign policy expressed even in the term "making" also resonates with the constructivists' stress on processes of social construction. Constructivists, however, disapprove of the way the FP/IP split developed, since agent and structure should never be torn apart nor should one be given priority over the other.

Constructivists differ on what to do about the latter tendency (Figure 1.3). Their differences undoubtedly stem from the fact that the terms agent and structure are controversial in sociology, whence they were brought to IR, as well as among constructivists in IR.

Figure 1.2   **Intellectual Influences on FP/IP**

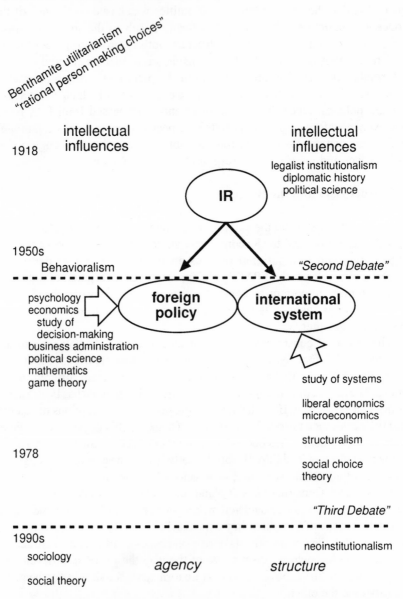

Despite appearances, the correspondence of the terms "agent" and "struc-ture" with FPA and IP respectively is as partial and misleading as the other pair categories, or binary oppositions, used to separate FPA and IP—namely, "micro-macro" and states as units versus the system of states. Looming over

Figure 1.3   **Agency and Structure and IP/FP Split**

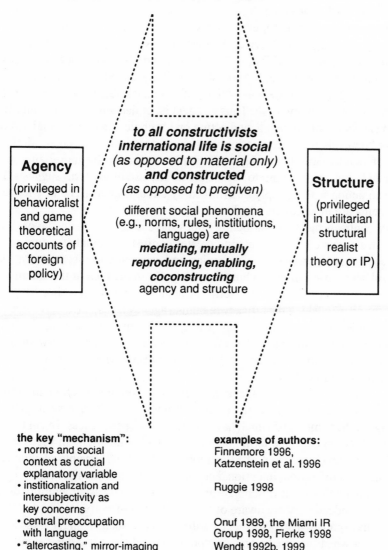

the key "mechanism":
• norms and social
  context as crucial
  explanatory variable
• institionalization and
  intersubjectivity as
  key concerns
• central preoccupation
  with language
• "altercasting," mirror-imaging

examples of authors:
Finnemore 1996,
Katzenstein et al. 1996

Ruggie 1998

Onuf 1989, the Miami IR
Group 1998, Fierke 1998
Wendt 1992b, 1999

these pairs are the great binaries of Western thought: subjectivity and objectivity, atomism and holism, free will and determinism. To compound the confusion, the terms "agent" and "structure" came to IR already burdened by an abundance of other concrete meanings in ordinary language—"agent" as in the KGB or CIA or as in "insurance agent," and "structure" as in architecture or a fixed, material inanimate object presumed always to have been there, primordial or given.

The origin of terms "agent" and "structure" gives some clues as to their abstract meanings in the service of constructivism. "Agent" derives from the Latin verb *agere*—"to drive, to lead, to act, to do"—and it means literally a "person doing something." And "structure" is derived from the past participle of the Latin verb *struere*—"to build"—and it refers to something that is in the process of being built. Thus an agent is, or depends on, a human being who is capable of choosing, and acting on his choice, in some social setting. I say "depends on," because human beings, as agents, can create fictional persons such as the state and grant these persons agency by authorizing some human being, as an agent, to act for them. The use of the term suggests that human action is not simply determined by circumstances. The key features of agents are intentionality and meaning.

In contrast, the term "structure" does have a deterministic flavor. Here too, structure's everyday meaning creates confusion. Social structure refers to recurring patterns of social behavior, and especially to those patterns that would seem to set limits on human agency. From the idea of the stability of patterned life conveyed by the term "structure" there is but a short step to a determinism in which the efficacy of human agency is lost. Structure, whether observable patterns or underlying principles, is separated from agent, but it still motivates social action. The effort to overcome the tension between these terms is characteristic of constructivism. So is disagreement on how the overcoming should be done.

Social action in which agents take part is a complex phenomenon. It is loaded with diverse meaning for agents, who act with diverse intentions, many (perhaps most) of which have unintended consequences. In contrast to "action" or "agent," the term "behavior," which was the main focus in the behavioral revolution and of FPA, refers strictly to observable phenomena, exclusive of reflection, intention, and meaning. Agency thus has distinct "social" connotations that IP scholars are disposed to view as structurally determined, if indeed they are aware of them at all. Constructivists say that FPA, and behavioralism in general, neglects the agent as a social being. FPA scholars neglect it when they make an assumption that behavior is a dependent variable, susceptible to objective assessment.

As I have suggested, the stress on agent and structure resonates with the philosophical question concerning the degree to which what happens in human affairs can be ascribed to free will and the degree to which it is determined by social or material constraints. Constructivists do not find a contradiction between human choices and material determination because they hold that international relations are social relations. By defining both foreign policy and international politics as social, they see that both must start with people interacting in, and with, a world that is inextricably social and material. This gives any social relation its dynamic nature and constructivism its ability to see social relations as constantly changing. Many constructivists reject the notion of seeing the social world as positivists do—as a world of reified relations, that is to say, abstract concepts and relations made into concrete objects, and natural laws of behavior waiting to be discovered. Instead constructivism attaches great significance to processes that are likely to affect each other in contingent and unexpected ways.

This is, however, where the similarity among constructivists ends. Constructivists offer different solutions to the artificial separation of agent and structure. Some have only a cosmetic change in mind, while others propose a radical rethinking of this duality, proposing instead their virtual fusion in an ongoing process in which agents and structures constitute each other as they go about whatever else it is that they do. Different styles of constructivism fasten on different social phenomena (for example, language, rules, norms, structures) variously mediating, mutually reproducing, enabling or coconstituting agency and structure. Figure 1.3 identifies the different intellectual sources that constructivists draw on in their efforts to solve the agent-structure problem. Chapter 3 develops the rule-oriented constructivism to which I subscribe. Chapter 5 shows on an exploration of one particular historical case just how different are the conclusions reached by mainstream as well as constructivist approaches.

Seven Questions

In Table1.1, I distill, in the form of seven questions, the characteristic ways in which FPA, IP, and constructivism deal with the perplexities of agent and structure in IR. I order these seven questions into four sets. The first set pertains to traditional, or classical, IR before it split into behavioral FPA and systemic IP, which are the subject of the second and third sets respectively. The fourth set consists of two questions pertaining to constructivism, but only one, the mainstream form of constructivism, is discussed in this chapter. Its discussion continues into the next chapter, which focuses on Alexander Wendt's structurally oriented constructivism. The eighth question is discussed indirectly in chapter 2 and takes up all of chapter 3.

Before the Split: Classical Realism (Question 1, Table 1.1)

As mentioned earlier, the classical tradition in IR lost, certainly in the United States, in the course of the Second Debate in the 1950s, to the scientific,

Table 1.1

Questions Asked by FP, IP, and Constructivists

	A. Foreign policy analysis focuses on attributes of units to reach conclusions about their relations (from parts to whole)	B. International politics as international system focuses on the system of relations to reach conclusions about system's attributes (from the whole to parts)
"Classical realism"	1. *What* does (rational actor) state A do to state B, C, D, E, etc. (and they to it) in response to (objectively existing) threats they individually or collectively represent to its national interest?	
Mainstream approaches: FPA and IP	2. *How* does individual decision maker acting on behalf of state A, based on his *subjective* perceptions, decide what to do to states B, C, etc.? 3. *Why* has individual decision maker acting on behalf of state A, based on his *subjective* perceptions decided what to do to states B, C, etc.?	4. *How* do (objectively existing rationally acting states A, B, C, D, E, etc. called a system) *behave* (based on biology, mathematics, general systems theory, cybernetics)?

5. Neorealist, structural realist approaches

How do (objectively existing rationally acting) states, A_1, A_2, and A_3... A_x behave under the constraints of X, Y, Z, etc., known as (material) *structure* (i.e., unequal distribution of capabilities across alike units—exogenously given constraints)?

6. Neoliberal, neoinstitutional approaches

How do rules/institutions created by states A_1, A_2, A_3, A_x mollify effect of X, Y, Z (structure) on (rationally acting) states A_1, A_2, etc. and enable their cooperation—despite exogenously given constraints?

7. Soft constructivism

What do states A, B, C, D, with their identities and interests not uniform and *not exogenously given* but *intersubjectively* agreed based on their different identities (i.e., NB no longer A_1, A_2, A_3 etc.) *intersubjectively* agree is the nature of X, Y, Z (structure) within which they exercise rational choice?

How do ideas change identities of states and thus their interests and policies?

8. Rule-oriented constructivism (see chapter 3)

behavioralist orientation that resulted in the FPA/IP split. The classical approach, epitomized in the work of Hans Morgenthau (1985 [1949]), managed to accommodate both FPA and IP. Morgenthau's realism was both FP oriented (Holsti 1998, 19) and aware of "contextual imperatives" associated with geography, history, economics, and politics (Pettman 1975, 34). According to his later critics, Morgenthau achieved this flexibility by using his theoretical framework in a rather cavalier manner. Drawing on historical and other descriptive materials, classical realism was based on several, often tacit, assumptions:

1. States are far and away the most important actors.
2. The actions of states could be analyzed as if states were unitary, monolithic actors.
3. States are rational actors. They choose the best available means to achieve their ends as unitary entities.

These three assumptions gave rise to the image of states as billiard balls in motion (Wolfers 1962; Keohane and Nye 1972; Wagner 1974). Their frequent collisions set them off on new trajectories and occasion further collisions. The billiard table does no more than set boundaries on a frictionless surface. This vivid imagery overlooked the fact that Morgenthau talked a great deal about responsibilities of leadership, thereby bringing the behavior of individuals in through the back door. Morgenthau also paid due attention to "national character" and thus to the quasi-personification of states. It is not very hard to see in Morgenthau and the classical tradition traces of the romantic nationalism characteristic of the nineteenth century. In its extreme form, glorification of nation-state went so far as to endow it with an independent soul, will to power, or superior rationality.

What makes the imagery of the billiard table so compelling is the simple way it conveys the mutual insecurity of states and the absence of superior political authority (a condition conventionally described as anarchy). States exist in an ever-present danger of war among themselves. Their actions are driven by a feeling of threat and a drive to secure survival. Therefore foreign policy must be security policy in the first instance, because survival is the first task of the state in an anarchical and violent environment. In this regard the "systemic perspective pervaded traditional analysis of foreign policy" (Singer 1969, 22–23). The vocabulary of national power, purpose, and interest reflected a homogeneous image of nation-states, and the dominance of the state's external environment over its internal environment left statesmen little latitude in the courses of action that they could rationally choose.

Rationality as a pervasive concept in modern Western thought has played a key role in Morgenthau's classical realist theory but particularly in the realism of its later scientific variety. Positivism has made rationality central to the study of the social world. As Ferguson and Mansbach put it, "[t]he assumption [of rationality] is . . . essential for the construction of general theory . . . . Denial of rationality or disagreement about its meaning . . . must inevitably force us to construct theory out of subjective factors and to reduce dramatically the prospects for fruitful comparison" (1988, 143).

Classical realism aspires to offer a general theory. It treats both states and statesmen as rational. Without the rationality assumption, it would be impossible for any statesman to act on the "national interest," which, for realists, is what puts states, as billiard balls, into motion. The assumption of rationality is also the starting point from which a dehumanized IP of the variety introduced by Waltz later developed. This is because the external behavior of the state was not explained as a series of decisions made on behalf of the state but in terms of an objective situation that all states would respond to in the same way. I cannot overstate just how crucial the concept of rationality is to realism and all those approaches that make the state into the most important actor. From a constructivist perspective, this is tantamount to making the agent an automaton—a stimulus-response machine—that responds in a merely mechanical way to externally generated impulses. As we shall discover in chapter 3, rule-oriented constructivism also sees agents as rational but in a conceptually very different way.

The Behavioral Side of the Split: Foreign Policy Analysis (Questions 2 and 3, Table 1.1)

Moving chronologically from classical realism to behavioralism, there is one particular book that stands out. In a monograph published in 1954, Richard Snyder and associates undertook to account for all factors relevant to the making of a foreign policy decision (reprinted in Snyder 1962, 14–185). This systematic account is usually taken as the turning point in the study of foreign policy. It is worth noting that FPA began in earnest by introducing certain elements that many constructivists and postmodern scholars would later take up. FPA opened up the state as a black box and turned attention to just those personal, ideational, and cultural factors affecting decision making that realism tended to minimize. It did so, however, by seeking to objectivize subjective phenomena through the methods of positivist science. Some scholars saw FPA's "decisionism" as a return nonetheless to idealism of sorts, through its study of ideas or ideological phenomena (Shklar 1964, 3–17). In James Rosenau's view, an emphasis on foreign policy decision making "crystallized the ferment and provided guidance—or at least legitimacy—for those who had become disenchanted with a world composed of abstract states and with a mystical quest for single-cause explanations of objective reality" (1967b, 202).

The problem was that when scholars looked inside the hard shell of the billiard ball and opened the black box of the state, the contents of the box soon looked—as Pettman (1975, 51) put it—like a filing cabinet, full of files with fascinating data but lacking an intelligible filing system. Almost a reversal from the previous practice had taken place: The presumably objective reality of rational action was replaced as a central concern with the "objective situation," consisting of a presumably objective description of subjective behaviors, whose sheer complexity made it unlikely that decision makers could respond to it rationally from any presumably objective observer's point of view.

As I suggested, the discovery that decision making is necessarily subjective anticipates aspects of constructivist and even postmodern scholarship. An emphasis on the complexities of agency points up the limits of science when applied to social phenomena. Among these complexities are:

1. the relationship between discrete decisions and the continuous processes of decision making (or foreign policy making—see chapter 4 below);
2. the relationship between the national interest and the subjective "definition of the situation" by particular decision makers;
3. the blurring of the distinction between domestic and international factors in any decision maker's "definition of the situation"; and
4. the relation between institutions and processes, and thus the relevance of two levels of analysis, or in Snyder's words (1962, 7), "psychological variables" and "sociological variables."

In short, FPA focused on the subjective situation of the decision maker in a group context, and tried to do so scientifically. That led scholars to social psychology for the relevant concepts, propositions, and methods. Imported concepts included "image" (Boulding 1956, 1959), "belief system" (Holsti, Ole 1962), and misperception (Jervis 1969), all of which became regular features of FPA. Conversely, FPA progressively tended to neglect the objective features of the decision maker's world. Harold Sprout and Margaret Sprout (1956), for example, tried to introduce balance by talking about not just the psychological "psycho-milieu" of decision making but also the "operational milieu" (objective environment). Nevertheless, the neglect of "structure" and social context increased over the years. As suggested by the formulation of question 2 in Table 1.1, which epitomizes this approach, the emphasis on decision making changed the question that scholars asked. Instead of asking questions about foreign policies as such, scholars turned their attention, though selectively, to the processes through which decisions were arrived at.

The ubiquitous concept of rationality, that constant shadow of the modern era, was never very far off in the wings. According to James Rosenau (in Charlesworth 1967, 211), the next important development in FPA in those heady days of enthusiasm was the introduction of game theory, which puts the rational agents in situations where they must make choices contingent on the choices that other rational agents make in anticipation of the former's choices. This is "strategic interaction," and it models adversarial situations with which IR is replete. (Nicholas Onuf considers strategic interaction from a constructivist point of view in chapter 4.) FPA joined the other behavioral sciences in developing game theory as the "formal study of the rational, consistent expectations that participants can have about each other's choices" (Schelling 1967, 213). Game theory is, or at least ought to be, of great relevance to constructivism since it must always identify the rules by which any game is played. In effect, game theory is "a book of instructions," a general plan, consisting of strategies, strategic decisions, involving a plurality of rational agents in situations that offer incentives for them to compete and to cooperate with each other or with others to varying degrees (Shubik 1967, 241).

Game theory fostered the development of a powerful analytic perspective that has come to be known as rational choice theory. Under its influence, foreign policy analysts joined a broad multidisciplinary movement that eventually transformed realism, once Waltz had reformulated it in structural terms, into neorealism. Rational choice theory also helped to transform liberal institutionalism, which realists had earlier dismissed as idealism, into what became known as neoliberalism. Indeed, it is rational choice that they both share that makes neorealism and neoliberalism barely distinguishable.

The formal model of rational choice, which is closely identified with classical economic theory, provides the common starting point of all of these approaches. This model stipulates that the rational decision maker has a stable, intransitive order of preferences and the ability to assess courses of action with sufficient reliability to bother going through the process. In these circumstances, the decision maker will always choose a course of action most likely to produce an outcome that the decision maker would prefer over any other likely outcome. Note that the inability to determine consequences with complete reliability, conveyed by the term "likely," complicates the calculus of choice, but does not make the process of choosing any less rational. The model breaks the process into the following steps:

1. perceiving a problem, or the need to make some sort of choice;
2. listing the possible consequences of whatever course of action that might be available for choice;

3. ranking possible outcomes in order of preference; and
4. choosing the best available outcome.

Scholars developing the decision-making model were quick to modify rational choice theory to suit the particular circumstances of foreign policy decision making and significantly relaxed it in contrast to its original formulation. Herbert Simon and other scholars soon indicated that rather than "optimizing," decision makers often choose the first viable option that is minimally acceptable even if such a less-than-optimal choice does not maximize their values or goals. This and similar modifications to rational choice theory were expressed in concepts such as "satisficing"or "bounded rationality" (Simon 1957), or Charles Lindblom's "disjointed incrementalism" or, more informally, "muddling through" (Lindblom 1959). I might note here that these qualifications add social context to rational choice theory, though not as much as most constructivists would want. Nevertheless, as Onuf and Collier show in their contributions to this volume, constructivists can deploy the assumptions of rational agency to good effect.

In this context it is important to mention one of the main texts in FPA, and one of the few imported from FPA to IR as a whole. Graham Allison's *Essence of Decision* (1971) systematically put rational choice in a social context specific to foreign policy decision making in large, powerful states such as the United States. He managed to summarize large bodies of FPA writing when he identified three approaches to the rational conduct of foreign policy. The first is the standard realist approach, which takes the state as a unitary, rational actor. The second approach emphasizes the limits on rationality that large, hierarchical organizations impose on decision making as a process. Here Simon's and Lindblom's insights are especially pertinent. The last approach sees foreign policy decision making in the context of multiple governmental bureaucracies, each of which exhibits the preference ordering that suits its functional mission. Threatening IP with irrelevance and promising to reorient IR as a scientific enterprise, Allison's book has had an influence far beyond FPA.

The Systemic Side of the Split: International Politics (Questions 4, 5, and 6, Table 1.1)

If it were not for Wendt's structure-oriented constructivism, and the closely related norm-oriented constructivism of Peter Katzenstein and his circle, we could halt the discussion at this point. In fact it might sound strange that many of these constructivists overwhelmingly favor IP over FPA as their critical point of departure. In the next chapter, Steve Smith offers as an answer to this puzzle Wendt's insistence on treating states once again as black boxes. There is too the fact that Katzenstein and his group style their work as falling into the category of "new security studies," and it is not on the FPA but on the IP side of the discipline that security studies, dealing with the context of the world, have always been located.

It is because of the attention that so many constructivists pay to the IP literature that I briefly discuss theories on the systemic side of the discipline, that is, early systemic theories, followed by structural realist theories and their rather limited modification as neoliberal theories. Besides, the terminology of structural realism (now better known as neorealism) even seeped into FPA as the latter diminished in vitality and coherence.

I now briefly turn to the right-hand column in Table 1.1. The distance between the two columns and the two orientations ought to be clear from the questions that they ask. In the hands of systemic theorists, IR becomes a study of systemic-structural constraints within which a rational actor makes his or her decision. Table 1.1 shows how these constraints deprive states of any semblance of individuality, or, to use a term much favored by constructivists, identity. I depict this situation by changing the symbols referring to states A, B, and C to the virtual clones A_1, A_2, and A_3, all of which are distinguishable only in the capabilities that they possess. The distribution of capabilities is itself held to be a defining feature of the structure (Waltz 1979). As I suggested earlier, rational choice enters the IP side of the split the way it does in liberal economic theory; namely, states make choices under the same sort of systemic constraints that individuals do in markets. As in the case of liberal economics, this way of thinking gives IR a static, conservative slant, since preferences are given and assumed, and change in them is deemed unlikely.

The "identity" of the state and its exogenous or endogenous determination are other concepts that at this point I need to introduce. Because classical realism is, in the first instance, a systemic theory, states are always in danger of losing their distinctiveness. Morgenthau compensated for this by attention to national character and statesmanship, but he undercut the coherence and power of his systemic theory by doing so. By contrast, structural realism makes a virtue of simplicity. Structural realists insist that states are like units with exogenously determined but intrinsically given interests and identities that are unchanging and interchangeable. These identities have four features: sovereignty (states are all alike in all regards except their capabilities), rationality (states are uniformly rational), vulnerability (states worry only about their survival, and their primary interest is to make themselves secure), and negativity (the lack of trust as to the motives of the others). Held in common, these features leave states a limited repertory of choices in their relations with other states. They fight, they form or leave alliances, and they act to increase their capabilities from within themselves, thereby affecting the distribution of capabilities in their favor.

This picture is not fundamentally altered by neoliberalism, which developed as a response to structural realism. What was initially a fierce debate between neoliberals and neorealists (Baldwin 1993) has faded away now, and, as an inseparable duo, they delimit what is often called the mainstream in IR. Neoliberalism complicates the simple elegance of structural realism by suggesting that an additional choice is available to states when they make rational choices in their relations with other states. When they choose to cooperate, as indeed they do when they form alliances, they often have good reasons to institutionalize cooperative relations. States with very large capabilities, as hegemons, are especially disposed to institutionalize relations that benefit them (and perhaps others because of the collective guides that these institutionalized arrangements create). Institutions tend to take on lives of their own, functioning as intervening variables between system structure and state agents (Keohane 1984). In the metaphorical language of the billiard table, they roughen up its surface or make it sufficiently uneven as to allow the balls to nestle together in hollows.

Neoliberalism in IR alters the structural realist framework, but timidly. Many scholars agree that the only remaining real difference between neorealists and neoliberals is that neoliberals think states seek absolute, and neorealists, relative gains in their relations with other states. With their commitment to free trade, free capital flows, and "open" world economy, neoliberals think any particular state does not mind if other states benefit from the relation so long as the state in question benefits more. Neorealists, in contrast, believe that states prefer a lesser benefit so long as other states are excluded from any benefits at all (Grieco 1988; also see Onuf 1989, 265–270, for a constructivist version of this argument). Neoliberals tiptoe in the direction of constructivism when they acknowledge that states act within institutional constraints of their own making, whether intended or not. As we shall see below, this comes nowhere close to the constructivist understanding of agent and structure.

Soft or Moderate, Structure- or Norm-Oriented Constructivism of Wendt, Katzenstein, and Others (Question 7, Table 1.1)

The end of the Cold War meant the end of a distribution of material capabilities that was more or less symmetrical between the two leading states. Unexpectedly rapid change in the distribution of capabilities exposed the weaknesses of neorealist and neoliberal theorizing, with its marked tendency toward structural determinism. Subsequent developments cast doubt on the assumption that states alone matter for theoretical purposes. Contrary to expectations, the most troublesome conflicts were no longer between states, nor were they strictly internal either. Although it is tempting to read this as indicative of the demise of states themselves (as do many theories of "globalization"), this, too, is an unwarranted simplification. It would be more accurate to say that the world has gotten more complicated. It is also surely right to say that the world was always more complicated than systemic theory was prepared to acknowledge, even when encumbered with auxiliary propositions about national character and institutional stickiness. Obviously structure matters—in this IP is right. Equally obvious, agents matter—FPA is no less right. Yet neither suffices, and something needs fixing. Enter constructivist repairmen. With at least one foot planted in the mainstream, structure- and norm-oriented constructivists think they know how to fix the problem.

Just as neoliberal institutionalism served to rescue a neorealist orthodoxy that had diverged too far from reality, it might well be the case that constructivism—at least the version of constructivism closest to the mainstream—can rescue IP from sterility and irrelevance. What we have here is not a fundamental change in framework but a shift from a stress on the capabilities of states, or the distribution of power as a structural property of the system, to a stress on the identity of states (a word that earlier did not have an important place in the vocabulary of IR since, as we recall, the system itself was thought to be exogenously given and uniform with identities of states also uniform). The shift from capabilities to identities has meant a shift from what states can do because of their position in a structure, to what they want to do because of how they see themselves in relation to others. According to mainstream constructivists, it is no longer capabilities, but identities, that are harnessed to interests. As such, the interests of states are no longer set by the structure of the system of states.

The introduction of the term "identity" is not without problems. The vast social science scholarship on identity is overwhelmingly based on individuals, who in their search for their "true selves" can assume and discard identities as if they were trying on masks. It is, in my opinion, a doubtful proposition that people can make themselves over as they choose. My doubts multiply when scholars talk about a group of people, and particularly a large and diverse group, as if they constituted a single self in search of a plausible identity. There is, however, a rather appealing way out of this impasse. Identifying "others" against whose alleged identity one forms one's own identity simplifies the equation, especially insofar as groups are concerned. Nizar Messari's contribution to this volume explores this process.

Some constructivists have already taken this route (Kowert 1998; Wendt 1999, 246–312). In simple terms, states create each other as enemies, rivals, or partners, and proceed to share their interpretations of their respective identities. They also act in accordance with each other's expectations of them. If they make themselves what they are together, then "anarchy is," as Wendt (1992b) so aptly observes, "what states make of it." In this constructivist reading, anarchy is not a particular configuration of states objectively existing and determining states' moves, but instead an intersubjective agreement among them.

It seems that scholars following this soft or moderate constructivist path are trying to bring states back into the systemic picture by having them follow an "endogenous" logic that derives from each state's identity. They see this logic as fostering an intersubjective agreement among states on the structure of their relations. In part reflecting material circumstances, any such agreement constitutes the state of affairs—anarchy, in this case—it alleges to describe. In other words, the structure of the system has the same properties that make identity, interests, and culture what they are. Thus Wendt (1999) claims to have changed structural realism (with its stress on material factors and the distribution of capabilities) into structural idealism (with its ideational structures that are intersubjectively created). The ever present problem of reconciling the subjective and the objective in the name of science is resolved by this form of constructivism by this interesting spin: The recognition of the subjective is accomplished by claiming that what is objective is really *intersubjective*.

According to Peter Katzenstein (1996, 24), identity is shorthand for varying constructions of nationhood and statehood (national ideologies, collective distinctiveness, and purpose). Many constructivists change the order of march, as it were, for their research. Instead of beginning with structure, which determines state's interest, as neorealists and neoliberals do, they proceed from identity to interest, and from interest all the way around again to structure, all of which, somewhat vaguely, constitutes culture. After fix-it constructivist repair, structure ends up in an inclusive category called culture, which nevertheless seems to be remarkably bereft of content aside from the identity that states give to each other in their relations.

Chapter 2 continues the argument from this point by examining the contribution that Wendt's structure-oriented constructivism makes to FPA and IP. Chapter 3 is, as I have already said, devoted to rule-oriented constructivism. Chapter 5 returns to the seven questions of Table 1.1 to show that the differences in approaches are not just theoretical, academic. When applied to a practical problem, they point to very different policies.

Notes

1. That it cannot be called International Political "Analysis" derives from the understanding of systems approach as holistic, not analytical, in temper (Waltz 1979).

2. The English language facilitated this process. In many languages, one word suffices for what in English requires two words, politics and policy. The term "policy," as in "insurance policy," is widely used, but it has a meaning unrelated to politics and is derived from the Greek word for "proof" (*apodixis*). In French, German, Spanish, Russian and other Slavic languages, and Farsi, for example, there is no separate word for policy as in "foreign policy." There is only the equivalent of "politics," as in *die Politik, la politique, politika*. These words are derived from the Greek word *polis*. In these languages, politics and policy are generally regarded as synonymous in the sense of "concerning or related to government" or "government" itself. Policy has an additional meaning, however, which in English denotes the "manner of governing, conduct, direction of a state, conduct in pursuit of one's interest, plan of action, wisdom, governing principle." The English language acquired the term "policy" by indirect means. It traveled from its origin as polis (political society) via its Greek derivation *politeia* (form of rule, arrangement of offices) into the Old French *policie*. The French meaning of policie was "civil administration" or "administration of public order." Edmund Burke used it in this sense, one that was imported from France as late as 1791. The English language preserved the meaning French gave it long after the French dropped it, however. The French kept only its derivative, using it to refer to police officers. (Hegel used *polizei* more broadly to refer to civil administration.) Only English kept both words, "police" and "policy." The Americans gave the latter term an additional meaning as in "policy oriented" or "policy relevant" to refer to knowledge that is professedly practical and useful rather than merely academic.

3. In addition to the definition of FPA just cited, these are some of the related definitions: the International Politics discipline claims to study only power *among* states, leaving the study of the power *inside* states to *political science*. What the state does inside its borders is also known as *public policy* in contrast to *foreign policy*, which refers to states' official contacts with other states. The distinction between foreign and public policy cannot always be made clearly. Unlike public policy, foreign policy targets goals outside of a state's exclusive jurisdiction. Unlike public policy, foreign policy is often veiled in secrecy (see chapter 4). *Security studies*, particularly *national security studies*, combine domestic policy, foreign policy, and international politics issues that can lead to war. Foreign Policy can also be confused with *Diplomacy*, and International Politics or Foreign Policy can be confused in turn with *Diplomatic History*. "Diplomacy" means communications between states. It is one form of foreign policy, but diplomacy is a more limited activity typically undertaken by a professional staff.

Students of *history* record sequences of concrete events, explaining an event in terms of what preceded it without looking, or at least, without looking consciously, for general or abstract patterns. Diplomatic History, too, may be confused with Foreign Policy. Unlike Diplomatic History, Foreign Policy as a field focuses on processes rather than outcomes.

References

Allison, G.T. 1971. *Essence of Decision: Explaining the Cuban Missile Crisis*. Boston: Little, Brown.

Baldwin, D., ed. 1993. *Neorealism and Neoliberalism: The Contemporary Debate*. New York: Columbia University Press.

Boulding, Kenneth. 1956. *The Image*. Ann Arbor: University of Michigan Press.
————. 1959. "National Images and International Images." *Journal of Conflict Resolution* 3(2): 120–131.
Brown, Chris. 1997. *Understanding International Relations*. New York: St. Martin's Press.
Charlesworth, James C., ed. 1967. *Contemporary Political Analysis*. New York: Free Press.
Checkel, Jeffrey. 1998. "The Constructivist Turn in International Relations Theory." *World Politics* 50: 324–348.
Clark, Ian. 1999. *Globalization and International Relations Theory*. Oxford: Oxford University Press.
Ferguson, Y., and Mansbach, R. 1988. *The Elusive Quest: Theory and International Politics*. Columbia: University of South Carolina Press.
Fierke, K.M. 1998. *Changing Games Changing Strategies: Critical Investigations in Security*. Manchester: Manchester University Press.
Finnemore, Martha. 1996. *National Interests in International Society*. Ithaca, NY: Cornell University Press.
Grieco, Joseph. 1988. "Anarchy and the Limits of Cooperation: A Realist Critique of the Newest Liberal Institutionalism." *International Organization* 42(3): 485–508.
Holsti, Kal. 1998. "The Study of the International Relations during the Cold War." *Special Issue: The Eighty Years' Crisis 1919–1999, Review of International Studies* 24(5): 17–46.
Holsti, O.R. 1962. "The Belief System and National Images." *Journal of Conflict Resolution* 6 (September): 244–252.
Jervis, Robert. 1968. "Hypotheses on Misperception." *World Politics* 20(3): 454–479.
Katzenstein, Peter J., ed. 1996. *The Culture of National Security: Norms and Identity in World Politics*. New York: Columbia University Press.
Katzenstein, Peter J., Keohane, Robert O., and Krasner, Stephen D. 1998. "International Organization and the Study of World Politics." *International Organization* 52(4): 645–685.
Keohane, Robert O. 1989. "International Institutions: Two Approaches." In R.O. Keohane, ed., *International Institutions and State Power*, pp. 158–179. Boulder, CO: Westview Press.
Keohane, R.O., and Nye, J.S., eds. 1972. *Transnational Relations and World Politics*. Cambridge, MA: Harvard University Press.
Kowert, Paul. 1998. "Agent Versus Structure in the Construction of National Identity." In Vendulka Kubálková, Nicholas Onuf, and Paul Kowert, eds., *International Relations in a Constructed World*, pp. 101–122. Armonk, NY: M.E. Sharpe.
Light, Margot. 1994. "Foreign Policy Analysis." In A.J.R. Groom and Margot Light, eds., *Contemporary International Relations: A Guide to Theory*. London and New York: Pinter Publisher.
Lindblom, Charles. 1959. "The Science of Muddling Through." *Public Administration Review* 19(2): 78–88.
Morgenthau, Hans J. 1985. *Politics Among Nations*. New York: Alfred Knopf, 1947.
Onuf, Nicholas Greenwood. 1989. *World of Our Making. Rules and Rule in Social Theory and International Relations*. Columbia: University of South Carolina Press.
Pettman, Ralph. 1975. *Human Behavior and World Politics*. London. Macmillan.
Rosenau, James N. 1967a. "The Premises and Promises of Decision-Making Analysis." In James C. Charlesworth, ed., *Contemporary Political Analysis*, pp. 189–212. New York: Free Press.
————. 1967b. *Domestic Sources of Foreign Policy*. New York: Free Press.
————. 1971. *Scientific Study of Foreign Policy*. New York: Free Press.
Ruggie, John. 1998. *Constructing the World Polity: Essays on International Institutionalization*. London: Routledge.

Schelling, T.C. 1967. "What Is Game Theory?" In James C. Charlesworth, ed., *Contemporary Political Analysis*, pp. 212–239. New York: Free Press.

Shklar, Judith. 1964. "Decisionism." In Carl J. Friedrich, ed., *Nomos VII: Rational Decision*, pp. 3–17. New York: Atherton Press.

Shubik, Martin. 1967. "The Uses of Game Theory." In James C. Charlesworth, ed., *Contemporary Political Analysis*, pp. 20–30. New York: Free Press.

Simon, H.A. 1957. *Models of Man: Social and Rational*. New York: Wiley.

Singer, J.D. 1969. "The Level-of-Analysis Problem in International Relations." In J.N. Rosenau, ed., *International Politics and Foreign Policy*, pp. 20–30. New York: Free Press.

Snyder, Richard C., Bruck, H.W., and Sapin, Burton. 1954. *Decision-Making as an Approach to the Study of International Politics*. Foreign Policy Analysis Project Series, No. 3, Princeton.

———, eds. 1962. *Foreign Policy Decision Making: An Approach to the Study of International Politics*. New York: Free Press.

Special Issue: The Eighty Years' Crisis 1919–1999, Review of International Studies 24(5).

Sprout, H., and Sprout, M. 1956. *Man-Milieu Hypotheses in the Context of International Politics*. Princeton: Princeton University Center of International Studies.

Taylor, Trevor, ed. 1978. *Approaches and Theory in International Relations*. New York: Longman Group Limited.

Wagner, R. Harrison. 1974. "Dissolving the State: Three Recent Perspectives." *International Organization* 28(3): 435–466.

Waltz, Kenneth. 1979. *Theory of International Politics*. Reading, MA: Addison-Wesley.

Wendt, Alexander. 1992a. "The Agency-Structure Problem in FPA." *International Studies Quarterly* 36(3): 245–270.

———. 1992b. "Anarchy Is What States Make of It: The Social Construction of Power Politics." *International Organization* 46(2): 391–425.

———. 1992c. "Levels of Analysis vs. Agents and Structures: Part III." *Review of International Studies* 18(2): 181–185.

———. 1994. "Collective Identity Formation and the International State." *American Political Science Review* 88(2): 384–396.

———. 1995. "Constructing International Politics." *International Security* 20(1): 71–81.

———. 1999. *Social Theory of International Politics*. Cambridge, UK: Cambridge University Press.

Wendt, Alexander, and Duvall, Raymond. 1989. "Institutions and International Order." In Ernst-Otto Czempiel and James Rosenau, eds., *Global Changes and Theoretical Challenges: Approaches to World Politics for the 1990s*, pp. 51–73. Toronto: Lexington Books.

White, B.P. 1978. "Decision-Making Analysis." In Trevor Taylor, ed., *Approaches and Theory in International Relations*, pp. 141–165. New York: Longman Group Limited.

Wolfers, Arnold M. 1962. *Discord and Collaboration*. Baltimore: Johns Hopkins Press.

2

Foreign Policy Is What States Make of It: Social Construction and International Relations Theory

Steve Smith

In this chapter I want to trace the development of social construction as an approach within International Relations (IR) theory. I start from the premise that a priori, social constructivism should be particularly relevant to foreign policy analysis (FPA), precisely because social construction starts from the assumption that actors make their worlds, and this assumption lies behind most of the foreign policy analysis literature. Foreign policy is what states make of it, to paraphrase Alexander Wendt. Thus, in contrast to those international relations approaches that focused on the structure of the international system as a cause of state behavior, foreign policy analysis starts from the perspective of the state-as-actor, and then looks inside that particular black box. In Singer's terminology, foreign policy analysis is a state-level account of world politics as distinct from a systems-level account. Indeed, as Singer noted in his celebrated discussion of this issue, one of the complications of the state-as-level-of-analysis was that it raised the question of how to treat the perceptions and intentions of those officials who made state policy (Singer 1961, 85–90). Regardless of how one interprets the phenomenological issues that lie at the heart of that particular question, it is nonetheless clear that foreign policy is a realm of (albeit limited) choice: actors interpret, decide, pronounce, and implement. Even if they do so through powerful belief systems or operational codes, or as a result of small group dynamics or groupthink, or as a response to their bureaucratic political setting, they nonetheless act. Foreign policy analysis is at the very least an arena of individual action, even if that action has structural or social drivers. Foreign policy is at least in part an act of construction; it is what the actors decide it will be. Social construction and foreign policy analysis look made for one another.

However, this tempting overlap may be more imagined than real: Although perhaps it should be the case that social constructivism and foreign policy analysis share core assumptions about both the nature of the social world and how to study it, my main claim is that this is not likely to be the outcome. I say this because I feel that a specific version of social construction is likely to dominate the literature; furthermore, this specific version looks as if it is being assimilated into the mainstream of the international relations litera- ture. Social construction, which in principle offers a potentially radical alter- native to the assumptions of the positivist mainstream literature, is thus in danger of becoming very restricted in its theoretical reach. In short, the radi- cal possibilities promised by social construction are in danger of being hi- jacked by a mainstream that can assign to it an unthreatening role of being an adjunct explanation for those things that the positivist mainstream finds dif- ficult to explain.

I will follow through this line of argument by focusing on the current status of social constructivism in international relations theory. I will try and show how it has become adopted by the mainstream, and how the version of social constructivism that the mainstream is treating seriously is in fact a very specific form. Indeed, let me be clear at the outset and say that the kind of constructivism represented by the Miami International Relations Group is very different from the constructivism that the mainstream finds acceptable. I see this as a significant cause for regret, since it is precisely the constructivism developed by Onuf (1989) and others (for example, see Kratochwil 1989) that offers both the possibilities of, and the intellectual underpinnings for, a more fundamental reassessment of the nature of the social world, of FPA, and of IR, than that provided by the form of constructivism deemed accept- able by the mainstream.

Let me, however, start by trying to categorize social constructivist approaches to international relations. Its intellectual lineage is a long one, having its philo- sophical roots in the writings of Husserl, Weber, and Wittgenstein. In the social sciences the first book to use the phrase "social constructivism" in its title was Berger and Luckmann's *The Social Construction of Reality* (1966), although the approach was central to the work of the sociologist Alfred Schultz, whose *The Phenomenology of the Social World* (1967) is the classic statement of a Husserlian/Weberian position. The major recent contributions to the debate are John Searle's *The Construction of Social Reality* (1995), and Ian Hacking's *The Social Construction of What?* (1999). Within international relations the key state- ments have been by Onuf (1989; and see Kubálková, Onuf, and Kowert 1998), Kratochwil (1989), Ruggie (1998), and Wendt (1992, 1999).

There are many attempts in the literature to classify the main currents of constructivist thought in international relations. Ruggie (1998, 35–36) distinguished three variants of social constructivism: *neoclassical,* based on intersubjective meanings and derived from Durkheim and Weber; *postmodernist,* based on a decisive epistemological break with modernism and derived from the work of Nietzsche, Foucault, and Derrida; and *naturalistic,* based on the philosophical doctrine of scientific realism and derived from the work of Bhaskar. Adler (1997, 335–336), building on the work of Lynch and Klotz, distinguishes four forms of constructivism: *modernist, rule-based, narrative knowing,* and *postmodernist.* For Katzenstein, Keohane, and Krasner (1998, 675–678), there are three versions: *conventional, critical,* and *postmodern.* Wendt (1992, 1999) relied at different times on two main strands of theoretical work, the symbolic interactionism of Mead and the scientific realism of, among others, Bhaskar.

The problem with these classifications is that they reveal two main features of social constructivist accounts of international relations: first, there is little agreement over what social constructivism entails, and second, despite all the differences, the lists point to very similar "fault lines," mainly those between what I have elsewhere (Smith 1995) termed "constitutive" and "explanatory" theory. For me this indicates that there are significant divisions within social constructivism over what may be termed philosophy of social science issues. In other words, these classifications seem to contain within the term "social constructivism" approaches resting on what I would call fundamentally opposed epistemological positions. Thus, even to talk of "a" social constructivism is problematic: there are many, and this poses the question of just how useful it is to use this blanket term, as is commonly done when talking of a "constructivist turn" in IR theory.

The reason for this division can, I think, be illustrated by Alexander Wendt's map of international theory (see Wendt 1999, 29; and the discussion in Adler 1997, 330–333): In his matrix (Figure 2.1) Wendt has two axes representing "holism-individualism" and "materialism-idealism," and he puts social constructivism in the holism/idealism box. But note that with it in that box he later adds the English School, World Society, Postmodernist IR, and Feminist IR (Wendt 1999, 32). My concern is that these are approaches with very different epistemological and ontological assumptions. These assumptions are so distinct in terms of their views of the social world that it is difficult to see how they can be classified together. More puzzlingly, it is not clear that the form of constructivism that Wendt advances can really be located on that "top right" box of his matrix: This is because he wants to propose a form of constructivism that involves causal analysis, and this seems to me to mean that his work is located in the "top left" quadrant of the matrix (holism/materialism). I will return to this issue later when discussing Wendt's work in more detail.

Figure 2.1 **Locating IR Theories**

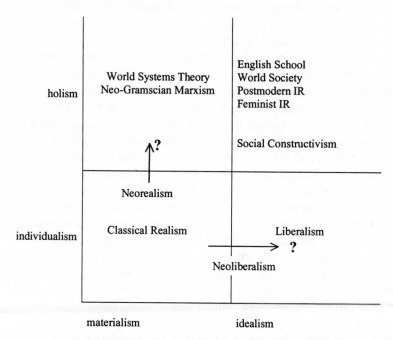

Source: Adapted from Wendt, 1999, *Social Theory of International Politics*, p. 32. Reprinted with permission from Cambridge University Press

Where, then, does social constructivism fit within international relations theory? My contention is that, in marked opposition to the intentions of key founding figures such as Onuf and Kratochwil, much of the approach has been subsumed into the mainstream, so that it looks increasingly likely to become part of that mainstream in the coming decade. In one important sense, however, this has been the intention of several leading constructivists, most notably Wendt (1992, 1999), Adler (1997), and Jørgensen (1997b). For these thinkers the aim has been, in the words of Adler, that of "seizing the middle ground." I will now turn to look at exactly what is this middle ground, and to what extent these writers have succeeded in their aim.

The last decade has seen the emergence of two main intellectual positions in IR theory. These are commonly classified as rationalism and reflectivism. *Rationalism* is the cover-all term given to what Ole Wæver has called the "neo-neo synthesis" (Wæver 1996, 163–164), namely the "debate" between neorealism and neoliberalism. Rationalism dominates the mainstream of the discipline, and, despite their differences, neorealism and neoliberalism share basically the same view of the world (ontology), and, crucially, the same view of what counts as reliable knowledge about that world (epistemology). The core differences between neorealism and neoliberalism concern the extent to which institutions can mitigate the effects of international anarchy, and whether the main actors in international politics (states) pursue absolute or relative gains. But in my view these differences mask a much wider agreement about the nature of international politics: It involves states as actors; it focuses on patterns of cooperation and conflict; actors are unitary and rational; and state interests, determined by the state's position in the international political system, drive foreign policy behavior. But as I have argued elsewhere (Smith 1995, 1996, 1997), the more important assumptions are epistemological ones, and it is these that are so important in rejecting much of the work of reflectivist scholars. The main epistemological assumptions are those of positivism, namely, (a) a belief in naturalism in the social world, that is to say that the social world is amenable to the same kinds of analysis as those applicable to the natural world; (b) a separation between facts and values, by which is meant both that "facts" are theory-neutral and that normative commitments should not influence what count as facts or as knowledge; (c) a commitment to uncovering patterns and regularities in the social world, patterns and regularities that exist apart from the methods used to uncover them; and finally, (d) a commitment to empiricism as the arbiter of what counts as knowledge.

Reflectivist approaches are united more by an opposition to this view of international politics than by any agreement over what should replace it. Reflectivism commonly includes postmodern, feminist, and Critical Theory approaches to international theory. Each of these approaches offers a very different set of answers to the key features of rationalism noted above. They define a range of different actors, define different patterns of relations, see the processes of policy formation in very different ways, and see a much wider set of interests determining the positions of key actors. But, again, I believe that a much more important issue than these ontological issues is the question of the theory of knowledge that underpins inquiry. Reflectivist approaches are often attacked for their epistemological assumptions. In particular they are criticized for not being social science and thereby not counting as reliable knowledge about the world. Reflectivists are thus presented by the mainstream as operating outside of the acceptable realm of academic study; they are not intellectually legitimate. Not surprisingly, they are therefore not well entrenched in North America, the homeland of the mainstream of the discipline. The most clear-cut attack on their epistemological assumptions came from Robert Keohane in his 1988 address as President of the International Studies Association. Keohane spoke of the need to be able to evaluate the rival research plans of the two main emerging approaches to IR, namely rationalist and reflective approaches. He called for this analysis to be based on their "testable theories" without which "they will remain on the margins of the field . . . [since] . . . it will be impossible to evaluate their research program" (Keohane 1989, 173–174). Note that this challenge was one issued on the epistemological terrain of rationalism, and it is difficult to see just how reflectivist accounts could conceivably provide answers that Keohane would accept given their epistemological starting points.

Social constructivism is commonly self-consciously portrayed as an approach that lies between rationalism and reflectivism, and as such can be seen as a middle ground or a *via media*. Writing from within the literature of social constructivism, Wendt's self-proclaimed aim is to build a bridge between the two IR traditions of rationalism and reflectivism by developing a constructivism that builds on the shared features of the liberalist wing of the rationalist tradition and the modern constructivist wing of the reflectivist tradition (Wendt 1992, 393–394). In his 1999 book, Wendt states his intention as wanting to defend a "moderate," "thin" constructivism against two positions: On the one hand he wants to argue against those in the mainstream who reject social constructivism as being tantamount to postmodernism; on the other he is opposed to those "more radical" constructivists who want to go much further than he does. He wants to develop a "philosophically principled middle way" between these positions (Wendt 1999, 2). Similarly, Adler sees constructivism, rather than any alternative such as the neoinstitutionalist focus on the role of ideas (see Goldstein and Keohane 1993), as the "true middle ground" between rationalist and relativist (his wording) approaches (Adler 1997, 322). Checkel, in his survey of "the constructivist turn" in IR theory, claims that "Constructivists thus occupy a middle ground between rational choice theorists and postmodern scholars" (Checkel 1998, 327). For a group of influential social constructivist scholars, then, one aim is self-consciously to position the approach so as to serve as a link between the two main research groupings represented by rationalism and reflectivism: along with rationalists, these social constructivists can agree that states are the main actors and that social science is the method of study. With reflectivists, these scholars can agree that ideas matter more than is represented by the neoinstitutionalists. In Wendt's memorable phrase, "Epistemologically, I have sided with positivists . . . our best hope is social science . . . [but] . . . on ontology—which is to my mind the more important issue—I will side with post-positivists. Like them I believe that social life is 'ideas all the way down' (or almost anyway . . .)" (Wendt 1999, 90).

Writing from within the mainstream of the discipline, Stephen Walt has commented on the position of constructivism in his state-of-the-art review of international relations theory for the influential U.S. journal *Foreign Policy*.

He argues that although the key debate in international relations theory has been, and continues to be, that between realism and liberalism, there is a third approach, constructivism, which he sees as the main alternative to these two. He sets out the main features of these three "paradigms" in a figure that represents a classical building with three pillars. Aside from the fact that his description of social constructivism is simplistic, and misleading, making adherents appear as latter-day utopians who think that things can be changed simply by changing our ideas about them, it is important to note that he assigns social constructivism a very limited, and augmental, role. In his words, the diplomat of the future should "remain cognizant of realism's emphasis on the inescapable role of power, keep liberalism's awareness of domestic forces in mind, and occasionally reflect on constructivism's vision of change" (Walt 1998, 44). By way of contrast, he notes that "realism is likely to remain the single most useful instrument in our intellectual toolbox" (Walt 1998, 43). In their major review of the state of the field in the fiftieth-anniversary issue of the influential U.S. journal *International Organization*, Peter Katzenstein, Robert Keohane, and Stephen Krasner offer a summary of the development of IR theory that portrays the current theoretical scene as one dominated by two theoretical traditions, rationalism and constructivism. Specifically, they argue that "constructivists have positioned themselves quite self-consciously between rationalist theoretical orientations, such as realism or liberalism, and postmodernist orientations"(Katzenstein, Keohane, and Krasner 1998, 678).

However, although this is the dominant portrayal of the place of social constructivism in contemporary international relations theory, my contention is that this view of social constructivism as "the middle way" is in fact deeply misleading. In my view, most social constructivism is far more "rationalist" in character than "reflectivist"; indeed, I would go so far as to say that social constructivism in its dominant (mainly North American) form is very close to the neoliberalist wing of the rationalist paradigm. This is precisely why it is seen by Walt, and by Katzenstein, Keohane, and Krasner, as acceptable. For these writers it is acceptable because it accepts both the ontology and, much more importantly, the epistemology of the mainstream. This is made absolutely clear in the following quote from Katzenstein, Keohane, and Krasner: "In contrast to. . . . constructivism, postmodernism falls clearly outside of the social science enterprise, and in international relations research it risks becoming self-referential and disengaged from the world, protests to the contrary notwithstanding" (Katzenstein, Keohane, and Krasner 1998, 678). *International Organization* had not published postmodernist work, because the journal "has been committed to an enterprise that postmodernism denies: the use of evidence to adjudicate between truth claims" (Katzenstein, Keohane, and Krasner 1998, 678).

A similar view can be found in the writings of some of the leading constructivists. Adler, in his powerful manifesto for a constructivist research agenda, is explicit in differentiating it from what he terms relativist approaches (Adler 1997, 330–337). These approaches are, he claims, based on "untenable" assumptions that essentially deny the separate existence of both foundational truth and an independent reality. As Jeffrey Checkel puts it: "It is important to note that constructivists do not reject science or causal explanation: their quarrel with mainstream theories is ontological, not epistemological. The last point is key, for it suggests that constructivism has the potential to bridge the still vast divide separating the majority of IR theorists from postmodernists" (Checkel 1998, 327). Wendt's work is explicitly based on epistemological assumptions shared with rationalist, not reflectivist, approaches (see Wendt 1987; 1992, 393–394, 422–425; 1994; 1999). As he comments in a recent paper coauthored with Ronald Jepperson and Peter Katzenstein, "The term *identity* here is intended as a useful label, not as a signal of commitment to some exotic (presumably Parisian) social theory" (Jepperson, Wendt, and Katzenstein 1996, 34). Similarly, Knud Erik Jørgensen, in outlining a constructivist approach to the study of European governance, argues that "Reflective scholars who wish to conduct theoretically informed empirical research on European governance cannot allow themselves the luxury of a comfortable, postmodernist position" (Jørgensen 1997a, 7).

Thus, although many leading social constructivist scholars want to present themselves as working in the space between rationalism and reflectivism, and although (maybe because) this is the view of constructivism held by many working in the mainstream, in my view social constructivism is mainly a rationalist enterprise, because it shares methodological and epistemological assumptions with rationalism (most obviously with neoliberal institutionalism). By contrast, the gap between social constructivism and reflectivist work is fundamental.

To illustrate this I want to look in some detail at Alexander Wendt's 1999 book, *Social Theory of International Politics*, which is both one of the most important books published in the last decade and the long-awaited statement of probably the most cited and quoted constructivist scholar. As I noted earlier, Wendt is very clear that he wants to position himself between rationalism and reflectivism; yet I think that he does no such thing and in fact, ends up writing a book that sits fairly comfortably within the mainstream of IR theory. Moreover, the version of constructivism that is developed in that book prohibits any linkage between constructivism and FPA because Wendt's notion of the state-as-actor removes any role for domestic influences on foreign policy behavior.

Before I look at Wendt's notion of the state I want to say something about the reasons why I think his form of social constructivism is closer to rationalism than it is to reflectivism. I have dealt with this elsewhere at length (Smith 2000) and so will only summarize my main arguments here. The main problem with Wendt's work is that he very explicitly wishes to construct a *scientific* account of international politics. I simply do not think that such an account is appropriate. More importantly, I do not think that many other social constructivists, certainly those from the Miami Group, would agree with that aim. Critically, note that the position Wendt wishes to occupy on his matrix (top right, i.e., holism/idealism) is decidedly not one that seems to fit with the quest for a social *science*. Indeed, that side of the materialism/idealism axis does not seem very promising for a social scientific account. I cannot think of another analyst who would be placed in that quadrant and who would see him- or herself as developing a scientific account of the social world. Certainly, none of the other approaches listed by Wendt as fellow occupants of that quadrant would see themselves as engaged in the science game. The underlying problem, then, is that Wendt adopts an approach to studying the social world that I feel is inappropriate. Now, in fact, I think that Wendt's starting position is not exactly where his analysis ends up. Wendt embeds his analysis of international politics in an approach known as scientific realism; as he puts it, he is "a strong believer in science . . . I am a positivist" (Wendt 1999, 39). The problem this causes is that scientific realism is decidedly not an idealist account of the social world (idealist here referring to philosophical not international relations usage). Moreover, most scientific realists argue that the approach is not suitable for the analysis of the social world; it is an account of the natural world alone, because it assumes that the reality it is dealing with is independent of the beliefs of humans. Yet, of course, the beliefs of humans lie exactly at the core of an idealist or intersubjective approach. Thus, whereas Wendt wants to claim that his approach is on the idealism side of the materialism/idealism axis, scientific realism lies on the materialist side.

This tension is evident throughout Wendt's book, since it leads to his adopting different, and contradictory, positions about the relationship between the ideational and the material at different points in his argument. Put simply, the problem is over whether material factors cause the ideational realm, or whether these material factors are themselves constituted by our ideas about them. At some points he argues the former; thus, he claims his aim is to "defend a 'rump' materialism which opposes the more radical constructivist view that brute material forces have no independent effects on international politics" (Wendt 1999, 110). In this light, "material forces are constituted independently of society, and affect society in a *causal* way. Material forces are not constituted solely by social meanings" (Wendt 1999, 111). Yet, at other times, Wendt argues very differently: Social constructivism "inquires into the extent to which ideas *constitute* these ostensibly 'material' causes in the first place" (Wendt 1999, 94). Hence, "The issue of 'how' ideas matter is not limited to their causal effects. They also matter insofar as they constitute the 'material base' in the first place" (Wendt, 1999, 135).

This strikes me as wanting it both ways, since at times the ideational constitutes the material, while at others the material has independent causal power. Underlying this is another concern, namely that he treats the two sorts of stuff (material and ideational, or natural and social kinds) as different types of things with different powers and attributes, whereas many scientific realists argue that the reason why that one approach can work is precisely that they conceive of a unity between social and natural kinds. Wendt seems ultimately unclear as to the relationship between the material and the ideational, and indeed over whether they are the same kind of stuff. This results in his being open to the criticism that, if they are different, then naturalism cannot hold, and that different types of theory are required to explain the two worlds. Let me conclude on this point by simply quoting Wendt's definition of his scientific realist account and then ask you the reader to say whether this view fits the social world. Scientific realism is guided by three principles: "(1) the world is independent of the mind and language of individual observers; (2) mature scientific theories typically refer to this world; (3) even when it is not directly observable" (Wendt 1999, 51). My view is that this cannot be a description of the social world, where the "stuff" of social interactions is intersubjective understanding that cannot be seen in any way as independent of the "mind and language" of actors: It *constitutes* those minds and languages. After all, if people stop behaving according to these intersubjective understandings, then they no longer exist!

This general worry leads into rather deeper philosophical water, and I do not want to say too much about this (for a more detailed discussion see Smith 2000, 156–161). There are two main concerns, and I will summarize them briefly. The first is directly related to Wendt's comments quoted above about the linkage between the ideational and the material, where he said that the ideational constituted the material, while the material had independent causal power. Wendt sees a distinction between constitutive and causal explanations: the former deals with the "how-possible?" and "what?" questions, whereas the latter deals with the "why?" and to an extent the "how?" questions. He claims that both natural and social scientists utilize both sorts of theorizing. He needs to make this move to maintain his commitment to naturalism, since causal analysis has traditionally been seen as having real difficulties when applied to the social world. Now, the difficulty here is that while he needs to introduce constitutive theory as a different form of *explanation* to that provided by causal theory, he then has to be able to define constitutive theory in a scientific way, when in its usual usage it is a term used to develop *understanding* theory; by these terms I simply mean that explanation and understanding are distinct forms of analysis and Wendt is therefore trying to move constitutive theory from one side to the other side of that divide. And, as Martin Hollis and I have argued repeatedly (see especially, Hollis and Smith 1990), these two approaches to the social world cannot be combined. In fact, Wendt redefines constitutive theory to become an adjunct to causal theory, so that it explains the social world only when linked to causal theory. It is for exactly this reason that scientific realists are usually seen as explainers, not understanders, since they ultimately want to explain the ideational world by reference to the material, and not the other way around. Wendt's constitutive theory therefore ends up being not an equal to causal theory but an account that provides the basis for causal explanations by accounting for how the ideational constitutes the meanings of the material forces on the world. This is a necessary move for Wendt, given his view that the social and the natural are different kinds of "stuff," but it is a move that makes the ideational of secondary importance to the material, and thus it is not "ideas all the way down," or even "ideas most of the way down."

The second philosophy of social science problem concerns whether reasons can be causes. Much hangs on this issue, since Wendt needs to show that they can be if he is to succeed in his quest for a naturalistic social science. He has already made a key move in distinguishing between causal and constitutive theories; this is key because reasons cannot be causes in the sense implied by standard Humean causal theory, in which causal relationships operate between separate objects, with that which causes occurring before that which is affected. Now, although it is fair to say that there are many philosophers of the social sciences who argue that reasons can indeed be causes, there are also significant objections to this claim. And, critically, these objections seem to me to fit much more clearly into the kind of theory offered by other key social constructivists, notably Nick Onuf. As you may deduce, I believe that this alternative form of social constructivism offers far more to FPA.

The main objections to the claim that reasons can be causes are twofold: first, there is the standard psychological concern over whether the reasons we give for our actions can be accepted as the "real" reasons. This is indeed complicated territory, but I hope it will suffice to say that disentangling the "real" motives for our actions seems to be very difficult indeed: To put it another way, are reasons causal in the sense of a specific reason for action being the cause of that action or does causation operate in the more limited sense of us being reasoning and intentional actors? The second concern is even more fundamental and it relates to the work of Peter Winch, specifically his interpretation of the later work of Ludwig Wittgenstein (see Winch 1958). For Winch, the notion of a cause is very different in the social and in the natural sciences; more precisely, Winch does not believe that reasons can be causal in the same way that causes operate in the natural sciences. The main difference is that behavior in the social world is essentially rule governed, and this involves interpretation and the possibility of making a mistake. What matters in all this is that action takes place in a social setting bounded and constructed by language, or what Wittgenstein called language-games. These language-games involve both regulative and constitutive rules, and it is these rules that shape and indeed construct identity. This is very different to the picture painted by Wendt, for whom reasons have to be causes.

We now come to the nub of the problem with Wendt's form of social constructivism: Put simply his view that reasons must be causes seems fiercely at odds with his insistence that he is located in the top right-hand box of his matrix (where holism and idealism combine) (see Figure 2.1). Surely, if reasons are ultimately causes, he is located in the top left-hand box (where holism and materialism combine). It is noteworthy that he barely discusses Wittgenstein in his book, and yet it is Wittgenstein who most philosophers of social science would define as the classic occupant of the top-right box. In a footnote in another article he goes so far as to note that "In saying that reasons can be causes I am taking one side in a debate . . . for an opposing Wittgensteinian view . . ." (Wendt 1998, 107, fn.18). And, note that it is exactly this Wittgensteinian perspective that Onuf places at the core of his version of social constructivism.

These, then, are significant problems with Wendt's version of social constructivism, and my central claim is that there are other forms of social constructivism that offer very different models of the social world, models that I think more accurately capture the essential features of what makes the social world different from the natural world. Thus, in contrast to Wendt, I do not think that naturalism is appropriate, although paradoxically I would place myself in exactly the same "box" that he places himself in. I hope I have shown why I believe his placing of himself in that box to be mistaken.

All of this brings us back to foreign policy analysis and to the problems that the dominant Wendtian version of social constructivism poses for any attempt to bring the two perspectives together. These problems are best illustrated by Wendt's treatment of the nature of the state-as-actor, which he discusses at length in chapter 5 of the book. His concern is to show how "states get constituted as the 'people' of international society" (Wendt 1999, 195).

This is, of course, a central concern for FPA, but Wendt's position seems to make foreign policy analysis redundant or even impossible. Wendt's position is that those who want to problematize the existence of the state as a separate and unitary actor are mistaken. This includes both liberals and "students of foreign policy decision-making" (Wendt 1999, 196). As he puts it: "states are real actors to which we can legitimately attribute anthropomorphic qualities like desires, beliefs, and intentionality . . . [the state] is an actor which cannot be reduced to its parts" (Wendt 1999, 197). He defines the state as "an organizational actor embedded in an institutional-legal order that constitutes it with sovereignty and a monopoly on the legitimate use of organized violence over a society in a territory" (Wendt 1999, 213), and argues that states should be seen as intentional actors that have generalizable national interests (comprising physical survival, autonomy, economic well-being, and collective self-esteem): "these interests are intrinsic to states; relative to the international system they are not social constructions" (Wendt 1999, 233–234). In this sense Wendt argues that "states are people too" (1999, 215), and in doing so he violates one of the central tenets of scientific realism, which argues that it is mistaken to ascribe human agency to social collectives.

In contrast to foreign policy analysis, Wendt's account of the foreign policy behavior of states leaves no room for domestic factors, since states are "presocial" and "exogenously given." States form "their identities and interests by interacting with each other" (Wendt 1999, 245); these are not the result of debates between domestic actors or even the domestic political process. As far as international politics goes, then, states are "ontologically prior to the states-system. The state is pre-social relative to other states in the same way that the human body is pre-social" (1999, 198). This means that social construction can explain international politics "only if such processes have exogenously given, relatively stable platforms" (1999, 198). In other words, Wendt sees the role of social constructivist theories of international politics as explaining how these pregiven and ontologically prior actors interact as unitary actors. There is precious little room for those theories central to foreign policy analysis. They cannot explain these interactions since they fail to treat the state as a unitary actor which is "a person"; or as he puts it four times on one page: "the ideas held by individual states . . . state cognition . . . states think . . . states have internalized" (1999, 372).

Thus Wendt's version of social constructivism offers little scope for the analysis of foreign policy. It is a theory of the foreign policy of states, but one that sees that policy constructed as a result of interactions between pregiven state actors. Their identities can change through interactions with one another, but not as a result of events in their foreign policy decision-making processes. There is no room for decision theory, or groupthink, or bureaucratic politics, or operational codes, or implementation theory. The actors are not the officials who make decisions, or the interest groups or companies, or political parties or military juntas. Rather, the actors are the states-as-persons, and there is no need to look into the black box of the foreign policy process. It is in this sense that foreign policy is what states make it.

I hope that my main concern is now evident: To the extent that Wendt's version dominates the literature of social constructivism and that it is this version that becomes the reference point for the debate between rationalism and constructivism, that debate will be very narrow. The most obvious example of this is the way in which rationalism and Wendtian social constructivism deal with the role of ideas in international politics: for both, ideas are important only as adjuncts to causal analysis. The overlap between, say, Goldstein and Keohane's (1993) treatment of the role of ideas in foreign policy and Wendt's (1999) version is enormous. Neither conceives of the role of ideas in anything like the way that both reflectivists, and, I would argue, some social constructivists (notably Onuf) conceive of it. The importance of all this is that I think Wendt and the rationalists see largely the same world, and, crucially, agree on how to study it. This world looks very different to the kinds of social worlds seen by reflectivist scholars: never mind the question of what furniture is in this social world, for me the crucial question is how we know about that world, and here Wendt sides with the positivist mainstream. Being a positivist on questions of knowledge means that analysis is limited to certain kinds of things, and, most significantly of all, analysis is based on the notion that naturalism prevails and that the social world can be analyzed by using the same methods as those used in the natural sciences. The problem with all this is that there is an important intellectual tradition that sees these worlds as distinct, requiring distinct and different analytical approaches. Wendt ends up painting a world that seems very similar to that painted by rationalists, and that is the alpha and the omega of the problem.

Now, what might a different worldview look like and how might this assist in the analysis of foreign policy? There are in fact many alternatives within social theory and international relations theory, most of which are covered by the label "reflectivism," that is to say postmodernist, feminist, and Critical Theory accounts. But for the purposes of this chapter it is most important to note that there is also a powerful tradition within social constructivism that both paints a very different view of the social world from that painted by Wendt, and opens up real room for the analysis of foreign policy. This, of course, is the strand of constructivism founded by Nick Onuf and carried on by the Miami IR Group.

There is no need for me to rehearse the main ideas of Onuf in this volume; those interested in following these up should look at Onuf (1989) and the contributions (especially that by Onuf) in Kubálková, Onuf, and Kowert, eds.1998. The key point of difference between this form of social constructivism and that offered by Wendt is that it sees a very different kind of social world, one in which actors, whoever they are, are governed by language, rules, and choices. This view of the social world has its intellectual roots in the work of writers such as Wittgenstein and Winch, and thus, it is a view that does not subscribe to the naturalism of Wendt. It is precisely this form of social constructivism that offers both a role for foreign policy, rather than treating the state as "a pre-social given" that forms its identity only through interactions with other states. Whereas Wendtian social construction offers little room for the social construction of foreign policy from within the state, the Miami IR Group version seems to me to offer an active role for the domestic construction of foreign policy.

This is supported by the main moves that Onuf makes in his 1989 book, *World of Our Making*, and also by his chapter in the 1998 volume edited by Kubálková, Onuf, and Kowert. Onuf's position is based explicitly on the notion of a speech act and on the claim that "saying is doing: talking is undoubtedly the most important way that we go about making the world what it is" (Onuf 1998, 59). Onuf focuses on three elements of the social world, namely individuals, society, and the rules that link them. A rule is defined as "a statement that tells people *what* we *should* do" (Onuf 1998, 59). Importantly, rules define who are the agents in society, and for Onuf these are people. Now, note that although Onuf thinks that social collectivities can be agents, he is clear that these collectivities are not presocial, as Wendt does. Rather, he sees them as produced by the rule-governed behavior of individuals. Agents, then, act in a goal-directed manner, with the goals defined by the rules of the language-game, and these may lead to the creation of institutions representing the relatively fixed pattern of expectations. In all of this, actors interpret rules and make choices over whether or not to follow the rule. The key point is that this looks like a very different type of social world from the kind that Wendt proposes. Remember that the key figures for Onuf (Wittgenstein and Winch) get virtually no mention in Wendt's work.

The upshot of all this is that whereas Wendtian social construction offers little room for domestic political influences on foreign policy (it is, after all, self-consciously a structural theory), the version adopted by Onuf and the Miami IR Group opens up the possibility for exactly this kind of domestic influence: indeed, it positively requires it because of how it sees collective social actors gaining agency. In this sense all agents follow rules because they live in a world that is socially constructed by these rules. This view of the social world fits well with the foreign policy analysis literature. That literature focused exactly on the linkage between social structures and calculating agents. Bureaucratic politics, for example, seems almost a paradigmatic example of social constructivism, as does Irving Janis's work on groupthink. In short, FPA looks at the interface between institutions, agents, and rules with the aim of showing how these led to the foreign policy choices made by the collective agents known as states. It is this interface that lies at the intellectual heart of Onuf's version of social constructivism.

All of this means that there is a version of social constructivism that offers the intellectual underpinning for the analysis of foreign policy. This underpinning would permit investigation into the ways in which foreign policy is rule-governed behavior, and would also give researchers the foundation for their empirical studies. Yet, my worry is that the genuinely exciting possibilities opened up by this approach will be stifled by the emerging linkage between Wendtian social constructivism and the rationalist mainstream. That linkage not only shares a similar worldview, but, more importantly, shares a view of how to study that world. Onuf's version of social construction sees a different kind of social world and holds to a view of how to study that world that is very different from the shared vision of Wendt and the rationalists. His version has much in common with the work of many reflectivist scholars. It will be interesting to see which version of social constructivism dominates the literature in the next decade. My view is that it will be Wendt's, precisely because it is the version that is still wedded to the canon of social science. This concerns me, for two reasons: First, it will limit the extent to which there will be social constructivist accounts of the foreign policies of states. These accounts will be limited to examining how states construct identities and interests through interactions, and will not delve deeper into the identity of the state than that. Second, the very fact that Wendt and the rationalists can talk so easily to one another means that more radical or far-reaching versions of constructivism will be ignored. Constructivism will therefore become an adjunct to the mainstream and will become the acceptable face of those who want to enquire into questions of agency, subjectivity, and the social construction of foreign policy and the social world. What this shows is that the real driving force of the U.S. study of international relations is not so much the issue of who acts over what issues, but how we construct knowledge of these actions. Because the U.S. discipline of IR remains committed to a social scientific account, the version of constructivism that that mainstream will deem acceptable is going to be the one that shares that same commitment. This not only proves the importance of epistemology, it also shows how what we find in the world is affected by what counts as knowledge about that world. Thus, despite the massive potential mutual benefits of a linkage between FPA and social constructivism, I fear that these will not be realized unless a more far-reaching social constructivism such as that offered by Onuf and the Miami IR Group gains ground in the discipline. The chances of that happening might be bleak, given the power of the commitment to social science in the discipline, but if we want to create these linkages, and, above all, this intellectual space, then we must keep our end of the conversation going. There is a lot more at stake than just the question of which version of social constructivism becomes predominant; at stake is how we think about foreign policy and, because of the link between rules and conduct in the social world, how these foreign policies actually get constructed. So much political power goes to those who, in the name of a "neutral social science," can see these foreign policies as no more than the required responses of "pre-social" actors. In that world foreign policy is not what states make of it since the questions of why and for whom they have agency are outside the analysis. It is for this reason that I prefer a form of social constructivism that deems these questions to be central to the analysis of foreign policy, and it is also exactly why that form of constructivism will be resisted by the mainstream. What does this tell us about the social construction of intellectual disciplines?

References

Adler, Emmanuel. 1997. "Seizing the Middle Ground: Constructivism in World Politics." *European Journal of International Relations* 3: 319–363.

Berger, Peter, and Luckmann, Thomas. 1966. *The Social Construction of Reality: A Treatise in the Sociology of Knowledge.* New York: Doubleday Books.

Checkel, Jeffrey. 1998. "The Constructivist Turn in International Relations Theory." *World Politics* 50(2): 324–348.

Goldstein, Judith, and Keohane, Robert, eds. 1993. *Ideas and Foreign Policy: Beliefs, Institutions and Political Change.* Ithaca: Cornell University Press.

Hacking, Ian. 1999. *The Social Construction of What?* Cambridge, MA: Harvard University Press.

Hollis, Martin, and Smith, Steve. 1990. *Explaining and Understanding International Relations.* Oxford: Clarendon Press.

Jepperson, Ronald, Wendt, Alexander, and Katzenstein, Peter. 1996. "Norms, Identity, and Culture in National Security." In Peter Katzenstein, ed., *The Culture of National Security: Norms and Identity in World Politics*, pp. 33–75. New York: Columbia University Press.

Jørgensen, Knud Erik. 1997a. "Introduction: Approaching European Governance." In Knud Erik Jørgensen, ed., *Reflective Approaches to European Governance*, pp. 1–12. Houndmills, UK: Macmillan.

Katzenstein, Peter, Keohane, Robert, and Krasner, Stephen. 1998. "*International Organization* and the Study of World Politics." *International Organization* 52(4): 645–685.

Keohane, Robert. 1989. *International Institutions and State Power: Essays in International Relations Theory.* Boulder, CO: Westview).

Kratochwil, Friedrich. 1989. *Rules, Norms, and Decisions: On the Conditions of Practical and Legal Reasoning in International Relations and Domestic Affairs.* Cambridge, UK: Cambridge University Press.

Kubálková, Vendulka, Onuf, Nicholas, and Kowert, Paul, eds. 1998. *International Relations in a Constructed World*. Armonk, NY: M.E. Sharpe.

Onuf, Nicholas. 1989. *World of Our Making: Rules and Rule in Social Theory and International Relations*. Columbia: University of South Carolina Press.

———. 1998. "Constructivism: A User's Manual." In Vendulka Kubálková, Nicholas Onuf, and Paul Kowert, eds., *International Relations in a Constructed World*, pp. 58–78. Armonk, NY: M.E. Sharpe.

Ruggie, John. 1998. *Constructing the World Polity: Essays on International Institutionalization*. London: Routledge.

Schultz, Alfred. 1967. *The Phenomenology of the Social World*. Evanston, IL: Northwestern University Press.

Searle, John. 1995. *The Construction of Social Reality*. London: Penguin Books.

Singer, J. David. 1961. "The Level of Analysis Problem in International Relations." In K. Knoor and S. Verba, eds., *The International System: Theoretical Essays*, pp. 85–90. Princeton, NJ: Princeton University Press.

Smith, Steve. 1995. "The Self-Images of a Discipline: A Genealogy of International Relations Theory." In Ken Booth and Steve Smith, eds., *International Relations Theory Today*, pp. 1–37. Cambridge: Polity Press.

———. 1996. "Positivism and Beyond." In Steve Smith, Ken Booth, and Marysia Zalewski, eds., *International Theory: Positivism and Beyond*, pp. 11–44. Cambridge, UK: Cambridge University Press.

———. 1997. "New Approaches to International Theory." In John Baylis and Steve Smith, eds., *The Globalization of World Politics*, pp. 165–190. Oxford, UK: Oxford University Press.

———. 2000. "Wendt's World." *Review of International Studies* 26(1): 151–163.

Waever, Ole. 1996. "The Rise and Fall of the Inter-Paradigm Debate." In Steve Smith, Ken Booth, and Marysia Zalewski, eds., *International Theory: Positivism and Beyond*, pp. 149–185. Cambridge, UK: Cambridge University Press.

Walt, Stephen. 1998. "International Relations: One World, Many Theories." *Foreign Policy* 110: 29–46.

Wendt, Alexander. 1987. "The Agent-Structure Problem in International Relations Theory." *International Organization* 41(3): 335–370.

———. 1992. "Anarchy Is What States Make of It." *International Organization* 46(2): 391–425.

———. 1994. "Collective Identity Formation and the International State." *American Political Science Review* 88(2): 384–396.

———. 1998. "On Constitution and Causation in International Relations." *Review of International Studies* 24 (special issue): 101–117.

———. 1999. *Social Theory of International Politics*. Cambridge, UK: Cambridge University Press.

Winch, Peter. 1958. *The Idea of a Social Science and its Relation to Philosophy*. London: Routledge and Kegan Paul.

3

A Constructivist Primer

Vendulka Kubálková

Constructivism can do a lot of things for International Relations (IR). The constructivism of the variety described in chapters 1 and 2 as soft, moderate, and inspired largely by the work of Wendt, is no more than a friendly Mr. Fix-it, who can provide the crumbling edifice of knowledge that we call IR with a new facade. It is not difficult to become a Mr. Fix-it: a bucket of paint and a brush and the novice constructivist is set! A little work can make an old style look new once a fashionable design is pasted onto the old surface and a fresh coat of a pastel color applied. The new facade and its ornamentation will give the old structure a new "identity" and locate it in a distinct, let's say art deco, "culture." In this sense, the soft constructivism is responsive to changing fashions (the world of scholarship too, as a sort of a culture in its own right, is inevitably sensitive to matters of vogue). But how long before we realize that the old crumbling structure has the same problems, only now thinly disguised by the coat of paint!

There is a more robust if less fashionable variety of constructivism—what we in this volume call rule-oriented constructivism—that can provide a much more lasting renovation than an art deco–style facade. This approach addresses the main problem of the old structure, namely, that it is so ill suited to the shifting sands of empirical research in which positivist social science forever seeks—and never finds—the solid rock of a foundation. Rule-oriented constructivists propose to build a new frame altogether, and it is this frame, not just the terrain on which it stands, that gives the edifice its strength. The new frame connects agents and structure at as many levels as agents decide on by giving structure to agency. In the new frame agents do what they have to do, still on rational grounds, but the scope of rational choice, and the meaning of what is rational, is recast. The structural conditions provide the social context within which agents find themselves and set the limits within which agents exercise judgment.

What does this mean? If the structure has no kitchen, because it is, for example, an office building, agents are likely to figure out that cooking dinner is a possible choice but not a rational one. If the structure has a limited number of bedrooms, the agents will not invite dozens of guests for a sleepover unless it is culturally acceptable that guests can sleep on the floor. It will be the structure, in other words, the particular structure that will set the limits, rather than any a priori framework that sets what is or is not regarded as rational. Since the new frame is a social structure, a space is opened for the consideration of humans as complex social creatures with multiple, often conflicting, goals and a great variety of skills and other resources available to them.

Rule-oriented constructivism can achieve all of this because it is not working alone. As Michael Collier explains in his contribution to this volume, it has the tremendous potential to welcome theories, and even entire disciplines, into its ambit, because it provides a way of joining them together. Above all, the new building will accommodate real people, without whom agency and thus social structure are impossible. The problem now—and the opportunity—is to convince scholars and students of the virtue of this project by making it possible for them to see how this kind of constructivism works and what it can do for them.

The following contains very little narrative and many tables. I suggest that, practically speaking, a rule-oriented constructivist proceeds in four steps, each one leading to the next.

The four easy steps are:

Step 1. *Learning to see the way a constructivist sees*—seeing the world as inextricably social and material, seeing people in their world as makers of their world; seeing the world as a never-ending construction project.

Step 2. *Learning to think the way a constructivist does*—learning constructivist categories.

Step 3. *Learning to translate familiar ways of talking into constructivist categories* in order to make use of existing scholarship.

Step 4. *Learning to ask the sorts of questions that a constructivist asks* and determining the best way to answer them.

I can explain these four steps in the context of the building metaphor. Seeing the world for what it is, taking the trouble to look at all, and then seeing it differently, is the first step without which we cannot begin to appreciate the circumstances and the condition of the old structure (whether it is

IR or any of the other social sciences). Only then are we going to realize that much more than superficial repairs are necessary. In the second step, we proceed to learning what the constructivist frame consists of so that we can identify its parts and get used to looking for them everywhere around us. The third step takes us to the materials that were used as the bricks and mortar in the old structure and bids us to figure out where and how, in the constructivist frame, they fit. Only then can we do what we understand to be empirical research. The fourth step, asking the most useful sorts of questions, often means asking what the rules are (since rules do the framing in rule-oriented constructivism), how they got made, how they define the terms of agency, how they set the conditions of rational choice, and how they constitute resources. It means asking how rules that are constantly changing constitute institutions that both resist and foster change in the process of structuring social relations. And it means asking how rules and thus institutions allow agents to exercise control over resources and other agents, thus affecting the distribution of benefits among agents. All of these questions can be cast in terms of the building materials to be found in other fields of knowledge, but materials used here in a different frame.

Before we do this however, we need to take the four steps. Each step requires a great deal of thought—in fact, thinking them through is the hardest part of all, although many students have claimed that constructivist thinking is closer to what they regard as common sense. It takes practice to think this way, but then any structured human activity takes practice before anyone, and not just scholars, can participate in that practice effectively. It is only because of past practice that the received ways of thinking, which all of us engage in daily, seem easy by comparison.

Seeing the Social World the Way a Rule-Oriented Constructivist Does

Seeing the social world the way a rule-oriented constructivist involves seeing the world as inextricably social and material, that is, seeing people in their world as makers of their world, and seeing the world as a never-ending construction project.

Seeing is not merely a matter of receiving and processing information about the world. This is the standard positivist sense of what it means to see, whether with our own eyes or with the help of various instruments and procedures. Let us practice it on an example, a story of a visit from another planet in which I paraphrase an account written for this purpose by a postpositivist contributor to this volume, Ralph Pettman. Then, and going somewhat beyond this step, I use a table to juxtapose and contrast side by side a checklist of the positivist and postpositivist ways of seeing the world (Table 3.1), no longer in Pettman's language of rocks but in the language of social science. Thus we come at the problem of seeing in two ways: a postpositivist commentary on seeing the world, and a new way of seeing, contrasted with the way we have already learned to do in IR or other social sciences. Rule-oriented constructivists do not deny the benefits of seeing as positivists do (at least for some purposes), but they agree with postpositivists that positivists don't see enough—they don't see that seeing is always a social, world-making activity.

A Story of Visitors from Another Planet and Two Humans

Imagine that a scientific expedition arrives on the earth from a distant planet called Positivia. The Positivians explore the earth's surface, measure, sample, count, and estimate. They observe with amazement the strange life taking place in territorially bounded feedlots of different sizes. They do not understand the signals that their inhabitants use to communicate with each other, but they impute to their life a logic from what they can observe. Two humans join the Positivians to help them in their research. The first one quickly learns the Positivians' ways and does exactly what they do. Although he speaks the language of humans, he accepts the Positivian wisdom as superior to his own and agrees with the Positivians that the speech of his fellow humans distracts from the research carried out from a higher, objective, Positivian perspective. Thus, he treats humans as Positivians do—as cognitively inferior to themselves. He, too, measures and reports and imputes the logic of what is going on from observed features, such as the different size of the feedlots. Since he learned all this from his extraterrestrial Positivian teachers, he calls himself a positivist.

The second human resists a conversion to the Positivian way. Positivians ask him to tell them what it is that he sees, and when he produces his report, they reject it as totally unbelievable, impossible to test, to measure, or to verify. I paraphrase here his non-Positivian, nonpositivist report:

> Everything we know, we make as well as find. All we can explain, in other words, we construct as well as discover. We are all constructivists, in this fundamental sense.
>
> This applies to our knowings of the natural world as well as to our knowings of those worlds of human invention we call "societies" and "cultures." Clearly, rocks don't have a society or a culture, and in this respect they can only be found, not made. But what do we find rocks with?
>
> Whenever we try to know about rocks, we do our knowing using senses already culturally and socially conditioned, and using intellectual appraisal prac-

tices already learned. These conditionings and learnings serve to make what we find. However hard we try to know rocks without them, for example, we cannot. We are all without exception cultural and social beings and the particular kind of cultural and social being we are will influence (some would say, determine) what gets known. However hard we try to eliminate such influences, we cannot eliminate them entirely.

This said, there is a difference between knowing the natural world and knowing the human one. Human beings are creative in a way rocks are not. The possibility of knowing rocks in a singular, eternal, and absolute way is a real one. There is a chance, by minimizing social and cultural influences, or more accurately, by choosing to prioritize that culture and society that objectifies, that we might come to know the Truth about rocks. But people? Of course, some analysts see what people do as the outcome of natural causes alone. To them the argument about the natural world applies to the human world, too. To everyone else, however, human creativity is seemingly endless and well nigh boundless, and this means that no single Truth can ever obtain about humankind. There can only be human truths that constantly change as people construct new ways to be.

This said, there are those, as noted above, who will adopt the wisdom of the Positivians and will try and "find" the human world regardless. Despite the extent to which this world is "made" (and remade in the very act of trying to find it), they will want to see how far they can get by assuming that foreign policy, for example, is a phenomenon already out there, already in the world, to be approached in a more or less scientific way. They believe that they can stand back and look at the world from an analytic vantage point that seems to them to be outside that world.

This is what "speaking of" foreign policy largely entails. We describe and explain what we see. We share with others what the objectifying mind-gaze reveals. We tell them about foreign policy after seeing how certain people behave. Standing back, we look for patterns of behavior, for "structures" that we can generalize and relate to other general patterns in causal terms. This we think constitutes the large structure of whatever it is that we're looking at. There is nothing wrong with this—as far as it goes (and, in the case of foreign policy, this hasn't been very far at all). As an alternative, we can move closer to people and pay attention to what they do (and one of the constructivist maxims is "speaking is doing"). Generalization ceases to be a meaningful possibility, but we end up with a much better sense of the (mostly small) ways that people, as agents, affect the world. Constructivists prefer to move back and forth, "zoom" in and out, in order to get some sense of the processes by which agents and structures affect each other. Nevertheless, every such stance presupposes an objective point of reference that we all know, as a matter of common sense, does not exist except as an idea.[1]

Thinking Like a Constructivist and Learning Constructivist Categories

The first step is also the last one that constructivists and most other postpositivist scholars are likely to take together. In fact, the long passage

Table 3.1

Seeing Like a Constructivist (Constructivist Ontology I)

	Mainstream IR Approaches	Constructivism
Background		By the use of the verb "construct" it intends to convey the active role of people "constructing" the reality, in contrast to stress mainly on "structure" or "agent" (see chapter 1), including idealist theories collectively referred to as action theories. Unlike some action theories, constructivism maintains that the construction is inseparable from the effect of that which is being constructed, that is, the social relations in turn "construct" or coconstitute people as social beings.
Ontological status of the "world" including IR	The world is "out there" to be found	Not "out there" to be found; stepping out to study the world is only provisional, the social world is being made by people (agents, that is, competent participants) who in turn are made. Not all of the world is social, only that part constructed by people.
Ontological status of people	Either detached, objective observers or people who are observed, their behavior (devoid of meaning, intentionality) reified into objects: their ideas, values, and so forth are excluded, all ideas and so forth are traced to material factors	—People as agents observing structures ("structure" refers to agents acting in institutions and consequences, intended and unintended, of their actions; Figure 3.3). —People as agents acting in institutions ("institution" refers to agents, rules, and consequences of acts), making rules, that is, influencing others, making other people do something.

(continued)

Table 3.1 (continued)

	Mainstream IR Approaches	Constructivism
Ontological status of language	Neutral medium, representing reality, studied only for its propositional content (Figure 3.2)	Has ontological status, it is one of the universals of the human species (together with reasoning): speech acts → deeds → their patterns = rules; rules in turn make agents, that is, competent participant, wielding influence, making the world; rules are of three categories (assertive, directive, commissive; Figure 3.3).
Objective of the research	Search for regularities in the world, establishing laws (connecting events) so that through their application the world, that is, events, can be explained, predicted, indeed by some accounts, controlled	1. Finding rules, identifying them as one of the three generic categories of rules 2. Identifying agent, institutions, and structure 3. Explaining their content, for example, "realism," "liberalism," and so forth, which is studied and analyzed as the content of the three categories of rules
What is studied	Events, their description and explanation	Rule-based relations and institutions identification of agent/structures/ rules (IR consists of commissive rules, studying their interface with rules of other states) rules, their main categories, mixes, support for them in other rules, in consciousness and culture study of rules' content
Status of realist assumptions (state centrism, anarchy, states' objectives, behavior, etc.)	Regarded as facts	Regarded as content of rules issued by agents in order to make the world in a certain way

written by Pettman that I have paraphrased above (and his epilogue to this book) suggests his abhorrence of the modernist rationalist project and its objectifying, reductive tendencies. Instead, he stresses the need to get closer and not just to see but to hear and feel as well. He certainly would not be happy to see conceptual thinking, which rule-oriented constructivists proceed to next, as the only step to take.

Rule-oriented constructivists regard conceptual thinking as a cognitive universal—a characteristic feature of the human species. It nevertheless depends on practice. Conceptual thinking is therefore also a social phenomenon. Categories are learned. In practice, we change them to suit our needs and experiences, devising new ones and abandoning old ones that no longer work for us as we see fit.

Step 2, thinking like a constructivist, depends on learning constructivist categories. These are categories that rule-oriented constructivists have devised and refined to complement a small number of core propositions, including this one: People are social beings because they make and use language to achieve ends that are still social even when they think of those ends as their own, that is to say, as their individual ends.

Three illustrations accompany this step. Figure 3.1 contrasts the standard positivist position that language can more or less faithfully represent the world as observed with the constructivist claim that people use language additionally to have an effect on other people. Thus, whether they acknowledge it or not, their claims to have represented the world contribute to its constitution. Figure 3.2 shows how using language makes the social world what it is by introducing such categories as speech act, rule, agency, institution, and structure, and by introducing the major claim that agents and structures constitute each other through the media of speech, policies, rules, and institutions.

It is, of course, one thing to say that agents and structures make each other, and quite another to explain how this actually works. Rule-oriented constructivism provides a way of handling this vexing issue by taking the "linguistic turn." The phrase "linguistic turn" was coined by Gustav Bergmann (1964), a language philosopher and member of the Vienna Circle, which, by giving positivism its final turn toward logical closure, exposed its limitations in studying social phenomena. In expressing his disdain for materialism, Bergmann called on philosophers to rethink the uses of language. Ludwig Wittgenstein, another philosopher with close ties to the Vienna Circle, did just this. The consequences for modern philosophy have been nothing short of revolutionary. Not all constructivists however, and certainly none of the mainstream constructivists, have taken the linguistic turn.

Rule-oriented constructivism follows Wittgenstein into the linguistic turn, though there are different ways to proceed beyond it. At least one constructivist

Figure 3.1   **Language in Positivism and in Constructivism**

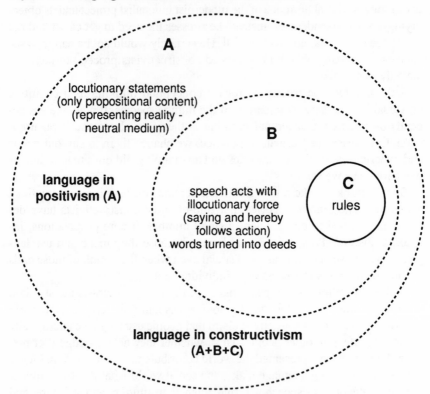

(Fierke 1998, 2001) follows Wittgenstein's treatment of rules in order to understand the "language games" that agents play on behalf of states over matters of security. By contrast Friedrich Kratochwil (1989), and especially Nicholas Onuf (1989), turn to speech act theory, which philosophers J.L. Austin (1963) and John Searle (1969) developed in order to explain how language accomplishes social ends.

Arguably Onuf's most important contribution to constructivism is his systematic effort to show that rules derive from, work like, and depend on speech acts, and that language and rules together (they can never be separated) are the medium through which agents and structures may be said to constitute each other. Thus, language and rules have, according to Onuf, an ontological status no different from that of the agent, and perhaps even more substantial than that of the structure. Language is one of the universal features of the human species, and the presence of rules is a defining feature of the human condition. To study international relations, or any other aspect of human existence, is to study language and rules.

Figure 3.2 **Thinking Like a Constructivist (Constructivist Ontology II)**

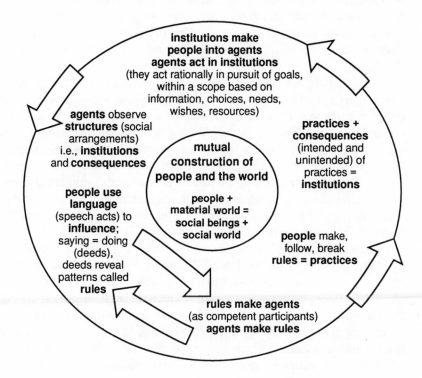

In claiming centrality for language, constructivists reaffirm the time-honored claim that reasoning, consciousness, and the ability to use language together constitute a distinguishing feature of our species. Does it not then make sense that language should figure centrally in IR as a field of study? If language is central, then so are rules. If rules are central, then so is the way that people arrange rules and deploy resources to the advantage of some people over others. As social creatures and language users, we never escape the condition of *rule*. When we scratch the surface of what we are told about such key concepts as power, interest, and anarchy, we find rules, including rules that turn the material features of the world into resources and the rules that turn our needs and wants into interests. We thus find that anarchy, the central concept of mainstream IR, is also a condition of rule.

Constructivism also tells us that in all social relations, people are agents because rules make it possible for them to act and put limits on the range of actions available to them. Chief among those actions is, indeed, speaking. When people speak, within the limits that agency imposes, what they say will have an effect on what other people, as agents, do, even if what they do is to speak to social effect in their turn. As agents, people decide how they will respond to what they hear other agents are saying to them. Speaking, however, never guarantees the social effect that people wish to achieve. The same is true when agents respond to what rules or policies tell them they should do.

In Onuf's rendition of speech act theory, there are three primary ways in which speech works to achieve these social effects. We may assert something about the world that others will accept (or reject, qualify, etc.). We may demand that others do what we say. We can make promises that have consequences for us if others accept them. These three ways that we, as agents, use language to affect others also mean that there are three categories of rules—Onuf calls them instruction-rules, directive-rules, and commitment rules—and three forms of rule—hegemony, hierarchy, and heteronomy. Anarchy as a description of the world of international relations mixes the first and third forms of rule, with a pinch of the second thrown in.

Onuf extends this tripartite scheme to many aspects of the social world, including culture and values. Table 3.2 provides a summary, and tries to explain as many of them as can be fitted into a table. The columns in this table present the three primary categories into which we organize our experiences, and the many rows give some sense of the scope or range of those experiences. Any change in any row within the column has ripple effects (and this is not a unilinear causal influencing, but more a dialectical mutual effect) on all of the other entries in the column. Similarly, changes within one column ripple across columns. This is because the categories, as containers, are conceptual devices, while the world around us typically exhibits varying mixes of whatever phenomena the rows seek to categorize.

Translating Familiar Ways of Talking/Thinking into Constructivist Categories

Step 2 includes the main categories of rule-oriented constructivism for the understanding of the mutual relation of agent and structure, the role of speech acts and rules, and the three categories of speech act and rules, and other elementary features of social relations. To repeat what we find in Figure 3.2, *agents* always act in an institutional context; action is intentional by definition. Agency is a social condition, and individuals act on behalf of themselves as social beings or on behalf of *institutions* to which we then impute agency.

Agents make and use *rules*, and those rules constitute institutions, which, in turn, constitute agency as a social condition. As agents, individuals always choose whether to act in accordance with those rules. As a matter of

Table 3.2

Constructivist Synoptic Table

Faculties of experience (a determinate set of three) / Paradigms of experience (not a determinate set, others can be added)	Category of existence and constitution/regulation of its meaning	Category of material control and its constitution agreement and exchange,	Category of discretionary endeavor, mutual constitution of agency
Speech acts (getting someone to act)	Assertive • Stating a belief that speaker hopes hearer to accept • X counts as Y (if Y is a value, then it is a principle) • The world is presented in words	Directives • Speaker presents hearer with his intention of some act to be performed • X person must do Y • Words indicate how the world ought to be and that X will do it	Commissive • Speakers commitment to a course of action, promise/offer: if hearer accepts speaker is stuck • I state I will do Y • Words indicate how the world ought to be and I will do it if you accept my proposition
Rules (repeated speech acts)	Instruction-rules	Directive-rules	Commitment-rules
Common phrases associated with these types of rules	"I state," "affirm," "report," "characterize," "attribute," "insist," "dissent," "declare"	"I ask," "command," "demand," "caution," "permit"	"I promise," "offer"
Strength of rules support/sanctions of rules	Normatively weak (needs support) internal consciousness	Normatively strong external	Normatively weak (needs support) internal/ other rules
Defining features of society	Status	Office	Role

	Hegemony	Hierarchy	Heteronomy
Rule (form of) (rules determine distribution of material resources and thus "rules yield rule")	Ideas and beliefs seem to do the ruling	Chain of command	• Agents' roles defined by roles of others • The association rules • Thus agents do not see rule in their role
Form of organization	Informal networks	Organizations	Associations
Social ambition, objective, interest	Standing	Security	Wealth
Main form of activity/ occupation	Prophecy "Priests and professors" (and their derivatives)	War "Warriors and diplomats" (and their derivatives)	Provisioning "Physicians and merchants" (and their derivatives)
Main form of reasoning	Conjecture/Abduction	Deduction	Induction
Typical logical procedures	• Metaphor, conjuration hypothesis," which is either — accepted on faith or — explained by referring to column 2 and 3 reasoning • Global comparison "I want to be the best" (of the rank ordered field of many)	• Analytico-deductive model • Scientific research justification • "Combat" • Binary comparison "I want more so that the other has less"(absolute gain)	• Academic research • Implication • "Clue finding" • Medical profession • Internal comparison "I want as much as I can get"(relative gain)
Feeling	Shame	Dread	Guilt

Primary categories of political practice	• "Manners" • Ethical conduct	"Virtue" to regulate individual appetite since coercion is allowed	"Rights" (deciding about conflicts involving rights)
Main exhortation	Tell the truth	Do no harm (since violence of sanctions is allowed)	Keep promises
Regime (form of)	Monitory regimes	Executive regimes	Administrative regimes privileging merchants and property owners
Examples of bundles of rules and their classification according to predominant rules • Cultures • Civilizations • Political systems • Modes of activities (all are mixes of all three categories but one is more strongly represented)	Premodern political systems Religions Religion based cultures and civilizations Nationalism, totalitarian and authoritarian political systems (in combination with hierarchical elements) Universities, media, educational bodies, religions Principles of identity of self and community high, internalized, leading to martyrdom (e.g., Shi'ism)	• "Warrior"-type occupations, army etc. • Natural sciences • Social sciences based on positivism • Analytico-deductive model Corporations Internalize directive rules, calculating responses fear/dread culture	• Western capitalist/ democratic/ liberal state (with sanctions and police) • Individualism • Liberal culture • Commissive culture of capitalism (rights and duties) • Material achievement Guilt culture, sense of responsibility, concern over performance and failure

Source: Based on Onuf's synoptic table of paradigms of experience and faculties, 1989, p. 290. NB: "Any change in a society's rules redefines agents, institutions, and their relation to each other; any such change also changes the rules, including those rules agents use to effectuate or inhibit changes in societies." Onuf, 1997, 7. Constructivists claim they cannot stand outside human experience and cannot offer a set of coordinates that "explain" the recurrence of consistent pattern for experience in a form of a table. However, for pedagogical purposes this "standard logocentric" exercise might be excused. Onuf, 1989, p. 290ff.

rational choice, they evaluate the consequences of either course of action; as a practical matter they have *internalized* many such rules, which they are prone to follow more or less routinely.

Culture consists of *beliefs*, or those rules that are widely internalized for any group of people, and the *practices* stemming from these beliefs. Even if action is intentional, it is likely to produce unintended consequences. These, in turn, often fall into patterns, or *structures*, which agents notice and, by acting on them, institutionalize. As such, they define the precise conditions of agency for affected individuals, and so we go around again. Figure 3.1 portrays this process as an uninterrupted circle. We might better think of it as a spiral, since each time around every element changes in relation to all the other elements.

Adding the three types of rules and extending them to the broader social context along the lines indicated in Table 3.2 amplifies the framework without altering the basic process as I have just conceptualized it. Figures 3.1 and 3.2 and Table 3.2 encapsulate quite a large number of concepts, and open room for others. Even if the framework seems fairly simple, it is suited to the study of social relations, ranging from daily life to international relations. The social reality that rule-oriented constructivism conveys is one of tremendous complexity. Yet the framework makes a place for everything.

Contrast this with the starkly simple framework that most IR scholars start with: States coexist in a condition of anarchy. Faced with a complex world, these scholars proceed to add elements in an ad hoc fashion: international regimes, norms and ideas, the social construction of interests, and, of course, the traditional realist notions of balancing and bandwagoning. Nothing fits together properly, and no one thinks that anyone else's research makes sense on conceptual grounds. Methodological competence is never enough.

Rule-oriented constructivists can avoid this sorry state of affairs. Once familiar with steps 1 and 2, and used to looking for agents, rules, their categories, structure, and so on, they can move on to step 3. After all, scholars learn comparable steps in order to be able to conduct positivist research competently and then take them for granted. Their problem is not the steps as such but the incoherence of the concepts that they step up to and learn. For positivists in IR, there is nothing comparable to step 3. Often enough it is here, however, at step 3, that constructivist research may begin without necessarily repeating and explaining steps 1 and 2.

It is important to remember that rule-oriented constructivism reaches across all of the social sciences, each of which has its own categories and schemes for classifying its subject matter. Whenever positivists leave the cozy confines of their disciplinary homes, they, too, must learn how to translate conceptually unfamiliar material wherever they encounter it. For constructivists, this will often seem to be a never-ending task, and one never to be shirked or shortchanged. Its importance cannot be overstated. Through the common denominator of constructivist categories, constructivists have access to the knowledge assembled by all other social science disciplines.

Our concern in this volume is with foreign policy, and, thus the conceptual premises of FPA provide the raw material for step 3. Onuf's chapter ("Speaking of Policy") is devoted almost entirely to examining the very concept of foreign policy, as used in ordinary positivist language, and to redefining it in constructivist terms. There are many other concepts and categories in FPA that need translation. Table 3.3 identifies quite a number of them for IR in general and FPA in particular. Many of the other contributions to this volume translate some of these, and other concepts as needed, and Table 3.3 (and Table 3.2 always) serve as guidelines.

The important caveat I want to repeat is that rule-oriented constructivism is merely a "way of studying social relations," a "system of concepts and propositions." It remains—as far as possible—on the level of ontology. It offers no theory about international relations or foreign policy. Instead, it helps us to make sense of what we have learned in studying IR by sorting this material into categories—agents, structures, institutions, rules, types of rule—that are systematically related. Rule-oriented constructivism does not offer any specific explanations for the way things seem to be related, but rather it "makes it feasible to theorize about matters that seem to be unrelated because the concepts and propositions normally used to talk about such matters are also unrelated" (Onuf 1998, 58).

Rule-oriented constructivism suggests links where none seemed possible heretofore. We have to be prepared to crisscross disciplinary boundaries to make use of categories less familiar to IR scholars than to anthropologists or sociologists, for example. In other words, an important distinction needs to be made between rule-oriented constructivism as a framework and those theories, wherever they are found or whenever they are devised, that can be used within the framework and linked through its categories to other, seemingly unrelated theories. Only theories, not the framework, will generate specific questions and point to appropriate methodologies.

Rule-oriented constructivism's ontology is the common thread in the ever-changing range of social activities in which people engage, shaping the world and in turn being shaped by it. Words, rules, and rule are the key elements in this ontology. With words people move effortlessly across the divide between "is statements" and "ought statements," in the process defying positivists who think that this divide can and should never be bridged. In doing so, they make rules, and with rules they organize system of rule.

All of this adds complexity but also flexibility, lacking in IR as it is cur-

Table 3.3

Translating into Constructivist Categories the Established Discourses: IP/FP

IR Discipline	Constructivism
International Politics as a *discipline* claims the topic of international relations as its *sole focus*. IR is one of the disciplines into which Western academy is fragmented. There is no main approach but three mainstream approaches. The singularity of focus on IR of mainstream approaches, neorealism in particular, means that they can devise elegant, simple (truncated) theories of international relations, uncomplicated by adding other types of relations.	In the tradition of Max Weber, Karl Marx, Talcott Parsons, Anthony Giddens— scholars who predated (and/or rejected) the specialization of Western academe into more narrow academic disciplines—constructivism is a *social theory* that claims to deal with most general principles on which societies, indeed humanity, not only IR, are based.
	IR as a particularly *important* category of social relations deserves a separate inquiry, is at the apex of multiple social relations of great complexity. IR constitute only one set of these relations, impossible to tear out of a broader context.
• Mainstream approaches are *structuralist*, that is, they emphasize the importance of structure, defined in neorealism as uneven distribution of capabilities across functionally same units	• Constructivism is *not structuralist*, it regards agent (and rules) of equal importance: structure to constructivism is any stable pattern of rules, institutions, and unintended consequences as observed by other agents (preferred label for structure is *social arrangement*).
• State is the main actor, "a territorially based political unit characterized by decision making and enforcement machinery, that is legally *sovereign* (i.e., it does not recognize any higher or lower unit of equal or superior strength) and that exists in a world of other similarly composed units."	• Constructivism unwraps the reified packages of positivism and presents states as social relations.
	• *Sovereignty* is a fiction: agents are always limited by rules that give other agents opportunity to act.
IP—relations of states in a unique environment of anarchy	*IP— a society of relatively self-contained societies constituted by different rules*

• *States are like units*, unitary and uniform: sovereignty and survival are fundamental parts of a state's identity; any other possible "identity" is irrelevant.

• International relations and *domestic politics* are fundamentally different, and domestic politics is relegated to study in other disciplines, for example, domestic politics to political science.

• *Anarchy* is a condition of rule, but constructivism disagrees that anarchy characterizes the states system; they see states system as characterized by *heteronomy*, a pattern of unintended consequences (rules are not directly responsible for agents' conduct).

• States differ from each other according to the *prevailing types of rules* on which they are based.

• International relations and *domestic relations* are mutually connected, made out of the same cloth (although of very different categories of rules). The parallel existence of states then as they interact and coexist brings them into a relation where they either "speak" to each other in commissive rules, obliging both of them. Because among them none would be agreed upon by the others to become an agent and rule, they understand that their relations are at best based on unintended consequences of input of all participants.

The difference in the functioning of state on one hand and relation of many states on the other would be in the type of rules and the existing agency.

Foreign policy deals with agents of one society and circumstances of making rules within one society, targeted at a society operating by other rules.

The *difference between FP and IP* is in the nature of rules: IP involves interaction of different societies (states are not uniform) based on different rules. IP rules are weak rules. A rule adopted by an agent of system of states will be accepted and incorporated differently in different societies, depending upon the internal support for these rules.

FP rules are used to evince responses from other states, that is, at a destination beyond the states' jurisdiction.

rently constituted. Indeed the field is so narrowly configured that it leaves itself very little to study: states as rational agents, varying only in size (capability) and engaged in a narrow repertory of behaviors from which there is no escape. Constructivists are not bound by any such set categories. Thus, they might conclude, for example, that in particular situations, the territorially bounded, law-based, Western-type state is no longer the central principle on which the actual conduct of international relations is based, given the presence of nonstate agents, failed states, and states serving as cover for nonstate agents engaged in activities such as terrorism that affect other states. Or, we might posit states whose agents regard states as transitory and insignificant features of the world. The point of departure for constructivists, in other words, cannot be a fixed notion of who or what actually matters in any given domain of social relations.

Asking Questions Like a Constructivist

Conducting research along constructivist lines means asking the right sort of questions. The reader will appreciate the complexity of this step and the impossibility of formulating in advance an authoritative list of questions. I suggested some of the more important questions when I introduced the four steps.

This is where we ought to return to the important distinction between constructivism as a framework, and the theories and methodologies that can be used within this framework. Only theories can generate specific research questions (although some positivists use specific methodologies to do so, with embarrassingly trivial results). It is these theories that can be linked together through the constructivist framework particularly by "filling in" Table 3.2, something of a centerpiece in constructivist research. The questions asked by rule-oriented constructivists are very different from those asked by positivists.

While positivists claim that their first question is, "What are the facts?" a constructivist will inquire, "Who are the agents; what are they doing [since saying *is* doing] and not doing [which is also a way of saying something]; what seems to be changing and what is not?" All these questions lead to, and away from, one other question, which for rule-oriented constructivists is often the first one to ask: "What are the rules and where do we find them?" In international relations, for example, should we look for rules in the talk of diplomats and statesmen? Or, in the official pronouncements of states or international organizations? Should we look at what the press has to say? Or IR texts? The choice will depend on the specific subject under investigation and the specific theory to be used within a constructivist framework. Answers to the question at hand are not likely to be obvious. As anthropologists have discovered, people usually know what the rules are, but they often do not think about them as rules. The same is generally true about the sources of information about international relations: The rules are there for the constructivists to discover, often enough between the lines, once they set out finding them.

Positivists start with facts as such, attaching great importance to methodological arguments over the status of facts: If "it" cannot be measured, is "it" a fact? How can we be sure that a fact is not contaminated by the fact of its being observed? Constructivists tend to be less fussy about these matters; they often do not subscribe to the "rules of evidence" required by positivists, because they think that these rules effectively count most of social reality out of consideration. The falsification of hypotheses and theories, as required by positivists, postulates a correspondence theory of truth between the "world and the word," between the "objective reality" and our representations of it. However, if language is constitutive of the world, as step 2 suggests, then we cannot really meaningfully compare it with that which it describes.

This is where we reach the key to the constructivist epistemology, that is, the answer given by constructivists to the question, "What counts as knowledge?" Constructivists shift from the positivist approach, where criteria can be imposed from outside, to looking for the relational context within which we interact with others (Fierke, 2001). Constructivists then attempt to identify the larger intersubjective context within which deeds of one kind or another appear to be reasonable and therefore justifiable. The soft/moderate constructivists also talk about intersubjectivity, but not the same way. To them, intersubjectivity is shared understanding, and this is something discernible, at least in principle, from the outside. By contrast, rule-oriented constructivists hold that intersubjectivity is a process, which makes all facts *social*. As such they are provisional claims, some better founded than others, but always dependent on the subject's (agent's, claimant's) ever-contingent position in an ever-changing stream of deeds.

As to methodologies, Onuf recommends using any methodology that suits a particular theory. Constructivists should not shy away from analytic rigor in particular settings just because the complexity of social reality defeats the effort to be rigorous. Thus, Collier's contribution to this volume illustrates the value of rational choice theory from a constructivist point of view. As Milliken (2001) shows, discourse theory can be made more rigorous without sacrificing its critical (and, therefore, postpositivist) intentions. The moderate/soft constructivists favor case studies, and they are not alone. Faced with a complex social reality, positivists often resort to case studies, and, as this volume illustrates, rule-oriented constructivists also find them exceedingly useful tools. One can use many of the qualitative methodologies assembled in the standard IR methodology courses, athough there is no one method that seems especially suited to the needs of rule-oriented constructivism. By engaging in the close reading of exemplary texts, or the thick description of emblematic situations, it is possible to give some sense of the intersubjective processes at work. We can tease out the rules that guide them. Obviously, rules always seem to matter, even if policies and other practices are not reducible to rules only.

I want to emphasize that there are any number of other questions that a rule-oriented constructivist might want to ask once steps 1, 2, and 3 have been taken. The topically diverse contributions to this volume illustrate the point. Step by step, rule-oriented constructivism takes practice. Speaking from my own experience, it is impossible not to ask questions like a constructivist after one has been doing so for a while!

Note

1. Ralph Pettman wrote this section specially for this volume.

References

Austin, J.L. 1963. *How to Do Things with Words*. Cambridge, MA: Harvard University.

Bergmann, Gustav. 1964. *Logic and Reality*. Madison: University of Wisconsin Press.

Fierke, K.M. 1998. *Changing Games, Changing Strategies: Critical Investigations in Security*. Manchester: Manchester University Press.

———. 2001. "Critical Methodology and Constructivism." In K.M. Fierke and K.E. Jørgenson, eds., *Constructing International Relations: The Next Generation*, pp. 115–135. NewYork, Amonk: M.E. Sharpe.

Kratochwil, Friedrich V. 1989. *Rules, Norms, and Decisions: On the Contradictions of Practical and Legal Reasoning in International Relations and Domestic Affairs*. Cambridge, UK: Cambridge University Press.

Milliken, Jenifer. 2001. "Discourse Study: Bringing Rigor to Critical Theory." In K.M. Fierke and K.E. Jørgenson, eds., *Constructing International Relations: The Next Generation*, pp. 136–159. New York, Amonk: M.E. Sharpe.

Onuf, Nicholas Greenwood. 1989. *World of Our Making: Rules and Rule in Social Theory and International Relations*. Columbia: University of South Carolina Press.

———. 1997. "A Constructivist Manifesto." In Kurt Burch and Robert A. Denemank, eds., *Constituting International Political Economy*. Boulder, CO: Lynne Rienner.

———.1998. "Everyday Ethics in International Relations." *Millennium: Journal of International Studies* 27(2): 669–693.

Searle, John R. 1969. *Speech Acts*. Cambridge, UK: Cambridge University Press.

4

Speaking of Policy

Nicholas Onuf

Few terms are more prominent in public discourse and political studies than "policy." Few terms are used more freely, with less attention to conceptual implications and empirical referents. Discussions of foreign policy illustrate the point. Here it is almost impossible to find a sustained connection between the use of the term "policy" and claims about specific policies made by reference to their origins, contents, targets, uses, and effects.

This chapter is a conceptual investigation of a term as elusive as it is familiar. Underlying the investigation is a constructivist framework, which I have developed elsewhere for making sense of the world (Onuf 1989, 1998a). In representing the way things are and how they work in relation to each other, language makes things (including ourselves as agents) what they are by making the world (any world of social relations) what it is. Each of us uses language as an instrument (one of many instruments that language makes available to us) to carry out our individual intentions—ends that we hold for ourselves and take to be within our capacities to achieve. Yet it is never possible for us to carry out those intentions without the participation of others, because of the language that we use together, and the world—the manifold of ends and capacities—that we make for ourselves collectively.

Policies do not exist apart from the words that we, as agents, use to characterize them. In this respect it does not matter whether we are acting on our own behalf or on behalf of others. Policies exist only when we put our intentions into words and frame courses of action, or plans, to achieve them. We can always form plans without communicating them to anyone else. In such cases, we can always change our plans as we see fit. While we may refer to our unspoken plans as "personal policies" (Bratman 1999), they are exceedingly unreliable as instruments for achieving our intentions.[1]

Speaking is an activity with normative consequences. When we speak, our words lead others to expect that we will act in a certain way—in accordance with our stated intentions—and that we ought to do so. Our words matter to us. Simply by being spoken, our stated intentions and plans have some degree of normative force in their own right.[2]

If we do not wish (intend) to be held to our stated intentions, it is better not to state them at all. Even then, other agents are obliged to make inferences about *our* intentions in order to be able to act on *their* intentions. They put words into our mouths and call them our policies. In this case, too, it is better not to affirm, or even deny, what others have to say about our intentions and the plans that we adopt for achieving them, if indeed we wish not to be held to them.

Often enough, we do not want to hold other agents in the dark about our intentions. Instead, we want others to hold us to standards of conduct that we accept for ourselves by stating our intentions. We welcome the normative force of stated intentions, and we state those intentions in ways that reinforce their normative effects. We declare our intentions; we go so far as to make pledges about our intentions. Paradoxically, these policy statements are so familiar that we tend to take them for granted when we detach ourselves sufficiently from any world of agents and intentions to observe it closely.

The first section of this chapter starts with undisclosed or misrepresented intentions and considers them from the point of view of rational agents who are engaged in strategic interaction.[3]

Strategically engaged agents must make inferences about the actual intentions of their counterparts in order to make choices best suited to achieving ends that they themselves are not disposed to reveal to others. The analysis of strategic interaction looks behind threats, lies, and promises to the commitments motivating such overt acts. Many threats and certainly most lies and promises are spoken. Analyzing their properties as speech acts tells us a good deal about agents' undisclosed intentions when they make strategic moves. Like policies, commitments exist only as inferences made by agents forced to anticipate what other agents who have obscured their intentions are going to do.

Strategic interaction often eventuates in agreements understood as acts of reciprocal commitment. The second section of this chapter again examines the properties of speech acts to show that many agreements do not depend on agents' exchanging promises. Instead, they are coordinated declarations of agents' intentions. Each such declaration is capable of standing alone. Individually and collectively they are policy statements, to which all agents accord great normative significance. They do the work of public standards, or rules.

The next section of the chapter shows that declarations of intention are comparable to gifts and shows how both relate to pledges. While the ceremonial aspects of social life seem far removed from strategic interaction, speech acts are common to both spheres. Speech acts have the properties that they do only in relation to agents' intentions. The concluding section looks into the wide space between disguised intentions and declared intentions, between bluffs and pledges (a space warped by the occasional convergence of bluffs and pledges). There we find policies attributed to agents who, for their part, often have good reason not to agree with or even acknowledge what others say. It is no surprise, then, that when we look closely, alleged policies vanish from view.

Commitments

To illustrate my claim that policies vanish under the gaze of any close observer, let me turn to the most thorough discussion of the term "foreign policy" that I have come across (Meehan 1971). For Eugene Meehan, "a 'policy' is by definition the instrument needed to make a reasoned choice in a specific situation," with "reasoned choice" further defined as "all human actions based on deliberate comparison of alternative possible outcomes in terms of known standards or principles" (Meehan 1971, 268, 269). Standards enable agents to set priorities among competing goals and order preferences. Policies are "intellectual tools" reworked for each use but always according to available standards (Meehan 1971, 275).[4]

To say, then, that agents know what their policies are is to say that they know how to fashion tools and use them in various situations in order to make choices. Observers are able to make appropriate inferences about agents' policies by examining those choices, no doubt in conjunction with information about relevant standards that agents can be supposed to have used for guidance. Of course, agents often make statements about situations, standards, preferences, and choices. To be sure, they have many reasons to be less than truthful about their policies. On Meehan's account, they rarely are truthful. "Policy statements," as Meehan (1971, 286) called them, "are not very useful as sources of information about policy."

Meehan's concern for the accuracy of policy statements misses the point of his own position. Policy statements should be "treated as *actions* (Meehan's emphasis) rather than policies," because policies are instruments that result in action (Meehan 1971, 286). Situations change, standards point to previously unconsidered courses of action, preferences assume new orderings, choices bear little or no relation to each other, and the diverse reasons that people give for making unrelated choices cannot be reconciled. If policies do not seem fixed because, as tools, they have many uses, then statements about particular policies must seem vague, deceptive, or fabricated when taken together. Agents may not intend this result, and observers are mistaken in assuming that ambiguity or deception must be intended or indeed that agents care what conclusions observers draw.

According to Meehan (1971, 287), "policy statements may contain lies, bluffing, and threatening information that can be highly beneficial to the actor, at least in the short run." Agents may indeed lie, bluff, or threaten, as a matter of policy, to achieve goals or solve problems. Yet Meehan never said that these acts—typically spoken—are statements of policy in their own right. What kind of statement they might be is another matter. Meehan's rather offhand reference to threat offers a clue.

Rational agents make threats and promises as strategic moves in interactions with other agents. These interactions make pairs of agents adversaries and/or partners, always dependent on the others' choices in making choices of their own. Moves communicate information about agents' intentions, sometimes tacitly (e.g., by aiming a weapon or dropping it) and often not reliably (because agents are lying or bluffing about their intentions). Typically, agents do not know if statements or other indications of intention are credible. They can simply accept such statements at face value and act accordingly. Or they can respond with the sort of move that forces other agents to act on, qualify, or repudiate their stated intentions.

No one has analyzed these interactions more effectively or accessibly than Thomas Schelling. "Policy" is not a term that figures in Schelling's game-theoretic vocabulary. Nevertheless, statements of intentions, which may indeed contains lies, bluffs, and threats, are policy statements, as Meehan conceived them. Schelling's term for what agents have in mind when they talk this way is "commitment."

Never precisely defined, commitment is "a *strategic* move, a move that induces another player to choose in one's favor." It should be "interpreted broadly" to include a variety of "maneuvers" (Schelling 1960, 122, 127, his emphasis). Yet it seems to exist independently of any particular move. Thus, a commitment "must lie behind" a threat (124).

Located in the minds of agents, commitments are beliefs that these agents are prepared to act on, or convictions. The stronger these beliefs are, the greater their normative force. They are also instruments available for many uses. Agents can suit these instruments to circumstances by making them more or less firm or inclusive, or by expressing them with more or less clarity or intensity. It is difficult to imagine policies that agents are not committed to, at least in some measure.

In Schelling's way of thinking, moves are events. By giving voice to policies, moves serve agents' intentions and reflect their commitments. At the same time, moves are policies. Agents' intentions and commitments exist only as moves express them. Even those moves intended to rescind agents' commitments or hide their intentions express intentions and commitments that exist only for that move.

Other writers have responded to Schelling's ambiguous terminology by using a neologism, "precommitment," that otherwise makes no sense.[5] Commitments are anticipatory by definition. This is so because they precede some state of affairs that agents intend to bring about through their actions. If commitments are simply acts that agents decide to take, then they anticipate other such events, including subsequent commitments. They cannot be *pre*-events.

If, however, commitment is some*thing*—a conviction—that agents possess, use, and act on in making commitments, then calling that thing a precommitment always distinguishes it from commitments-as-events. Thus, Nicholas Rowe (1989, 23) could say that an "agent who rationally follows a rule acts *as if* he had precommitted his actions," and make perfect sense. The agent treats the rule's content as a firmly held belief. Acting on a rule, or acting on one's convictions, is an event, a rationally chosen move. As an instrument, precommitment eliminates the need to make some other sort of move, or series of moves quite possibly including commitments, in situations covered by the rule. Precommitment also explains behavior that would otherwise seem to be irrational. To avoid the impression of granting causal efficacy to a disposition or mental state, Rowe covered himself by adding the "as if."

Awkward, self-conscious word choices tell us that strategic analysts are not comfortable speaking about commitments-as-beliefs and commitments-as-instruments. When they make events the subject of discussion, their word choices seem less forced. Schelling (1960, 35–52, 123–137) used familiar terms, "threat" and "promise," in his discussion of commitments-as-events, and substantiated their meaning with a variety of vivid illustrations. Other writers have followed suit. Yet even here ambiguities arise. By turning to the properties of those acts—hereinafter, *speech acts*—through which agents convey threats and promises, we can see what these ambiguities are.[6]

Most moves consist of a bundle of acts, and many of those acts are likely to be speech acts. For example, agent A will make an assertion about agent B's last move: "Your country has been massing troops along the border—your actions speak for themselves." Agent A goes on to say, "On behalf of my country, I demand that you send your troops back to their barracks and desist from all other expressions of hostility." Finally, agent A says, "If you do not comply with these demands, we will take appropriate measures." Only when these three speech acts are taken together, in series, do they constitute agent A's move, which would seem to answer a threat with a threat.

The first statement is an assertive speech act. It presumes to match words (a proposition about some state of affairs) and the world (an actual state of affairs) by having agent B agree with the proposition as stated (making it an actual state of affairs for agents A and B). The second statement is a directive speech act. It seeks to (have agent B) change the world in conformity with that statement's propositional content. Finally, the third statement is another assertive speech act. It predicts a state of affairs that agent B will surely regret. Agent B may accept this assertion as credible or construe it as a bluff.

One might think that the third statement in A's move is not an assertion, but a commitment to effectuate the proposed state of affairs. Commissive speech acts specify states of affairs that agents intend to bring about. These agents propose to do so, not by using words to change the world (*you should* change it), but by speaking of a world that will have changed, thanks to their commitment (*we will* change it). As spoken, agents' words fit promised worlds.

Commissive speech acts constitute promises, however, only if other agents accept them. Rejected or ignored promises bear no consequences for the agents offering them, even if those agents remain committed (we might say, as a matter of policy) to goals that such acts were intended to achieve. Clearly, agent B is not likely to construe agent A's prediction ("we will take appropriate measures") as a promise that, if rejected or ignored, agent A will feel no need to fulfill. Quite the opposite: Ignoring agent A's prediction may well inspire agent A to act as if a promise had been accepted.

There are only three fundamental categories of speech acts: assertive, directive, and commissive.[7] Speech acts help speakers to achieve goals through their effect on others: They are necessarily social. Speech acts belong to the categories that they do because of the ways that they work. Assertive speech acts ask for hearers to accept their propositional content; rejecting or ignoring assertions limits their effect on the state of the world. Directives would have hearers accept indicated tasks as theirs to perform; rejecting or ignoring directives thwarts speakers' efforts to change the world. Commissives call for hearers to accept speakers' intentions to change the world; rejecting or ignoring commissives does not thwart speakers so much as it relieves them of what would have been an obligation to change the world.

Obligation is clearest in the instance of a promise accepted. Obligation is implied when hearers accede to a directive: By their consent, they are obligated to change the world. Even the acceptance of an assertion suggests an obligation to affirm that assertion as opportunity arises. Obligation is the beginning of normativity, but only a beginning. When hearers refuse to accept speech acts, they deny obligation in any measure. Speakers will bundle speech acts to increase the likelihood that any one of them will be accepted and obligation secured. One of the most familiar bundles is a directive supported by a *conditional* assertion—an assertion of probable consequences if the hearer does not accede to the directive.

The directive followed by a conditional assertion is the model for a legal rule in positivist legal theory. The rule is a general order (Hart 1961, 18–25); not simply a speech act, or event. Invoking a rule is a move, normally in the form of a speech act, that puts the rule to use. In theory, this move is most likely to succeed, and the rule demonstrated to be effective, if it includes an assertion about consequences, or sanction. The sanction may well be a rule on its own—a general order directing any agent properly invoking the rule to bring specified consequences about—and all the more credible for being so. Obligation attaches to legal rules directly; not just to the speech acts that agents use to invoke them.

Agents use rules the way that they use policies and commitments to affect other agents' conduct. For the most part, those other agents are deterred from conduct not consistent with the standards reflected in the rules. When rules do not work, agents bring sanctions to bear. Sanctions need not be negative from the point of view of the agents to whom they are directed. Positive sanctions, or inducements, may be available, and they may cost less than negative sanctions to use.[8]

Clearly, moves that feature negative sanctions threaten punishment. Should we say, then, that positive sanctions promise rewards? Schelling (1960, 133) remarked that the "definition of a promise—for example, in distinction to a threat—is not obvious. It might seem that a promise is a commitment (conditional or unconditional) that the second party welcomes," and thus a positive sanction. Jon Elster (1989, 40, n. 40) was less tentative when he spoke of "promises to reward and threats to punish." Schelling waffled. "A better definition, perhaps, would make the promise a commitment that is controlled by the second party," in which case it is not a sanction at all (Schelling 1960, 134).

As we have already seen, Schelling was right the second time. As an alternative to issuing directives backed by assertions about consequences, agents can make unconditional promises that, if accepted, bring consequences of their own. Both moves change the world, but they do it differently, by obligating different sets of agents. For Schelling, unconditional promises rarely commend themselves in strategic situations.[9] If moves include so many bluffs, lies, and deceptive assertions that agents know better than to trust each other, we can only agree with him. In such circumstances, however, agents are unlikely to agree on very much of anything that they say to each other.

Agreements

Even if unconditional promises are strategically unpromising, agents nevertheless do come to agreement. Indeed, "agreement" is a familiar but undefined term in Schelling's work, as it is in most discussions of strategic interaction. As we shall soon see, there are three different ways that agents come to agreement. If one of them tells us a great deal about strategy, yet another tells us just as much about policy.

Schelling seems to have thought that agreement results from pairing conditional promises. Such promises are "bilateral (contractual) commitments given against a quid pro quo that is a promise in return."[10] If benefiting from others' promises depends on keeping promises made to those other agents, then both sets of agents have an incentive to abide by their promises. In the instance of "spot contracts" providing for the immediate discharge of obligations, cheating is least likely to be a problem (Kratochwil 1995, 76). To the contrary, successful spot contracts are events that agents have an incentive to repeat. Success breeds success, and many successes breed trust; agents earn reputations that they have an incentive to protect (Rowe 1989, 36–59).

As Schelling himself demonstrated (1960, 89–113), conventions arise as agents succeed in coordinating moves. Conventions are not agreements; agents have no control over the obligations they create. Accepting an unconditional promise does not constitute an agreement in any but the weakest sense of the term. Even the reciprocal obligations of a spot contract fall short of constituting an agreement, insofar as the term suggests a lasting arrangement. Conventions are instruments, not events. So are agreements. Schelling made just this assumption, and so has everyone else writing on the subject.

The longer an agreement is intended to last, the less likely it is to specify all possible contingencies, and the more opportunities agents will have to cheat (Kratochwil 1995, 75–79). Schelling drew the obvious conclusion (1960, 131): "Enforceable promises cannot be taken for granted. Agreements must be in enforceable terms and involve enforceable types of behavior." Charles Lipson (1991, 508) put the matter in even stronger terms: "In international affairs, then, the term 'binding agreement' is misleading hyperbole. To enforce their bargains, states must act for themselves." Notice that this sort of claim parallels the legal positivist claim that laws, as general orders, depend on sanctions to back them up. Its rhetorical power derives precisely from the reader's recognition that enforcement is a property of legal orders.

If one believes that the anarchic world of states and their agents is largely lawless, then agreements cannot last, and the obligations that they create are bound to wither. If one believes that the international legal rule *pacta sunt servanda* (treaties must be observed) brings into play an impressive set of tools for agents of states to use in defense of their agreements, then all such agents have disincentives to cheat on the obligations that they have agreed to. Schelling's conclusion that everything depends on enforcement may seem obvious, but it is not the only one possible. Nor indeed is his conclusion that agreements are best thought of as jointly conditional promises, or contracts.

Two properties of lasting agreements (more generally, properties of speech) affect the likelihood that agents will perform their obligations: specificity and formality.[11] Schelling himself alluded to the property of specificity when he said that agreements must be rendered in enforceable terms. The more specific the terms of an agreement, the more difficult it is for agents to avoid doing what they have promised—or so it would seem. The problem comes in trying to make agreements so specific that their obligations are inescapable. The process itself becomes interminable as the specification of particular contingencies brings to light other, even more particular contingencies in need of specification. Specificity risks irrelevance; the complexity of so many interlocking terms invites confusion; the sheer density of a fully specified agreement deters agents from taking it seriously. Beyond some point, the quest for specificity is self-defeating.

As an alternative, agents can make their agreements formal. The more formal their agreements, the more difficult it is for them to claim that they did not intend to be obligated by their words. Formality is not a relevant property of promises as such; an informal promise is no less a promise than a formal promise is, however (in)formally either is accepted. The effect is always the same. Agents keep promises by changing the world, not with the words constituting their promises, but through other acts (which may include speech acts of high formality). If formal agreements are more likely to be honored than informal ones, then it would seem that these agreements are not, or not just, the reciprocal promises, or contracts, that Schelling took them to be.

Schelling has had good company. Early in the seventeenth century, Hugo Grotius held that treaties are analogous to contracts in civil law. Ever since, lawyers have affirmed that treaties work the same way that contracts do to create obligations (Lauterpacht 1927, 155–80; Onuma 1993).

"International treaties are agreements, of a contractual character, between States or organisations of states creating legal rights and obligations between the Parties." Thus begins the chapter on treaties in the century's foremost English language treatise on international law (Oppenheim 1955, 877, footnotes deleted). By inference, then, any "international" instrument that reciprocally obligates must be a treaty. Joint declarations are not treaties, despite their formality, if "they are intended as formulating general statements of principle and policy rather than legal obligations" (900). Conversely, treaties may take any number of forms; formality has no effect on obligations that arise from exchanging conditional promises.

The difficulty comes with unilateral declarations. In some instances, at least, these highly formal acts have been construed to create legal obligations. Yet they cannot do so as conditional promises because obligations arise only when such promises are reciprocated. More plausibly, they are unconditional promises, obligating their makers only insofar as other agents construe them as promises, accept them as such, and proceed to rely on them. In this case, however, they are not agreements at all, and they are classified as treaties only because lawyers think it makes even less sense to classify them as customary legal rules.[12]

If unilateral declarations are unconditional promises, then it seems rather odd for them to be rendered in declaratory form. Their formality suggests that it does not matter to the agents making such promises whether they are accepted by other agents. If agents intend their words as promises, they would couch them in such terms as to elicit acceptance. Formality calls for a response in kind—a counter-declaration that would turn the pair of declarations into an exchange of promises—or no response at all.

The most plausible way of all to look at unilateral declarations is as assertions and not promises of any kind. The advantage of doing so is to shift focus from the intentions of agents in accepting promises, or not accepting them, to the intentions of agents when they make such declarations. According to John Searle (1979, 16–20, 26–127), declarations are neither assertives nor commissives, but a category of speech acts in their own right. They differ from all other speech acts because the act of declaring some state of affairs is complete and sufficient.

Declaring something makes it so. For example, to say, "I declare a state of emergency," brings such a state into existence, then and there. As Searle pointed out (1979, 18), it does so only if some "extra-linguistic institution" gives me the authority to issue such a declaration. Declarations differ from assertives for this reason alone.

What Searle failed to realize is that the credibility of any assertion depends, at least in measure, on the status of its speaker (also see Mühlhäusler and Harré 1990, 41–42). Status is an extra-linguistic institution. Declarations, then, are assertions for which there exists an extra-linguistic institution that makes them *formally* complete and self-fulfilling. Declarations of independence may constitute a special case insofar as they create the extra-linguistic institution giving them their force.

Acceptance is beside the point. When I declare a state of emergency, no one in particular needs to accept it (except, of course, subordinates who are obliged to consider my declaration a directive speech act). Even if the declaration does refer to particular agents, their acceptance is irrelevant. Take this example: "We declare war on you."

Such a declaration brings a state of war into existence at that moment, and not in the future as a consequence of promised hostile conduct. Agents to whom the declaration refers are perfectly free to ignore it. They are more likely to match it with their own declaration of war. Taken together, the two declarations resemble an agreement that both sides will treat *as if* it produces obligations that cannot be ignored.

Gifts

If indeed paired declarations produce obligations, they are obligations that agents have created for themselves, not each other. These obligations have the force they do both because of the formalities of agency and the formality with which agents assert states of affairs. Association with extra-linguistic institutions also contributes to the normative force that declarations unilaterally bring to bear, insofar as those institutions create obligations in their own right. In this respect, no institution seems more important than the gift.

Declarations resemble gifts in a number of respects. First, gifts need not have designated recipients, even if they often do. Second, there are always rules telling agents when, and to whom, they are free to give gifts, obliged to do so, or indeed sometimes obliged not to do so. Third, there are counterpart rules for accepting gifts. Fourth, there are rules, often quite elaborate, telling agents when they are obliged to exchange gifts.[13] The first two sets of rules parallel extra-linguistic institutions placing some agents in a position to issue declarations and others in a position to receive them. The third set of rules reflects the general norm of reciprocity that every society seems to have.[14]

Such a norm does not require an exchange of gifts, or declarations, on every occasion for which giving a gift, or issuing a declaration, might be appropriate. When agents are formal equals, and when occasions are themselves formally marked, the rule of reciprocity is most likely to apply. Holidays call for reciprocity in giving gifts; declaring war calls for, but does not compel, a declaration of war in return. Reciprocity fosters a shared commitment to live by agreements taking the form of exchanged promises, and it fosters a shared appreciation of paired declarations as agreements of another kind.

Just what kind of agreements they are remains to be clarified. We often think of agreements as propositions that agents have actively accepted. Consent is one way to respond to directive speech acts, although we rarely think of such exchanges as agreements. Assenting to others' assertions—"I agree with you"—is a different matter. Yet agents often assent to propositions that no one in particular has asserted: "I agree that war is sometimes the best policy." To say, "I agree with you (when you say) that war is the best policy," does not signify an agreement between us to go to war. Our agreement is passive, and it reduces to its two constituents—what I say and what you say—with no loss of meaning.

Our passive agreement differs from a contract—for example, an agreement by each of us to go to war if the other does—in two respects. First, our agreement says nothing about our intentions, while the other agreement is centrally concerned with intentions. Second, our agreement consists of unconditional assertions, while the other consists of conditional promises. Now we can easily see a third possibility: agreement in the form of parallel unconditional assertions about our respective intentions. When we both assert, "I intend to go to war," we have jointly agreed to do so, without having actively accepted, or assented to, the agreement, or having committed ourselves to each other.

This third possibility is precisely the kind of agreement represented by paired declarations. After all, declarations are formally self-sufficient assertions, and it is this property that marks their unconditional nature. Formality functions for speakers the way that consent does for hearers. "I declare my intention to go to war" and "I consent to (your directive that I) go to war" are statements of comparable normative force—they both obligate me more than most other speech acts do—but their normativity comes from different directions, so to speak, and they constitute agreements of different kinds.

We might see agents' intentions behind acts of consent, just as we do with hostile acts, and call those acts policies. Of course, we can always be mistaken in such inferences. Alternatively, we might call assertions of intentions policy statements and expect to see future acts consistent with those statements. Again, these expectations might be misguided, because these statements might well be bluffs or lies. When assertions of intention are given the formal completeness of declarations, and even more when agents intend them to coincide with other agents' declarations, they gain in normative force, and our confidence in them increases.

When, centuries ago, crowned heads conjointly declared their intentions, their agreements were not treaties on the model of contracts. Yet these agreements "were nevertheless considered sacred and binding," not simply "on account of religious and moral sentiment" (Oppenheim 1955, 878), but more specifically because exalted beings had given their word. Typically they did so in the form of an oath. "The practice of concluding a contract by oath-taking and inserting expressions of oath in treaties is believed to have continued until the eighteenth century" (Onuma 1993, 198, footnote deleted; also see Akashi 1998, 52). Intentions thus declared are beyond doubt. Declarations of intention are policy statements of the most emphatic sort.

When agents of the highest status issue declarations of intention together, these agreements have normative effects perhaps more powerful than those that arise from exchanging promises. Indeed, by giving their word, they have exchanged gifts on an occasion charged with significance. To this day, agents of states put great store in ceremonial exchanges. Their treaties often contain general provisions that, though declaratory in name or thrust, are fully as normative as specifically contracted obligations are.

Contemporary international relations offers other examples. The General Assembly seems like a lawmaking organ because some few of its resolutions, styled declarations, exhibit the normative force of a great many coordinated declarations of intention.[15] Although the Helsinki Final Act is expressly not a treaty, the normative force of its provisions is hardly lessened for this reason and perhaps enhanced.[16] Even if such instruments depend on acts of assent in the form of affirmative votes for their adoption, such acts do not indicate consent to be bound. Instead they create agreements that we might fairly call collective policy statements. As such, they set public standards and engender expectations about compliance. They do the work of formal rules, or law, whatever legal positivists might call them.

Whatever policies may be, policy statements assert or, more likely, declare agents' intentions. Sometimes agents may themselves prefer to make their assertions of intention highly formal in order to make their intentions altogether clear. The point of assertive speech acts is to persuade other agents that any proposed state of affairs is credible. In the instance of propositions about agents' own intentions, the point is to persuade other agents that speakers are sincere in their expressions of intention—they will do as they say. When agents declare their intentions, instead of merely asserting them, they signal an intention to be taken seriously, with a commensurate gain in the credibility of whatever they say about their intentions. If acceptance is the point, then declarations are more likely than assertions to succeed as speech acts.

Declarations are more formal than assertions by degree. Pledges, oaths, and vows are declarations of intention expressed in the highest degree of formality that agents, as speakers, are capable of giving them. They possess all the normative force that speakers can give their commitments (as beliefs and as instruments) without the help of other agents. In other words, pledges do not have other agents as targets and are not intended to elicit from them speech acts, such as consent or an offer of a promise, that would confirm or increase the normative force behind whatever is pledged. When Searle (1979, 22–23) classified pledges as commissive speech acts, he was mistaken for this very reason: Other agents need not accept pledges, oaths, and vows for these speech acts to do their job.[17] Promises, for their part, cannot be promises without agents for indirect objects.

Consider an example of Searle's (1979, 22): "I pledge allegiance to the flag." In expanded form, this sentence becomes, "I declare publicly, but to no one in particular, my intention to perform a variety of acts associated with flag and nation." It could also become "I promise myself to perform such acts," I myself being the only plausible candidate for an indirect object. Agents often make promises to themselves and accept them for themselves, not publicly, but silently. Such acts are not social and usually limited in normative force, as evidenced by the likelihood that they will soon be broken. The sorry fate of most New Year's resolutions makes the point. If we make our self-promises public, then we translate them into declarations of intention, thereby making our concerns for reputation a source of normativity.[18]

Searle's second example, "I vow to get revenge," would seem to supply an agent for the indirect object and therefore qualify as a commitment. In expanded form, this sentence could become, "I vow to you that I will get my revenge." If you (the indirect object) are also the object of my revenge, then your acceptance is irrelevant. If you are not, then there would seem to be little point in my offering such a promise and in you accepting it. Either way, the promise means little if anything. As an alternative, we could have this sentence say: "I vow publicly, solemnly, but to no one in particular, to take my revenge on you." Normative force depends on my vow, even though you are the focus of my intentions.

Pledges, oaths, and vows are an integral part of social life and a significant factor in making it normative. They make gifts of words: "I give my word that I intend to honor the nation," "uphold the Constitution," "exact my revenge." Presents make their presence known; pledges, oaths, and vows draw attention to speakers' intentions. When agents want their intentions to be known, assertions are the appropriate vehicle. Declarations are better than mere assertions, and pledges best of all. Ceremonial occasions, formal speech, the incidents of status: all of these enhance policy statements and make them more useful instruments.

Observers

Sometimes agents do *not* want their intentions known. To achieve them, they plan strategic moves that work only if other agents do not know what their intentions are. Indeed, successful moves may depend on deception, with respect both to intentions and to the circumstances that agents have taken into account in forming their intentions. Occasionally, agents will make pledges that they intend not to honor, thinking a pledge may work better as a bluff than a mere assertion would. If, however, other agents call the bluff, a broken pledge can be a costly move.

Deceptive assertions tend to be informal in order to limit normative implications for future conduct. When agents cannot avoid speaking on formal occasions, they take refuge in generalities. Such statements afford agents the greatest possible interpretive leeway for whatever they say or do subsequently. In most such situations, saying nothing, or as little as possible, is the best "policy."

Agents will have relatively fixed intentions, or policies, that they have never announced and endeavor to hide. Other agents are forced to make inferences about those policies from limited and often misleading evidence in order to choose their moves. Observers are in the same position, even though they often feel that agents have an obligation to disclose policies or even seek approval for them. Obligation may stem from electoral promises, parliamentary practices, statutory requirements, or, indeed, policy statements that agents had reason to make at other times. Close observers tend to feel that their own professional status and responsibilities suffice to obligate agents to explain their conduct.

Faced with agents' reluctance to make policy statements in some situations, observers will claim that their inferences fairly represent agents' policies. If agents were to declare themselves, to say anything at all formal about their intentions, then, observers assert, this is what they would say. Agents in their turn can ignore these assertions, only to have observers interpret silence as assent. Or agents can repudiate words that observers have put in their mouths, at the risk of disclosing more than they would like about their intentions. Sometimes, of course, agents benefit from the cacophony of claims about their policies, because it gives them the cover they need to act on their undisclosed intentions.

However agents respond, policy statements of obscure provenience and questionable content will proliferate. Casual observers will assume that agents have policies that bear a systematic relation to the many policy statements to which everyone is constantly exposed. As observers look more closely, they discover that many policy statements are fictions, and that many agents are not talking. The closer they look, the less they find. In the end, observers are left with what agents want observers (and other agents) to know about agents' intentions, as manifest in their pledges and declarations, singular and collective, and the confusing evidence of their strategic moves.

In the wide space between glittering generalities and indecipherable events, there may be no policies to be found—at least, no *foreign* policies.[19] There is much else to be seen and heard. Agents may refuse to declare their intentions publicly, but they still have to rely on other agents to carry out their moves. At minimum, agents must convey their intentions to subordinates through the medium of directive speech acts.

Information that moves up and down a chain of command is often hard to keep from public view. Multiply chains in complex organizational arrangements, and the opportunities for leakage also increase, no doubt exponentially. Directive speech acts intended only for subordinates' ears provide far better evidence of agents' intentions than their strategic interactions are likely to. Inferences about agents' intentions are more plausible, and they are harder for agents to repudiate without confusing their subordinates.

Keeping one's policies from view is frequently difficult. Disclosing policies may be a good move for practical reasons. As we have seen, agents also have principled reasons to declare their intentions. They make policy statements with the intention of being held to them. Oaths of office, major speeches, summit oratory, resolutions of public bodies, and agreements as coordinated unilateral declarations are just some of the many examples of such policy statements. On all such occasions agents treat all hearers as observers, and all observers as judges. When agents take these occasions to speak, they tend to be sincere in what they say.

Furthermore, they are likely to remain so for the sake of their reputations. Observers find it easy to draw inferences from policy statements—inferences that they, as agents, can rely on. In the absence of evidence to the contrary, highly formal policy statements, as declarations of intention, *are* policies. Even though these policies are often highly general and, therefore, permissive in practice, they have the normative force to make the world— any world of agents and intentions—what it has become and can ever be.

Notes

I am indebted to members of the Miami International Relations Group for many help-ful comments.

1. As are commitments to one's self (see pp. 89–90 above of this text) and private rules. William Kincade prompted me to consider the relation between plans and policies, but see Bratman (1999, 52–56) for a different conclusion.

2. Hereafter I use the term "normative force," in preference to "binding force" (as in "the binding force of speech acts"; Johnson 1993, 81), to make it clear that normativity is a relative condition. By contrast, positivist legal theory and ordinary language both take the condition of being bound to be absolute. One is either bound or not.

3. "A situation is strategic if an actor's ability to further its ends depends on the actions that others take" (Lake and Powell 1999, 8, footnote deleted). See pages 6–20 for a helpful introduction to the study of strategic interaction.

4. Students of public policy have made instruments a focus of attention, but they do so on the assumption that policies are set in place and ready to be carried out (Peters and van Nispen 1998). In these circumstances, agents devise regulatory, financial, and infor-mational instruments whose properties suit the mechanics of program administration and use them accordingly. Clearly this focus has little bearing on Meehan's conception of policies as tools.

5. Jon Elster (1979, 37) seems to have coined the term, which he used, rather nar-rowly, to express the concept of "binding oneself" directly and not through strategic inter-action; "*precommitment* is a generic technique lending credibility to threats and prom-ises" (Elster 1989, 278, his emphasis, footnote directing attention to Schelling deleted) and, therefore, available for strategic use (170–172).

6. James Johnson (1993, 80–82) has pointed out that speech acts have properties—specifically normative properties—that the analysis of strategic interaction should take into account. As far as I know, neither he nor anyone else has followed up on this suggestion.

7. I defend this claim in Onuf (1989, 82–94). It depends on, but departs from, John Searle's taxonomy of speech acts (Searle 1979, 1–29; Searle and Vanderveken 1985, 13–15, 51–62).

8. "The sanction might consist in the manipulation of symbols (praise or censure), or in the redistribution of goods and services, or in the use of violence, or, generally, speaking, in reward or punishment by way of any value whatever. The sanction is *positive* when it enhances values for the actor to whom it is applied, *negative* when it deprives him of values" (Lasswell and Kaplan 1950, 48–49, their emphasis).

9. Thus Schelling's two examples (1960, 132–133) are both desperate measures.

10. To similar effect: "once an agreement has been concluded, the contracting parties will feel an obligation to fulfill their promises." In saying this, Jon Hovi (1998, 80) intended to cast doubt on the claim but not the terms in which he couched it.

11. Elsewhere I have argued that these are also properties of rules (Onuf 1998b, 175–176). Cf. Kratochwil (1995, 84–92), where explicitness, openness, and formality are the relevant properties of agreements. With Lipson (1991, 527–532), I believe that formality brings openness (see n. 90 above).

12. Not that unilateral declarations are irrelevant to the emergence of customary rules. In Schelling's terms (1960, 54–58), they can serve as "focal points" for the tacit coordination of strategic moves, with conventions resulting. Also see Kratochwil (1995, 91).

13. Also see Mauss (1967, 37–43), on "The Three Obligations: Giving, Receiving, and Repaying" (section title).

14. "Gifts and goods pervade our lives. So do evils and injuries. Everywhere, in every society of record, there is a norm of reciprocity about such things. Returns are expected: good for good received, hostility for hostility" (Becker (1990, 73).

15. On the legal issues, see Falk (1966) and Onuf (1970); on normative force, see Jones (1992) and Onuf (1998c, 690–691).

16. Cf. Lipson (1991, 533) and Kratochwil (1995, 88), for whom the Helsinki Final Act is "informal" because it is not a legal instrument. Kratochwil's assessment of the Final Act is nevertheless unassailable: "Having all nations solemnly declare, so to speak, unilaterally, the inviolability of post-war boundaries added considerable legitimacy to the status quo."

17. We might plausibly construe pledges as the best possible evidence of commitments as strongly held beliefs and then use the terms interchangeably. Robert Jervis (1997, 83) did just this in a discussion of self-commitment in strategic interaction. When Zeev Maoz and Dan Felsenthal (1987, 187) defined a *self-binding commitment* as "a unilateral credible commitment to act in a certain way regardless of what other players do," they could have called this move, and the commitment behind it, a pledge.

18. While Searle failed to comment specifically on declarations of intention, J.L. Austin, who pioneered the analysis of speech acts (1975), thought that declaring one's intention, giving one's word, and pledging (not to mention agreeing and consenting) are all commissive speech acts (157–158). Note, however, that Austin's typology of speech acts has no place for declarations as such. Perhaps Searle considered pledges to be commissive speech acts and not declarations (of intention), because he associated intentionality with commitment as a state of mind. Austin even thought that "intend," as a verb, is a commissive speech act (1975, 158), but Searle corrected him: "Intending is never a speech act; expressing an intention usually, but not always, is" (1979, 9).

19. Students of public policy who assume that governments adopt formal policies openly and carry them out routinely will find little relevance in this discussion. That same assumption limits any contribution on their part to discussions of foreign policy.

References

Akashi, Kinji. 1998. *Cornelius Bynkershoek: His Role in the History of International Law*. The Hague: Kluwer Law International.

Austin, J.L. 1975. *How to Do Things with Words*, rev. ed. Cambridge, MA: Harvard University Press.

Becker, Lawrence C. 1990. *Reciprocity*. Chicago: University of Chicago Press.

Bratman, Michael E. 1999. *Faces of Intention: Selected Essays on Intention and Agency*. Cambridge, UK: Cambridge University Press.

Elster, Jon. 1979. *Ulysses and the Sirens*. Cambridge, UK: Cambridge University Press.

———. 1989. *The Cement of Society: A Study of Social Order*. Cambridge, UK: Cambridge University Press.

Falk, Richard A. 1966. "On the Quasi-Legislative Competence of the General Assembly." *American Journal of International Law* 60(4): 782–789.

Hart, H.L.A. 1961. *The Concept of Law*. Oxford: Clarendon Press.

Hovi, Jon. 1998. *Games, Threats and Treaties: Understanding Commitments in International Relations*. London: Pinter, 1998.

Jervis, Robert. 1997. *System Effects: Complexity in Political and Social Life*. Princeton, NJ: Princeton University Press.

Johnson, James. 1993. "Is Talk Really Cheap? Prompting Conversation between Critical Theory and Rational Choice."*American Political Science Review* 87(1): 74–86.

Jones, Dorothy V. 1992. "The Declaratory Tradition in Modern International Law." In Terry Nardin and David R. Mapel, eds., *Traditions of International Ethics*, pp. 42–61. Cambridge, UK: Cambridge University Press.

Kratochwil, Friedrich. 1995. "Contract and Regimes: Do Issue Specificity and Variations of Formality Matter?" In Volker Rittberger, ed., *Regime Theory and International Relations*, pp. 77–93. Oxford: Clarendon Press.

Lake, David A., and Powell, Robert. 1999. "International Relations: A Strategic Choice Approach." In David A. Lake and Robert Powell, eds., *Strategic Choice and International Relations*, pp. 3–38. Princeton, NJ: Princeton University Press.

Lasswell, Harold D., and Kaplan, Abraham. 1950. *Power and Society: A Framework for Political Inquiry*. New Haven, CT: Yale University Press.

Lauterpacht, H. 1927. *Private Law Sources and Analogies of International Law* (with Special Reference to International Arbitration). London: Longmans, Green.

Lipson, Charles. 1991. "Why Are Some International Agreements Informal?" *International Organization* 45(4): 495–538.

Maoz, Zeev, and Felsenthal, Dan S. 1987. "Self-binding Commitments, the Inducement of Trust, Social Choice, and the Theory of International Cooperation." *International Studies Quarterly* 31(2): 177–200.

Mauss, Marcel. 1967. *The Gift: Forms and Functions of Exchange in Archaic Societies*. Ian Cunnison, trans. New York: W.W. Norton.

Meehan, Eugene J. 1971. "The Concept 'Foreign Policy.'" In Wolfram F. Hanrieder, ed., *Comparative Foreign Policy: Theoretical Essays*, pp. 265–94. New York: David McKay.

Mühlhäusler, Peter, and Harré, Rom. 1990. *Pronouns and People: The Linguistic Construction of Social and Personal Identity*. Oxford: Basil Blackwell.

Onuf, N.G. 1970. "Professor Falk on the Quasi-Legislative Competence of the General Assembly." *American Journal of International Law* 64(2): 349–355.

———. 1989. *World of Our Making: Rules and Rule in Social Theory and International Relations.* Columbia: University of South Carolina Press, 1989.

———. 1998a. "Constructivism: A User's Manual." In Vendulka Kubálková, Nicholas Onuf, and Paul Kowert, eds., *International Relations in a Constructed World,* pp. 58–78. Armonk, NY: M.E. Sharpe.

———. 1998b. *The Republican Legacy in International Thought.* Cambridge, UK: Cambridge University Press.

———. 1998c. "Everyday Ethics in International Relations." *Millennium* 27(3): 669–693.

Onuma, Yasuaki. 1993. "Agreement." In Yasuaki Onuma, ed., *A Normative Approach to War: Peace, War, and Justice in Hugo Grotius,* pp. 174–220. Oxford: Clarendon Press.

Oppenheim, L. 1955. *International Law: A Treatise,* 8th ed. H. Lauterpacht, vol. 1. New York: David McKay.

Peters, B. Guy, and van Nispen, Frans K.M., eds. 1998. *Public Policy Instruments: Evaluating the Tools of Public Administration.* Northampton, MA: Edward Elgar.

Rowe, Nicholas. 1989. *Rules and Institutions.* Ann Arbor: University of Michigan Press.

Schelling, Thomas C. 1960. *The Strategy of Conflict.* Cambridge, MA: Harvard University Press.

Searle, John R. 1979. *Expression and Meaning: Studies in the Theory of Speech Acts.* Cambridge, UK: Cambridge University Press.

Searle, John R., and Vanderveken, Daniel. 1985. *Foundations of Illocutionary Logic.* Cambridge, UK: Cambridge University Press.

II

Constructivists at Work

5

Soviet "New Thinking" and the End of the Cold War: Five Explanations

Vendulka Kubálková

Constructivism as an approach to International Relations (IR) and Soviet "new thinking" as a phenomenon of the final years of the Cold War barely crossed paths, since constructivism was coming into existence as an approach just as the other, "new thinking," together with its main author, Mikhail Gorbachev, were about to exit international relations. Soviet "new thinking" is associated with Gorbachev's tenure of office as the General Secretary of the Communist Party of the Soviet Union (CPSU). This ran from the mid-1980s until the disintegration of the Soviet Union in 1991. Nicholas Onuf introduced constructivism in his book *World of Our Making* in 1989, and it was only in 1992, a year after the formal dissolution of the USSR, that Alexander Wendt referred to "new thinking" in his article "Anarchy Is What States Make of It" as "one of the most important phenomena in [recent] world politics" (Wendt 1992, 419). It is in this same article, as we noted in chapters 1 and 2, that he also used the term "constructivism," a term he borrowed from Onuf. Other, freshly converted constructivists followed in Wendt's footsteps and, as evidence of the strength of their new approach, they often used "the DNA of the deceased," Soviet "new thinking" and other artifacts and stories related to the Cold War, which—with its main protagonist gone—was over. "New thinking" figures prominently again in Wendt's theoretical book on constructivism, where it is probably the empirical case that he handles in a more sustained manner and devotes more time to than any other case or example (Wendt, 1999).

There are multiple ironies here. While the USSR and its bloc existed, Soviet thinking, new or otherwise, was never a topic, certainly not as "thinking" at any rate, since it could not count as thinking. The positivist ontological and epistemological premises of the Western social sciences decreed it possible to have only one truthful and accurate representation of objective reality. They saw to it that Westerners have that key and find that truth. Anything contradicting that truth simply could not be "thinking": It had to be an intellectually inferior and deficient construct, a bunch of fabrications, distortions, and/or ex post facto justifications—in short, an ideology, concocted not to shed light on reality but to fool millions of Soviet and East European citizens who, by implication, must have been intellectually inferior not to see through it.

Having been raised myself as a "Soviet thinker," that is, having not known anything else for the first half of my life other than what was taught at the Soviet empire's Prague Charles University outpost, and having then studied in the West after fleeing there, I was never able to accept either of the corollaries of the positivist view. I could never accept that the thinking I was raised in was not thinking or that we were all fools. My university teachers in particular were not fools. Quite the contrary, they showed a great deal of personal courage and ex cathedra heroism, a quality we academics in the West are never called upon to demonstrate. While the Soviet Union was in existence I argued this point frequently and in vain in a number of my works on Soviet "new thinking" (particularly in a book entitled *Thinking New About Soviet "New Thinking"* [Kubálková and Cruickshank 1989b] and other works dealing with Soviet thinking in general [e.g., Kubálková and Cruickshank, 1977, 1978, 1980a, 1980b, 1981a, 1981b, 1983, 1985a, 1985b, 1989a, 1989b; Kubálková 1979, 1990, 1994]).

The USSR's political and economic system was always regarded as unique, and its high national security relevance made for a separate social science subdiscipline. Sovietology was a field for the study of all things Soviet; its sister field, Comparative Communism, for the study of East European satellites. As a superpower, the USSR and its foreign policy also loomed large in most of those areas of IR studied as International Politics (IP) or Foreign Policy Analysis (FPA) (see chapter 1). The end of the Cold War revealed Sovietology to be trapped in its own kind of old thinking. Collections of misguided predictions about the long life expectancy of the USSR made as late as two years before the USSR's demise by well-known Sovietologists are now considered amusing reading (Puddington 1990; Harries 1991; Karatnytsky 1992; Mueller 1995). As their subject "died" on them, Sovietology and Comparative Communism were the hardest hit of the social science fields and subfields and had to drastically scale down their operations and rename themselves. Although the events took the entire IR discipline by surprise and no area of IR escaped unaffected, nothing as drastic as scaling down or renaming took place in other fields.

Another irony in the rediscovery of "new thinking" as a topic is that it is not brought before us by former Sovietologists, but by IR theorists for whom Soviet "new thinking" has become something of a *cause celebre* to demonstrate the need for a constructivist approach to the post–Cold War era. What is most ironic, however, is that the Wendtean form of constructivism, which in this volume I have called "soft" constructivism, gets Soviet "new thinking" wrong. This may be of little consequence as far as the history of the Soviet Union is concerned. I doubt very much that future students of Russia, or of Eurasian studies, or of the history of ideas more generally, will pay much attention to work on their subject written by IR specialists. Different disciplines and subdisciplines develop in blissful ignorance of each other's concerns and achievement. Scholars of one discipline or field do not read, as a rule, much outside their own field of study.

However, the inability of the Wendtean constructivism to handle "new thinking" and presenting it as a litmus test of the prowess of soft constructivism becomes serious if this form of constructivism is to be the response that IR scholars in the United States make to the post–Cold War world. That this may happen is not so difficult to imagine if we consider how constructivism has become elevated to one of the three main IR approaches. We referred in earlier chapters to this meteoric rise. Steven Walt, for example, actually goes so far as to replace globalist, dependencia, Neo-Marxist, and World System approaches with a constructivist one, next to realist and liberal approaches (introduction, Figure 1.1), and he clearly refers mainly to soft constructivism. The elevation to prominence of this brand of constructivism, replacing in the process an entire tradition, is certainly an indication of how seriously constructivism is treated, or how badly it is perceived to be needed. The message conveyed by this switch is that we do not need approaches drawing to our attention world inequalities in the post–Cold War era because either the world inequalities have ceased to exist or, if not, constructivism can adequately handle them. Unfortunately, this is not the case.

It would seem that the mainstream American IR discipline made three changes to adjust to the blunders of failing the "end of the Cold War" test. All three are related to constructivism, and all three underscore the interpretation of mainly soft constructivism designated as the IR approach to the post–Cold War era. First, there was the recognition that such phenomena as Soviet "new thinking" might have held some clues missed by the approaches extant at the time of the Soviet Union's unraveling, and—equally important— occurrences of similar phenomena might not be uncommon after the Cold War's end. Thus, a bundle of new themes was added to the list of IR concerns. All of these themes have to do with what two prominent neoliberal writers called "ideational" factors (Goldstein and Keohane 1993), the quirky developments of the "agent" in the juxtaposition of agent and structure that Wendt introduced the IR audience to in 1987. I have explained these terms in chapter 1; they all have to do with the recognition of the "voluntaristic," undetermined aspect of IR, in which people, rather than material forces, play a role. The new IR topics, which soon became the biggest and most popular IR topics of the post–Cold War era, have been identity, intersubjectivity, meaning, motivation, interest, and culture. These happen to be the main topics of the soft constructivism.

The second adjustment is closely related. Namely, recognition that topics such as "new thinking" escaped the attention of both FPA and IP as they were originally conceived and as I have explained them in chapter 1. This has led to the creation of a new home for constructivism in "national security studies," a field straddling and combining elements of both FPA and IP without having to redefine either of them (Katzenstein, ed. 1996). Finally, the third change is the elevation of constructivism to one of the three main approaches to IR. It amounts to recognition that a large number of topics and concerns were unaccounted for in the gamut of topics covered in the main approaches to IR whose names even undergraduates had to learn and recite. Thus, the trio realism, pluralism, and globalism—more recently relabeled as neorealism, neoliberalism, and globalism—has been changed to neorealism, neoliberalism, and constructivism.

For all practical purposes it would appear that this triple change wraps up the Third Debate, at least for the mainstream. Unrelated to the demise of the Cold War, the Third Debate discussed in chapters 1 and 2 could be said to have prepared the ground for this triple change. Perhaps "overprepared" is a better word, since many IR scholars, under the influence of Third Debate themes and expectations, might be reading more into these changes than they warrant.

The triple change I describe is only tenuously related to the Third Debate. None of these changes is antipositivist, while the Third Debate was mainly an assault on positivism in the IR discipline. The nonpositivist glimpses that most versions of constructivism provide are fleeting at best and the positivist framework has been never seriously challenged. It is as if for a few brief moments, the traffic swung to the left, only to return immediately to the right side of the road. Needless to say, all of the other traffic has kept driving all the time, or most of the time, on the right.

All of this would be of little consequence if it were not for one detail; namely, that we do not have one constructivism but several. There is the post–Cold War soft constructivism encouraged and elevated by the academic politics of the aftermath of that discipline's glaring failure. And there are other constructivisms, which emerged out of the Third, that is, the postpositivist, Debate in the IR discipline. The leaders of the mainstream have forewarned that the test as to which version of constructivism will make it will be played out in positivist terms, that is, on the grounds of empirical utility, and this is the test we face now (Keohane cited in chap. 2). Postmodern constructivism, the other form of constructivism that emerged out of the Third Debate, however, disqualifies itself from such a contest based on its antifoundationalist claim denying that discourses have a reality behind them to be checked against. Rule-oriented constructivism accepts the challenge.

This chapter is the tale of two constructivisms (Kubalkova 2001), the soft and the rule oriented; the one that emerged from the post–Cold War adjustment of the IR mainstream and the other, a product of the Third Debate. The chapter is the tale of these two constructivisms but also of the different tales that they and other approaches tell about Soviet "new thinking." Poststructuralists would say that this is, of course, unsurprising and it cannot be any other way: Story telling or narrative construction is a way of bringing order to an otherwise messy reality. Consequently, argues Karin Fierke (2001), we may have any number of stories about any one set of events or historical context, each of which provides the structure of a particular story. Likewise, in the political world, actors in different positions are likely to tell very different stories: about the past, about what they and the other are doing, about the reasons for their actions, about what is possible in the future. The outcome, in this case, is multiple narratives about the end of the Cold War, for instance, from Western leaders, former Soviet leaders, from different scholars, and from peace and human rights activists. Western leaders, as the most powerful, the poststructuralists would argue, were successful in imposing their narrative and marginalizing the others. If the poststructuralists are right, then it is even more important to discover those stories that we never hear.

About This Chapter

I use for the structure of the discussion the sequence of approaches I introduced and explained in chapter 1 so that readers can flip back and forth should they require a reminder of the meaning of some of the concepts. The structure of the chapter is based on Table 1.1, which summarizes the main questions characteristic of individual IP/FPA approaches. I reproduce that table here in a more specified form as Table 5.1 and reprint the relevant question along with the answer offered by individual approaches.

Table 5.1 is divided into two vertical sections indicating the split between FP and IP, one of the main themes of this book. It was in chapter 1 that I explained the split between the Foreign Policy Analysis and international relations studied as a system, IP. This was a division that crystallized with

Table 5.1

Questions Asked by FP, IP, and Constructivists

	A. Foreign policy analysis focuses on attributes of units to reach conclusions about their relations (from parts to whole)	B. International politics as international system focuses on the system of relations to reach conclusions about system's attributes (from the whole to parts)
"Classical realism"	1. *What* does (rational actor) state A do to states B, C, D, E, etc. (and they to it) in response to (objectively existing) threats they individually or collectively represent to its national interest?	
Mainstream approaches: FPA and IP	*Sovietology* 2. *How* does individual decision maker acting on behalf of state A, based on his *subjective* perceptions, decide what to do to states B, C, etc. ? 3. Why has individual(s) decision maker acting on behalf of state A, based on his *subjective* perceptions decided what to do to states B, C, etc.?	(4. *How* do [objectively existing rationally acting] states A, B, C, D, E, etc. called systems *behave* [based on biology, mathematics, general systems theory, cybernetics?]) 5. *Neorealist, structural realist approaches* How do (objectively existing rationally acting) states, A_1, A_2, and A_3... A_x behave under the constraints of X, Y, Z, etc., known as (material) structure (i.e., unequal distribution of capabilities across alike units—exogenously given constraints)?

6. *Neoliberal, neoinstitutional approaches*

How do rules/institutions created by states A_1, A_2, A_3, A_x mollify the effect of X, Y, Z (structure) on (rationally acting) states A_1, A_2, etc., and enable their cooperation—despite exogenously given constraints?

7. *Soft/moderate constructivism*

What do states A, B, C, D, with their identities and interests not uniform and ***not exogenously*** given but intersubjectively agreed based on their different identities (i.e., NB no longer A_1, A_2, A_3, etc.) *intersubjectively* agree is the nature of X, Y, Z (structure) within which they exercise rational choice?
How do ideas change identities of states and thus their interests and policies?

8. *Rule-oriented constructivism*

What are the relevant rules? Are the relevant rules assertive, directive, or commissive? How did they get made? How do they define the terms of agency? How do they set the conditions of rational choice? How do they constitute resources? How do rules that are constantly changing constitute institutions that both resist and foster change in the process of structuring social relations? How do rules and thus institutions allow agents to exercise control over resources and other agents and affect the distribution of benefits among agents? What are the relevant "paradigms of experience" (Table 3.2, p. column 1), that is, form of rule, organization, regime, social ambition, values, and culture, consistent with the rules identified and pointed to by the used theory?

Soft / moderate constructivism

the conversion of IR in the United States, in particular to behavioralism, and its commitment to make the study of IR scientific, along the lines of scientific achievements of natural sciences. The split was not evident before the scientific—or behavioral—revolution, and the classical realism typified in the work of, for example, Hans Morgenthau accommodated both aspects of IR.

The attempt to bridge the split is evident in some approaches and would be one of the important contributions of rule-oriented constructivism. I simplified the FP/IP approaches into one or two questions showing the range of their concern and reproduced these seven questions in Table 5.1. I added a summary of the rule-oriented constructivism based on chapter 3, representing it with a number of characteristic questions. Thus, the overview of the approaches as they handle Soviet "new thinking" can be seen at a glance.

I follow the approaches in chronological order, focusing first on those that were contemporaneous with the "new thinking" and only then those that were developed later, after the end of the Cold War: the improvements to the neoliberal neoinstitutional approaches and then, finally, the main forms of constructivism.

Following this scheme, the chapter is divided into three parts. In the first one I discuss Cold War historiography, neorealist and Sovietological approaches, and their handling of Soviet "new thinking." I then proceed to this process's culmination in the development of soft constructivism. I note that certainly if the example of the Soviet "new thinking" is anything to go by, the mainstream constructivism is very similar to the neoliberal approach in its conclusions concerning "new thinking." Insofar as the latter is compatible with the neorealist approach as well, then mainstream constructivism, I will argue, is nothing more than mainstream IR adapted for the post–Cold War era. To use Ruggie's formula combining the two "neo's" into one, we have a utilitarian approach modified by a dose of voluntarism.

Finally, I show the differences in the treatment of the same Soviet "new thinking" reread in line with my "four steps" by constructivists of the rule-oriented variety (chapter 3). Here I use mainly my own work on "new thinking" based on the actual Soviet discourse.

Trained to Ignore: The "New Thinking" and Western Scholarship Before the USSR's Collapse

If Wendt is right in saying that Soviet "new thinking" was one of the most important phenomena of our time, how is it that only a few years before Wendt made that statement, his IR colleagues thought that they could ignore it?

Let me illustrate the magnitude of this issue using the following parallel. Let us imagine that the president of the United States, with the help of his speechwriters and advisors and the entire academic IR mainstream elite, came

up with a public statement that he formally enunciated and then kept returning to for his entire term of office. (President George Bush, true enough, did
come up with the concept of a New World Order, but without the imprimatur
of the academic IR mainstream, which is significant in terms of my comparison.) Let us imagine that this president revealed in this important speech his
understanding of what the world is about and his vision of the shape it should
assume into the next millennium. Also imagine this vision as a strikingly
new one, indeed as somewhat strange, coming as it did from the pen of the
leader of a superpower. It included rather unprecedented ideas for a president of the United States that seemed to undermine U.S. interests and its
position as a superpower. For example, it contained the notion that the world
was no longer a state system, but that it had become globalized, that it was
now a world society, and that the states had been eclipsed as the system's
main building blocks. The world now shared values in common, and there
was no longer such a thing as "threat." This strange plan proceeded, furthermore, to put forward a detailed timetable for demilitarization and world disarmament to be carried out within a short period of fifteen years, thus
proposing to modify irreversibly one of the key features of the 300-year-old
Westphalian state system. The new ideas did not stop there, but included
ideas about the redistribution of wealth and the rethinking of territoriality as
a principle of global organization. Nor was all of this just talk: there was a lot
of action consistent with these statements. The president started making unprecedented unilateral cuts in military spending. To the consternation of all,
he lifted every embargo still in place, forgave foreign debts, and made other
unexpected friendly gestures, for example, visiting erstwhile foes such as
Fidel Castro and Saddam Hussein.

Such a president would suffer overwhelming public criticism. The
country's academics would have a field day tearing his program to shreds.
Dissertations would be written for years to come on the subject. It is incon-
ceivable that academics would refuse to read the president's statements or
insist that they already knew what it all meant since they knew the constraints under which he operated and could impute to him what he was really
thinking and doing. Nor could they dismiss his statements on the grounds
that the president was still new to his job, anxious to set himself apart from
his predecessors and to sweep away the past with a "new broom."

This is what happened to Gorbachev's "new thinking." Gorbachev's "new
thinking," I repeat, is no longer at issue. However, with the same academic
attitudes unchanged, it could easily happen again that a major change of
thinking originating from a culturally different place, like China, Iraq, Iran,
or North Korea, could be given the same treatment. We might pick up familiar words and impute the real "thinking" to foreign leaders based upon our

own study of their actions and our own understanding of how the world works rather than what they actually say. Are we wired into monitoring only particular facts (IP) and kinds of behavior (FP), and can we continue ignoring the rest as mandated by the discipline within which we function? Are we likely to argue that there is ample evidence, in cases of "thinking" originating from dictatorships and nondemocratic societies, to confirm the fact that statements by politicians originating from these societies do not reveal their intentions and that they, or their academic elaborators, can never make a heuristic contribution to our understanding of the world? There has been a long history of experience with secretive, totalitarian, authoritarian regimes paranoically disguising their intentions, which does predispose such an argument.

The academics traditionally put their own spin on this type of positivistic reasoning, namely, that a country without academic freedom produces inferior or no scholarship. Thus, Stanley Hoffmann, in his important article, "An American Social Science: International Relations," excused the neglect of Soviet and Chinese IR scholarship on the grounds that it would be hard to speak of free social science and scholarship in those societies (1977, 48), while Michael Banks declared Soviet scholarship to be simply "intellectually inferior" (1984). In the case of Soviet thinking, with rare exceptions such as Alker and Biersteker (1984), who treated it even when it was only "old" as a counterpart to our IR theories, IR theorists have paid no attention whatsoever to Soviet thinking on IR, old or new.

An additional justification for the studied ignorance of sources like Soviet "new thinking" is provided by the existence of academic disciplines and subdisciplines. Such a topic might be deemed to fall into the domain of several disciplines or none at all. IR, for example, has traditionally refused to study domestic politics, and scholars may have deemed "new thinking" an internal affair, a synonym for "perestroika," the domestic reform.

As an "important phenomenon," to use Wendt's words, "new thinking" should have been noted in a large number of academic disciplines, particularly if it were not quite clear what it was: Sovietology, comparative communism, a history of the Cold War, FPA, the foreign policy of the United States and of the USSR, political theory (which should have noted a change in Soviet ideology), and theory of IR. It was noted in some, evaded in others, and misunderstood in most of them.

Historiography of the Cold War, IR Neorealism, and Soviet "New Thinking"

How do (objectively existing rationally acting) states, A_1, A_2, and A_3 . . . behave under the constraints of X, Y, Z, etc., known as (material) *structure* (unequal distribution of capabilities across alike units—exogenously given constraints)?

The beginning of the Cold War and its initial interpretation in the United States predated the split between FPA and IP and their quest to become scientific. Before the IP/FPA split and their elimination of subjective and other elements that would thwart their scientific claim, Cold War historians, U.S. decision makers and even many IR specialists saw the U.S.–USSR confrontation as first and foremost a clash of two totally opposed systems of ideas, democratic on one side and expansionist communist on the other. The mirror image of this interpretation on the Soviet side was provided in the Soviet theory of IR based on Lenin's theory of imperialism (Holsti 1972): Accordingly, the domestic nature of a state determined its foreign policy, and capitalism made states by definition aggressive and imperialist while the Soviet system, lacking the capitalist drive, was inherently peaceful. On the U.S. side, the Cold War historiography was confirmed by the traditional Sovietological interpretation of the Soviet Union as totalitarian or authoritarian. In the détente years, this form of Sovietology gave way to a more liberal approach that characterized its final decades as "détente Sovietology."

By the time "new thinking" developed, most of IR, certainly in the United States, and unlike the Cold War historiography, dismissed subjective, ideological factors as a characteristic of the USSR and of the Cold War. The reigning neorealist paradigm talked not so much of the Cold War as more neutral bipolarity of the two superpowers and the constraints on their behavior in terms of material capabilities. Something specifically called "thinking" would thus by definition attract little attention.

At a first glance and in an odd way the disregard that welcomed Soviet "new thinking" in the IR discipline was not that different from postmodernists' treatment of the mainstream discourse, that is, the consequences of the mainstream's neglect of Soviet "new thinking" were again asymmetrically similar to the postmodern attitude to the mainstream! The Soviet side was treated as though it was effectively mute: It was deemed incapable of using the language to represent the state of affairs fairly and accurately. This is what postmodernists do when they dispute the "hegemonic discourse" of the West and the capacity for its linguistic representations to correspond to any "objective" world. Similarly, western scholarship denied Soviet "representations" of the world any utility. Soviets were seen as creating by their words a world of their own that had no social (or material) effects, a world true only to itself, a make-believe world of propaganda and lies designed either to fool or to scare a rather unintelligent and docile population kept in obeisance by coercive totalitarian or authoritarian methods. This dismissive attitude fully consistent with positivistic beliefs also fails to recognize the tremendous importance of "words" in the legitimization of nondemocratic regimes of all sorts, as I will discuss later on.

The problem with the neorealist IR position, the dominant approach to IR at the time of the Soviet new thinking and summarized in Table 5.1 as question 5, is that it makes two static "snapshots" of the world, one before and one after the collapse of the USSR. It has no way of connecting the two.

Take the snapshot of Gorbachev at the helm of the USSR. No matter what he might have said, to IR theorists, it did not matter. The Cold War was a bipolar structure, and this determined the Soviet Union's interests in a way that could not be overridden by any amount of talk and wishful thinking. Neorealism, by definition, shuts out consideration of domestic features of individual states, relegating them to the theoretical margins. In his famous *Theory of International Politics* (1979), Kenneth Waltz was prepared to consider Lenin's theory of imperialism as a theory—albeit a flawed one—of IR, but he could not consider it as a foundation stone of a Soviet theory of IR competing with his own theory. The world ran to the design that he had discovered. As he put it, if there is a theory of IP, it is the balance of power.

What then could Soviet "new thinking" possibly mean to neorealists? The answer: nothing. When in 1988 I presented a paper at Berkeley about Soviet "new thinking" in the presence of Kenneth Waltz, he agreed that "new thinking" "looked like" a theory of IR. No theory however can "wish away" Newton's law of gravity and make objects fall upward instead of downward. Neorealists cannot possibly see how any amount of thinking can alter the material structure (the Cold War) under which Gorbachev had to make his rational choices.

A systemic change/transformation as momentous as the end of the Cold War was deemed. by neorealists at any rate, impossible short of superpower war (Lebow and Risse-Kappen 1995, 1). By the logic of Hobbesean anarchy and the logic of the balance of power, exogenously imposed on the United States as well as the Soviet Union, Gorbachev had to do everything he could to protect the Soviet position in the structure as defined by Waltz. He should have balanced, formed alliances, and tried to regain his country's strength. Instead, the Soviet Union literally gave away its territorial holdings, the geopolitical acquisitions of the Second World War, and actively encouraged East European satellites to go their own way. For the first time since the Sino-Soviet split, a Soviet leader got on well with a Chinese leader. The newly fashioned Sino-Soviet entente and alliance was not put to the use that it should have been in realist terms. The Soviet Union made passes at the United States, but not of the sort expected by realists. Somehow, Gorbachev "defied," or tried to defy, the exogenous forces under which he was deemed to be laboring.

Take a second neorealist snapshot, this time of the end of the Cold War after the collapse of the USSR. The ex post facto explanation of this collapse is that internal problems weakened the Soviet Union to the point that they changed the structure of bipolarity. Thus, the conclusion: "we have won." A realist of Morgenthau's variety might have argued that Gorbachev paid the price of his *irrational* behavior, and so did the Soviet Union (for which Russians now hate him!). Neorealism however makes no place for irrational behavior, thus the leap between the two snapshots and to the conclusion of claiming victory of this terminal contest, though realists were not fully aware at the time that the contest was actually terminal!

The message that "we have won" is very important though, since it serves to legitimize the hegemonic unipolar world structure that resulted with its single superpower and its broad mandate for NATO activities, as some authors claim, in the resultant world.

"New Thinking" in Sovietology and in the "Domestic Sources of Foreign Policy" Approach to FPA

How does individual decision maker acting on behalf of state A, based on his *subjective* perceptions, decide what to do to states B, C, etc.?

Why has individual decision maker acting on behalf of state A, based on his *subjective* perceptions, decided what to do to states B, C, etc.?

Although Sovietology as a study of all things Soviet, its domestic politics as well as foreign policy, had little to do with the IR discipline, Sovietology and the discipline of IR have had a great deal in common. They were both of high national security relevance and close to the US government. When the going was good, that is, when the Cold War was "cold," Sovietology certainly received more than its share of government and other funding in comparison to fields such as sociology or anthropology. The "politically significant" national security fields tended to become too closely tied up with the political fortunes of their subject matter, however. Sovietology kept changing and its fortunes fluctuated with the particular stage of the Cold War in which it found itself (Cohen 1985).

Having been given a historical, political, and methodological shape similar to classical realism of the Morgenthau variety, Sovietology never developed a left wing. At first its dominant mode of thought was of the USSR as "totalitarian" and then as changed due to détente. Once these positions were reached, however, within Sovietology as a discipline, there was a consensus and little controversy. Although there was a brief spell of a "neototalitarian Sovietology" for the couple of years after the "new Cold War" response to the USSR's invasion of Afghanistan in 1979, Sovietology put that brief interval behind it once Gorbachev got into power and Sovietology returned to its main, "détente," read liberal, mode.

Tending to lag behind comparative politics, and borrowing approaches and ideas already out of fashion elsewhere (Fortescue 1986), Sovietologists saw the USSR as a postindustrial society, with striking similarities in this respect between the two superpowers. Sovietologists tended to downplay the actual threat the USSR represented, while seeing it as a very stable type of society. Although Sovietology was liberal in orientation the behavioral revolution and its commitment to making Sovietology into a science reached Sovietology very late and never completely. The behavioral revolution reached Sovietology only insofar as Sovietologists tried to deideologize both their approach and their subject matter.

Lagging behind IR, which, as a discipline, had begun to recognize its left wing in the 1980s, Sovietology never considered seriously the mainly Marxist (in the classical sense), Trotskyist, or Western Marxist Soviet watchers (Kubálková 1994, 24). This "left Sovietology" had in common with the then minority traditionalist/totalitarian Sovietology a keen interest in Soviet pronouncements, unlike their liberal Sovietologist colleagues. The left Sovietologists read the Soviet pronouncements for evidence of growing distance from Marxism and the traditionalist totalitarian and neototalitarian Sovietologists for signs of aggressive intent. It was only left Sovietology that insisted on the pending demise of the USSR, an insistence somewhat devalued by the fact that they had made that claim ever since the USSR had come into existence in 1917.

What, then, was "new thinking" to a positivist, liberal, "détente" Sovietologist on whose perspective depended the FPA approach identified in chapter 1 (called traditionally "domestic sources of FP")? What did they study? (see Table 5.1, questions 2 and 3). How and why had Gorbachev changed his foreign policy, and what, if anything, had Soviet "new thinking" to do with it?

A great deal was written on Soviet new thinking at the same time as it came into existence. There were different definitions of what "new thinking" meant, even in those studies specifically dedicated to its analysis in the United States, United Kingdom, Germany, and China (see, e.g., Berner and Dahm 1987/88; Dallin 1987; Evangelista 1987; Glickham 1986; Legvold 1988a, 1988b; Light 1987, 1988; Meissner 1986; Miller 1988; Sestanovich 1988; Shenfield 1987; Snyder 1987/88; Valkenier 1987; Wettig 1987; Zhi and Zhang 1988). No Sovietologist disputed that something had changed, but the identifying of that something remained constrained by the positivist premises on which mainstream Sovietology, as well as mainstream IR studies, had become based.

Simply put, and consistent with positivist premises, "new thinking" seemed to be the new style of the new broom. Gorbachev was new. The Sovietologists meticulously listed all of the ways in which Gorbachev represented a break from the "old style," that is, from the "old thinking" of the Brezhnev variety. He was much younger, he changed the entire diplomatic establishment, and he traveled a great deal (his geriatric three predecessors—Brezhnev, Chernenko, and Andropov—had all died in office and were too elderly to travel). Not only did he travel, but he also took his wife with him. His predecessors' wives had made their first appearances at their husbands' funerals. Gorbachev and his wife looked, dressed, and sounded like Westerners.

There were Sovietologists who specifically cautioned against paying any attention to the Soviet concept of Soviet "new thinking." For example, Robert Legvold, chairman of the Task Force on Soviet New Thinking and director of the Harriman Institute for Advanced Study of the Soviet Union at Columbia University, put it very strongly:

> It is important when considering the foreign policy implications of Gorbachev's initiatives and statements *not to focus unduly on the concept of "new thinking" as such*, which has been advanced by Gorbachev and his associates as a general rubric for the General Secretary's approach to international affairs. Any new thinking takes place within a historical context of adaptation by the Soviet leadership to external realities. It is this broader pattern, and not any particular slogan, that should be the focus of Western attention. . . . The "new thinking" label itself confounds understanding more than it helps, and it might be better to set it aside and look for formulations that have more solidity and focus. (Legvold 1988b, 4, 8, emphasis added)

Despite this cautionary note, there were Sovietologists who noted that Soviet "new thinking" consisted of a number of points or principles. These were differently identified, however. Thus, Margot Light, for example, listed six main points (1988); Alexander Dallin four (1987); Charles Glickham, about seven (1986); and Jack Snyder, none (1987/88). Legvold (1988b), meanwhile, found "new thinking" to mean changed attitudes in four regards: (1) security, (2) interdependence, (3) the Third World, and (4) socialist states.

According to Stephen Sestanovich, "new thinking" meant "devaluation of ideological precepts, a more complacent assessment of outside threats, a re-examination of national interests and heavier stress on global 'common' interests, a cap on resource commitments, a search for less expensive policy instruments, a more flexible and less demanding stance in negotiations, and an arms-length attitude toward friends in need and an insistence that they do more to help themselves, avoidance of actions that adversaries can treat as provocations, and so forth" (1988, 4). Sestanovich thought that Gorbachev freed "Soviet foreign policy from ideological preoccupations and constraints"

(1988, 5). Characteristically, both Legvold and Sestanovich used their own words in formulating and reformulating what "new thinking" and its principles were, and not the words of any Soviet writer or spokesman, except, of course, terms such as "deideologize"—apropos of Gorbachev—to which, in my view, they gave the traditional Western, rather than the totally different Soviet, meaning.

Since there was in the West no agreement about the content of Soviet "new thinking," any IR expert could borrow whatever he wanted. Thus, "new thinking" was seen not only as a new foreign policy style but also as a new strategic doctrine. The foreign policy analysts placed whatever these principles might have been in the context provided by the FPA and by the neorealist understanding of the constraints under which whatever it was that was happening in the Soviet Union was taking place.

The disintegration of the USSR surprised Sovietologists just as much as it surprised IR specialists. The enormous difficulties with its transition to capitalism contradict the "convergence" notion, the idea that the United States and the USSR, as large, bureaucratic countries, would gradually begin to look alike, and the dilapidated condition of the Soviet economy contradicts any idea of relative prosperity and stability under the Communist Party's control.

The final consensus among Sovietologists, immediately preceding the demise of the USSR, was based on a somewhat lopsided convergence theory admixed with a greatly stressed declinism, a mixture popularized by Samuel Huntington, according to whom both the United States and the USSR were declining, although the USSR was doing so faster than the United States. The declinist or convergence view rested on an understanding of Soviet foreign policy as an expression of problem-ridden Soviet domestic politics, rather than on the traditional communist-expansionist view, which had been a diagnosis characteristic of the earlier "traditional" Sovietology, and by the time of Gorbachev had been totally discredited.

When the end came, as one observer put it, Sovietologists "were in Moscow talking to the wrong people, 'wired' into wrong sources of information" (Karatnytsky 1992, 34).

Sovietology was not around for the "postmortem" snapshot that is the subject of the following section of this chapter.

After the USSR's Collapse: Neoliberal Institutionalism and Soft Constructivism and the "New Thinking"

(a) How do rules/institutions created by states A_1, A_2, A_3, A_x mollify the effect of X, Y, Z (structure) on (rationally acting) states A_1, A_2, etc., and enable their cooperation—despite exogenously given constraints?

(b) What do states A, B, C, D, with their identities and interests not uniform and *not* **exogenously** given but *intersubjectively* agreed based on their different identities (i.e., no longer A_1, A_2, A_3, etc.), *intersubjectively* agree is the nature of X, Y, Z (structure) within which they exercise rational choice? How do ideas change identities of states and thus their interests and policies?

Once the Cold War had ended and the dust had settled, it became obvious just how big a social change the world had undergone. Scholar after scholar expressed surprise: Why would the USSR give up the Brezhnev doctrine and let East Europe go? Katzenstein (1996) asks, why let the Warsaw Pact disintegrate when, under the same strategic conditions earlier on, it would never have considered doing so? Many IR scholars with liberal leanings suspected that the key issues were out of the conceptual reach of neorealism and even of liberalism, and that what went on in the USSR under the label of "new thinking" might hold the clue.

Two germinal pieces concerning these questions, and separated by only one year when they appeared, were both obviously inspired by the end of the Cold War. Wendt wrote his famous constructivist article in 1992. Another book of innovations, this time neoliberal institutionalist, came out on the heels of Wendt's piece, namely a book entitled *Ideas in Foreign Policy: Beliefs, Institutions, and Political Change* (Goldstein and Keohane 1993). Adding to this literature is Katzenstein's collection of case studies published in 1996. There followed a number of other studies, which used one or other of these frameworks or fused the two, making it difficult to distinguish them. In addition to the chapter on Soviet "new thinking" in Katzenstein's collection (1996), I also refer to the book on the subject by Checkel (1997) and to the collection of essays dedicated to the Soviet "new thinking" inspired by either neoliberalism or constructivism and edited by Lebow and Risse-Kappen (1995). Wendt returns to "new thinking" again in his 1999 book.

How did scholars argue their new case? "Reigning realist and liberal explanations cannot adequately account for 'new thinking's' revolutionary character," Robert Herman says, for example. Realism, he continues, is too preoccupied with material capabilities, the structural constraints on political actors. Liberalism, too, marginalizes the "social processes that spawned the core ideas of mature New Thinking" (Herman 1996, 272). How do we suddenly know, however, that "new thinking" (read, the "new style" of the "new broom") was so seemingly "revolutionary" that it had passed through stages enabling it to "mature"?

Most authors of this genre explicitly state that their wish is not to contradict but to complement the liberalist and realist approaches. The impression one gets is that they want to complement/qualify the rather awkwardly argued neorealist argument that "we have won" the Cold War. Neorealists, as I have tried to show in the previous section, did not, or could not, shed light on how this process of social change became possible. The question in this section is to determine to what extent the neoliberal neoinstitutionalists and mainstream constructivists have succeeded in their stead.

The literature I am referring to originated from the 1990s. By then Sovietology was gone. Its détentist, liberalist conclusions lingered on, however. What is striking is how little and superficial was the search for evidence by those engaged in this new wave study of "new thinking." This confirms my impression that conclusions drove the search, rather than the other way around (i.e., the search for evidence resulting in a new conclusion).

What, then, do the two approaches identified above conclude was the nature of "new thinking" and its role in ending the Cold War and in the collapse of the Soviet Union? Both neoliberal institutionalists and constructivists take away some of the glory of a U.S. victory in the Cold War claimed by neorealists, and/or they spread and apportion the credit for the victory in such a way as to include others and other factors, not just the United States and its various policies. It is the question of producing evidence that is troubling. It is as though there is a temporary amnesty to scholars who are self-avowedly positivist, to allow them to eschew positivist rigor and to issue the command: Go and find whatever evidence you can and bring it in, it will be accepted.

The shades and details may differ, but the "helpers" in the victory the United States had are all liberal favorites. They include the tremendously contagious ideas of democracy, freedom, and so forth that when tasted, or simply heard about, people never get over. These ideas penetrated the Soviet Union, goes the argument, in the détente years when academic exchanges took place. Or, they simply "rubbed off" on the Soviet elites as a result of interdependence and the "learning" that it inevitably brings (Gross Stein 1995). Or, it was Mikhail Gorbachev himself who took steps facilitating the United States victory, either as a liberal reformer himself, or simply as a rational leader. For some scholars he did it alone, for others, there was pressure from local elites. Accordingly, argues Herman, "new thinking" represents a "genuine reconceptualization of interests grounded in new collective understandings about the dynamics of world politics and in actors' evolving identities." The "turn in Soviet international policy," he goes on, "was the product of cognitive evolution and policy entrepreneurship by networks of Western-oriented in-system reformers coincident with the coming to power of a leadership committed to change and receptive to new ideas for solving the country's formidable problems" (Herman 1996, 273). Checkel seems to concur, putting the role of reform and democratic ideas, and the "subversive" role of U.S. academics, into a "neorealist context": Changes in a state's external environment create "windows of opportunity through which policy entrepreneurs . . . jump," when the domestic institutional setting "affects their ability to influence policy" (1997, 7). "As structures weaken, [Checkel explains], access to policymaking increases . . . , [thus] creat[ing] a greater number of pathways for promoters of new ideas" (ibid.).

Who are these promoters? How do we measure their influence? What exactly triggers an "ideational change?" Herman continues: Liberal specialists developed new understanding about cause-and-effect relationships in international politics (1996, 274). The principles governing the relations among the Western democracies and within those societies, he goes on, were transmitted to Soviet reformers through the kind of transnational contacts with Western, liberal-Left counterparts that flourished in the 1970s and survived détente's precipitous decline (275). Out goes the objectivity of the academy, which hereby plays the role of agent of influence, with the responsibility for subverting one of the world's superpowers as its contribution to world peace.

Wendt's conclusion is less enthusiastically put and more sober. His argument is more complicated, but he is not that far from some Cold War historians who, having regarded the Cold War to be a matter of clashing ideas, conclude that when Gorbachev "changed his mind," Cold War ended (Mueller 1995). Wendt, too, gives almost full credit for the victory of the United States in the Cold War to the Soviets. The Soviets won it for the United States. He argues that Gorbachev's "new thinking" was the policy that allowed the change from a competitive to a cooperative security system. He covers his bets by saying that the existence of this new cooperative relationship may still be in doubt, and may not last. It developed, according to Wendt, in a four-stage process, namely,

1. The breakdown of the consensus about identity commitments inside the USSR resulting from the giving up of an aggressive posture, and bolstered by reassurances from the West that it would not attack the Soviet Union.
2. These changed ideas then led to rethinking the Soviet identity, the discovery of "new selves" by the Russians, and the recognition of how much the old selves fed the old competitive structure.
3. Then, there followed "altercasting," that is, the presentation of the Soviet Union by Soviet elites (now with new identity) in such a way as to change the identity of the United States as well. This was accomplished by such actions as withdrawal from Eastern Europe and Afghanistan, that is, by reducing in turn the U.S. need to perceive the Soviets as a threat.

4. And, finally, the establishment of a firm intersubjective basis between the United States and the USSR for their understanding of
   their changed relationship (Wendt 1992, 419–422).

Wendt returns to the "new thinking" in 1999. Gorbachev's "new thinking," he argues, was

> a deep conceptual reassessment of what the U.S.-Soviet relationship "was." It
> was constitutive theorizing, at the lay level, and based on it the Soviets were
> able to end, unilaterally and almost overnight, a conflict that seemed like it had
> become set in stone. It may be that objective conditions were such that the
> Soviets "had" to change their ideas about the Cold War, but that does not change
> the fact in an important sense those ideas were the Cold War, and as such chang-
> ing them by definition changed the reality. (1999, 374)

For, he argues, "reality is being caused by theory rather than vice-
versa" (1999, 76). Thus, he is quite right when he described his approach
as structural idealism, an inversion of the approach of the structural
realists, whom he criticizes as those "wedded to the blind forces model
of intentional action."

> Certainly the economic and military pressures on the Soviet state were a cru-
> cial impetus for change. However, a structural pressures theory alone cannot
> explain the form the Soviet response took (ending the Cold War rather than
> intensifying repression) or its timing (the material decline had been going on
> for some time). And it also ignores the role that the leadership's realization that
> its own policies were part of the problem played in conditioning that response.
> Structural conditions did not force self-awareness on the Soviets. Soviet be-
> havior changed because they redefined their interest as a result of having looked
> at their existing desires and beliefs self-critically. The reflective model of in-
> tentional explanation captures this process more naturally than the blind forces
> model. (1999, 129)

And, this is how he explains the "reflective model":

> When social kinds are reified there is a clear distinction between subject and
> object. However, there are occasions when collectives become aware of the
> social kinds they are constituting and move to change them, in what might be
> called a moment of "reflectivity": for decades, for example, the Soviet Union
> treated the Cold War as a given. Then in the 1980s it engaged in "New Think-
> ing," an important outcome of which was the realization that aggressive for-
> eign policies contributed to Western hostility, which in turn forced the Soviets
> to engage in high levels of defense spending. By acting on that understanding
> to conciliate the West, the Gorbachev regime virtually single-handedly ended
> the Cold War. In effect, if a social kind can "know itself" then it may be able to

recall its human authorship, transcend the subject-object distinction, and create new social kinds. (Wendt, 1999 76)

Soviet "new thinking," Wendt argues, serves as an example that "even states are capable of . . . thinking reflexively" (1999, 374). It is also an example of a situation in which, he argues, "deliberation can generate dramatic 'preference reversals' even while structural conditions remain constant" (374). And so the cognitive and deliberative arguments may overlap. The principles informing Soviet "Reason" were not wholly independent of beliefs about the identity of the Soviet state, the feasibility of certain actions, and even about right and wrong. Deliberation about national interests takes place against the background of a shared national security discourse, in other words, which may substantially affect its content (Wendt 1999, 129).

Relative to the amount published about "new thinking" at the time of its occurrence, the post–Cold War studies are very few, and often not by former Sovietologists. Most are amazingly selective in choosing the sources they cite (and mix). Nor are there any guidelines given as to what type of evidence should or should not be brought to bear and the standard positivist strictures are obviously set aside.

Except to pick up little snippets here and there, this rather unpositivist attitude is largely due to the reluctance to go "inside the USSR." Both neoliberal and mainstream constructivists abide by the strictures of keeping domestic and international politics separate. Despite the stress on things ideational, they did not change the standard Sovietological approach of treating the Soviets as if they were mute. Reformers or not, therefore, Soviets are presumed not to talk. Their words are not cited. They are described in our own terms. Remember, even when they were reformists (according to the old Sovietologists), they only "spoke ideology." We can only quote them, even now, when they speak like we do.

True enough, the Soviet Union is gone, and its case is used now not by Sovietologists or post-Sovietologists but by theorists of IR, who want only to demonstrate the validity of the emerging neoliberal and constructivist frameworks for handling social change. Besides, many of the authors are not Sovietologists by training or trade and neither is their audience. Thus, nobody picks up their mistakes (e.g., Herman is simply wrong when he argues that "other central elements" of "new thinking," e.g., the relationship between peace and socialism, and between class values and "values common to all mankind," were the products of ongoing debate within the socialist bloc [1996, 275]). Positivist standards would lead one to expect some documentation would be offered as to who were all these "new thinkers," before attaching the label to some only, and without any explanation as to why to them and not to others. By positivist standards, it could be expected that these authors would recognize and acknowledge differences among their sources and minimally explain why they rely on some sources (or only their parts) and ignore the rest, or other sources.

Thus, Wendt (1992, 420) for example, cites my argument (Kubálková and Cruickshank 1989b), but uses it to reach different conclusions. He does not acknowledge that that particular argument, which he takes from my book, crucially important for his constructivist framework, completely contradicts the consensus of the Sovietological literature on which he at the same time draws. Essentially, I argued that Gorbachev gave up Lenin's theory of imperialism in 1986 at the Twenty-Seventh CPSU Congress but did so without referring to either Lenin or the theory of imperialism. The theory of imperialism at the core of Soviet thinking on IR mandated all Soviet leadership to sustain a conflictual, very expensive policy toward the capitalist United States. Most Sovietologists argued either that in 1986 the Soviet Union was already deideologized, or that Gorbachev's 1986 speech, in which, I argued, he announced the surrender of Lenin's theory of imperialism, was boring and brought "nothing new." Wendt quotes my argument but takes it out of its context. He explains Gorbachev's "change of mind" in material, rationalist, functional, institutionalist efficiency terms, namely, that an aggressive posture was too difficult to sustain in material terms. He never explains why he chooses to overlook other, or additional, explanations offered by the Soviets themselves that he could have found in the same source that he quoted.

How, indeed, do you determine which information to use and which to set aside? Even the bit Wendt uses does not fit into his four stages. If he agrees (with me) that the change (which all Sovietologists missed) took place as early as 1986, at the very beginning of Gorbachev's tenure of office, when exactly and between whom did the process equally central to his argument take place, namely "an intra-elite process by which the alteration of Soviet identity" was reached? If Wendt accepts the discarding of the theory of imperialism, and puts it at a later date than 1986, how does he reconcile this with the notion that by 1986 the Soviet Union had already deideologized its foreign policy? Why not consider those alternative explanations offered by the Soviets themselves to explain their making conciliatory measures meant to soften would-be adversaries' perceptions of hostile Soviet intentions, alternatives, that is to say, to the axiomatically postulated jettisoning of Marxist-Leninist ideology as a guide for defining state interests and lapsing into behavior stipulated by rational choice theory? Why postulate an essential compatibility with the mainstream approaches when the conclusion that Gorbachev somehow deliberately contributed to or conspired to engineer the collapse of the USSR contravenes all realist and neorealist theories? It implies Gorbachev's surrendering of the national interest or survival of his country, in the name of his changed understanding of the world and his learning of liberal ideas, which he somehow managed either himself directly or with help from his advisors, who, in turn, had help from U.S. academics. Is this compatible with rational choice theory?

Not for the sake of further analysis of this particular historical incident, but for future reference, I will now summarize the frameworks that generated this discussion. Even in the simplified summary of these two approaches used in Tables 1.1 and 5.1, neoinstitutionalist liberalism and mainstream constructivism appear to be very different, which they must be, if they are the alternative paradigms that they are claimed to be.

Judging from the analysis of Gorbachev's "new thinking," differences between the two approaches are substantively negligible. I concur with Jennifer Sterling-Folker that mainstream constructivism does not offer a paradigmatic alternative to neoliberal institutionalism (Sterling-Folker 2000, 98). As she points out, both constructivists and neoliberals are interested in much the same things as "potential evidence." They share the same ontology and same epistemology and they rely on the same post hoc explanations (100). Both are positivist and emphasize that their purpose is not to replace, let alone discredit the mainstream approaches but to complement them. Thus, I agree that they are no more than complementary theories within the larger framework of liberal IR theory (100). She reaches this conclusion mainly on the argument that both neoliberal institutionalists and mainstream constructivists depend on the same mechanism of functional, institutional efficiency in order to account for social change. Let me, in conclusion and for the record, summarize the two frameworks side by side (Table 5.2).

Like neorealists, neoliberals subscribe to the idea that states' actions are restricted by the overpowering "logic of anarchy," but they concede that institutions, namely organizations or patterns of recurrent relationship, can also act as constraints, thus possibly modifying the material constraints stressed by structural realists. Goldstein and Keohane argue that ideas can become a significant independent variable, that is, the factor that may help to explain or predict the dependent variable, in this case foreign policy. International institutions, they argue, can transform state identities and interests.

The framework offered by both aims at reducing the element of unpredictability in the event that a state like the Soviet Union, following a different logic from that of the neorealist "logic of anarchy," suspends the rigors of positivism. Both of these approaches set out to correct the focus on material structures in the explanation of a state's foreign policy. Both agree that one also needs to examine *ideational* factors in addition to those emphasized by neorealism, that is, such material forces as bipolarity, and other

Table 5.2

Neoliberal Institutionalism and Soft/Moderate Constructivism Compared

	Framework	New topics and key words	Ideas are	States' identity and interests	States' rationality	Explanation of social change	Domestic politics	Language
Neoliberal institutionalism	Both positivist: insisting on empirical testing of propositions/hypotheses against facts	Both approaches: norms, ideas, learning, identity-formation and transformation (inconsistent with neoliberal premises—identity should be held constant), institutions, interests	Independent variables but limited role, placed within rationalist framework as road maps and preferences in cost-benefit calculations. Impact of ideas on objective reality not studied	Rationalist-behavioral, exogenously given by the anarchical (bipolar cold war) material structure that has causal power: USSR as a superpower restricted by the cold war and has to rationally follow these external dictates in its FP, but some institutional modifications are possible (by "new thinking")	Yes, maximizing interests or utility	Both approaches: the same mechanism of functional / institutional efficiency and causal logic	Not studied	Not studied
Soft constructivism		Constructivism adds: agency, process, social structure, intersubjectivity	Not pure rationalist (cost-benefit calculations) but reflectivist, taking ideas and understandings into account in relation to interests that influence decision making and choice of action. Ideas regarded as capable of changing objective reality	Identity and interests are endogenous to interaction, i.e., not given, dependent variable, i.e., and therefore can be transformed. Anarchy, cold war, structure are socially constructed by collective meanings. Thus, states can transform competition into cooperation: "new thinking" could change the superpower game	Yes, once interests are established (through acceptance of ideas and changed identity) Consider also psychological insights			

differences

balance-of-power considerations, as well as institutional developments added by the neoinstitutionalist mainstream theorists. Policy choices and behavior are constrained/dictated by both these material *and* institutional factors. Most authors begin with a declaration to this effect, namely that material forces, by themselves, cannot account for actual policies. A new focus is needed to ascertain how ideas, norms, rules, and learning affect decision makers' preferences and, ultimately, foreign policy outcomes. Or, to use the neoliberal jargon, particular circumstances (both systemic and domestic) create the foundation (scope conditions) for policy change and the implementation of new ideas (Goldstein and Keohane, 1993, 30). All of these authors seem to concur that material structures coexist with social structures and that they codetermine a state's behavior, thus opening up an avenue for the investigation of factors previously excluded. Stressing the need to adopt an "institutional-ideational" framework to account for foreign policy outcomes, Checkel (1997, xi), for instance, examines the "interaction between ideas, political institutions, and the international system" to explain the process through which ideas have shaped Soviet/Russian foreign policy.

The common denominator of these studies is the acknowledgement that ideational factors, in addition to material ones, shape elite preferences, interests, and policies. Hence the need to scrutinize the exact relationship between these factors, that is, how structures and institutions constrain foreign policy, but also how they leave a range of choice (the possibility to articulate different policy paths), so that ideological factors like beliefs, culture, or "historical narratives" need to be looked at as well.

Table 5.2 enables me to skip the technical detail of the subtle differences between the two approaches in theoretical terms. I compare the two approaches, focusing on their similarities and differences. In regard to their commitment to positivism, rational choice, the explanation of social change, the attention to domestic politics, and to language, they do not differ. I mark in the middle of Table 5.2 the areas where they differ, namely in regard to processing ideas, interests, identities, and so forth. Constructivists of the Wendt variety are "reflective," and their argument goes deeper than that of neoliberals who simply place ideas in the rational context *tout court*. To Wendt it is a more philosophically erudite process; that is, for him the objective world becomes intersubjectively available, and disciplined inquiry can make intersubjective understanding more reliable. His constructivism goes no further, however. Thus, it can be absorbed into the hegemonic discourse of North American IR without undue discomfort on either side.

The conclusion reached by both neoliberal institutionalists and mainstream constructivists seems to be counterintuitive. It also flies in the face of the facts: The main beneficiaries of the collapsed Soviet Union and its bumpy transition were from the beginning the former party officials in what is now an overwhelmingly corrupt economic system. It takes a leap of faith to argue with any degree of conviction that any Soviet leader would have agreed on behalf of his country to plunge into the disarray characteristic of the transition in which the former Soviet Union still finds itself.

Neither neoliberals nor constructivists have come up with any other suggestion, however.

Soviet "New Thinking" and Rule-Oriented Constructivism

From Common Sense to Rule-Oriented Constructivism

At the beginning of this chapter I noted that constructivism was introduced in 1989 when the Cold War was ending and the Soviet Union was soon to be formally disbanded. How can I now claim that I can use my research on the subject of "new thinking" published also in 1989 for a rule-oriented constructivist analysis, when "new thinking" predated its introduction?

The answer is simple. Rule-oriented constructivism comes very naturally to a person who studies, here in the West, the culture/religion/ideology from which he/she hails. Or to a person who takes seriously the work of insiders in the areas he/she studies. That in itself is a step in the direction of acknowledging that the world is constructed differently in its different parts. Studying Soviet pronouncements, as I have done, is a step in the direction of recognizing that words matter. To those of us who were "insiders" somewhere else before becoming "insiders" in the United States, constructivism is simply common sense and need not be learned. Positivism, in contrast, has to be learned, and, in my experience, the learning is by no means easy.

I shall never forget how taken aback I was when, after completing my British Ph.D., I was welcomed into my first job in the West by the head of the department that had hired me as a specialist in IR and Soviet studies. He said I was "in the wrong job," something he was prompted to say by my having said—in answer to his questions concerning my experience and background—that I woke up one day with the Warsaw Pact tanks under my window, that I was soon after torn out of the social arrangements in which I had been raised, and that I was one of tens of thousands who fell through the cracks created by the Cold War. In his view, I was too "emotionally involved" in both of my areas, IR as well as Soviet studies, to make a good (positivist) scholar and teacher. And yet all I was describing was the Brezhnev doctrine from the perspective of someone on the receiving end of it, as I had found myself when the Warsaw Pact troops invaded Czechoslovakia in 1968. I have heard similar remarks many times since from positivist colleagues who claim that personal experience constitutes "inadmissible evidence," contaminated as it is by the subjective fashion in which it is acquired. This subjectivity ostensibly disallows a scholar from making any generalizations or from performing any of the other exercises in which positivist scholars engage, such as formulating objective hypotheses, identifying dependent and independent variables, collecting data, measuring, refuting, falsifying, verifying, and so on. I discovered that to be a social scientist working in IR or in any other Western social science means keeping one's personal concerns, experiences, and political commitments very much to oneself, and certainly out of one's work. Personal experience is suitable for writing memoirs or belles lettres, not for scholarship. Social scientists apply the same sanitized, dehumanized approach not only to themselves but also to their subject matter, purging it of people. As I described in chapter 1, one way to achieve this is simply to study not people, but reifications, that is, objects made up of people. Another way is to observe people's behavior. In both cases the point is to forget that it is people, with their intentions and meanings, that are involved.

Objectivity, and the elimination of subjectivity, requires another crucial step: imputing uniform, a priori, given, inescapable rationality, either to every human being—American, Czech, or Russian—or to every reified institution made up of Americans, Czechs, or Russians. The positivist scholar is taught to speak and write in the passive voice (or to use the royal "we"). This is regarded as appropriate since the pursuit of knowledge is scholarly, that is, objective, value free, and untainted by any subjective biases. This precept has been taken to heart by generations of academics, which accept it as given. The department head in my first academic job was no exception.

I was baffled by his comment because I did not think that he actually could have meant it. I was used to the old Marxist notion of the unity of theory and practice axiomatically postulated in the Soviet bloc, and I failed to see how one could go without the other or how one could harm the other. Only later I discovered that it was quite common for Ph.D. scholars, for example, to defend dissertations on Soviet subjects but not know properly, or at all, the Russian language and not have visited the USSR (Pettman 2000). Research was based on translations into English and on secondary sources. When the USSR topped the list of priorities on the national security agenda, Soviet materials were extensively translated into English. Now that Russia does not loom so large, one wonders how research proceeds, considering that the basic approach has not changed. The same approach will be difficult to defend in the post–Cold War era, in a world dotted with alien cultures and religions, of the sort that characterize many of the "states of concern" (formerly rogue states). There are too many such states to open a translation service of the magnitude the USSR warranted when it occupied the number-one slot in the list of national security concerns (Kubálková 2000).

As originally an "insider from elsewhere," I was, in other words, close to constructivism of the sort Ralph Pettman called "commonsense constructivism" (Pettman 2000). This approach lends itself to extension to rule-oriented constructivism, and in itself provides a perspective quite at odds with American social science. For years my work was based on this form of commonsense constructivism, as I continued reading Soviet materials, taking them as seriously as Sovietological secondary sources. My "common sense" was also telling me that things were happening "in IR," and were not restricted to the state-centric perspective characteristic of the mandatory focus of the IR mainstream.

The Soviet rendition of the world was very different from the one I learned from Western IR specialists. Instead of states and anarchy and balances of power, the Soviets regarded "states" as a level of abstraction too general to permit any meaningful generalizations. Although it was cast in socioeconomic terms, the Soviet approach emphasized the need to distinguish among states, depending on their identity. It was this that determined their different interests and therefore behavior (does this sound familiar to soft constructivists?). The Soviets did not use the concept of anarchy and of the balance of power. They viewed the world in terms of "correlations of forces" instead—a reading they took at any particular moment of the entire system of relations, which was one that they viewed in a state of constant flux. The correlation of forces included not only the material capabilities of states but also domestic or nonstate factors and such intangibles as moral and ethical considerations. The entire Soviet view of the world was underpinned by Lenin's theory of imperialism, which placed their thinking into the "second image" category Kenneth Waltz created, namely, one where the domestic nature of a state determines to a large extent that country's foreign policy (Waltz 1954). To anticipate an important point I am going to make later on, let me say that the effect of Lenin's theory of imperialism was that relations of states were "ideologized": States were enacting roles assigned to them by their respective ideology and, thus, in their relations with other states were protagonists of class struggle. The framework of Soviet thinking resembled—although in an inverse form—the Cold War historians' view of two blocs based on different ideas/ideologies. Unlike Cold War historians who saw this conflict as based on different ideas/ideologies with states poised in a relation called "Cold War," Soviets saw this conflict in deeper socioeconomic terms. They preferred to call the Cold War "peaceful coexistence of states of socialist and capitalist socioeconomic formation." In East-West, North-South terms, the Soviets equated the West with the North. The East-West axis was complemented by the North-South axis in a very similar way to that of dependencia (based on Lenin's theory of imperialism). The relations among states of different groups were guided by different rules. The relation among socialist countries, for example, was known as socialist internationalism, referred to in the West (but not by the Soviets) as the "Brezhnev doctrine." Far from contravening the International Law, the Brezhnev doctrine type of intervention such as "happened to me" was in fact mandated by the "Socialist International Law" applicable among socialist countries and overriding the "general international law," which played a subsidiary role. Nobody among the Sovietological or IR scholarly community took any of this seriously, however, since it was only "ideology" or "propaganda." I was wasting time, they said, by treating it as if it were theory. I argued repeatedly—in vain—that it was an honest statement of Soviet intentions, and that as such it offered an insight into Soviet foreign policy that was just as useful as that offered by U.S. scholars.

Soviet "New Thinking" from the "Horse's Mouth"

My study of new thinking was one of the most exciting projects that I have ever undertaken. At the time of its inception I was engaged in another project, namely figuring out what the Soviets meant by "new international law." However, something else, also called "new," suddenly began beaming out of the Soviet Union's texts and speeches, promising—to me at any rate—to supersede all else.

I began collecting all Soviet sources as they were published—articles, speeches, and later also books—on the subject of "new thinking." The concept of "new thinking" crystallized in the first year of Gorbachev's tenure of office of General Secretary of the CPSU. In fact, other authors high up in the Soviet hierarchy wrote on the subject first, before Gorbachev took up the concept. There was confusion among the Soviet decision-making elite as to what it was (Petrovskij 1986). There must have been concern that the Soviet population at large might not understand it either. Thus, *Pravda* published a series of political cartoons putting it in clear and graphic terms for everybody to see (Kubálková and Cruikshank, 1989b, Appendix).[1] I carefully tracked the writers on the subject in a flowchart of the Soviet State and Party organization. I studied their biographies to discover their professional/intellectual/educational backgrounds, to find out whether they did or did not study outside the USSR, or what their previous assignments were. I tried to read as many publications by these authors as possible. This proved to be a daunting task: Georgi Shakhnazarov, one of Gorbachev's closest advisors, wrote more than fifty books, some under the nom de plume "G. Shakh." I paid particular attention to whom these writers cited and who were their Western sources of inspiration. I kept track of the personal changes Gorbachev made to the leading state and party institutions by moving personnel and creating new bodies. I took careful note of the tasks assigned to different research outfits and confirmed some of these developments in discussions with Soviet defectors. I found it interesting that Gorbachev's wife, Raisa, was a professor of Marxist-Leninist philosophy and had introduced her husband to a circle of her colleagues and their philosophical discussions, which apparently he enjoyed. Gorbachev elevated at least one of this circle beyond mere academic status.

The Duality of the "New Thinking's" Sources

Right off the bat, I found a little puzzle; the meaning of the actual words "new thinking." Soviet authors stressed it tirelessly—and equally tirelessly, their Western "watchers" ignored them. In the West, as I came to argue, the meaning of the term "new thinking" was set in terms of its antonym, "old thinking," understood to be the old Soviet, Marxist-Leninist, inflexible, aggressive, Brezhnevite type of thinking. Gorbachev's group acknowledged that they were trying to depart from some of Brezhnev's practices and from those of other Soviet leaders. However, as Gorbachev and his team repeated, the term "new thinking" was borrowed from Albert Einstein, who had coined it for the Pugwash Peace movement. Specifically, it was used for the manifesto written jointly for Pugwash by Einstein and Bertrand Russell. "New thinking's" antonym—the "old thinking" that was to be supplanted by the "new thinking"—was not the Soviet thinking. Rather, "new thinking" was to replace what we here in the West call realist, state-centric thinking, the Westphalian system that Gorbachev agreed with Einstein had become untenable (with its reliance on the use of violence) in the nuclear era. The mainstream realism we teach and propagate here in the West was, in this view, tantamount to war propaganda and should be banned! Western analysts could not possibly have missed the meaning the Soviets were trying to convey with the term "new thinking." "New thinking" was not to be Soviet thinking only, but the thinking of humanity in general in the nuclear age. However, Western analysts chose to set it aside. They probably regarded it as not important enough to deserve comment, or as thwarting the spin that they chose to put on what "new thinking" meant.

There were many other differences between the Soviet meaning and the Sovietological interpretation of "new thinking." Most of its associated concepts, as I documented in detail, had a dual source, one Soviet, one Western. Apart From Einstein and Russell, they included Herman Kahn, Willy Brandt, Jonathan Schell, Niels Bohr, Olaf Palme, Richard Falk and his WOMP project, and even the pope and the Catholic Church (e.g., Plimak 1987, 74). I kept jotting them down as they emerged. I also started collecting the work of Sovietologists on the subject, not restricting myself to the U.S. or English literature, but including also German and Chinese authors. My reading of the Soviet texts led me to the conclusion that the term "new thinking" had ten regular conceptual associates. There were, in other words, ten aspects to Soviet "new thinking," and only the inclusion of all of them gave a clear idea of what the Soviets meant. They were

1. the global problems of mankind, or "global human problems" (nuclear catastrophe, ecological disaster, poverty, etc.);
2. the interdependence for survival of mankind in a world regarded as one interrelated totality;
3. the renunciation of war (there was therefore no such a thing as a Soviet "threat");
4. the concept of peace as the highest of humanity's values;
5. the regarding of the security of all states as global and indivisible;
6. the attainability of security not by military but political means, not on the basis of the "balance of power" but of the "balance of interests" in a comprehensive system of security;
7. the reduction in the level of military confrontation in all areas;
8. the size of military arsenals to be based on "reasonable sufficiency" to repel aggression,
9. the stress on flexibility in international relations so as to reflect the realistic assessment of them;
10. the coexistence of socialism and capitalism in one interrelated and interdependent world (where the mode of thought that continued to distinguish socialism from capitalism was Marxist-Leninist historical materialism based on dialectics).

Taken in isolation from each other, this mixed bag of points and ideas would have baffled many an analyst. Some authors thought these points were mutually contradictory. Thus many authors picked only one or two points and ignored the rest. A focus on only point 9 for example, led to appreciation of a new approach/new style of foreign policy. Points 5–9 suggest a new doctrine of national security. Points 1–4 were usually listed by Sovietologists at the end of any discussion of "new thinking" and dismissed as propaganda. Points 5–8, taken in isolation, could be seen as indicating no more than a fresh wave of rhetoric. Point 10 was seldom cited at all, and then only to argue that it conflicted with the rest.

My interpretation was different. I saw the ten points as just the tip of an iceberg—a small part of a profoundly significant and far-reaching intellec-

tual/ideological change and reorientation. I interpreted the ten points of Soviet "new thinking" as consisting of essentially of four things:

1. a new Soviet ideology,
2. a new form of Marxism,
3. a new theory of IR,
4. a new guide for foreign policy action.

My case rested on very shaky ground by the standards of positivist scholarship, however. I had to prove, first, the validity of my hypothesis that Soviet "new thinking" pertained to these ten principles, and second, that it originated from the pens of decision- and policy-making elites close to Gorbachev.
My other "evidence" was based on a comprehensive survey of all sources
and a flowchart indicating the location of authors of "new thinking" in the
Soviet apparatus. My evidence included a collection of cartoons from *Pravda*
showing what the Soviet elites wanted the Soviet population to associate
with the concept. My evidence included an "intersubjective consensus"
among a small handful of analysts, most of them from outside the United
States. It was not enough. Thus, I was delighted to find that Glickham's
analysis came close to mine; that some German analysts concurred that "new
thinking" was not a foreign policy expedient (Meissner 1987, 3) or disinfor-
mation (Wettig 1987, 144); that, like me, two other German scholars also
thought that new thinking was "a grand theory" (*Grosskonzeption*) (Berner
and Dahm 1987/88, 5); and that Chinese analysts concurred that new thinking was a formal repudiation of Lenin's theory of imperialism. I cited for
support some American Sovietologists who agreed that Gorbachev could
not have been a closet democratic reformer because he understood by "democracy" something very different from the idea of it imputed to him. By
democracy, Gorbachev meant, at best, grass-roots democracy at the
microsocietal level, that is, free elections at the enterprise, primary party
organization, and local soviet levels—but not at the macroinstitutional level,
which included state and party organs (Bialer 1987, 64). Another commenta-
tor pointed out that the "democratization" of the interstices of the party advocated by Gorbachev, which some Western observers mistook for a genuine wish to democratize the entire Soviet society, excluded nonmembers of
the party. It meant no more than democratization of the rule by whites in
South Africa, that is, it did not affect apartheid in any way and maintained
the policy of excluding black voters (Handleman quoted in Bialer 1987, 33).
None of this was evidence that satisfied the positivist consensus either. Until
constructivists took it out of the mothballs, Soviet "new thinking" had ceased
to exist, and the debate about it was closed.

Rule-Oriented Constructivist Interpretation

> What are the relevant rules? Are the relevant rules assertive, directive, or com-
> missive? How did they get made? How do they define the terms of agency?
> How do they set the conditions of rational choice? How they constitute re-
> sources? How do rules that are constantly changing constitute institutions that
> both resist and foster change in the process of structuring social relations? How
> do rules and thus institutions allow agents to exercise control over resources
> and other agents and affect the distribution of benefits among agents? What are
> the relevant "paradigms of experience" (Table 3.2, p. column 1), i.e. form of
> rule, organization, regime, social ambition, values, culture, consistent with the
> rules identified and pointed to by the used theory?

I should stress right at the outset that there are two ways a constructivist can
proceed: go either for the big picture or for its fragment. As we have pointed
out before (Kubálková, Onuf, and Kowert 1998), constructivism presents a
picture of social reality of enormous complexity. That does not rule out the
possibility of "zooming" in on one or more aspects of this complex picture,
however. It is this approach that Koslowski and Kratochwil pursued in their
1995 study, the first ever rule-oriented constructivist interpretation of an aspect of Soviet "new thinking." In it the authors singled out one rule, the
Soviet Internationalism (aka the Brezhnev doctrine), and showed how a
change in one rule affected the entire system. I fully agree with the conclusions they reached. (see Koslowski and Kratochwil, 1995). However, by
comparing the range of approaches to "new thinking" in this chapter, I have
committed myself to the other, broader, option. Even so, I limit myself to a
particular aspect of the issue, to do mainly with the understanding of
Gorbachev as agent and the social structure from which he arose, and the
context of the rational choices he made. I refer to my larger study on the
subject, on excerpts from which the following discussion is based (1989b).

Constructivism has nothing to say directly about "new thinking" per se or
about Gorbachev. What it does do is direct our research to certain areas of
social relations. A positivist scholar would only reluctantly consider the material I have just summarized in the previous section. This, though, is the
starting point for rule-oriented constructivists. It is the preliminary to what
in chapter 3 I called step 3. Constructivism's first concern is to find "rules,"
understood here as a crucial form of human and social activity that enables
us to see people as interacting in, and with, an inextricably social and material world. Thus, while "ideology" or "propaganda" are not regarded by positivists as admissible evidence, to constructivists they contain rules, and these
rules need to be sorted out not only in terms of their relation to agents and to
structure, but also by their type (instructive, directive, and commissive). This
categorization offers insight into nonlinguistic aspects of the social world

(chapter 3, Table 3.2), which, unfortunately, space limitations preclude me from pursuing.

Soviet Ideology

In my earlier "commonsense constructivist" work, I argued against the point-blank dismissal of Soviet ideology. I argued that Soviet ideology ought not to be viewed as amorphous or homogeneous, but rather as consisting of a highly structured body of ideas whose various roles were played out with respect to their overall position within a whole ideological framework. To simplify the argument, that framework can be represented in pyramidal form, with different ideas corresponding to different levels of the pyramid (Kubálkova and Cruickshank 1985a;1989a, 71ff; 1989b, 15ff).

The ideas at the apex always performed a largely rhetorical, ceremonial, propagandist, and legitimizing role, while also acting as the binding agent for the whole structure. This function remained unchanged throughout Soviet history. But the pyramid had other levels that performed other roles. As the axiomatic value of all levels declined, the heuristic potential of the pyramid's lower levels rose, and the number of elements open to debate and research increased.

There had always existed a degree of mobility and flexibility in the pyramidal structure, as old axioms were opened up for debate, or as ideas developed by those whose research was more unconstrained began percolating upward. This is not to deny that change was a rare and painful process, which had to wait years to be officially promulgated, usually from the platform of Congresses of the CPSU. More than five thousand delegates attended congresses. They did not lend themselves to anything other than announcements. In the welter of largely ceremonial speeches major doctrinal change could easily get lost, such as the change that took place under Gorbachev's leadership at the twenty-seventh CPSU Congress in 1986. This, incidentally, was a change that Western Sovietologists mostly missed.

The main idea at the ideological apex was that of communism as the "future of mankind." The definition of communism played a central role in the rituals and symbolic ceremonial practices of the Soviet regime. It was crucial to any understanding of the other parts of Soviet ideology, for two reasons at least. First, the notion that communism was the future of mankind took the form of an instruction rule that required acceptance on faith. The Soviets argued that historical materialism allowed them to predict "scientifically" that communism was the future of humanity. They saw their predictions as being based upon a scientific understanding of the past and as a scientific projection of the pattern that historical materialism had uncovered onto the future. At the same time, however, communism was not just a social goal. Following Lenin's definition in 1920, it was an ethical and moral standard for the world as well.

These ideas about communism formed the core of Soviet Marxist Leninist ideology, remaining largely unchanged after 1917, and, indeed, being largely unchangeable, having been lifted virtually verbatim from the work of Karl Marx. They were used to show how in the Soviet way of thinking the normative and the descriptive elements were merged. The ideas concerning communism were also unconfirmable and unfalsifiable, however. They were more akin to articles of faith, and generation after generation accepted these notions on faith. If they had changed, the entire system would have become something else, as was borne out in due course when these notions were changed.

In my constructivist reading, these ideas took the form of instruction rules that made the form of Soviet rule predominantly hegemonic (see Table 3.2). Soviet ideology had a strong moral component, and its instruction rules were unusually strong as a consequence. Its hegemonic character was that of a secular religion. This character was modified, but was not completely obliterated, by coercive sanctions in the form of directive rules, meted out to those who did not comply with the "faith." The goal was to fully internalize the instruction rules whereby Soviet Marxism-Leninism was presented, though it never quite worked out like that, despite the decreeing of a "moral code" for "builder[s] of communism" in 1960, for example, the Soviet equivalent of the Ten Commandments.

The reason I mention the hegemonic nature of the Soviet society, in the sense in which this category is used by Onuf (Table 3.2), is to explain why some of Gorbachev's changes were doomed to fail. I will refer to these at a later point. Here I simply want to note that the introduction of democratic and capitalist rules into Soviet society, albeit in the strictly controlled manner Gorbachev "promised" in his various international commitments (a form of commitment rules), required for their success the presence in the domestic context of corresponding rules. These were totally absent, however (see Table 3.2, column 3). The classical example often given is that in order for a modicum of "free market" to be introduced, an entrepreneurial spirit in individuals or simply individualism is necessary. Throughout the existence of the Soviet system, what we understand as "entrepreneurial spirit," that is, finding a niche in the market where there exists a need and a profit can be made, was banned in the Soviet criminal code as a crime of "speculation" carrying years in prison as a penalty. Gorbachev did not get enough time to attend to the necessary rule changes.

The second important role the core Marxist-Leninist ideas played was a legitimizing one. Since its inception, Soviet ideology had been for the Soviet Union what democratic processes and elections are for Western democracies today, or what filial relations are for monarchies. The Soviet system's legitimacy was based on what was deemed the "superior" way of thinking that Marx thought only the proletariat (and Lenin, the proletariat under the guidance of the Bolsheviks) were capable of. The leadership of the Communist Party, in other words, had its epistemological roots deep in Marx's ideas about private property as alienating those who owned it and as impairing their ability to think in an undistorted way.

The importance, from my point of view, of this second aspect of Marxist dogma is that, together with the relevant practices, it became part of the social structure called the Soviet Union. The social knowledge and the search for the Truth had nothing to do with I.Q., as borne out by the strict class criteria for admission of children, as I myself could testify, to schools, and universities in particular. The children of proletarian class origin enjoyed a privileged epistemological position and did not need to excel academically. Conversely, academic success was no indication or guarantee of suitability for higher learning.

Gorbachev's Social Structure

Gorbachev inherited this social structure, which Onuf prefers to call a social arrangement (see chapter 3), and his agency was defined in these terms. Gorbachev was not answerable or accountable to the people as he would have been if the USSR were a democratic state. Instead he and the party were vested with a superior way of knowing and could always be paternalistic toward the people, who needed to be led and guided. Like the priesthood in religious societies, the Communist Party, the agent here, was entrusted "by history" with the task of leading the society along the path of transformation to communism, as defined in terms of the negation of all the injustices and inequalities capitalism wrought and, above all, the abolition of private property.

The social structure of which Gorbachev was the agent also contained cumbersome and inefficient political and economic institutions, however. The latter in particular, despite incessant attempts to reform them, were incapable of providing food for the Soviet population in most years. This social structure provided the main constraints on Gorbachev when he took over from his predecessors. As an agent, as a human being, with the ability to choose and to act on his choices, Gorbachev gave the structure a dynamic social element. As an agent, he gave it an intentionality and meaning. He could not just "jump out" of the social arrangement he inherited, however, because in rule-oriented constructivist terms, the rules of that arrangement made him a part of it. The social structure represented the full range of values and principles, the recurrent patterns of social behavior, and the institutions and practices that weighed him down. He sought to make his choices under this weight. It was this structure and not some abstract a priori notion—as formulated by Western rational choice principles, for example—that defined for him the nature of his agency, as well as what might constitute the meaning of rationality and rational action on his part. As agent he was separate from the structure, but the structure dominated his ability to act and, in fact, it demanded that he act. The structure also set, on its own behalf, the range that Gorbachev's rational choices could enjoy.

Gorbachev never conceded that the goal of his society and humanity was not communism. Figuring out how to achieve this goal legitimized his position as an agent. Moreover, Gorbachev never stopped reiterating his commitment to this goal. Nor did he ever sign off on any document that used the term "private property," a term that directly negated the concept of communism. A constructivist understands Gorbachev's position perfectly well: What was or was not rational for him was determined by the structure in which he was embedded, and not by some a priori quasi-natural law.

A society whose apex derives its legitimacy from its relations with other layers provides an equally revealing example of constructivism at work. In the Soviet case, the further down toward the base of the pyramid we move, the more numerous the rules become, and the more flexible and changeable are the strategies and policies they contain (always allowing for consistency with the layers below and above). Occasionally, the changes taking place in rules on lower levels percolated up. There was the switch from the "socialism in one country strategy" to the "peaceful coexistence," for example, that Khrushchev inaugurated in 1956. Building on reforms of Khrushchev, Gorbachev's reforms were bold and far reaching. They stopped short of the pyramid's apex, however.

He had to make changes to preserve the social structure. "New thinking" represented changes on behalf of a crippled Soviet superpower that was casting around to survive, let alone remain on the "one true path." It was a daunting task, not only because of the pitiful condition of the Soviet society and economic system but because as agent, Gorbachev wore multiple hats. Gorbachev was agent in a multitude of social arrangements; his public statements were addressed simultaneously to a range of constituencies, including the Soviet population, the Communist Party, his internal foes, the international community, Western governments, Western populations, and the U.S. administration. Holding supreme agency in the social structure of the Soviet Union and wielding supreme influence through the speech acts and rules, he embodied a number of overlapping social arrangements. The same words conveyed different messages to these different social arrangements; it was the same message but it served as different rules for different hearers. Sometimes this resulted in misunderstandings. Glasnost, for example, was intended as a rule addressed to the Soviet workforce to overcome alcoholism-related absenteeism, to improve working morale, and to raise workplace standards. This was to be achieved by encouraging people to "voice" (root of "glasnost"—"glas" meaning voice) complaints concerning their coworkers and management. This in turn was to improve performance standards in the workforce. When this rule was intercepted in the West, it was promptly translated into English, somewhat inaccurately, as "openness," and taken—quite mistakenly—as an early indication of democratization taking place in the entire Soviet society.

Western observers saw the Soviet superpower as being constrained by the bipolar structure of the Cold War. This structure, they believed, allowed Gorbachev to make only certain moves. This missed a large part of the picture, by setting aside the multiple contexts that Gorbachev represented. Space precludes me from developing this line of argument, but it is clear that the stress on this or that social structure of which he was an agent, notable in terms of who he was addressing first and foremost at the time, kept changing. In my opinion, the tremendous popularity that he received in the West led him to place greater stress on his role as international agent, to the detriment of the other contexts of which he was an agent and which he should have tried to reconcile in terms of rules and speech acts that he made. The concept of "new thinking" holds the key to understanding the rescue strategy he devised on behalf of the Soviet superpower.

The "Breakthrough"

Gorbachev certainly made enough noises on this subject to dispel any notion that "new thinking" was just a label. He stressed that "new thinking" was neither his brainchild nor a product of glasnost. Nor was it a product of free debate among Soviet foreign policy specialists. It was not "hastily put together," the "fruit of improvisation." It was, he argued, "profoundly considered and nurtured" (*Pravda*, 9 Dec 1988). None of these comments makes sense if "new thinking" was what it was taken to be in the West, however.

Gorbachev no doubt realized the tremendously difficult situation in which he found himself. Mindful of the central Marxist notion of the unity of theory and practice, he obviously felt the importance of thinking one's way out of practical problems. In his own words, Gorbachev hazarded all hopes and the future of his country on making a "theoretical breakthrough." In his view, "new thinking" was this theoretical breakthrough.

It is at this point that the utility of my textual analysis of "new thinking" might become apparent. In making this analysis I made a list of ten points. I did not try and decide which one did or did not merit being included, based on my own rational evaluation rather than Gorbachev's. I did this consistently with constructivist argument that what was or was not "rational" to him was not to be found in Western texts but in his own social structure. That said, it should come as no great surprise that "new thinking," particularly given the stress on point 10 (p. 129), was cast in Marxist terms. Gorbachev knew nothing other, or very little other, than Marxism of the Soviet variety. It takes a very large leap of faith to postulate that Western democratic liberal principles are somehow primordial, and were therefore known to him personally, or that he learned them from his relatively brief exposure to them overseas, and, subsequently, allowed them to override or supplant his lifelong commitment to and knowledge of Marxism. I would argue, as a consequence, that the historical parallels drawn in the West between Gorbachev and Woodrow Wilson, Olaf Palme, and Willy Brandt were quite erroneous.

Almost nobody in the West saw Gorbachev as borrowing from Antonio Gramsci's ideas about "counterhegemonic" strategies. The German Sovietologists Berner and Dahm, who like myself did note the unmistakable Gramscian element in Gorbachev's ideas, trace these influences to that of Soviet apparatchiks assigned to the Communist parties of France and Italy during the (also Gramscian inspired) Eurocommunist years (Berner and Dahm 1987/88). The formal rehabilitation of Gramsci at this time, who had hitherto been viewed in the Soviet Union with suspicion for contradicting Lenin and for being too popular in the West, is indicative in this regard. Gramsci's popularity in the West ceased to matter under Gorbachev, and Gramsci was effectively rehabilitated in the 1980s. His work was translated into Russian, with introductions that stressed its consistency with that of Lenin. My discussions with Soviet defectors confirmed that work on Gramsci was commissioned in these years in various Soviet think tanks, together with the works of, for example, Jürgen Habermas and the Frankfurt School. It is when considered as a form of Marxism that the extraordinary array of Gorbachev's initiatives begins to fall into place.

In noting the connection with Gramsci, and the use of the concept of counterhegemony, I am not trying to suggest that Gramsci's works, such as *Prison Notebooks*, were Gorbachev's blueprint for saving the Soviet Union. It is important, however, to stress that in the annals of Marxism, there did exist a Marxist strategy for dealing with Marxism under duress, and that it makes sense to think that Gorbachev would have availed himself of this strategy's arguments and example. In devising a strategy for Marxists in a weak and defeated situation, Gramsci thought that there was a Marxist way to move from the traditional emphasis on overtly coercive class struggles to an emphasis on culture and consciousness instead, and the molding of consensus along lines set by a "historical bloc" of intellectuals. The parallels with Gorbachev's "new thinking" are arguably too obvious to miss.

Gramsci's work, produced in a Fascist jail, contained an explanation as to why Bolshevik-style revolution did not/could not work in Western Europe in the 1920s. He argued that the approach so successfully adopted by Bolsheviks in their October Revolution in Russia in 1917, which he called a "war of position," was condemned to fail in the context in which he lived. As a result, he advocated a much more subtle approach, one that combated capitalism using the same mechanisms by which capitalism in Western Europe had established itself, and by which it had made itself immune to the Bolshevik penchant for "going for the jugular." Gramsci suggested a counterhegemonic strategy instead, one that—once again—was Janus-faced and looked a bit like a social democratic/liberal compromise but was nothing of the sort. He offered an array of methods to penetrate and conquer the "civil society" that—according to Gramsci—was the factor that had so much strengthened capitalism in Europe in the 1920s. In order to break the hegemonic rule of capitalism, Gramsci believed it was necessary to use the same methods by which civil society itself worked. It was necessary to penetrate (and subvert) its activities, and particularly those of the educational and religious bodies it contained. This was the only method by which capitalism could be conquered. I advanced this thought as a possible Marxist strategy before the adoption of "new thinking" when I emphasized Gramsci's prescient counsel in regard to the shift from the "war of position" to what he called a "war of maneuver and 'counter-hegemony'. . ." the only agency he believed to be capable of "restructuring the states-system [as] the Machiavellian Centaur, a mix of coercion and consent, of authority and hegemony, violence and civilization" (cited in Kubálková 1985 and 1989a, 203–204).

Let us reread, in these counterhegemonic terms, the ten points I identified as summarizing Soviet "new thinking." There is, first of all, the apparently meaningless reference to "world society." Here Gorbachev added—after a complicated debate on the subject in the USSR regarding the compatibility of global and class issues—an additional "hat," as agent of yet another social structure, to the multitude that he already wore. Global issues were found to be prior to class issues at humanity's present stage. By stressing these global problems Gorbachev began talking to humanity as a whole, or, rather, to what Hedley Bull understood to be "world society" (Bull 1977). The Soviets actually used the term "world society," and it is more than likely that they were familiar with its Western usage. I have reason to believe that they followed with great interest Western theories of IR: The reason I initially came to the West was to study IR theory to see whether it is compatible with historical materialism. The only difference in the Soviet understanding of world society was that rather than seeing the world bound together in positive terms and by positive values held in common, values that Bull thought were going to be those of modernity, Gorbachev talked in negative terms about the miscellaneous forces threatening the existence of humanity on this planet (see point 1). He saw these global problems as binding humanity into a world society in which the state system and its attendant "old thinking," that is, Western realism, were rendered obsolete and were downright dangerous, even fatally so.

It is at this point that the relevance of Gorbachev's renunciation of Lenin's theory of imperialism also came in. If Lenin's theory of imperialism—as I argued earlier, in a deliberately simplified way—"ideologized" international relations by vesting states with an ideological mission, now came the time to "deideologize" IR. Sovietologists, in my view, took this expression out of context when they took it to mean that the USSR gave up its ideology and its aggressive posture. Hence the significance of the one sentence from the thousands of pages of documents coming from the Twenty-Seventh CPSU Congress in 1986 (and missed by the Soviet watchers) that said that the "peaceful coexistence of states of different socio economic nature was no longer a form of class struggle" (Speeches 1987).

Using Einstein's dictum that the nuclear age needed "new thinking," Gorbachev tried to reverse the order of the goals and conditions of agency set for him by the Marxist principles that informed the social structure in which he lived. Class struggle was always supposed to be the first priority for the proletariat and for the Soviet state, largely because it was assumed that states and the system of states would inevitably collapse once the class structure of Western societies was smashed. Gorbachev reinterpreted historical materialism (removing the Leninist component from the Soviet social structure in the process). He argued that in the light of the global problems threatening humanity's existence, world society had assumed a greater significance than the class struggle, which he then put in second place. Instead, Gorbachev concluded that the major threat to humanity was the further existence of the states system, with the grant it gave to sovereign states of the legitimate use of violence. Thus, in addition to being a Gramscian form of Marxism, "new thinking" was also a theory of international relations that declared the state system to have been effectively superseded by world society. The Soviets tirelessly stressed that they no longer meant to be a threat to others. They proposed a reduction in armaments, changes in their strategic doctrine, and eventually complete disarmament as ways of effectively abolishing the *ultima ratio regnum* of the Westphalian system, with its sovereign states and the legitimacy it gave to the use of violence in IR.

It is at this point that the duality of the sources of Soviet "new thinking," an innovation unprecedented in the history of Soviet Marxism-Leninism, begins to make sense. In the context of world society, "new thinking" was not simply Soviet "new thinking" but was thinking about and of humanity as a whole. Gorbachev's book—a best-seller in the West—conveyed this in its title: "Perestroika and new thinking for our country and the world" (Gorbachev 1988). The authors of "new thinking" were not just Soviets but also the Western intellectual elites from whom Gorbachev had borrowed not only the label "new thinking" but also most of its content. "New thinking" was the thinking of what Gramsci called the transnational "historical bloc." It was ostensibly shared by both Soviet and Western intellectuals. This was the breakthrough. The initiative taken by Gorbachev, needless to say, granted him a moral platform from which, despite the weakness of the Soviet superpower, he could espouse a continuing role for it, defined now not in military or economic terms, but in moral terms instead. This was another innovation. Instead of balancing power, the Soviets proposed to balance only interests, another point of the "new thinking" (see p. 129).

Just as it had proved for the Italian Communist Party in the 1930s, the Gramscian model appeared to be the only sensible option for the Soviet Union, given the circumstances in the USSR at the time. It was the only way that a weak and failing superpower, with nothing but military muscle to support its geopolitical gains, could go. Gramscian theory moved the issue of conflict and confrontation beyond the power realist promotion of force and the threat of force. It also moved it beyond the usual Western understanding of Soviet propaganda, however. It represented a shift from Gramsci's war of maneuver to a war of position, the former ultimately assuming invasion and occupation (and being very expensive), the latter targeting societies in their "homes" (and being much less profligate). Thus, it is quite correct to say that Gorbachev single-handedly dismantled the Cold War structure, as Wendt noted. It is also possible to see why it was in his interest to abolish the Socialist Internationalist (Brezhnev) doctrine, as noted by Kratochwil and Kozlowski (1995) and to set free, in some cases by force, the East European satellites as a way of making more credible his plans to move into "our common European home," a postterritorial notion reminiscent of Deutsch's security community idea.

Gorbachev never tired of stressing that his wish was not to dissociate himself from his Marxist predecessors or to give up Marxism as the Soviet state ideology. If the Brezhnev line was un-Marxist and a Marxist aberration—as Western Marxists agree—then this was a Marxist renaissance. There was very little of orthodox class or economic determinism in "new thinking," but that, in itself, as Western Marxism bears out, was no proof of the

Soviets giving up Marxism. It can be seen instead as an attempt to bring the Soviet variant of Marxism back from its "barrack version" (as Gorbachev called Soviet Marxism-Leninism), toward the Marxism of its estranged Western cousins.

My answer, then, to the question regarding the significance of Soviet "new thinking" and the end of the Cold War is this: The collapse of the Soviet Union, and the disintegration of the social structure called the Soviet Union, were unintended consequences of rational choices that Gorbachev made (because of the complexity and multiplicity of the social arrangements he presided over) in the wrong order or too late. Although he was working on his "new thinking" from the beginning of his agency, he was far too slow in that area of his structure that was notoriously weak, namely, the area of nationalities. He had to change the rules for the Soviet federation from directive to commissive ones, dissolve the existing arrangement, and allow all the Soviet republics to sign a confederative or federative treaty. He planned to do so, but he ran out of time. He left totally unprepared his other constituency, the Soviet population at large. He failed even to begin to change the rules that governed the everyday activities of the population. These were firmly embedded in the existing social structure. Without the support for the commissive rules the changing relationship with Western countries provided, he could not implement domestic alternatives. In my view, this is what left the living legacy (and nightmare) of that social structure, which survives in the successor states everywhere in the former Soviet bloc, lending itself to the worst possible abuse in what an increasing number of even Western observers see as a total failure of any transition to a Western political and economic model (Cohen 2000).

To a constructivist, the suggestion that Gorbachev was a closet democrat who wanted to reform the Soviet Union and make it a replica of a Western capitalist democratic state, or to give up Marxism in order not to lose the Soviet state's status as a superpower, makes no sense. The main role of rule-oriented constructivism is not to decry Western triumphalism. The Soviet state is, indeed, gone, and this no doubt deserves celebration. What rule-oriented constructivism does do is decry the enthusiasm exhibited by the "add on," fragmentary, and misleading explanations I surveyed earlier in this chapter. The world is full of other societies whose structures give their agents different kinds of rationality that might well produce surprises in the future (Kubálková 2000). We were lucky that the Soviet superpower collapsed due mainly to the unintended consequences of a range of policies implementing Soviet "new thinking." Some voices in the West have begun to claim that the rest of the world is yet to feel these unintended consequences when it is fully appreciated that our policies vis-à-vis the Soviet Union and its successor states have been a failure. Whatever happens, next time we may not be so lucky. IR scholars ought to prepare themselves better, so as to handle such a possibility with greater intellectual insight.

Note

1. *Pravda* published a series of cartoons popularizing the main ideas behind "new thinking." I managed to reproduce a sampling of these cartoons during the Cold War when the issue of copyright did not arise (Kubálková and Cruickshank 1989b, Appendix), but with *Pravda* now in disarray it seems impossible to obtain copyright permission and reprint them again. The associations that the cartoonists seek to create with "new thinking" are salvation of the world and escape from the nuclear impasse, nothing to do with the domestic situation in the Soviet Union. The world is portrayed as a personified globe. The globe is depicted as threatened, diseased, and being saved from its predicament, not by a worker, as one could have expected from a Soviet cartoon in *Pravda*, but by Dr. Novoe Myshlenie (*New Thinking*), who prescribes a nostrum; or by a crane-truck labeled "new thinking" that lifts the globe from a quicksand of weaponry. "New thinking" is the sun that melts the snowman of the cold war and dissolves the notion of Soviet threat."New thinking" is also the palette with whose rosy colors the globe (portrayed as a smiling boy) paints new idylls.

References

Alker, H.E., and Biersteker, T.J. 1984. "The Dialectics of World Order: Notes for a Future Archeologist of International Savoir-Faire." *International Studies Quarterly* 28(2) 121–142.

Banks, Michael. 1984. "The Inter-Paradigm Debate." In M. Light and A.J.R.Groom, ed., *International Relations: A Handbook of Current Theory*, pp. 7–26. London: Frances Pinter.

Berner, Wolfgang, and Dahm, Helmut. 1987/88. "'Neues Denken' in der Aussenpolitik der UdSSR mit Dokumentation." *Berichte des Bundesinstituts für Ostwissenschaftliche und International Studien* 46: 1–81.

Bialer, Seweryn. 1987. "Gorbachev's Move." *Foreign Policy* 68(Fall): 59–87.

Bovin, A. 1986. *The Imperative of the Nuclear Age.* Moscow: Novosti.

Brown, Archie. 1986. "Change in the Soviet Union." *Foreign Affairs* 64(5): 1048–1065.

Bull, H. 1977. *The Anarchical Society.* London: Macmillan.

Checkel, Jeffrey T. 1997. *Ideas and International Political Change.* New Haven, CT: Yale University Press.

Cohen, Stephen F.1985. *Rethinking Soviet Experience: Politics and History Since 1917.* New York: Oxford University Press.

———. 2000. *Failed Crusade: America and the Tragedy of Post-Communist Russia.* New York, London: W.W. Norton.

Dallin, Alexander. 1987. "Soviet New Foreign Policy." *Radio Liberty Research Bulletin* 2.

Deutsch, Karl W. et al. 1957. *Political Community and the North Atlantic Area.* Princeton, NJ: Princeton University Press.

Evangelista, Matthew. 1987. "'New Thinking' in Foreign Policy." *The Nation*, 13 June.

Fierke, K.M. 2001. "Critical Methodology and Constructivism." In K.M. Fierke and K.E. Jørgensen, eds., *Constructing International Relations: The Next Generation*, pp. 115–135. Armonk, NY: M.E. Sharpe.

Fortescue, S. 1986. *The Communist Party and Soviet Science.* London: Macmillan.

Friedrich C.J., and Brzezinski, Z.K. 1956. *Totalitarian Dictatorship and Autocracy.* New York: Praeger.

Glickham, C. 1986. "New Directions in Soviet Foreign Policy." *Radio Liberty Research Bulletin*, Supplement 2/86, 6(September): 1–26.

Goldstein, Judith, and Keohane, Robert, eds. 1993. *Ideas and Foreign Policy: Beliefs, Institutions, and Political Change*. Ithaca, NY: Cornell University Press.

Gorbachev, Mikhail. 1988. *Perestroika: New Thinking for Our Country and the World*. New York: Harper and Row.

Gramsci, Antonio. 1971. *Selections from the Prison Notebooks of Antonio Gramsci*. London: Lawrence and Wishart.

Gretskii, M.N. 1987. "Gramshi i Sovremennost" (Gramsci and the Present). *Voprosy Filosofii* 4: 114.

Grinko, V.S. 1983. "Problema Cheloveka v Rabotakh Antonio Gramshi" [The problem of man in the world of Antonio Gramsci]. *Filosofskie Nauki* 2: 33–42.

Gross Stein, Janice. 1954. "Political Learning by Doing: Gorbachev as Uncommitted Thinker and Motivated Learner." In Richard Ned Lebow and Thomas Risse-Kappen, eds., *International Relations Theory and the End of the Cold War*, pp. 223–259. New York: Columbia University Press.

Harries, Owen. 1991. "Communism, the Cold War, and the Intellectuals." *Commentary* 92(4).

Herrmann, Richard K. 1995. "Conclusions: The End of the Cold War–What Have We Learned?" In Richard Ned Lebow and Thomas Risse-Kappen, eds., *International Relations Theory and the End of the Cold War*, pp. 259–285. New York: Columbia University Press.

Herman, Robert G. 1996. "Identity, Norms, and National Security: The Soviet Foreign Policy Revolution and the End of the Cold War." In Peter J. Katzenstein, ed., *The Culture of National Security: Norms and Identity in World Politics*, pp. 271–316. New York: Columbia University Press.

Hoffmann, Stanley. 1977. "An American Social Science: International Relations." *Daedalus* 106(3): 41–66.

Holsti, Ole. 1972. "The Study of International Politics Makes Strange Bedfellows: Theories of the 'Old Right' and the 'New Left.'" Center for Advanced Study in Behavioral Sciences.

Karatnytsky, Adrian. 1992. "Getting It All Wrong: The Fall of Sovietology." *Freedom Review* 23(2): 20–38.

Katzenstein, Peter J., ed. 1996. *The Culture of National Security: Norms and Identity in World Politics*. New York: Columbia University Press.

Koslowski, Rey, and Kratochwil, Friedrich V. 1994. "Understanding Change in International Politics: The Soviet Empire's Demise and the International System." *International Organization* 48(2): 214–247.

Kubálková, V. 1979. "Moral Precepts of Soviet Politics." In R. Pettman. ed., *Moral Claims in World Affairs*. London: Croom Helm; New York: St. Martin's Press.

———. 1990. "Soviet Thinking on International Relations and the 28th CPSU Congress." *The Oxford International Review* I(2).

———. 1994. "A Requiem for the Soviet Union." In M. Mesbahi, ed., *Russia and the Third World in the Post-Soviet Era*, pp. 19–44. Gainsville: University Press of Florida.

———. (with Onuf, N., and Kowert, P.). 1998a. "Constructing Constructivism." In V. Kubálková, N.G. Onuf and P. Kowert, eds., *International Relations in a Constructed World*. Armonk, NY: M.E. Sharpe.

———. 1998b. "Reconstructing the Discipline: Scholars as Agents." In V. Kubálková, N.G. Onuf, and P. Kowert, eds., *International Relations in a Constructed World*, pp. 193–201. Armonk, NY: M.E. Sharpe.

———. 1998c. "The Twenty Years Catharsis: E.H. Carr and IR." In V. Kubálková, N.G. Onuf, and P. Kowert, eds., *International Relations in a Constructed World*, pp. 25–57. Armonk, NY: M.E. Sharpe.

————. 2000. "Towards an International Political Theology." *Millennium, Special Issue on Religion and International Relations* 29(3 Fall): 675–704.

————. 2001. "A Tale of Two Constructivisms at the End of the Cold War." Note de recherche/Working paper 9, REGIS (Groupe d'Etude et de Recherche sur la Securite Internationale/Research Group International Security), University of Montreal, McGill University, pp. 1–44; also on *Columbia International Affairs Online*, http://ww2.mcgill.ca/regis/gersipub.htm.

Kubálková V., and Cruickshank, A.A. 1977. "A Double Omission." *British Journal of International Studies* 3(October): 286–307.

————. 1978. "The Soviet Concept of Peaceful Coexistence: Some Theoretical and Semantic Problems." *The Australian Journal of Politics and History* XXIV(2): 184–199.

————. 1980a. "Detente: Not with Hindsight." *Australian Outlook* 34(2): 131–141.

————. 1980b. *Marxism-Leninism and Theory of International Relations*. London and Boston: Routledge and Kegan Paul.

————. 1981a. *International Inequality*. London: Croom Helm.

————. 1981b. "Marxist Perspectives in Studies of International Relations: A Rejoinder." *Review of International Studies* 7: 51–57.

————. 1983. "The Brezhnev Doctrine and Eastern Europe." *World Review* 22(2): 21–32.

————.1985a. *Marxism and International Relations*. In S. Lukes and Raymond Williams, eds., Marxist Introductions series. New York: Oxford University Press.

————. 1985b. "The Soviet Idea of Peace and Peaceful Co-existence." In J.D. Frodsham, ed., *Interdisciplinary Approaches to Peace*, pp. 233–249. Sydney: PWPA.

————. 1989a. *Marxism and International Relations*. Oxford Paperback. Oxford: Oxford University Press.

————. 1989b. *Thinking New about Soviet "New Thinking."* Berkeley: University of California/Berkeley, Institute of International Studies.

Kubálková V. Onuf, N., and, Kowert, P., eds. 1998. *International Relations in a Constructed World*. Armonk, NY: M.E. Sharpe.

Lebow, Richard Ned. 1995a. "The Long Peace, the End of the Cold War and the Failure of Realism." In Richard Ned Lebow, and Thomas Risse-Kappen, eds., *International Relations Theory and the End of the Cold War*, pp. 23–57. New York: Columbia University Press.

————. 1995b. "The Search for Accommodation: Gorbachev in Comparative Perspective" In Richard Ned Lebow and Thomas Risse-Kappen, eds., *International Relations Theory and the End of the Cold War*, pp. 167–187. New York: Columbia University Press.

Lebow, Richard Ned, and Thomas Risse-Kappen. 1995a. "Introduction: International Relations Theory and the End of the Cold War." In Richard Ned Lebow and Thomas Risse-Kappen, eds., *International Relations Theory and the End of the Cold War*, pp. 1–23. New York: Columbia University Press.

————, eds. 1995b. *International Relations Theory and the End of the Cold War.* New York: Columbia University Press.

Legvold, Robert. 1988a. "The Emerging Revolution in Soviet Policy." Collin Miller Lecture, Berkeley, 25 February.

Legvold, Robert, and the Task Force on Soviet New Thinking. 1988b. *Gorbachev's Foreign Policy: How Should the United States Respond?* Headline Series No. 284, Foreign Policy Association, April.

Light, M. 1987. "'New Thinking' in Soviet Foreign Policy." *Coexistence* 24(3): 233–243.

————. 1988. *The Soviet Theory of International Relations*. London: Wheatsheaf Books.

Matveev, S. 1985. "Problemy Vzaimosviazi Politiki, Kultury i Mirovozreniia v 'Tiuremnykh Tetradiakh' A.Gramshi" [Problems of relations of politics, culture and worldview in the prison notebooks of A. Gramsci]. *Filosofskie Nauki* 6.

Meissner, Boris. 1986. "Gorbachev's Foreign Policy Programme." *Aussenpolitik* 37(2): 107–120.

———. 1987. "Gorbachev's Perestroika: Reform or Revolution?" *Aussenpolitik* 38.

Miller, J.F. 1988. "Gorbachev's 'New Thinking': The Diplomatic and Military Implications." *Quadrant 32*, 7(296): 15–19.

Mueller, John. 1995. *Quiet Cataclysm: Reflections on the Recent Transformation of World Politics.* New York: HarperCollins.

"October Revolution, Peaceful Coexistence." *New Times*, 9 November 1987.

Onuf, Nicholas. 1989. *World of Our Making.* Columbia: University of South Carolina Press.

Oye, Kenneth A. 1995. "Explaining the End of the Cold War and the Failure of Realism." In Richard Ned Lebow and Thomas Risse-Kappen, eds., *International Relations Theory and the End of the Cold War*, pp. 57–85. New York: Columbia University Press.

Petrovskij, Vladimir. 1986. "Moscow's Foreign Policy Initiatives." *Soviet Analyst* 15(16): 33–35.

Pettman, Ralph. 2000. *Commonsense Constructivism, or the Making of World Affairs.* Armonk, NY: M.E. Sharpe.

Plimak, E.G. 1987. "Novoe Myshlenie: Perspektivy Sotsialnogo Obnovleniia Mira" [New thinking—perspectives on the social renewal of the world]. *Pravda*, 14 November.

Puddington, Arch. 1990. "The Anti-Cold War Brigade." *Commentary* (August).

Risse-Kappen, Thomas. 1995. "Ideas Do Not Float Freely." In Richard Ned Lebow and Thomas Risse-Kappen, eds., *International Relations Theory and the End of the Cold War*, pp. 187–223. New York: Columbia University Press.

Sestanovich, Stephen. 1988. "Gorbachev's Foreign Policy: A Diplomacy of Decline." *Problems of Communism* 37(1): 3–17.

Shenfield, Stephen. 1987. *The Nuclear Predicament: Explorations in Soviet Ideology.* Chatham House paper 37. London: Routledge and Kegan Paul.

Smirnov, G. 1980. *Antonio Gramsci. Izbrannye Proizvedeniia* [Antonio Gramsci, collected works]. Moscow: Novosti.

Snyder, Jack. 1987/1988. "The Gorbachev Revolution: A Waning of Soviet Expansionism?" *International Security* 12(3): 93–131.

———. 1995. "Myths, Modernization and the post-Gorbachev World." In Richard Lebow and Thomas Risse-Kappen, eds., *International Relations Theory and the End of the Cold War*, pp. 109–127. New York: Columbia University Press.

Sterling-Folker, Jennifer. 2000. "Competing Paradigms or Birds of a Feather? Constructivism and Neoliberal Institutionalism Compared." *International Studies Quarterly* 44(1 March): 97–119.

Speeches to Plenary Meeting of the CPSU Central Committee, 25–26 June 1987. Moscow: Novosti.

TASS, 2 November 1988; FBIS-SOV-88–215, 7 November 1988.

Valkenier, E.K. 1987. "New Soviet Thinking about the Third World." *World Policy Journal* 4(4): 651–674.

Waltz, Kenneth. 1954. *Man, the State, and War.* New York: Columbia University Press.

———. 1979. *Theory of International Politics.* Reading, MA: Addison-Wesley.

Wendt, Alexander. 1992. "Anarchy Is What States Make of It: The Social Construction of Power Politics." *International Organization* 46(2): 391–425.

———. 1999. *Social Theory of International Politics.* Cambridge, UK: Cambridge University Press.

Wettig, Gerhard. 1987. "Gorbachev and 'New Thinking' in the Kremlin's Foreign Policy." *Aussenpolitik* 38(2): 144–154.

Zhi, Rong, and Zhang, Wuzhuan. 1988. "Gorbachev's 'New Thinking' and Foreign Policy Adjustments." *Beijing Review* 15–21 August: 19–24.

6

Thus Spoke Franco: The Place of History in the Making of Foreign Policy

Gonzalo Porcel Quero

> The struggle of man against power is the struggle of memory against forgetting.
>
> —*Milan Kundera (1981, 3)*

> Yesterday's and tomorrow's history is yet to be written.[1]
>
> —*Antonio Machado (1997, 155)*
> *El Dios Ibero*

In this chapter I explore the foreign policy of Spain under the Franco regime. My revisiting of the Franco regime[2] and its foreign policy is premised on the assumption that rule-oriented constructivism has much light to shed upon both.[3] Such an exploration also allows me to engage in a dialogue with the past. The willingness of any society to face its past, I will argue, is an indication of the strength of its democracy. From the outset of Spain's still-young democracy, many have argued against establishing any dialogue with the past, fearful that one would be opening a Pandora's box that can hold only resentment and hostility. Yet without such a dialogue, many of the present debates about Spanish historiography are meaningless, as is any conceptual discussion of foreign policy that does not elucidate the origins (i.e., history) of present policy. Thus, I hope to contribute not only to the development of Foreign Policy Analysis (FPA), but also to the elucidation of an important period of Spanish history.

At the expense of reiteration, I will offer a brief and general characterization of constructivism. I will then articulate the specific premises upon which this chapter relies and develop a basic organizational plan to explore the foreign policy of the Franco regime. Thereafter, I will advance some preliminary thoughts on the relationship between forms of rule and regime type. Finally, I will conclude with a discussion of the *politics of memory* and its relevance for foreign policy and constructivism.

At its barest, rule-oriented constructivism holds that "people and societies construct or constitute, each other" (Onuf 1989, 36).[4] This process is called *co-constitution* and takes place through speech acts (assertive, directive, and commissive), which in turn yield three types of rules: instruction, directive, and commitment rules. These rules emerge as speakers perceive that what they collectively say to each other and do as a result begins to rise to the level of convention and to contain added normativity.[5] Broadly stated, speech acts can be defined as "the act of speaking in a form that gets someone else to act" (Onuf 1998, 66). For this reason, constructivists believe that language has performative capacities. In other words, *"speaking is doing."* If this is so, these rules are at once

> instances of behavior as well as social acts. [. . .] and they occur at the nexus of biology, psychology, and sociology. But constructivists take biological, psychological, or social performance one step further. They argue that people strive not only to make sense out of their world and to act within it, but also to communicate their understandings to others. At the same time, the process of communication is a process of making sense. This extends the syllogism offered above: speaking *is* doing *is* knowing. As communication is a social act, so is knowledge. This is precisely the bridge that constructivism offers between *ontology* (the socially constructed world) and *epistemology* (our ability to know something about it). (Kowert 1998, 104; emphasis in the original)

Thus, I see the production of knowledge, and particularly the formulation of knowledge claims, as a historically and socioeconomically situated process, rather than as an aseptic and harmonious production of theories by seemingly impersonal and ahistorical agents. This stance, which I believe to be congruent with constructivism, has paramount methodological and *epistemological* implications, Onuf's and Kubálková's assertions to the contrary notwithstanding.[6] This position bears witness to the social nature of knowledge. More importantly, if knowledge is social, the traditional debate in philosophy (as well as all of its spillover debates into the social sciences) between rationalists and empiricists shifts ground, and the foundations that both camps so eagerly searched for, and thereby erected, crumble in the absence of an empty slate for sensory data or presocial ideas. What we are left with is the capacity to use linguistic categories embedded in the neurological, mostly unconscious, functions of the brain to construct ourselves, and to be constructed, through our interaction with others.[7]

Having briefly sketched the basics of the constructivist ontology, I will now postulate that foreign and public policy are not separate domains, but rather different facets of the generation of *rule*, a premise shared by some of the other contributors to this book. Once the separation between public and foreign policy is overcome, the separation between domestic and foreign/ international politics is also called into question. This chapter renounces both dualisms.[8] When policy is formulated, whether public or foreign, its constituent parts are always the same: linguistic performances[9] (declarations, affirmations, commitments, etc.) intended to bring about a state of affairs by eliciting some form of response to them, understanding passive and oppressive compliance as a form of negative response.[10]

My investigation relies on a careful consideration of the linguistic performances made by Franco during the course of his regime (see appendix for a sample). Analyzing these performances will shed light on the regime's intentions and the coherence of its policy goals.[11] Yet to speak of policy goals, one must first deal with the thorny question of what a policy is. I resolved to overcome much of the conceptual ambiguity of the term *policy* by focusing on the use of language in formal settings where highly specific statements are issued. We find here the ontological source of both public and foreign policy (see Onuf's chapter in this book).

It is easier to bridge the conceptual distance between dictatorships and questions of legitimacy, power, and memory, but what can dictatorships contribute to debates about policy? Dictatorships illuminate more clearly the intricate links between public and foreign policy, because they concentrate decision making in fewer hands, reducing thereby the scope of actors to consider as sources of policy. The sense of grandiose historical destiny conveyed by Franco's linguistic performances (the notion of *Hispanidad* and its use by Franco is one of the most visible examples) and his largely uncontested leadership after Spain's civil war also provide a magnifying glass that clarifies the sources of policy, the interplay between domestic and foreign politics, and the impact of external and domestic constraints upon policy. This seems to suggest that a criterion for the selection of policy statements and actors needs to be accompanied by a historical narrative of the context of rule surrounding policy statements.

Thus, I argue that the historiography of Franco's regime, and our understanding of his policies, can also benefit from a narrative that relates how the dictatorship justified its origins, explained its "unavoidable" evolution in the quest for survival, and witnessed its eventual decay[12] as an exhausted dictatorship. Here I hope to show how one may proceed to carry out a historically informed inquiry into the field of foreign policy. While the study of such a long period of *rule* poses many challenges, my focus on foreign policy provides a thread through time with which to weave together the different stages of the regime. This is so because Franco saw foreign policy as one more instrument to legitimate and perpetuate his stay in power[13] (Armero 1978). Even though this chapter is intended as an exercise in "foreign policy analysis" rather than as a reappraisal of the regime, it will become obvious that much of the narrative also addresses, if only as a necessity posed by the inherent link between public and foreign policy, the nature of the regime itself.

For the sake of clarity, this chapter is divided into two sections, a historical narrative of the foreign policy of the Franco regime and a constructivist analysis thereof. This division is arbitrary, however, since each part depends heavily on the other. The explicit link between the two sections is my understanding (1) of history as the contested ground where the struggles over the collective memory of a people play themselves out (Cox 1981);[14] and (2) of social arrangements as the more or less institutionalized spaces where agents deploy rules in a parallel and ongoing process of contestation. In short, our understanding of history has consequences for the social body in that it informs future deployments of one's agency. Our understanding of how social relations work, *how rule is generated and maintained*, influences the historical accounts we provide as well as our notions of the role that language plays in them. I develop this position about the relationship between history and social action elsewhere under the label of "historical constructivism" (Porcel Quero 2001).

Historical constructivism advocates a type of social theory that becomes "empirical" by placing greater emphasis on language use in context. As an approach, it represents my attempt to see where memory intersects with language, how they mutually constitute each other, and how this process allows for the formulation of a more empirical constructivism. By "empirical" I do not wish to postulate the possibility of falsification, but rather the evaluation of knowledge claims against the contextual backdrop from which they emerged. Context, as Fierke shows, does not unveil mechanisms of causality or solve the puzzles that surround social action, but it does give us some clues as to what explanations of the puzzle are even plausible under a given set of circumstances and actors (Fierke 1998). Context, by demanding that we look at specific events and give meaningful accounts of them, directs our attention to the interplay between the synchronic and diachronic aspects of the process of social construction. By looking at the temporality of rules and how it affects their institutionalization, we find new and important ways to break into the process by which agents and structures constitute each other. Context forces us to pay attention to how language is used in the specific practices and rituals that make up social life. Memories are frail and often fail, but where memories fail, many language practices, and the rules to which they give rise, survive.

Whenever possible, I will refer readers to specific statements and declarations of policy that they may wish to explore on their own. After all, reading is also a social activity, even if not often thought of in those terms. As such, it positions the reader as an active agent in the process of social construction: She can criticize a text or acquiesce to its content (I see indifference as a form of intended or unintended acquiescence). Regardless of which route the reader follows, intertextuality ensures that these texts remain socially efficacious. Intertextuality refers to the relationship of one text to another text. According to Roland Barthes and Julia Kristeva, a text can be read only against a background of other texts we have already encountered.[15] *Texture* is defined as a finely interwoven web of textual relationships (a textual environment) that binds both a text and its reader. Intertextuality and intertextual awareness has a ripple effect on the mind of the reader by creating expectations about the text to be read as well as by recasting, *"resemanticizing,"* texts previously read in light of the new material. It is therefore useful to remember that my interpretations of Spain's foreign policy under Franco are equally embedded in intertextual relationships. One of my conscious entry points to those texts comes from Giddens' important account of the production of knowledge as originating from the double hermeneutic, which he characterized in the following terms: "sociological knowledge spirals in and out of the universe of social life, reconstructing both itself and the universe as an integral part of that process" (Giddens 1990, 15–16).[16] Yet, as relevant as sources are, the list of unknowable sources and life experiences that inform a reader's interpretation of a text is what makes intertextuality a powerful social and personal experience. Therefore, pointing to textual sources is not tantamount to relinquishing or holding interpretive independence/authority. All of the above suggest, that because language mediates our knowledge claims, and because these claims have constitutive power and are rendered from specific historical and socioeconomic conditions, multiple readings will continue to offer spaces of historical resistance and contestation. [17]

The Foreign Policy of Franco: A Crusader Without a Cause[18]

> The dictatorship dictates in order to endure and it endures in
> order to dictate. . .
>
> —*Salvador de Madariaga (1992, 7)*[19]

Although the number of works dealing with Franco's dictatorship has increased exponentially in the past twenty-five years, its historiography can still benefit from greater interdisciplinarity and from a refusal to take histories produced during Franco's time at face value.[20] I see my work as helping to erode the consensus that had been built around the official historiography of the regime. For this purpose, I introduce an alternative ontology for the study of Franco's foreign policy that casts light on the social arrangements that held the regime together for almost four decades.

The official historiography purported to create a historical ensemble that would justify the regime on the basis of an "unavoidable" civil war (see appendix). The inevitability of historical outcomes that made Franco's messianic intervention a necessity was a running theme on which the regime drew for both domestic and international legitimacy. Thus, my starting point is the outbreak of the civil war, for this is the most contested historical event of Spain's contemporary history and the common frame of reference for apologists and detractors of the regime.[21] It is also the backdrop for Franco's foreign policy statements, particularly during the early stages of his regime.[22]

What do we know about the civil war? We know the civil war was an armed conflict triggered in July 1936 by the insurrection of a section of the Spanish military against the legal and democratically elected government of Spain. We know that both sides of the conflict engaged in cruel killings and that the asymmetrical war capabilities between the sides determined the outcome. We know that these asymmetries stemmed largely from the considerable support, financial and military, that Franco received from Hitler's Germany and Mussolini's Italy.[23] We know that the common good was forgotten for the private self, and that, in turn, the private self of one man, Franco, was projected in the aftermath of the war into the auditorium of a desolate country as the arrival of the "Sentinel of the West," the knight in shining armor.[24] Finally, we know that the victorious side remained in power for almost forty years. It did so by silencing disagreement and condemning to exile any potential source of internal dissidence. It initially silenced *the other,* and rarely is this postmodernist buzzword as fitting as it is in this context, by ruthless means, but ruthlessness alone could not provide the *instrumental* arguments needed for the legitimation of the regime. Subsequently, any alternative narration of the events that started in July 1936 was drowned out by the unbearable heaviness of words: words that pounded the minds of Spaniards in every radio station and newspaper, in every official declaration, with every deed that followed every mandate (directive speech act) for complete submission to the *Crusade.*[25]

It is therefore relevant to ask about the origins of Franco's Crusade. Historically speaking, the imagery is revealing of how Franco construed social and political relations. There were two groups: the heretics who had brought about the wreckage of the "motherland" and the saviors who would restore *her* to the honor and glory of the days of yore. This binary division corresponds with the in-group and out-group categories that cognitive psychologists interested in social identity have identified.[26] If "placing people in situations of objective conflict" (Kowert 1998, 106) tends to foster the creation of distinct group identities, then Franco brought about his (di)vision of Spain by providing the belligerent conditions that turned it into a self-fulfilling prophecy.

Franco was not a man of ideas. Irrespective of his strong military and dictatorial impulses, his vision of Spain faltered at the beginning of the military uprising and was oftentimes expressed in vague terms until his fervent adoption of fascism.[27] Franco's version of fascism would become a mix of the totalitarian influences of Germany and Italy and his own traditionalist views. Its main ingredients were: totalitarianism, nationalism, Catholicism, and corporatism (Armero 1978). Giddens's words regarding totalitarianism are particularly germane in understanding the changes that would take place in Spain and their long-lasting consequences: "totalitarian rule connects political, military, and ideological power in more concentrated form than was ever possible before the emergence of modern nation-states" (Giddens 1990, 8).

Franco saw Germany and Italy not only as reliable allies, but also as models for the construction of the totalitarian state. Subsequently, Franco's hagiographers would endeavor at great length to disassociate Franco from any connection with Hitler's Germany and Mussolini's Italy by crediting him with, among other things, Spain's "neutral" position during WWII. This task has nonetheless proven a difficult one, for the overwhelming evidence shows that Spain was neither neutral during WWII, nor indifferent to the destinies of the Axis powers. In an article based on documents recently released by the Spanish Ministry of Foreign Affairs, Paul Preston (1997) shows how Franco gave ongoing and enthusiastic strategic and industrial support to the Axis Powers during World War II, convinced until the very last moment that they would prevail. After the war, Spain became a haven for escaped Nazis, Fascists, and supporters of the Vichy government in France. Indeed, war criminals were expeditiously granted Spanish nationality so as to avoid their deportation and placate the raging Allied protests. "By the device of granting nationality to war criminals, it was possible to deny that they were given asylum" (Preston 1997, 84). Even though a thorough report produced by a subcommittee of the United Nations Security Council on May 31, 1946, concluded that there were two thousand to three thousand German Nazi officials, agents, and war criminals with substantial financial holdings in Spain, no real sanctions were adopted beyond the symbolic withdrawal of ambassadors from Madrid (Preston 1997, 85; see also Preston 1996). Even this response was provisional. On November 2, 1950, President Truman, who was known to be a strong critic of Franco, declared that it "would be a long, long time before there is an ambassador in Spain" (Byrnes 1999, 264). Yet a few weeks later, on December 27, Stanton Griffis was designated as the new American ambassador to Spain. This change of policy is generally attributed to the intense and successful lobbying campaign of the Spanish government in Washington, the conflicting interests within Washington's bureaucratic politics, and the changing perceptions brought about by the beginning of the Cold War.

This complete about-face in U.S. foreign policy was not without consequences. At a critical moment, the United States guaranteed the international legitimacy that the regime so badly needed and put an end to the precarious economic and political isolation in which Franco was mired. These events contributed to the long-term survival of the regime. Moreover, because Franco had not significantly altered his policies, he was able to claim that the *Truth* had been affirmed, and that the very nations that had shunned Spain had eventually shifted their position to recognize that they were in error (see appendix).

If we consider the outcry against communism and the "capitalist" conspiracy of the Masons to be at the heart of Franco's stated Crusade, then this shift in American policy is particularly striking: Truman was a known Mason.[28] Moreover, the United States had recently launched the Bretton Woods institutions, and it had given serious consideration to a number of plans proposed by the Spanish Republican emissaries to the State Department to oust Franco from power and reestablish democracy. Ultimately, it had not been that long since Franco had exclaimed: "What joy to see the German bombers one day punishing the insolence of the skyscrapers of New York" (Byrnes 1999, 264).

How can we explain this dramatic shift in U.S. policy? The onset of the Cold War helped produce a change of mindset in American foreign policy. The East-West confrontation turned Spain's geopolitical location into an asset in its search for international recognition. Franco knew this and used it to considerable advantage as a negotiating tool, aware that the survival of his regime depended on the reformulation of American foreign policy (see appendix).

Hastily, the United States "relaxed" its demands for expedient regime change and decided to pursue a "pragmatic" foreign policy. The United States went from pressing to establish a UN embargo on Spain to supporting Spanish UN membership. While Spain was not a beneficiary of the Marshall Plan, it did receive some U.S. financial and military aid. Spain reciprocated by signing in 1953 the Madrid Pact, which consisted of a number of agreements allowing the establishment of military bases in Spain. Franco thus placed Spain's security at serious risk, subordinating the interests of the Spanish people to the goal of regime perpetuation. As Pollack notes, "Whilst there existed the possibility of becoming embroiled in a generalized East-West conflict, there was no guarantee of support in the case of reprisals against Spanish territory or during conflict within a scenario particularly threatening to Spain" (Pollack 1987).

The logic of self-perpetuation underpinning the policies of the regime at times bordered on a perverse irony. While Franco's anti-Communist crusade led to severe domestic repression and to the U.S.-backed international rehabilitation of his regime, it did not preclude him from eventually seeking to establish diplomatic relations with most Eastern bloc countries and with the Soviet Union itself. From time to time, an outcry against Communism would be accompanied by the signing of a commercial, trade, or educational agreement with a Communist government. This policy brought uncertainty and tension to U.S.-Spanish relations, particularly at the height of the Cold War. To add to the ideological paradox, Franco had a very cordial relationship with Castro's Cuba, which he presented as the inevitable outcome of Spain's historical links with the island. He also maintained very friendly ties with the Arab world, which led him to refuse recognition to Israel, despite strong U.S. pressure to do so. Franco's relations with the Arab world brought Spain very few tangible *rewards,* but served the regime well in its legitimation strategy. In the early isolated and, as a result, isolationist years, the periodic visits of foreign envoys allowed Franco to play the simulacrum of respectability before the Spanish audience. The service rendered by the Arab world was not free. Franco found himself supporting the Arab world in its clashes with Israel. The irony is that Franco's policy was taking place while the United States would ship military supplies to Israel via Spain.

Thus, Franco's opportunistic overtures to the Communist world only exacerbated the growing uncertainty in U.S. foreign policy circles as well as his poor relationship with most of Spain's European neighbors, many of whom still had serious misgivings about Franco's credentials. The many reservations of most West European countries kept Spain out of Europe for all practical purposes. If the success of a state's foreign policy may be partially assessed by considering whether it is a member of international organizations in which its interests are at stake, then Spain's foreign policy under Franco must be characterized as an absolute failure. Spain under Franco was never allowed to join NATO or the European Community and only managed to extract a preferential trade agreement from the latter. It joined the Council of Europe two years after Franco's death. It was not a beneficiary of the Marshall Plan. It did not participate in the drafting of the UN Charter and was only permitted to join the UN after much maneuvering.

In short, the world still frowned upon the nature of the Franco regime.

Yet Franco was not about to renounce *his* way of doing politics to win the favors of the Western world, as shown by his decision to carry out a number of executions in the last stages of his regime (1975), and the subsequent resolution by most states to remove their ambassadors from Spain (Mesa 1988, 10).

In reviewing the period from 1936 to 1975, I have to a large degree personified the regime. I believe that doing so is warranted by the nature of the regime and by the fact that Franco set himself up as the ruler and arbiter of every locus of political and social activity. To give an example, Article 6 of the Organic Law of the State read: "The Head of State is the supreme representative of the Nation; he is the embodiment of national sovereignty and exercises ultimate and absolute political and administrative authority."[29] From his command over an amalgamated coalition of supporting actors with little real power in the aftermath of the civil war to his shifting economic policies and alliances to his hand-picked selection of a personal successor,[30] Franco was the main formulator of policy.[31] In this regard, Fernando Morán stated that "the foreign policy of the Francoist period (1939–1975) is, at the end of the day, a policy defined, inspired and overseen by Franco himself" (Armero 1978, 15; my translation).

The emphasis on Franco's role does not deny a certain reduction of his role in the 1960s with the emergence of a more sophisticated economic technocracy or the role that dissident organizations played in effecting change in the regime. Rather, it indicates that economic policy still was meant to support the overall goals of the Franco regime as well as the political structure in place (see Franco's shifting economic policy statements in appendix), while dissident organizations had to confront a monolithic pattern of rule.

Put in abstract terms, the hierarchical nature of the institutions Franco commanded can hardly be denied. Directive rules are the most salient type of rules in "executive regimes" (Onuf's term, 1989) with a hierarchical structure of rule. Executive regimes are in turn characterized by a small group of actors who make all or most policy decisions. Yet, Franco did not secure hierarchy by issuing directives exclusively. In order to explain this paradox, an understanding of how rules make rule is necessary. In the case of Franco, the large number of assertive speech acts that he issued resulted both in hegemony in the realm of opinion, and hierarchy in the social and political milieus. This, as the next section shows, he did by relying on extralinguistic institutions and status.

To summarize and to return to my first assumption, dictatorships are forms of hegemonic and hierarchical rule characterized by small-group decision making that tend to make the links between public and foreign policy more discernible.

The Generation of Rule in Franco's Spain: Consequences for Foreign Policy

In order to understand Franco's regime and foreign policy, we need to go beyond historically problematizing the deeds of his regime to ask ourselves how these deeds were institutionalized into a pattern of rule. As far as rule and rules are concerned, the Franco era can be divided loosely into three periods (1936/39–1950; 1950–mid-1960s; mid-1960s–1975). While each of these periods was shaped by many overlapping rules, I argue here that in each period a single rule type was dominant. In between these periods were transition years in which the rule mix began to shift, as there were recurrent lapses into earlier types of rule. These stages, above all, are the result of historical contingency, rather than the consequences of any preordained outcome. Nonetheless, earlier social arrangements distributed resources in such a way as to make certain outcomes likelier than others.

Before I discuss the rule mixes of the three main phases of the regime, a brief discussion about the interplay among these rules is particularly germane. Instruction rules are usually normatively weaker than directive rules. Therefore, they rely more heavily on performance and actualization to maintain a condition of rule. The social efficacy of directives, on the other hand, is not as closely tied to the ongoing performance of directive speech acts, but rather, once a rule has been established, to the ability of the issuer to sanction behavior in such a way as to encourage compliance. We can thus derive a general principle about the relationship between normativity and performance: instruction rules rely on ongoing performance and the status of the issuer; directives on sanctioning power; commissives on the acceptance, performance, and renewal of commitment.

For our purposes, it is important to recognize that Franco's assertive statements were directives for everyone else in his government. His status, as well as the other extralinguistic institutions that he could bring to bear made them so. Assertives that are backed up by extralinguistic institutions have strong normative force. This leads me to think that what I call *hierarchical hegemony* was the predominant form of rule in Franco's regime. Let us now turn to the three types of rules that characterized the periods suggested above.

Assertive speech acts and the rules derived from their ongoing performance would characterize the early parts of the regime. This is without a doubt the most declaratory stage of the regime and the one in which the most grandiose statements were issued. Evidence of this stage is perhaps most visible in Franco's staunch defense of his personal Crusade. As I suggested in the first section of this chapter, by believing the world to be divided, he made it so (see appendix). This is the nature of assertive speech acts: The world that they refer to comes about as it is represented. When Franco deployed material resources to bring his assertions to fruition, first by fostering a military uprising and then by securing the financial and military support necessary to wage a civil war, he supported what the world of speech had already constructed. When assertives are most salient, hegemony results.

> Hegemony refers to the promulgation and manipulation of principles and instructions by which superordinate actors monopolize meaning which is then passively absorbed by subordinate actors. These activities constitute a stable arrangement of rule because the ruled are rendered incapable of comprehending their subordinate role. They cannot formulate alternative programs of action because they are inculcated with the self-serving ideology of the rulers who monopolize the production and dissemination of statements through which meaning is constituted. (Onuf 1989, 209–210)

Nonetheless, the declassification of material about the civil war by the U.S. State Department in the 1960s, the huge emigration wave of the late 1950s and 1960s, and increasing contact with the outside world through tourism eventually broke the monopoly of truth. Aware of this, the regime gradually shifted from a declaratory approach and a disproportionate reliance on assertive speech acts to a policy-making style that was less public but just as effective. One style of rule does not completely vanish or become supplanted by another one. Franco continued to craft all foreign policy engagements for domestic consumption and the customary high-sounding speech about the "historical uniqueness" of the Spanish regime was the usual accompaniment to these engagements.

Directive speech acts and the rules derived from their ongoing performance were more visible during the second stage of the regime. As the regime began to expand its administrative bureaucracy in order to run everyday life, the number of formal directives also increased. Yet, as has been argued, the regime had been hierarchically ruled all along. In this sense, constructivism benefits from explicitly stating what is usually implied: that competent agents are able to learn which rules are in place, even if these rules have never been *officially* issued. They do so by observing social consequences. Thus, sanctioned silence and the remarks of a head of state whose standing was difficult to challenge effectively secured rule. What this tells us is that sanctions do not need to be formally stated to foster compliance with rules and to be collectively acknowledged. Yet, acknowledgement does not entail willful acceptance. The paradox here is that while the normative strength of directives is contingent on the status of the officer issuing them, their legitimacy, understood as social consensus about their issuance and use, is not. Chains of commands and bureaucracies are perceived to be legitimate when they have been enacted by agents whose standing has been secured through collectively approved means, usually elections. If heteronomy is the illusion of autonomy, then it is a useful illusion inasmuch as agents see the institutions of rule as derived from the legitimate *contests of wills*, rather than from the enforcement of authoritarian practices. If rule is the inescapable fact of social life, the illusion of autonomy is the basis for its contestation. Agents, by believing themselves autonomous, may act to enhance their autonomy. To return to the bureaucratic politics of the Franco regime is to acknowledge that the institutions of the regime tried to develop some independence on grounds of technocratic expertise. This was only partially achieved, as in the economic liberalization programs of the 1960s. When it came to matters of foreign policy, these institutions often had to find out which agreements "they" had signed or which rules "they" had put forth by reading the newspapers. This practice included some watershed events in foreign policy (Viñas 1984, 298).

Commitment rules are more conspicuous in the third stage of the regime. As the regime realized that its early attempt at autarky was not feasible, it relinquished some of the paraphernalia of self-sufficiency and began to embrace market capitalism. While this led to a period of directive rule, it would eventually signal a transition from the hegemonic rule of the state apparatus to heteronomous rule. Although the regime was determined to isolate domestic politics from foreign policy as well as from the economic reforms upon which the regime was embarking, this separation would prove untenable. The exchange of economic goods also introduced the commodification of culture (cultural goods to be precise), the control of which had been fundamental for the maintenance of a hegemonic regime. As the regime ceased to have complete control over the dissemination of statements, new loci of contestation gradually emerged. These began to strengthen the underground trade unions and political parties and gave rise to new spaces for the articulation of alternative programs. These programs coalesced into a loose form of open opposition to the regime. Suddenly, even the Church began to be more self-critical, failing to condemn the support that some of its priests were lending to the dissidents. A working contract between Spain's civil society and the regime's dissidents slowly emerged. The return of civil society began to take place (Pérez-Díaz 1993). As it happened, the instruction rules that had made Franco's regime a stable social arrangement became meaningless and his status as a crusader a historical anachronism.

We can finally draw some conclusions about the relationship among the three forms of rule, of which the Franco regime offers a good example. Hegemony legitimizes hierarchy, whereas hierarchy often provides the bureaucratic structure for the implementation of hegemony. In more liberal regimes, heteronomy provides the material basis for hegemony (Onuf 1989, 219). To the limited extent that the dictatorship (*dictadura*) can be said to have become a *dictablanda* (and this remains only a possibility of which I am not altogether convinced), and to the extent that Franco adopted market reforms intended to improve the economic performance of his regime, heteronomy also functioned—at least in the early 1960s—to legitimize hegemonic social arrangements. Yet heteronomy also had the unintended consequences described above that would be key to the downfall of the regime.

Because a market economy is not the exclusive property of democracies,[32] I am tempted to think of dictatorships as a combination of what Onuf called executive and monitory regimes.[33] It is worth noting that heteronomy is not a dominant form of rule in dictatorships, by which I mean that it is not usually the main form of rule mediating the relationship between the state and civil society. The state may nevertheless be engaged in heteronomous relations with other states. Yet, those who live under a dictatorship are under no *illusion of autonomy*, no matter how successful indoctrination of belief might have been. Therefore, if commitment rules are the backbone of heteronomous relations, it is clearly not in the interest of the authoritarian state to encourage them, considering that even asymmetrical commitments create rights and duties for the parties entering them, something a dictatorship would logically not desire. This helps explain why as commitment rules became slowly more prominent in the final stage of the regime, the rug was pulled from under its previously heavy feet.

A critical reader may still be wondering how constructivism improves our understanding of history and foreign policy beyond casting both in different terms. Perhaps the primary historical justification of the regime, the *problem of order*, the prevailing chaos that made waging a civil war necessary, is nothing but a powerful metaphor. By explicating the construction of this metaphor, constructivism allows me to shed needed light on this critical aspect of the historiography of the regime.

> To assert that order is a problem is to propose that the speaker thinks, and the hearer accepts, that order is a natural condition which is both desirable and achievable as a social condition. Figuratively "real," the natural condition of order is different from, but still subject to comparison with, an implied, necessarily figurative representation of a state of affairs we might call "disorder" or "anarchy" (but not "chaos," which would be incomparably different). (Onuf 1989, 157)

Following Onuf, I propose to conceptualize order differently, not as a problem for which there is a solution, but as a stable arrangement with distributional consequences that favors the promulgators or defenders of the order (Onuf 1989, 158). To put it even more bluntly, if order is an arrangement, who has arranged it and for what purposes? In the specific context of the Franco regime, the much sought-after order becomes far more problematic and questionable, for its purveyors (*rhetorical exercises* notwithstanding) were not indifferent to the type of order being sought. Because the type of order Franco sought was very narrowly defined and excluded in the formulation process and in its consequences many of those who made up the collectivity known as Spain, order cannot be described as a collectively desired good, but as a useful self-justifying metaphor. Order understood as a metaphor that calls for its own justification can be fully grasped only if we revisit and expand my initial characterization of language as performative. In this extension of the role of language, "performative speech is also figurative speech [which] means that the ongoing (re)construction of reality is rarely distinguishable from the known, felt, lived-in world we 'really' inhabit" (Onuf 1989, 157). This is possible because

> insofar as any figure of speech is persuasive—it persuades us to see what we hear—it shifts whatever is undergoing construction into the realm of what the speaker guesses is already "real" to the hearer. When human beings speak performatively, we also speak figuratively, thereby shielding ourselves and others from the provisional nature of our assertions, directives, and commitments. (Onuf 1989, 157)

Franco's dictatorship is a case in point of this dual nature of language. After his long regime, the world of speech/reality had changed to such an extent that writers who no longer had to work around the censorship machinery of the regime found it hard to get rid of the language mannerisms and habits, and the worlds these had created and represented, even though such linguistic devices were no longer necessary after the arrival of democracy. Some Spanish authors have referred to this ominous legacy as *Franquismo sociológico* or sociological Francoism (Alba 1978; see also 1980). Some of it may still be with us today (Jáuregui and Menéndez 1995).

Conclusion

As claimed at the outset, a democratic society that has not *consciously* called its past to testify as witness to its present policy making can hardly call itself democratic. Spanish historiographers and policy makers, fearful that revisiting the past would put in danger what they presume to be a frail democracy, have often failed to do just that.

A reading of Spanish foreign policy and of Franco's regime from a constructivist perspective has allowed me to put a contemporary school of thought, constructivism, in a very peculiar historical conjuncture: Could it provide forceful accounts of social relations that occurred prior to its own constitution as a set of concepts and propositions about the world? Could constructivism walk out of the narrative of social theory and into the forms of narration that are more closely associated with "history" yet remain forceful and coherent? As I hope to have demonstrated in this chapter, I believe that it should do so for empirical and normative reasons. To do so, constructivists and IR scholars alike will need to focus not only on what people construct, but also on what they think it is legitimate to construct within the internalized experiences of their history, society, and culture.

In writing a historical piece of this nature, much of my concern has been with memory and legitimation. This concern arises out of my belief that human beings always try to justify their actions by referring to some institutionalized past. By thinking of the past as an institutionalized backdrop, we engage in the appropriation of collective memory and, inevitably, in the *politics of memory* (Hirsch 1995; Thelen 1990; Barahona de Brito 2001).[34] The politics of memory sees collective memory as a contested site, because "the past is always constructed out of materials, as perceived in the present, and memory may be viewed as related to politics in the sense that 'images of the past commonly legitimate a present social order' (Connerton 1989, 3) and are used to justify present policy (White 1973, 332; Nietzsche 1957, 209)" as cited by Hirsch (1995, 23). Moreover, we find memory political for two reasons. First, the meaning of the past is never unproblematic, especially in a dictatorship that emerged out of a bloody civil war. Second, developing an identity is inherently tied to our ability to act socially and demands from us that we interpret our place in the world. As Gillis reminds us, "identities and memories are not things we think about, but things we think with. As such they have no existence beyond our politics, our social relations and our histories" (Gillis 1994, 5). We write and *speak* our histories and construct our social relations by fitting words to world, world to world, and world to words. Foreign policy is no exception to this.

The formulation of foreign policy often requires the appropriation of the past. To the extent that policy makers must take stock of where they are in order to propose policies that represent the prospective fulfillment of their intentions, they must understand how they got there. In doing so, they will tend to create self-serving readings of the past, and not just any past. The past becomes then a coherent whole where history has moved relentlessly to make their proposed policies a de facto necessity.

The responsibility for producing the homogeneous past that results from unilinear assumptions about history lies both with policy makers and scholars. In writing about history, I am aware of the dangers posed by periodizing history. I am perhaps even more keenly aware of the pitfalls of narrativizing a past that was far more heterogeneous than a chapter of this length has allowed me to convey. Guilty as I am of having broken Franco's regime into periods, I hope my readers will find merit in the focus on rules that it allows. Parsing these rules reveals social arrangements that are always historically contingent. Rules help us see the inherent contingence of all social arrangements, thus providing a way to go beyond the rigid vision of the past that periodization imposes.

I do not deny the possible narrativization of events as I told the story of the Franco regime. In fact, I have grave doubts about whether it is possible to *narrate* and not *narrativize*. These two terms represent for historians a conceptual and epistemological fault line that runs parallel to many contemporary debates in the philosophy of science and philosophy of language. I believe that this divide can be tentatively overcome by taking stock of the performative and representational properties of language (see previous section) and by postulating a different understanding of history. Thinking of history as the contested ground over collective memory, as historical constructivism urges us to do, sheds light on the fact that history has no inherent linearity and rather needs to be understood in two ways. First, history is a struggle over the appropriation of resources, by which I mean any tool that can be put to social use. One of the most fundamental social tools is language. Second, it is the subsequent or parallel discursive and social practices used to legitimate and justify this appropriation.

If collectivities expend resources on the politics of memory, it is because they have a stake in how the past is remembered. That collectivities care about how the past is remembered shows that "co-constitution," the process by which people and society make history (Onuf 1989, 42), can only give us a ruled rendition of the past. History as contested ground, then, is synonymous with "*contests* of *wills*" or "struggle" (Onuf 1989, 5) over collective memory. These contests of wills generate rule by *directing,* understood as the use of resources to affect the disposition of a matter (Onuf 1989, 5; emphasis added).

> *Direction* results when some member or members prevail. What they say serves as a direction to others, with consequences that we think of as mapping the direction in which a matter goes [. . .] Finally, the directiveness of politics suggests that contests and consequences are asymmetrical. Some members of a social unit prevail more often than others do, and they benefit more from having done so. (Onuf 1989, 5; emphasis added)

If directing is political and if remembering is at the core of politics, as suggested above, then it follows that directing is inextricably tied to (the politics of) memory. Furthermore, if directiveness is asymmetrical, then so

---

Box 6.1
Evolution of Spanish Foreign Policy in Franco's Spain

I have grouped the following statements in a box because they summarize quite well some of the changes in Spanish foreign policy over the years. My comments are in bold type. They can be found in Viñas (1984, 209, 288).

From the Isolationist Years and the Advantages of Autarchy

Spain is a privileged country: we are entirely self-sufficient. We have all we need to live and our production is abundant enough to ensure our livelihood. We do not need to import anything. (August 18, 1938)

Our victory is the triumph of those economic principles that are in complete opposition to the old liberal theories which allowed the colonial patronage to take over many sovereign nations. (June 5, 1939)

We are facing two fronts, Western sectarianism and Asian Communism. They both promote the foreign campaigns against the motherland. . . . The Truth and Reason will always be on Spain's side. Yet, it is not the peoples of these nations that are against us, but rather the sectarian politics of the opinion machinery of these states [. . .]. (May 14, 1946)

Spain regains a place in the world. Defending our independence not only serves our supreme national interest, but we are also the strongest buffer zone against communism. Therefore, when Western Europe criticizes us, it is undermining its future security. (October 1, 1946)

What unfortunate destiny awaits a nation that has trust in the good will of other nations! We must only trust ourselves. We must be ready to defend ourselves and to tighten our belts, should it become necessary [. . .]. (May 15, 1947)

To the Early Attempts to Join the EEC

We are central to any notion of Western resistance. We, as a country, first defeated communism. We are the most solid fortress of the Western world. (May 28, 1962)

The economic life of a people cannot exist in isolation from the world around it. It is rather closely tied to the economic life of other states. (December 13, 1947)

As a European country, we have decisively contributed to the formation of the idea of Europe. We cannot be left by the wayside of the great unifying project that is currently taking place [in reference to the EEC]. (December 30, 1969) will be the politics of memory, that is, the struggles over the collective memory of a people. Finally, if ruling is about directing contests of wills, and if we suppose a memory of past events, then the creation of patterns of rule over time has something to do with the ways in which collective memory is individually and endogenously internalized and produced and exogenously reinforced or weakened through formality and institutionalization (Onuf 1989, 127). These two processes—internalization and externalization—take place simultaneously and neither has causal or temporal primacy.[35] Thus, collective memory as a social practice and as an institutionalized backdrop for future individual and collective action is also co-constituted. This is an insight of importance for foreign policy analysis.

If this is a sound conclusion, then one may begin to see constructivism not only as a tool to redescribe the world as it is, but also as a useful roadmap to redescribe and revisit the past. To do so, constructivism will have to embrace its conceptual cognate, historical constructivism, which explicitly sets out to deal with the temporality of social action and the questions it raises. Yet one does not revisit just any past. Historical constructivism presents a landscape populated by people and the things they do. Normative considerations, no longer a threat to the human activity we call research, take central stage as one begins to ask who is doing the ruling and for what purposes. In answering these questions, we discover that different policy alternatives rely as much on different assumptions and justifications about the past as they do on prospective policy goals and the means to achieve these. In this respect, Onuf's account of policy making in this book misses one very important point. Understanding the making of policy cannot proceed solely from an analysis of the statements of assertion, direction, and commitment made by speakers engaged in strategically interactive games.[36] It must first and foremost offer an account of how history has shaped the speakers' perceptions of what statements could or should be legitimately made. Neither can foreign policy analysis be reduced to the process of "getting inside someone's head" (a dubious empirical exercise), as foreign policy analysts have often attempted. Rather, what is needed is an understanding of how ruled renditions of history are socially sanctioned and of how this process in turn affects the making of foreign policy.

Thus, I propose that foreign policy analysis must first grasp how policy makers attempt to bring their policy goals into line with the internalized experiences of the polity whose collective good they claim to represent and pursue. It is just as important to study the ways policy makers try to reconstruct the collective experience of a polity in terms more favorable to their policy goals. Only then can foreign policy analysis search for the ways interaction has shaped the rules of the games in which different players find themselves.

By focusing on history and memory, FPA scholars and constructivists alike will be able to ask fresh questions and maybe build bridges between their specialized literatures. Constructivists who often call attention to agency might find in the study of memory a chance to see the human face of social construction. Foreign policy analysis may gain relevance by renouncing the quest for generality, so endemic to the positivist enterprise, in favor of the study of contextual decision making. Were this prescription to be taken seriously, both groups of scholars would strengthen through their pursuits one of the foundations of democratic society: its ability to face the past.

Appendix[37]

This appendix is a small but illustrative collection of statements made by Franco. It is not intended to be final in any manner. On occasion, I have included a few statements by key actors to provide necessary context. The reader should note that while the content of the statements is faithfully reproduced, it sometimes may not be found in the same category of speech as in the original. This, however, should be a minor concern, since the majority of the statements here reproduced are collections of assertives, which tend to lend themselves readily to the task of transculturation and translation.

Ours is not a civil war, a partisan war, an "insurrectionist" war. It is rather a *Crusade* of men who believe in God, who believe in the human soul, who believe in goodness, who believe in idealism, who believe in sacrifice, against those men who lack faith, morals, or honesty. (Viñas 1984, 60)
—General Franco, November 16, 1937

Our conflict goes beyond national borders and becomes a *Crusade* where the future of Europe will be decided. (Viñas 1984, 141)
—General Franco, July 18, 1938

Spain's war is not an artificial thing: it is the culmination of a historical process. It is the fight of the motherland against the anti-motherland, of unity against secession, of morality against crime; of the spirit against materialism. The only possible outcome is the triumph of the pure and eternal principles over the bastardized and anti-Spanish ones. (Viñas 1984, 98)
—General Franco, August 27, 1938

Dear bishops [. . .]:
You know better than I that the History of Spain is intimately tied to that of its monasteries; they helped our monarchs wrestle with their problems and pointed our saints and caudillos to God's path. They were also our trusted

champions of unity. I fulfill with my visit a tradition of Heads of State in Spain: to happily pay homage to the Virgin who witnessed so many of our feats. At her service I only fulfilled my duties: I lent my arm and will. But, victory, victory only God can give, moved undoubtedly by your prayers. After liberating Spain from the Red hordes and reestablishing the worship of God and opening up the doors of the monasteries, we still have some unfinished work: to safeguard the motherland. A nation-state only exists when it has a Head of State, an army to defend her and a people to aid her. Our Crusade showed we have the Head of State and the Army, we need now a people. We only have a people when there is unity and discipline in a nation. The battle has therefore not ended. Thus, I ask for your collaboration and prayers in service of God and for the greatness of the motherland. (Armero 1978, 28)

—General Franco, January 25, 1942

The army constitutes the backbone of our fatherland. . . . The sacred mission of a nation's armies consists in maintaining order, and this is the mission which we have accomplished. (Gallo1974 11)

—General Franco, April 28, 1956

[. . .] these children are not responsible [for what happened]. And they represent the Spain of the future. We want to *teach* them to say some day: true, Falangist Spain shot our fathers, but it was because they deserved it. On the other hand, it gave us care and comfort in our childhood. Those who in spite of everything might still hate us at twenty would be the worthless ones. The dregs. (Gallo 1974, 106)

—The above statement was made by Carlos Croocke,
Head of Informaciones e Investigaciones
(the *Falange* police)

Notes

Nicholas Onuf's important contributions helped lay the foundations for historical constructivism, the approach to the study of history and foreign policy that is central to this chapter. Vendulka Kubálková encouraged me to proceed with the development of historical constructivism when it was still in its embryonic stage. Paul Kowert went above and beyond the call of collegiality in giving me thoughtful commentary on this chapter. Pamela Blackmon first brought to my attention Herbert Hirsch's work, for which I am very thankful. I am also thankful to the members of the Miami IR Group for creating an intellectually challenging community out of a barren academic landscape. Finally, my deepest appreciation goes to Martha Arrázola and Claudia Grigorescu for their love, friendship, and support. The usual disclaimer applies.

1. My translation of the sentence *"No está ni el mañana—ni el ayer- escrito"* found in Machado's poem *El Dios Ibero* (Machado 1997, 155).

2. I take to heart the cautionary remarks made by Nicholas Onuf with regards to the casual use of the term "policy." See Onuf (1999) and his chapter in this book.

3. Unless otherwise stated, when I speak of constructivism in this chapter, I am referring specifically to rule-oriented constructivism.

4. For a thorough exposition of constructivism as an alternative ontology and for a review of its conceptual and intellectual antecedents, see Onuf (1989).

5. See Michael Collier's chapter for a useful summary of how rules function in constructivism: "Rules tell people what they should do, what they must do, and what they have a right to do." Using rules always has normative and distributional intended and unintended consequences. Thus, constructivism links agents' intentions and actions to the material world.

6. See Steve Smith's chapter in this book for a position closer to mine. Also Smith (1996, 1–37).

7. Some of the latest findings in cognitive science seem to support this view. See George Lakoff and Mark Johnson (1999). Lakoff and Johnson's research seriously undermines the traditional separation in philosophy between reason and emotion, brain and mind, and so forth. If their findings hold, nothing short of a complete revision of the assumptions of Western philosophy should follow. One suspects that cognitive psychology, linguistics, semiotics, and most of the social sciences would also do well to revise their basic assumptions about what it is to think and to be rational.

8. For a different view on this issue, see Wendt (1999) and (1996). Because Wendt downplays or even denies the role that domestic politics can play as a source for and a context from which foreign policy emanates, he disqualifies himself for the type of historical social theory that I am interested in. See Smith's chapter in this book and Smith (2000) for an outstanding critique of Wendtian constructivism. Rule-oriented constructivism not only does not deny these influences, but it provides an empirically viable approach for the study of history and foreign policy as I intend to show in this chapter.

9. In constructivist terms, language is performative because it allows us to "perform social acts and achieve ends by making statements of assertion, direction, and commitment." See Onuf (1989). One of the earliest uses of the term "performance" can be found in Chomsky's generative grammar. For Chomsky, performance refers to "the actual use of language in concrete situations" as opposed to competence, or "the speaker-hearer's knowledge of his language" (Chomsky 1965, 4). For a critique of the division between competence and performance and of Chomskian linguistics, see Robinson (1973). For a useful review of Chomsky's Universal Grammar, see Cook (1994).

10. I define a negative response as the type of response given to policy declarations that are not issued to elicit an active reaction or an expression of consent, but rather passive compliance, either by coercive or oppressive means or on the promise of a scenario that adherence to them is supposed to create.

11. Heywood's words on the issue of consistency are revealing of the usual and unwarranted divide between foreign policy and domestic politics that most IR scholars espouse: "Under the dictatorship Spain's foreign policy had been subordinated to the domestic demands of the regime, leading to a lack of internal coherence" (Heywood 1995, 261). On the fixity and coherence of policies, and on the inferences of observers about policies, see Onuf's chapter in this book.

12. Please note that I did not hasten to use the word "demise." The rough draft of the epitaph of the Franco regime may only be said to have been written after the inauguration of the Constitution of 1978. Even then, as the attempted coup of 1981 proved, the dead were still rolling in their graves (many would say that they still are).

13. While I agree with Armero on this point, I believe his study of Spain's foreign policy would have been much more fruitful had he not established the customary and unjustified separation between public and foreign policy. Having said this, his book does not share any of the structuralist realist assumptions that would become so widespread with Waltz's publication of *Theory of International Politics* in 1979.

14. Cox makes the following useful remarks about the link between memory and history: "Mind is [. . .] the thread connecting the present with the past, a means of access to a knowledge of the changing modes of social reality" (Cox 1981, 130). For a review of the challenges that historical narration presents, see White (1992).

15. Constructivists can make good use not only of more mainstream work, that is, game theory and interactionism, but also of many of the insights developed by poststructuralist scholars. See Barthes (1976), Kristeva (1986), and Orr (1991).

16. See also Giddens (1976).

17. I find myself here at a paradox: I find Habermas's theory of communicative action useful in attempting to explain the "adjudication and sanctioning" of validity claims, at least within Western societies, yet I share with antifoundationalist scholars an emphasis on language as not only performance but also as play. I also share their preoccupation with power/knowledge. Giddens's comments on power and the use of knowledge are illustrative of this concern, albeit from a strictly "modernist" position. See Giddens (1990, 44). Also instructive for students and scholars interested in pursuing/clarifying this paradox is Habermas's exploration of the tension between validity and facticity as he searches for the "conceptual or internal relation, and not a simply contingent historical association, between the rule of law and democracy" (Habermas 1998, 449).

18. For declarations regarding the Crusade, see the Appendix. Note that Franco's appropriation of this term was aided by the use that the top of the Catholic hierarchy made of it. The bishops of Pamplona, Vitoria, and Salamanca referred to Franco's insurrection as such (see Armero 1978, 36–37).

19. Madariaga's work is a tour de force of compelling evidence about Franco's abuses in the formulation and subsequent justification of domestic and foreign policy. The book compiles a collection of chronicles that were aired through Radiodifusion Française into Spanish territory between 1954 and 1957. The significance of this undertaking lies in that it was one of the few attempts to counteract Franco's propaganda campaign by providing thoughtful and critical commentary and accurate evidence of how Franco's misinformation campaign worked.

20. A couple of good examples are Fontana (1986) and Payne (1987).

21. Current scholarly interest in the civil war as well as political divisions over the writing of its history serve as an indication of how unsettling and divisive an event it remains. For instance, Spain's ruling party, the conservative Partido Popular, met with hostility a recent proposal by all the remaining parties represented in the Spanish Congress to condemn the "fascist uprising that led to the civil war." For a chronicle of this particular event, see Larraya (1999). For a recent book on the death, retaliation behind the front lines, and repression that Spaniards endured as the result of the civil war, see Juliá and Casanova (1999).

22. Mesa claims that the defining feature of Spain's foreign policy was its unwavering support for the ideology that emerged victorious in the civil war (see Mesa 1988, 19; Grugel and Rees 1997).

23. See Viñas (1984). Viñas's well-researched book is one of the best sources for the links of the Franco Regime to Hitler's Germany and Mussolini's Italy. It also provides an insightful comparative economic history of the civil war and of the "first stages" of the regime.

24. Galinsoga's "work" is possibly the best example of the attempted appropriation of

collective memory (Galinsoga 1956). For an interesting overview of work on public memory, please see Thelen (1990).

25. The historical symbolism and relevance of the Crusade lies in its link to a previous mode of political organization, that is, the beginning of the empire, which had been established following national unification in the fifteenth and sixteenth century. The symbolic resonance of Latin America as a previous imperial enclave is particularly salient in Franco's formulation of Hispanidad as an alternative worldview opposed to Anglo-Saxon capitalism.

26. For an interesting review of the literature, see Kowert (1998). Note that this same analytical distinction was implied by the expression "*las dos Españas*," which both pro-Franco and critical historiographers have used at length.

27. Franco's speeches of July 17 and 25 of 1936 are full of ambiguity and even contradictions. One of them ends with "Long live the Republic" (see Armero 1978, 23).

28. Franco's hostility for Masonry never waned. On the last speech he ever made, delivered at the Plaza de Oriente on the 1 October 1975, he referred again to the dangers posed to the regime by freemasonry.

29. *Artículo Sexto de la Ley Orgánica del Estado* (my translation).

30. According to Morán and the classified documents he was allowed to consult, Franco took direct clues from Mussolini regarding the education of the prince of Spain and his designation as Franco's successor (see Fernando Morán in the prologue to Armero's book [1978, 15]).

31. Legislative bills and decrees would be routinely read and passed by the make-believe parliament. They would sometimes vote, as in the case of Spain's asymmetrically disastrous military agreements with the United States, without specific knowledge of what they entailed.

32. Onuf's comments on the reach of heteronomous relations are particularly germane here: "Political Economy is limited to the study of heteronomy, but heteronomy is not limited to the market" (Onuf 1989, 224). Also of interest is the growing consensus in the field of International Political Economy to suggest that democracies have fewer transaction costs and are therefore more friendly to the market.

33. Onuf's discussion of regimes referred primarily to international actors (Onuf 1989, 144–154). Yet, since his form of constructivism calls into question the boundary lines between the national and international, I do not see any good reasons for not extending his three categories of regimes to other social settings. Thus, I use the term "regime" in the standard non-IR sense of a prevailing social system. By doing so, we extend the conceptual reach of regimes to include systems of rule at any level of social construction. I believe this is consistent with general constructivist tenets, with my methodological approach to the study of the making of foreign policy, and with my discussion of legitimacy. Note that Onuf groups monitory regimes under "the category of existence and the constitution/regulation of its meaning in space and of time." Executive regimes fall under "the category of material control and the constitution/regulation of modalities of control." See his synoptic table named "faculties of experience" (Onuf 1989, 291).

34. For a very revealing analysis of the Spanish Civil War and the subsequent strategies deployed by different parties in the disputes to which the politics of memory gave rise, see: Aguilar Fernandez (1998, 52, 1996a, 1996b).

35. For a discussion of externalization and internalization of rules, see Onuf (1989, 130–131).

36. For a different discussion of games, of the importance of history and context, see Fierke's (2001) Wittgensteinian contribution.

37. Because all of these extracts were taken from speeches that are readily and freely available in the public realm, I believe that my quoting from some of the sources below constitutes a 'fair use' as provided for in section 107 of the U.S.

Copyright Law. The primary reason for quoting from these sources is to facilitate access to them, since it would be easier for an American reader to locate these than the actual statements. Whenever possible I have turned to documents published by the Spanish government. I have provided all translations unless otherwise noted, with the exception of statements found in Gallo (1969). I identify in parenthesis the source where the statement was found.

References

Aguilar Fernández, Paloma. 1996a. *Collective Memory of the Spanish Civil War: The Case of the Political Amnesty in the Spanish Transition to Democracy*. Madrid: Instituto Juan March de Estudios e Investigaciones.

———. 1996b. *Memoria y Olvido de la Guerra Civil Española*. Madrid: Alianza Editorial

———. 1998. "The Memory of the Civil War in the Transition to Democracy: The Peculiarity of the Basque Case." *West European Politics* 21(4): 52.

Alba, Victor. 1978. *Transition in Spain: From Franco to Democracy*. New Brunswick, NJ: Transaction.

———. 1980. *Todos Somos Herederos de Franco*. Barcelona: Planeta.

Archer, Margaret S. 1996. *Culture and Agency: The Place of Culture in Social Theory*. Cambridge, UK: Cambridge University Press.

Armero, José Antonio. 1978. *La Política Exterior de Franco*. Barcelona: Planeta.

Barahona de Brito, Alexandra. 2001. *The Politics of Memory and Democratization*. Oxford, UK: Oxford University Press.

Barthes, Roland. 1976. "From Work to Text." In Josue V. Harari, ed., *Textual Strategies: Perspectives in Post-Structuralist Criticism*. Ithaca, NY: Cornell University Press.

Byrnes, Mark S. 1999. "Overruled and Worn Down: Truman Sends an Ambassador to Spain." *Presidential Studies Quarterly* 29(2): 263.

Carr, E.H. 1961. *What Is History?* London: Penguin Books.

Chomsky, Noam. 1965. *Aspects of the Theory of Syntax*. Cambridge, MA: MIT Press.

Connerton, Paul. 1989. *How Societies Remember*. New York: Cambridge University Press.

Cook, V.J. 1994. *Chomsky's Universal Grammar*. Cambridge, MA: Blackwell.

Cortada, James. 1980. *Spain in the Twentieth-Century World: Essays on Spanish Diplomacy, 1898–1978*. Westport, CT: Greenwood Press.

Cox, Robert W. 1981. "Social Forces, State and World Orders: Beyond International Relations Theory." *Millennium: Journal of International Studies* 10(2): 128–137.

Del Río Cisneros, Agustín. 1968. *Discursos y Mensajes del Jefe del Estado: 1964–1967*. Madrid: Publicaciones Españolas.

Fierke, Karin. 1998. *Changing Games, Changing Strategies: Critical Investigations in Security*. Manchester, UK: Manchester University Press.

———. 2001. "Critical Methodology and Constructivism." In Karin Fierke and Knud E. Jurgensen, eds., *Constructing International Relations: The Next Generation*. Armonk, NY: M.E. Sharpe.

Fontana, Josep, ed. 1986. *España Bajo el Franquismo*. Serie General Temas Hispánicos. Barcelona: Editorial Crítica.

Galinsoga, Luis de. 1956. *Centinela de Occidente: Semblanza Biográfica de Francisco Franco La Epopeya y sus Héroes*, ed. con la colaboración del Teniente General Franco Salgado. Barcelona: AHR.

Gallo, Max. 1974. *Spain Under Franco: A History*. Jean Stewart, trans. New York: E.P. Dutton.

Giddens, Anthony. 1976. *New Rules of Sociological Method: A Positive Critique of Interpretative Sociologies*. New York: Basic Books.

————. 1990. *The Consequences of Modernity*. Stanford, CA: Stanford University Press.
Gillis, J.R. (1994). "Memory and Identity: The History of a Relationship." In J.R. Gillis, ed., *Commemorations: The Politics of National Identity*, pp. 3–23. Princeton, NJ: Princeton University Press.
Grugel, Jean, and Rees, Tim. 1997. *Franco's Spain*. New York: Arnold.
Habermas, Jürgen. 1998. *Between Facts and Norms: Contributions to a Discourse Theory of Law and Democracy*. William Rehg, trans. Cambridge, MA: MIT Press.
Heywood, Paul. 1995. *The Government and Politics of Spain*. New York: St. Martin's Press.
Hirsch, Herbert. 1995. *Genocide and the Politics of Memory: Studying Death to Preserve Life*. Chapel Hill: University of North Carolina Press.
Jáuregui, Fernando. 1995. *Lo Que Nos Queda de Franco: Símbolos, Personajes, Leyes y Costumbres, Veinte Años Después*. Madrid: Temas de Hoy.
Juliá, Santos, and Casanova, Julián, eds. 1999. *Víctimas de la Guerra Civil*. Madrid: Temas de Hoy.
Katzenstein, Peter, ed. 1996. *The Culture of National Security: Norms and Identity in World Politics*. Ithaca, NY: Cornell University Press.
Kristeva, Julia. 1986. *The Kristeva Reader*. Toril Moi, ed. New York: Columbia University Press.
Kowert, Paul. 1998. "Agent Versus Structure in the Construction of National Identity." In Vendulka Kubálková, Nicholas Onuf, and Paul Kowert, eds., *International Relations in a Constructed World*, pp. 101–122. Armonk, NY: M.E. Sharpe.
Kundera, Milan. 1981. *The Book of Laughter and Forgetting*. Michael Henry Heim, trans. New York: Knopf.
Lakoff, George, and Johnson, Mark. 1999. *Philosophy in the Flesh: The Embodied Mind and its Challenge to Western Thought*. New York: Basic Books.
Larraya, José Miguel. 1999. "El PP se Queda Solo en el Congreso y No Condena la Sublevación de Franco." *El País Digital*, 15 September. http://elpais.es.
Little, Douglas. 1985. *Malevolent Neutrality: The United States, Great Britain, and the Origins of the Spanish Civil War*. Ithaca, NY, and London: Cornell University Press.
Lizcano, Pablo. 1981. *La Generación del 56: La Universidad contra Franco*. Barcelona: Grijalbo.
Machado, Antonio. 1997. *Poesías Completas*, 25 ed. Colección Austral A33. Manuel Alvar, ed. Madrid: Espasa Calpe.
Madariaga, Salvador de. 1992. *General, Márchese Usted*. Madrid: Grupo Libro 88.
Mesa, Roberto. 1988. *Democracia y Política Exterior en España*. Madrid: EUDEMA.
Nietzsche, Friedrich. 1957. *The Use and Abuse of History*. Adrian Collins, trans. New York: Bobbs-Merrill.
Onuf, Nicholas Greenwood. 1989. *World of Our Making: Rules and Rule in Social Theory and International Relations*. Columbia: University of South Carolina Press.
————. 1998. "Constructivism: A User's Manual." In Vendulka Kubálková, Nicholas Onuf, and Paul Kowert, eds., *International Relations in a Constructed World*, pp. 58–78. Armonk, NY: M.E. Sharpe.
————. 1999. "Speaking of Policy." Paper presented at the National Conference of the International Studies Association, Washington, DC, 16–21 February.
Orr, Leonard. 1991. *A Dictionary of Critical Theory*. New York: Greenwood Press.
Payne, Stanley G. 1987. *The Franco Regime 1936–1975*. Madison: University of Wisconsin Press.
————. 1996. *El Fascismo*. Barcelona: Altaya.
Pereira, Juan Carlos. 1983. *Introducción al Estudio de la Política Exterior de España (siglos XIX y XX)*. Madrid: Akal.

Pérez-Díaz, Víctor M. 1993. *The Return of Civil Society: The Emergence of Democratic Spain.* Cambridge, MA: Harvard University Press.

Pollack, Benny. 1987. *The Paradox of Spanish Foreign Policy.* New York: St. Martin's Press.

Porcel Quero, Gonzalo. 2001. "Towards Historical Constructivism: An Analytical Framework for the Study of Culture and Identity." Paper presented at the Annual Convention of the International Studies Association, Chicago, 20–24 February.

Preston, Paul. 1996. *A Concise History of the Spanish Civil War.* London: Fontana Press.

————. 1997. "Franco's Nazi Haven." *History Today* 47(7): 8–10.

Robinson, Ian. 1973. *The New Grammarians' Funeral: A Critique of Noam Chomsky's Linguistics.* Cambridge, UK: Cambridge University Press.

Searle, John R. 1969. *Speech Acts: An Essay in the Philosophy of Language.* London: Oxford University Press.

————. 1979. *Expression and Meaning: Studies in the Theory of Speech Acts.* Cambridge, UK: Cambridge University Press.

————. 1983. *Intentionality: An Essay in the Philosophy of Mind.* Cambridge: Cambridge University Press.

Smith, Steve. 1996. "The Self-Images of a Discipline: A Genealogy of International Relations Theory." In Ken Booth and Steve Smith, eds., *International Relations Theory Today*, pp. 1–37. Cambridge, UK: Cambridge University Press.

————. 2000. "Wendt's World." *Review of International Studies* 26(1): 151–163.

Sueiro, Daniel, and Díaz Nosty, Bernardo. 1985. *Un Imperio en Ruinas: Historia del Franquismo (I).* Barcelona: Editorial Argos Vergara.

————. 1985. *Las Corrupciones del Poder: Historia del Franquismo (II).* Barcelona: Editorial Argos Vergara.

Thelen, David, ed. 1990. *Memory and American History.* Bloomington: Indiana University Press.

Tusell, Javier. 1996. *La Dictadura de Franco.* Barcelona: Altaya.

Viñas, Angel. 1984. *Guerra, Dinero, Dictadura: Ayuda Fascista y Autarquía en la España de Franco.* Serie General Temas Hispánicos. Barcelona: Editorial Crítica.

Waltz, Kenneth. 1979. *Theory of International Politics.* Reading, MA: Addison-Wesley.

Wendt, Alexander. 1987. "The Agent-Structure Problem in International Relations Theory." *International Organization* 41(3): 335–370.

————. 1996. "Identity and Structural Change in International Politics." In Yosef Lapid and Friedrich Kratochwil, eds., *The Return of Culture and Identity in IR Theory*, pp. 47–64. Boulder, CO: Lynne Rienner.

————. 1999. *Social Theory of International Politics.* Cambridge, UK: Cambridge University Press.

White, Hayden. 1973. *Metahistory: The Historical Imagination in Nineteenth Century Europe.* Baltimore. MD: Johns Hopkins University Press.

————. 1992. *The Content of the Form.* Baltimore, MD: Johns Hopkins University Press.

7

Failed Policy: Analyzing Inter-American Anticorruption Programs

Michael W. Collier

> Once widespread corruption in both civic and personal affairs becomes established, reestablishment of the necessary equilibrium in affairs of state is nearly impossible because the rise of corruption means that the [republic] already is lost when both its leaders and ordinary citizens lack civic virtue.
>
> —*Montesquieu,* Spirit of the Laws, *1748*

Recent corruption scandals reached the very top of many governments in the Americas. In 1992, Brazilian president Fernando Collor de Mello was forced to resign over a corruption scandal concerning kickbacks in exchange for public contracts and favorable government decisions. In 1996, Colombian president Ernesto Samper was charged with knowingly financing his election campaign with U.S.$6 million donated by the Cali drug cartel. The Colombian Chamber of Deputies, tainted by their own bribes from the drug lords, later exonerated Samper of these charges. In 1997, after only six months in office, Ecuadorian president Abdala Bucaram, along with most of his cabinet, fled into exile in Panama after fleecing over U.S.$100 million from Ecuadorian government accounts. These few examples of corruption are just the surface of a much deeper regional problem.

Under increasing international and domestic pressure to do something about their corruption problems, the thirty-four heads of state and government attending the 1994 Miami, Florida, Summit of the Americas I (all states except Cuba attending) included *Combating Corruption* as one of the twenty-three individual action items in their final declaration. This led to the March 1996 signing of the Organization of American States' (OAS) Inter-American

Convention Against Corruption. By the late 1990s, however, the regional interest in anticorruption programs had waned. At the 1998 Santiago, Chile, Summit of the Americas II, the *Combating Corruption* action item received only minimal discussion. By mid-2000, over four years after its initial signing, only eighteen OAS member states had ratified the OAS Convention. At the same time, no OAS member had adopted the comprehensive package of domestic legislation required for the Convention's full implementation.[1] Why are Inter-American anticorruption programs failing? Finding an answer to this question is a task that lends itself well to a rule-oriented constructivist analysis.

Corruption, the abuse of public office for private gain, is an extremely complex social behavior and so far no theory has managed to come to grips with its many faces. To fully understand corruption requires a theory of its causes that encompasses its many political, economic, and cultural factors. In my view, Onuf's (1989) rule-oriented constructivist approach provides an analytic frame that allows the development of just such a comprehensive theory. It does this by allowing the linkage of several partial agency and structural theories of corruption into one comprehensive social theory.

This chapter develops a comprehensive theory of the causes of corruption. I do this by linking several different agency and structural theories that partially explain the corruption phenomenon. In the first part of my analysis, after a review of several major rule-oriented constructivist tenets, I develop the normative and behavioral perspectives on corruption. I review where the normative principles and beliefs (instruction rules) concerning corruption originated. I then draw on a large scholarly political culture literature and show how specific political cultures differ in their social rule structures and the forms of societal rule they engender. Using the corruption scholarship of Heidenheimer (1970), I develop the perceptions of specific corrupt behaviors in different political cultures. I then use my normative and behavioral analysis as part of a rational choice agency analysis to establish the range of corrupt behaviors expected in differing societies. The rational choice analysis incorporates enterprise theory used in criminal justice analyses.

While the first part of my analysis provides a powerful explanation for corrupt behavior—it is still only a partial explanation based upon political culture and limited agency factors. A comprehensive constructivist analysis must consider all the key political, economic, and cultural factors concerning the phenomenon under investigation—including the role material resources play in explaining the social behavior. Therefore, in the second part of my analysis, I discuss other key agency, structural, and material resource factors related to corrupt behavior in the Americas. Many of these factors I draw from Johnston's (1994) comparative corruption scholarship.[2]

Finally, my analysis is summarized in a synoptic table of the coordinates of corruption. This table, along with the tenets of constructivism and rational choice theory, establishes the framework for a comprehensive theory of the causes of corruption. The most important contribution of my analysis is that it demonstrates the ability of constructivism to link several seemingly unrelated theories into one comprehensive theory. Additionally, my analysis reveals constructivism's ability to transcend the often contentious problem concerning agency and structural explanations in theory development. Integral to my analysis is a case study that investigates why Inter-American anticorruption programs are failing. This imbedded case study reveals the usefulness of the comprehensive theory of the causes of corruption.

The Constructivist Analytic Frame

Understanding Onuf's rule-oriented constructivism (hereafter just constructivism) first requires an understanding of his conceptualization of social rules.[3] A major tenet of constructivism is that complex institutions, like corruption, consist of a constantly changing mix of different categories of social rules associated with the three principal forms of speech acts—assertive, directive, and commisive. Each of his categories of social rules performs distinct functions.[4] First, instruction rules emerge from assertive speech acts and delineate the *principles* and *beliefs* that inform agents of an institution's purposes. Instruction rules tell agents what they *should do*. Second, directive rules emanate from directive speech acts and provide *specificity* to the instruction-ruled principles and beliefs. Directive rules support instruction rules by telling agents what they *must do*. In order for directive rules to be effective, they must be supported by other rules (sanctions) that stipulate the consequences when agents do not follow a particular directive rule. Third, commitment rules associated with commissive speech acts *create roles* for agents. Commitment rules tell agents what they have a *right* or *duty to do*. Commitment rules give some agents well-defined powers, while assuring other agents that those powers will not be abused. How well the three categories of rules perform their assigned function depends upon their strength and formality. A rule's strength is determined by how frequently agents follow the rule. A rule's formality refers to a variety of conditions that set the rule apart and emphasize its importance.

Onuf argues that a society's mix of the three different categories of rules results in three distinct forms of rule—or methods that govern society. While all three categories of rules exist in every society, those societies with a higher proportion of instruction rules are ruled by hegemony. The concept of hegemony used here follows the analysis of Gramsci, who argues that a ruling class had to persuade other classes in society to accept its moral, political, and cultural values, making culture and ideology central to the ruling system (see Gramsci 1971). As Onuf describes:

> Hegemony refers to the promulgation and manipulation of principles and instructions by which superordinate powers monopolize meaning which is then passively absorbed by the subordinate actors. These activities constitute a stable arrangement of rule because the ruled are rendered incapable of comprehending their subordinate role. They cannot formulate alternative programs of action because they are inculcated with the self-serving ideology of the rulers who monopolize the production and dissemination of statements through which meaning is constituted. (Onuf 1989, 209–210)

Societies with a higher proportion of directive rules are ruled by hierarchy. Onuf argues:

> Hierarchy is the paradigm of rule most closely associated with Weber because, as an arrangement of directive rules, it is instantly recognizable as bureaucracy. The relations of *bureaux*, or offices, form the typical pattern of super- and subordination, but always in ranks, such that each office is both subordinate to the one(s) above it and superordinate to the ones below. . . . The visualization of this arrangement of ranks linked by directives is the familiar pyramid of organization charts. (Onuf 1989, 211)

Societies with a higher proportion of commitment rules are ruled by *heteronomy*. The use of this term is traced to Kant, who referred to heteronomy as a condition of not having autonomy (see Onuf 1989, 212). Heteronomy defines a condition where rational decision makers are never fully autonomous, and where their decisions toward particular ends are bounded both by societal rules and their material means. Commitment rules stipulate *promises* by some agents, promises that become the rights (i.e., promises kept) of other agents. Conditions of strong and formal commitment rules massively restrict agent autonomy. My following analysis makes extensive use of the different categories of constructivist social rules and forms of rule.

Normative and Behavioral Perspectives of Corruption

Instruction rules pertaining to corruption can be traced to the republican thought of ancient Greece and Rome and their preoccupation with ensuring liberty and justice while resisting corruption. Resisting corruption meant resisting forms of government that served selfish private interests rather than the common good (Wilson 1989, 1). Corruption was a topic central to Machiavelli's (1469–1527) discourses on republican government (see Onuf 1998, 44–47). In analyzing Machiavelli's works, one analyst argues:

One dimension of [Machiavelli's] political corruption is the privatization both of the average citizen and those in office. In the corrupt state, men locate their values wholly within the private sphere and they use the public sphere to promote private interests. (Shumer 1979, 9)

Rousseau (1712–1778) also embraced the idea that government officials, selected by the people to manage society's business, should carry out their duties in a manner transcending personal interests (Rousseau 1978, 59–64). Noonan's (1984) historical treatise on bribery and corruption reveals that as the concept of official bribery developed from ancient times, it became correlated ever closer with the idea that public officials (monarchs, judges, elected executives, legislators, senior officials, etc.) should put aside their private interests when dealing with public matters. In his conclusion Noonan offers:

The notion of fidelity in office, as old as Cicero [Roman, 106–43 B.C.], is inextricably bound to the concept of public interest distinct from private advantage. It is beyond debate that officials of the government are relied upon to act for the public interest distinct from private advantage. (Noonan 1984, 704)

As Western ideas of good governance evolved, a primary anticorruption instruction rule emerged asserting the normative principle that public officials should separate their public duties from their private interests. Nevertheless, the directive and commitment rules that different societies developed to support this fundamental anticorruption instruction rule vary widely. This difference in rules leads to the issue of *cultural relativity* in studying corruption—the situation where behavior seen as corrupt in one culture may not be seen as corrupt in another.[5]

Mexican Nobel laureate Octavio Paz once remarked, "[t]he Rio Grande . . . marks the divide 'between two distinct versions of Western civilization.' In the Anglicized north, the work ethic, enterprise, the critical spirit, democracy, and capitalism prevailed; in the Iberian south, hierarchy, ritualism, centralism, orthodoxy, and patrimonialism reigned . . ." (quoted in Leiken 1996, 64). Paz was referring to the differences in cultures in the Americas. Culture defines the social rules of lifestyles, beliefs, customs, and values that influence a society's pursuit of its goals. Political culture, a subset of overall culture, defines the social rules developed by a society to reach its political goals (i.e., decisions about who gets what, when, and how; see Lasswell [1950]). Since Almond and Verba's (1963) groundbreaking work on culture and modernization, there have been many attempts to both classify various cultures and to use culture as a key factor in explaining corruption (see Huntington 1968; Scott 1972; Johnston 1983; Putnam 1993). Understanding the different categories of political cultures helps us deal with corruption's cultural relativity issues and is a first step toward understanding the complex corruption phenomenon.

Categorizing Political Cultures

Based upon my overview of political culture literature, I identify three principal categories of political cultures—*collectivist, individualistic,* and *egalitarian*—each with its own dominant category of social rules.[6] Collectivist (traditional) cultures generally exist in societies with hegemonic forms of rule and are dominated by instruction rules. Collectivist societies are simple and segregated. Social and economic transactions in collectivist societies are organized around small groups defined by familial, kinship, tribal, ethnic, religious, class, linguistic, or other social relationships. Each group tends to have its own narrow base of interests. Paternalism is the main intragroup controlling concept in collectivist cultures; that is, the father or group leader decides what is best for the family or group. The best interest of the group is the single most important governing rule in collectivist societies. Loyalty to the group and maintaining the traditional status quo are other important rules in collectivist cultures. With most social and economic transactions carried out within groups, intergroup social trust in collectivist cultures is extremely weak. Paz's description of the Iberian south corresponds to the characteristics of collectivist cultures that exist in most Latin American and Caribbean states.

Collectivist political cultures place power in the hands of a small and self-perpetuating governing elite who often inherit the right to govern through family ties or social position (Elazar 1966, 92–93). The hegemonic rule in collectivist societies is often personalistic—based upon one paternal maximum leader. The method of rule often relies on strong patron-client systems of informal reciprocity, where the clients (citizens or specific groups) pledge their economic and political support to patrons (governing elite) for access to government resources (Klitgaard 1988, 69–74). Political competition in collectivist societies takes place primarily among the small group of self-perpetuating governing elite. Politics is considered a privilege in collectivist political cultures and those active in politics are expected to benefit personally from their efforts. Collectivist polities are centrally organized with the powerful governing elite constituting the central core of the most dominant societal group. The rule of law is weak in collectivist political cultures, focused primarily on controlling the masses, while offering little accountability of the governing elite.

Individualistic cultures exist in hierarchically ruled societies and are dominated by directive rules. Individualistic societies are more integrated and complex than collectivist societies. Within individualistic cultures, social and economic transactions are conducted among people from different groups. Individuals frequently shift from one group to another and have a broader range of interests. Individual self-interest is the governing rule of these societies. The need to interact with persons from other groups in order to serve one's own self-interest results in a moderate level of social trust. Characteristics of individualistic cultures are found among the stronger democratic states in the Americas: French-speaking Canada, Chile, Costa Rica, some sections of the United States, and in a few of the Anglophone Caribbean states.

Individualistic political cultures view government as strictly utilitarian—providing those functions demanded by the citizens it serves (Elazar 1994, 230–232). Individualistic political cultures see politics as a business—another means by which individuals can improve themselves socially and economically. Political competition revolves around individual attempts to gain and maintain political or economic power. Politicians in individualistic societies are more interested in public office as a means for self-interested advancement than as a chance to build a better society. Political life in individualistic political cultures is based upon systems of mutual obligation rooted in personal relationships. Systems of mutual obligation are usually harnessed through the interactions of political parties and interest groups. Citizen participation in political decision making is carried out through networks of political parties and interest groups that attempt to influence government policy. Patron-client relationships generated by the system of political parties, interest groups, and large government bureaucracies emerge in individualistic political cultures. Individualistic political cultures are extremely legalistic. However, the rule of law, while stronger than in collectivist societies, remains focused primarily on controlling the masses and generates only limited accountability of the governing elite.

Egalitarian (civic) cultures exist in societies ruled by heteronomy and dominated by commitment rules. Egalitarian societies are the most integrated and complex. Social and economic transactions in egalitarian cultures are conducted widely among a variety of differentiated groups. Individuals belong to several political, economic, and social groups and have a large array of interests. Due to the widespread horizontal interactions across differentiated groups, high levels of social trust develop in egalitarian cultures. Egalitarian cultures characterize Paz's Anglicized north and are generally found in states receiving both their population stream and political ideology from northern Europe—in English-speaking Canada and some sections of the United States.

Egalitarian political cultures see politics as a public activity centered on the idea of the public good and devoted to the advancement of the public interest. The search for the common good is the controlling rule of politics.

Egalitarian political cultures view politics as healthy and promote the wide-scale involvement of civil society in political decision making. Egalitarian political officials vie for power just as those in other societies; however, their ultimate objective is not self-interested advancement but the search for the good society. Egalitarian political cultures flatly reject the notion that politics is a legitimate realm for private economic enrichment. While political parties and interest groups exist in egalitarian political cultures, their influences on political decision making are weaker and they have less impact on government policy than in individualistic societies. Political competition is focused on societal issues. Egalitarian government structures are organized hierarchically; however, their bureaucracies tend to be smaller than similar sized individualistic societies, and their political decision-making processes tend to be more horizontal, including both public and private groups. The rule of law is strong in egalitarian political cultures, applying equally to the masses and governing elite.

Classifying Corrupt Behavior

Each of the above three categories of political culture—collectivist, individualistic, egalitarian—generates different views about corrupt behavior. Heidenheimer (1970, 18–28) provides a useful method to demonstrate these differences. He classifies a society's perceptions regarding corruption along a normative continuum using three categories: white, gray, and black. White corruption denotes that the majority of both elite and mass opinion would probably not support attempts to punish a particular behavior. Gray corruption indicates that some elements, either the elite or certain mass groups, may want to see a particular behavior punished, while others may not, and the majority of elite and mass opinion may well be ambiguous. Black corruption signifies that the majority consensus of both the elite and masses would condemn a particular behavior and want it punished.

Table 7.1 lists ten typical types of behavior commonly associated with the Western normative standard of corruption and rates each in terms of its incidence and evaluation (white/gray/black) across the three classifications of political culture. The types of corrupt behavior in Table 7.1 correspond to typical abuses of public office for private benefit. The types of behavior range from minor deviations from the rules to benefit friends and supporters, to outright theft from the public treasury. Table 7.1 was compiled from a loose content analysis of corruption literature by Heidenheimer (1970) that was updated and adapted for this chapter. Table 7.1 reveals a significant variance in both the incidence and evaluation of corruption across different cultures. Collectivist cultures have the most frequent incidence of the listed behaviors and the most lenient (white) evaluation of the behaviors being corrupt. Egalitarian societies, on the other hand, have the lowest incidence of the listed behaviors and the strictest (black) evaluation of the behaviors being corrupt. Individualistic societies fall between the collectivist and egalitarian evaluations. When included in a rational choice (agency) analysis, Table 7.1 helps illustrate the range of corrupt behavior expected of a governing elite. The tenets of enterprise theory are useful in advancing this rational choice analysis.

Enterprise theory provides a useful model for classifying the range of governing elite corrupt or noncorrupt behavior (Smith 1980). Enterprise theory posits that there is a spectrum of social activity—ranging from illegal to legal—along which individuals or groups (agents) operate. The behavior of agents may be totally illegal, a combination of illegal and legal, or totally legal, classified by Smith (1980) as *pirates, pariahs,* or *paragons,* respectively. Like other rational choice–based theories, enterprise theory assumes that agents are rational utility-maximizers. It assumes that agents act in their own best interests after weighing the costs and benefits of their actions. Using simple cost-benefit analyses, enterprise theory is able to classify the likely behavior of agents faced with different legal/illegal decision situations, such as those faced by a state's governing elite concerning corrupt behaviors. My analysis assumes that a governing elite's (agent's) first priority is to gain or retain political power through their access to public office. It assumes a governing elite's second priority is to maximize their respective personal receipt of the society's social surplus, which can be accomplished only through their access to public office. Social surplus is an abstract concept defining a society's political, economic, and cultural resources that are available for distribution for the public good (see Weingast 1997, 247). My analysis also assumes that governing elite do not hold power indefinitely, but can be either voted out of office or overthrown by force. When combined with the above descriptions of differing political cultures and the Table 7.1 evaluation of corrupt behaviors, the above assumptions help shape a simple rational choice cost-benefit model explaining the range of corrupt behavior expected of governing elite in different societies. The model allows an evaluation of agent (governing elite) utility calculations that compare the costs (loss of power) to the benefits (access to social surplus) of corrupt behavior. The model also allows the linkage of the enterprise theory classifications of behavior—pirates, pariahs, and paragons—with societal patterns of corrupt behavior.

In collectivist cultures, there is virtually no sustained elite or mass opinion against the Table 7.1 corrupt behaviors. Without elite or mass opinion to condemn corrupt behavior, there exists little threat to the governing elite's access to office if they engage in corrupt behaviors. The governing elite are

Table 7.1

The Incidence and Evaluation of Corrupt Behavior

Types of corrupt behavior	Collectivist		Individualistic		Egalitarian	
	Incidence	Evaluation	Incidence	Evaluation	Incidence	Evaluation
Governing elite deviates from the rules for the benefit of friends or supporters.	SOP	W	SOP	W	FI	G
Unregulated gifts, or other benefits, accepted by governing elite for private gain.	SOP	W	SOP	G	OI	B
Unregulated campaign contributions solicited and accepted by governing elite.	SOP	W	SOP	G	OI	B
Nepotism or political cronyism in government appointments and contract awarding.	SOP	W	FI	G	OI	B
Citizens compensate governing elite for advancing administrative due process.	SOP	W	OI	G	OO	B
Governing elite profit from state decisions through sideline occupations or kickbacks.	SOP	W	OI	G	OO	B
Governing elite tolerate or cooperate with organized crime for private gain.	FI	G	OI	B	OO	B
Governing elite ignore convincing proof of political corruption.	FI	G	OI	B	OO	B
Governing elite steal or misuse state resources (land, property, etc.) for private gain.	FI	G	OI	B	OO	B
Governing elite steal from or otherwise misuse state treasury for private gain.	OI	G	OI	B	OO	B

Source: Adapted and updated from Heidenheimer (1970).
Key: SOP = standard operating procedure; FI = frequent incidence; OI = occasional incidence; OO = rare incidence, without regular pattern; W = white corruption; G = gray corruption; B = black corruption.

thus free to extract most of the society's social surplus for their own private use. In collectivist cultures, the governing elite are most likely to act as pirates—social predators free to exploit their own societies and to pillage the social product. Patterns of such corruption are categorized as *systemic*, "a situation in which the major institutions and processes of the state [society] are routinely dominated and used by corrupt individuals and groups, and in which many people have few practical alternatives to dealing with corrupt officials" (Johnston 1998, 89).

In individualistic cultures, the governing elite must take a more strategic approach to corrupt behavior and avoid or successfully hide those behaviors rated black in Table 7.1. Without a strategic approach, the corrupt behavior of individualistic governing elite could generate a coalition of adverse opinion threatening their access to office. Individualistic governing elite can extract substantial social surplus from the society, but must ensure they retain an alliance of elite or citizen groups to maintain their power base. In individualistic cultures, the governing elite are most likely to become pariahs (outcasts) if their corrupt behavior is uncovered. Patterns of such corruption can be categorized as *institutional*, indicating that they are symbiotic with many of the society's political, economic, and cultural institutions.

In egalitarian cultures, both elite and mass opinion are so averse to corrupt behavior that almost any behavior listed in Table 7.1 would threaten the governing elite's access to office. Due to the higher proportion of commitment rules in egalitarian cultures, the governing elite come under strong influence to honor their duties to remain noncorrupt, or face immediate removal from office fostered by a coalition of elite and mass opinion. The governing elite are thus influenced to ensure that a society's social surplus is distributed toward the common good. In egalitarian cultures, the governing elite are most likely to become paragons—model rulers acting in the noncorrupt roles that civic society expects them to play. In a world of self-interested utility-maximizers, there will never be zero corruption. Thus, in egalitarian societies, corruption should be only *incidental* to the regular political behavior.

It is interesting to note how the above classifications of governing elite behaviors apply to the Americas. Table 7.2 provides the 1997–1999 corruption ratings of twenty-one of the thirty-five regional states. Transparency International, a Berlin-based nongovernmental organization dedicated to eradicating corruption, compiled the ratings. The Table 7.2 numeric ratings provide the perception of corruption associated with foreign business transactions in each state.[7] The numeric ratings are supplemented with the overall evaluations of corrupt behavior by rough groupings of states based on the above discussion. Table 7.2 provides striking evidence of the magnitude of the corruption problem in the Americas.

Table 7.2

Corruption in the Americas

State	1997 Score	1997 Std. dev.	1998 Score	1998 Std. dev.	1999 Score	1999 Std. dev.	Corrupt behavior
Canada	9.1	0.5	9.2	0.5	9.2	0.5	*Paragons/* Incidental
United States	7.6	1.0	7.5	0.9	7.5	0.8	
Chile	6.0	0.7	6.8	0.9	6.9	1.0	
Costa Rica	6.6	1.3	5.6	1.6	5.1	1.5	*Pariahs/* Institutional
Peru	2.9	0.4	4.5	0.8	4.5	0.8	
Uruguay	4.1	0.8	4.3	0.9	4.4	0.9	
Brazil	3.6	0.7	4.0	0.4	4.1	0.8	
El Salvador	2.8	0.7	3.6	2.3	3.9	1.9	
Jamaica	na	na	3.8	0.4	3.8	0.4	
Cuba	3.5	0.7	na	na	na	na	
Mexico	2.7	1.1	3.3	0.6	3.4	0.5	
Guatemala	3.9	2.2	3.1	2.5	3.2	2.5	*Pirates/* Systemic
Nicaragua	4.2	1.8	3.0	2.5	3.1	2.5	
Argentina	2.8	1.1	3.0	0.6	3.0	0.8	
Colombia	2.2	0.8	2.2	0.8	2.9	0.5	
Venezuela	2.8	0.7	2.3	0.8	2.6	0.8	
Bolivia	2.0	0.9	2.8	1.2	2.5	1.1	
Ecuador	3.4	1.7	2.3	1.5	2.4	1.3	
Paraguay	1.7	0.7	1.5	0.5	2.0	0.8	
Panama	1.7	0.7	na	na	na	na	
Honduras	2.0	1.0	1.7	0.5	1.8	0.5	

Source: Transparency International (1997, 1998, 1999).
Note: Scores range from 10 (no corruption) to 0 (totally corrupt).

In developing a comprehensive theory of the causes of corruption, the above analysis partially addresses the issues of agency and structure. The enterprise theory rational choice cost-benefit analysis details the likely corruption patterns of agents in various cultures. Moreover, political culture, as a structural factor, partially explains the range of corrupt behavior in the Americas. Those who advocate culture as the primary cause of corruption would stop here—but not constructivists. Still missing from a constructivist theory of the causes of corruption is a deeper understanding of other factors affecting agency, political and economic structures, and material resources— factors that must be considered in developing a comprehensive theory of the causes of corruption.

Additional Factors Impacting Corrupt Behavior

The purpose of Inter-American anticorruption policy is to strengthen the boundaries between public office and private interest. The goal of Inter-American anticorruption policy is to transition all states to the Western normative standards of strong (black) boundaries between public office and private interest (Table 7.1). Beginning with the basic speech acts associated with the Inter-American anticorruption policy, this section looks deeper into the agency, structural, and material resource factors that affect the corruption phenomenon and that help explain why Inter-American anticorruption programs are failing.

Evaluating Governing Elite Interests

The 1994 Miami Summit of the Americas *Combating Corruption* action plan initiative provides the keystone for constructing Inter-American anticorruption programs. The *Combating Corruption* declaration constitutes an assertive speech act—a first step in establishing an instruction-ruled principle of separating public office from private interest. The Summit leaders' assertive speech act matched an actual state of affairs—the problem of regional corruption—with a proposition about some state of affairs—we will do something about it. The normative significance of this 1994 Miami Summit assertive speech act is clear when measured by its formality (all thirty-four leaders eagerly signed it), specificity (leading to the OAS Inter-American Convention Against Corruption), and visibility (extensive press coverage and a plethora of follow-on meetings and conferences).

Following the 1994 Miami Summit, the 1996 OAS Convention constitutes a directive speech act by giving more detail to the Summit proposition that we will do something about corruption and by seeking to change the world in conformity with its own propositional content—by providing an outline of an anticorruption program for regional states. Table 7.3 summarizes the OAS Convention's key elements. The Convention encompasses the majority of anticorruption measures championed for years by both academic and public policy officials. Similar to most multilateral international agreements, the Convention lacks several elements that diminish its role as an effective collective policy statement. First, the Convention lacks specific requirements. Compliance depends on the interpretation of each state "[s]ubject to its constitution and the fundamentals of its legal system. . ." (OAS 1996). Table 7.1 suggests these state interpretations may vary widely depending upon the political culture of individual states. Second, the Convention is short on obligation. The Convention includes no commissive speech acts that make promises or otherwise obligate signatories. The Convention mandates no compliance dates, no promises of bilateral or multilateral action among signatories, and no enforcement measures (directive-ruled sanctions) activated by a state's noncompliance with the Convention's provisions. These omissions weaken the Convention as a foundation for states in building anticorruption directive and commitment rules. In retrospect, the OAS Convention, the centerpiece of Inter-American anticorruption policy, is nothing more than a set of unilateral declarations that it appears most states never intended to implement. To determine why states made these anticorruption declarations that they never intended to implement requires a deeper look at anticorruption agency, structural, and material resource factors.

One of the key components of constructivist agency analysis is to determine the interests of individual agents. Onuf (1989, 258) argues that there are three principal interests that govern all social behavior—*standing*, *security*, and *wealth*. Standing entails an agent's status or reputation among other agents and engenders feelings of esteem or envy. Where instruction rules dominate, standing is the agent's principal interest. Security as an interest presents the agent with an awareness of threat (war, physical threat, job security, etc.). Where directive rules or their sanctions dominate, security becomes the agent's principal interest. Wealth as an interest includes not only money, property, and so forth, but any item of value. Where commitment rules dominate, generating societal wealth becomes the agent's principal interest. An agent's rational decision processes include consideration of all three of these interests. However, one interest will dominate the final behavior based upon the situation's dominant rule structure.

Standing was the principal interest behind the thirty-four regional leaders signing the 1994 Miami Summit of the Americas action plan. In the excitement of the 1994 Miami Summit process, launching *Combating Corruption*

Table 7.3

OAS Inter-American Convention Against Corruption

Parties to the Convention agree to:
1. Establish standards of conduct for public officials.
2. Implement asset disclosure for public officials.
3. Ensure transparency in government procurement, hiring, and revenue collection.
4. Improve government accounting and auditing standards.
5. Establish dedicated oversight bodies (ombudsman, inspectors, auditors, etc.).
6. Encourage civil society and nongovernmental organization participation in anticorruption efforts.
7. Issue domestic law against corruption, including the criminalization of bribery and illicit enrichment.
8. Criminalize transstate bribery and deny favorable tax credits for those bribing foreign officials.
9. Make corruption offenses extraditable.
10. Increase transstate cooperation and assistance to corruption investigations.

Source: Author's summary of 1996 Inter-American Convention Against Corruption (OAS 1996).

as an instruction-ruled principle for regional behavior presented the leaders with no immediate threats to their security and caused little concern for wealth. The leaders benefited from signing the summit action plan in terms of their standing as an equal among other OAS state leaders both to other state leaders and in the eyes of their own citizens. Once the leaders returned to their home-states, and the policy process leading to the OAS Convention began, the leaders were suddenly faced with the threat the anticorruption policy presented to their security—their potential loss of political power. The primary security concern of most politicians is the same, they want themselves (or their party) to be elected or reelected (Geddes 1991, 374). The threat of losing an election makes security a politician's principal domestic interest. Thus, the directive-ruled behavior of politicians surrounding elections—what they must do to get elected or reelected—is a primary interest in explaining anticorruption policy.

Geddes (1991, 1994) provides a compelling analysis of the security-related interest structure surrounding electoral victories in the Americas. Using simple game-theory models (agency models), Geddes (1991) demonstrates how the requirement for electoral resources prevents the reform of political patronage networks in the Americas. Patronage, the use of government resources (contracts, jobs, licenses, legislation, etc.) to award loyal political supporters, underlies the power structures in states throughout the Americas. Normally legal, patronage behavior obscures the boundaries between public office and private interest—a behavior that is antithetical to Western normative standards of good governance and a behavior Inter-American anticorruption programs hope to reform. Geddes (1994, 42) describes the region's patronage reform situation as part of a "politician's dilemma." Politicians may truly want to offer patronage reform; however, they face the dilemma that they cannot afford the cost of reform due to the loss of electoral resources that threaten their political survival. She submits:

> In order to maintain their electoral machines, politicians need to be able to "pay" their local party leaders, ward heelers, precinct workers, and campaign contributors with jobs, contracts, licenses, and other favors. What kinds of payments are common or even possible depends on political traditions, legal constraints, and the amount of state intervention in the economy among other things. Where state intervention has customarily been high, politicians depend heavily on the distribution of state largess to cement party loyalties. (Geddes 1994, 40–41)

In a study of small Caribbean Westminster parliamentary democracies, Peters (1992) found similar situations. In analyzing Caribbean leader incentives, Peters observed, "[t]he overriding objective seems to be centered on remaining in power" (Peters 1992, 85). Peters describes how, immediately upon election, Caribbean politicians begin to campaign for the next election through a system of government patronage and concerted efforts to victimize both opposition politicians and supporters of the opposition party (Peters 1992, 178–181). Along with their primary incentive of political survival, Caribbean political elite behavior is also motivated by a strong wealth interest. Peters offers "[t]he majority of politicians in the Caribbean rely on their position as elected officials for their sole source of income" (Peters 1992, 41). He observes that because the transition back to a nongovernmental role is so difficult for Caribbean politicians not reelected:

> lower income nonprofessional individuals elected to [Caribbean] government will do anything necessary to remain in power as long as possible. During that period, they spend their entire term in office campaigning for the next term and try to amass as much capital as they can in order to guarantee their economic survival after they lose power. (Peters 1992, 41)

The failure of states to implement the Inter-American anticorruption programs is thus partly explained by their unwillingness to reform behaviors such as patronage systems that are discouraged by Western standards of good governance. Political officials cannot ensure their standing or access to individual wealth without first ensuring their political survival—and political survival requires patronage in most democratic political systems in the Americas. Based solely on the need for patronage, Geddes's simple game-theory (agency) analysis helps explain the willingness of officials to engage in the

Table 7.1 corrupt behaviors associated with gathering patronage resources. Still missing from the analysis, however, is an investigation of the structural opportunities to be corrupt. To examine such opportunities requires a closer look at the structure of elite accountability and material resource factors.

Appraising Elite Accountability

Onuf's constructivism argues that directive rules (what agents must do) require the support of sanctions in case the agent decides not to follow the applicable rules. The analysis of anticorruption sanctions speaks to elite accountability. Assuming a state fully implemented all of the requirements in the OAS Convention (see Table 7.3), it would then fall upon the state's existing system of sanctions to ensure elite compliance. A lack of accountability provides increasing opportunities for the elite to act corruptly. In appraising a society's level of elite accountability there are two dimensions that must be addressed: answerability and enforcement (Schedler 1999, 14).

Answerability concerns the obligation for public officials to keep citizens informed about their activities and to explain public decisions (Schedler 1999, 14). This includes public officials providing information, facts, and data on public activities, more commonly referred to as freedom of information. Answerability also requires a free media (radio, television, newspapers, magazines, etc.). The media is not only the primary purveyor of information to the public, but also is the public monitor (watchdog) that reports public activities and initiates discourse on the topics most important to society. Lastly, answerability requires public officials to make themselves available in public or private forums to provide information, answer citizen questions, and explain public decisions.

Throughout the Americas, there are major restrictions upon freedom of information, media freedom, and the answerability of public officials to their citizens. Few states in the region have freedom of information laws. On the contrary, regional states often go to great lengths to restrict information from their media and citizens. Most of the Anglophone Caribbean states have adopted legislation similar to the British Official Secrets Act (see Thurlow 1995). Such legislation prohibits the release of any information not sanctioned by the government—defined as the prime minister and cabinet officials. Caribbean officials justify holding information release at such high levels as a means to ensure the executive remains responsible for the actions of his subordinate civil service. In reality, the restricted release of information is more to keep the sitting government from being embarrassed by government mismanagement and officials' illicit behaviors, especially just before elections. While theirs may not be as formal as the Official Secrets Act, most other states in the region have similar policies restricting the release of government information.

Besides restricting the release of information, regional states often go to great lengths to control the media (see Sussman 1999). In many states, the media is restricted outright through either state ownership or concentrated ownership by interests in alliance with the government. States also use systems of media and journalist licensing, special media taxes, and the withdrawal of government advertising as methods of controlling information. Numerous media outlets and journalists have found their licenses revoked on short notice for reports deemed harmful to governments. For example, in 1998 in Peru, an Israeli-born television manager had his station closed and his naturalized Peruvian citizenship revoked when he broadcast reports about state corruption. States also have strict defamation, slander, and libel laws—many dating to the authoritarian military rule in parts of the Americas prior to the 1980s. Throughout the region, the media finds itself the target of harassment and violence. Radio and television stations and newspaper offices are frequently bombed. Moreover, almost two hundred journalists were killed in the Americas during the 1990s and scores of others injured in violent attacks. In this atmosphere of constant harassment, it is not surprising that self-censorship is a major problem with media freedom in the Americas. In an atmosphere of restricted information, it is also not surprising that few government officials make themselves available to answer citizen questions and explain public decisions. Thus, answerability of the governing elite is a major problem throughout the Americas.

Enforcement, the second dimension of elite accountability, concerns the capacity of a state to impose sanctions upon officials who have violated their public duties (Schedler 1999, 14). When official behavior is called into question, it must eventually be investigated and punished if appropriate. To not punish misdeeds results in a state's loss of standing—it appears weak and toothless in the eyes of both its citizens and international observers. Sanctions (punishment) resulting from enforcement actions include those contained in the state's administrative-bureaucratic, electoral, and criminal justice systems. Administratively, a state must have the capacity within its political structure and bureaucracy to uncover suspected corruption (by inspections, audits, whistleblowers, etc.) and then take appropriate administrative action. This may include censures, fines, or removal from office. Electorally, when corruption is perceived as a problem, the citizens must be able to remove suspected officials, that is, "throw the crooks out," during the course of regular or special elections. When an official's corrupt behavior violates criminal statutes, the state's criminal justice system must be able to investigate, bring to trial, and punish convicted wrongdoers. As with answerability, the enforcement dimension of elite accountability in the Americas is a significant problem.

Administrative systems in developing states throughout the Americas tend to be nontransparent and inefficient. Such administrative problems are usually associated with the region's authoritarian-democratic governments (i.e., a form of hegemonic rule), which engender little accountability of the governing elite. An authoritarian-democratic government is one where although the leaders may be elected democratically, after elections the government's decision making becomes authoritarian as it falls under the control of the president or prime minister and his or her closest advisors. While all states in the Americas (excepting Cuba) are recognized as democracies, the vast majority of regional states present authoritarian decision-making structures. For example, in the presidential systems of the Americas' Spanish-speaking states and Haiti, with the possible exceptions of Chile and Costa Rica, there are few effective democratic checks and balances. Through a combination of presidential decrees, strong veto powers, and the exclusive right to initiate legislation in key policy areas, regional presidents can effectively control or bypass their legislatures and thus rule in an authoritarian manner (see Shugart and Mainwaring 1997, 41–52). In the Westminster parliamentary systems of the Anglophone Caribbean, prime ministers and cabinet ministers, drawn from the elected legislatures, actually perform a dual function of executive and legislature, as the parliaments are too small to offer effective loyal oppositions to the ruling governments (see Lijphart 1990, 328–332). In Anglophone Caribbean states, there is often little formal public debate of government activities as government decision making is concentrated in the hands of the prime minister and his or her key advisors. Corruption reforms that might hold a governing elite administratively accountable are not likely in hegemonic systems characterized by authoritarian decision making.

Elections throughout the Americas are often tainted by charges of fraud and corruption. The OAS and Emory University's Carter Center have developed a regular industry around monitoring regional elections. Despite this international oversight, governing elite continue to have considerable influence over the electoral process in their respective states. Even if elections are fair and free, there is no guarantee that electorates will vote out corrupt officials. For example, McCann and Dominguez (1998) found that despite widespread knowledge of the ruling Institutional Revolutionary Party's (PRI) corruption, in Mexican elections (1986–1995), the electorate repeatedly voted the PRI back into power. These PRI victories were based upon two primary elements. First, the PRI obtained votes through their own extensive patronage networks. Second, with the expectation that election fraud would return the PRI to power anyway, those voters most likely to vote for the opposition failed to come to the polls (McCann and Dominguez 1998, 498–499).

In the vast majority of states in the Americas, the criminal justice systems lack the basic processes and efficiency expected in developed states (Salas and Rico 1993, 48). Governing elite are seldom held accountable in criminal justice systems that lack openness. Moreover, the judicial systems lack independence as they are often dependent upon executive branches that control not only the budgets, but also the selection, promotion, and discipline of judges. Without a political base of their own outside the executive, such criminal justice systems are unlikely to hold the governing elite accountable. Thus, even if states were to pass all the legislation required to implement the OAS Convention, there is little chance that the governing elite in the Americas would be held accountable for violations.

Appraising elite accountability is a new topic in political research. Adapting the work of O'Donnell (1999), three categories of accountability can be identified: *circular, vertical,* and *horizontal.* Circular accountability is characteristic of collective political cultures and symbolizes informal answerability and enforcement of societal rules within the individual's respective group. Elite accountability is thus the preserve of the small group of governing elite in collectivist cultures. Government bureaucracies, elections, and criminal justice systems would likely have no role in circular accountability. For all but the most egregious offenses, punishment in collectivist political cultures would likely entail the official's removal, often only temporarily, from the group of governing elite. Vertical accountability is characteristic of individualistic cultures and signifies that answerability and enforcement measures originate in and travel through the society's vertical bureaucracy. Offenses for which elite are held accountable would be serious (black in Table 7.1), and once the offenses were made known to the public there would be a universal call for punishment within the confines of the society's administrative, electoral, or criminal justice systems. Horizontal accountability is characteristic of egalitarian cultures and indicates that answerability and enforcement originate not only within the society's bureaucracy, but also from groups outside government. Democratic balance-of-power and loyal opposition structures are key aspects of horizontal accountability. A free media (press) and civil society, especially nongovernmental organizations, take on primary roles in corruption oversight and have horizontal access to all levels of the government. Individuals reporting corruption (whistleblowers) are protected and do not have to follow bureaucratic chains of command to make reports. Maybe the most important component of horizontal accountability, however, is the involvement of a strong civil society.

Johnston (1998) argues that social empowerment is an essential element in preventing corruption. Social empowerment means "strengthening civil society in order to enhance its political and economic vitality, providing more orderly paths of access and rules of interaction between state and society, and balancing economic and political opportunities" (Johnston 1998, 85). Where civil society is weak, citizens become vulnerable to exploitation. Where civil society is strong, citizens are able to build coordination mechanisms across groups that are essential to elite accountability. A strong civil society fosters the development of anticorruption commitment rules. These commitment rules lead to self-enforcing mechanisms where governing elite make it their duty (promise) not to behave corruptly and civil society takes this promise as their corresponding right. As discussed previously, the governing elite know that if they break this promise and behave corruptly, civil society as a whole will automatically challenge the elite's actions—the self-enforcing aspect of the strong civil society. Therefore, the strength of civil society becomes a key horizontal accountability mechanism preventing corruption.

Assessing Material Resource Factors

Material resource factors are the final constructed social phenomenon considered in this analysis. No constructivist analysis is complete without consideration of how material resources impact upon the social behavior under investigation. Social rules turn raw materials into material resources. Material resource availability plays a major role in agent decision processes. Material resource factors help define the opportunities available for a governing elite to act corruptly. Here we look at rules pertaining to routine material resource factors, or how a society's economy is structured and how state-owned resources are managed.

Beginning with the writings of Adam Smith (1723–1790 A.D.), David Ricardo (1772–1823 A.D.), and other liberal nineteenth- and twentieth-century economists, theorists argue that to achieve economic efficiency a society's political interests must be prohibited from subverting market forces. A noninterventionist government with open and free markets reduces the opportunities for rent seeking or outright theft of public resources. An unintended consequence of an open and free market system is a reduction of corruption. Building from this logic and the previous discussion, three categories of state material resource systems can be constructed: *patrimonial, statist,* and *market.*

Patrimonial material resource systems are dominated by instruction rules and normally found in collectivist societies. Patrimonial material resource systems foster maximum government control by limiting the classes of citizens (normally only the governing elite) that have access to material resources. In these systems the small governing elite tightly control the economy and decide, often capriciously, how state-owned resources are distributed. Patrimonial material resource systems are usually not transparent and provide unlimited opportunities for rent seeking activities. The governing elite are given the opportunity to use the national treasury and state-owned resources as if they were their own personal property, and decide what, if any, resources may be distributed for the public good. To maximize their access to societal resources, governments with patrimonial material resource systems maintain strict control over their economies, usually including high levels of protectionism of foreign trade (high tariffs, etc.), high personal and corporate taxes, government ownership of major enterprises (public utilities, basic foodstuff production, etc.) and infrastructure (ports, airports, railroads, etc.), strict wage and price controls, and a variety of regulations (licensing, contracting, customs procedures, etc.) that allow maximum rent seeking by government officials. One analysis of corruption in underdeveloped societies found that where extensive patrimonialism existed, "the majority of the population are more or less permanently excluded" from the benefits of state resources (Theobold 1990, 91). In the Americas, Cuba and Haiti most resemble states with patrimonial material resource systems, with several other states possessing at least some patrimonial characteristics (Johnson, Holmes, and Kirkpatrick 1999).

Statist material resource systems are dominated by directive rules and found in individualistic societies. Statist material resource systems find less government control of a state's economy and state-owned resources. Statist systems utilize a mix of patrimonial and free market mechanisms to manage their economies, while still providing the governing elite ample opportunities for rent seeking. Knowing that their opportunities to accumulate capital are dependent upon their control of the state's resources and economic processes, governing elite in statist systems strive to ensure that they play key decision-making roles in economic and state resource management. Statist material resource economic management includes some protectionism of foreign trade, some government ownership of key enterprises and infrastructure, and a special emphasis on regulations (licensing, contracting procedures, etc.) that allow substantial rent seeking by government officials. In effect, the governing elite in statist systems view the state's economy and state-owned resources as their own private business resources and regulate them in a manner providing ample opportunity for illicit capital accumulation (see Manzetti and Blake 1996). Theobald (1990, 95) found that even among developed societies, corruption levels soar when the state becomes so involved in economic management "that in the absence of adequate alternatives the state apparatus becomes the main vehicle of economic advancement and capital accumulation" for those in power. In the Americas, thirty of the thirty-five independent states fit solidly into the statist category (Johnson, Holmes, and Kirkpatrick 1999).

Market material resource systems are dominated by commitment rules and found in egalitarian societies. Market material resource systems present the liberal ideal of free and open economies and efficient state-owned resource management. Taking their lead from the works of Smith (1937) and Ricardo (1960), market systems view the only role for the state in the economy as providing public goods that the market is unable to provide (monetary systems, public transportation infrastructure, etc.). State ownership of enterprises is contemplated only if the enterprise has no competition and state-ownership is in the public's best interest. Market economies enjoy maximum transparency and openness. State-owned resource management is also highly efficient and transparent. Overall, the market resource system presents the fewest opportunities for government elite rent seeking. In the Americas, only three states display true market systems—the Bahamas, Canada, and the United States (Johnson, Holmes, and Kirkpatrick 1999).

The Need for Anticorruption Commitment Rules

Table 7.4 provides a synoptic table of the coordinates of corruption. The table summarizes the factors addressed in the constructivist agency and structural analyses presented in this chapter. Along the bottom of Table 7.4 is a hypothetical corruption index modeled on the 0 (totally corrupt) to 10 (no corruption) scale used by Transparency International to annually rate state corruption levels (see Table 7.2 and Endnote 7). Table 7.4, combined with the constructivist tenets and rational choice assumptions presented in this chapter, provides the framework for a comprehensive theory of the causes of corruption. The resultant theory is probabilistic and not deterministic. By evaluating the characteristics of the Table 7.4 agency and structural factors present in a society (i.e., the society's social-ruled makeup), a vertical and horizontal interpolation of those characteristics provides a probable evaluation of that society's corruption pattern and corruption index score. Thus, the table provides a conceptual method to explain a society's corruption pattern and to predict a society's rating on the annual Transparency International Corruption Perception Index. The 1999 Transparency International Corruption Perception Index ratings for several American states are shown on the corruption index at the bottom of Table 7.4.

A number of theoretical propositions may be constructed using Table 7.4 and the constructivist tenets and rational choice assumptions presented in this chapter. However, one proposition is central—*to reduce its overall level of corruption, a society must increase its proportion of anticorruption commitment rules.*

Table 7.4

Coordinates of Corruption

Speech acts	Assertive	Directive	Commissive
Dominant social rules	Instruction	Directive	Commitment
Rules' purposes	Principles, beliefs	Specificity, sanctions	Create roles
Rules' function: what agents	Should do	Must do	Right/duty to do
Forms of societal rule	Hegemony	Hierarchy	Heteronomy
Political cultures	Collectivist	Individualistic	Egalitarian
Elite accountability	Circular	Vertical	Horizontal
Material resource factors	Patrimonial	Statist	Market
Public/private boundaries	White	Gray	Black
Agent interests	Standing	Security	Wealth
Agent behaviors	Pirates	Pariahs	Paragons
Corruption patterns	Systemic	Institutional	Incidental

Corruption Index:

0	HO 1.8	VE 2.6	JM 3.8	CR 5.1	CH 6.9	US 7.5	CA 10 9.2

Note: 1999 Transparency International Corruption Perception Index scores shown for Honduras (HO), Venezuela (VE), Jamaica (JM), Costa Rica (CR), Chile (CH), United States (US), and Canada (CA).

Building anticorruption commitment rules in the structural factors sum-marized in Table 7.4 (form of societal rule, political culture, elite account-ability, and material resources) is the key to reducing corruption—but doing so presents significant challenges.[8] While commitment rules creating roles and establishing rights and duties can be legislated or implemented through new legislation or regulations, more often commitment rules are built over time through the formal and informal interactions of agents (elite and masses) who see that, once established, the intended roles, rights, and duties will be honored. A first step in building stable commitment rules is usually to imple-ment a strong system of directive rules and their corresponding sanctions. Strengthening anticorruption directive rules (i.e., increasing the frequency a governing elite follows the directive rules), allows a society to build stable anticorruption duties and rights that constitute commitment rules. Within a robust directive-ruled structure, anticorruption commitment rules will not only develop and become stronger, but will also increase in formality (i.e., they will assume a status and importance of their own). This process of build-ing commitment rules takes time and is far from easy.

To construct effective anticorruption commitment rules, a society must first have the political will and political capacity to establish a full range of anticorruption directive rules and their associated sanctions. Political will concerns the society's (elite and citizenry's) acceptance of the Western (black) standards of boundaries between public and private and their willingness to take action to change conditions not congruent with these Western (black) standards. Political capacity concerns the ability of a society to follow through on their political will and fully implement a comprehensive array of anticor-ruption directive rules, including the enforcement of directive-ruled sanc-tions when members of the governing elite do not follow these rules. Additionally, over time, a society must evolve to where the incentive for the governing elite to follow the anticorruption directive rules is not just based on the threat of directive-ruled sanctions, but where following the rules be-comes the moral commitment (duty) of the governing elite. Simultaneously, over time, a society's citizenry assumes it is their right to be represented by an honest governing elite. The difficulty in building commitment rules ex-plains why this process takes significant time.

Neglecting the construction of anticorruption commitment rules has led to the failure of Inter-American anticorruption programs. First, the failure of states to generate the political will or political capacity to implement the 1996 OAS Inter-American Convention Against Corruption is explained by regional governing elite whose primary interests are instruction-ruled stand-ing and directive-ruled security. Governing elite in states with systemic and institutional corruption patterns (see Table 7.2) lack the egalitarian interests associated with generating societal wealth (i.e., the commitment-ruled condition). Geddes's (1991, 1994) and Peters's (1992) analyses demonstrate how governing elite in the Americas rely upon systems of political patronage to obtain the resources used to generate voter support and ensure their security—their hold on political power. Corruption reform programs like those in the OAS Convention threaten these political patronage systems and thus directly impact a governing elite's main source of political power. As long as electoral systems in the Americas allow political power to be tied to patronage-based resources, regional societies will likely never attain conditions of strong and formal commitment rules where a governing elite's interests center on societal wealth generation. Thus, the elite competition factor of how elections are funded becomes the primary explanation for why Inter-American anticorruption programs are not being implemented in accordance with the OAS Convention.

Second, where American states have found the political will to adopt anticorruption programs, they also face failure as the Inter-American programs do not address the full range of political, economic, and cultural factors that cause corruption. Building commitment rules requires that the full array of factors in Table 7.4 be addressed simultaneously. The 1996 OAS Convention (see Table 7.3), and similar corruption reform programs, focus too narrowly on the construction of directive rules meant to change a society's corruption boundaries and improve administrative-bureaucratic elite accountability. Table 7.4 reveals, however, that while addressing corruption boundaries and improving administrative-bureaucratic accountability are necessary, they are not sufficient to arrest the corruption problem. Also needed are parallel programs to modernize forms of societal rule and political cultures, implement freedom of information and freedom of the press programs as components of elite accountability and answerability, improve electoral and criminal justice systems as components of elite accountability enforcement, and transition states to open market economies. Also important is the strengthening of civil societies and the building of social trust needed to reach conditions of commitment-ruled horizontal accountability. The 1996 OAS Convention neglects these other important Table 7.4 structural factors.

Conclusion

This chapter's purpose is to illustrate the value of using Onuf's constructivist analytic frame in analyzing foreign policy issues. I demonstrate the power of the constructivist analytic frame to combine several seemingly unrelated theories of political, economic, and cultural behaviors into one comprehensive social theory. My analysis also investigates why Inter-American anticorruption programs are failing. It reveals that while interests of international standing influence state leaders to sign international anticorruption agreements, the leaders later fail to act upon these agreements when they threaten their domestic power structures. Additionally, my analysis demonstrates how anticorruption programs must consist of long-term efforts to build commitment rules in a society's political, economic, and cultural institutions. Overall, my analysis highlights the utility of using the constructivist analytic frame to investigate complex foreign policy questions.

Notes

The theoretical framework in this chapter was drawn from a paper that was the cowinner of the 1999 Alexander George Award for best graduate paper in the Foreign Policy Analysis Section, International Studies Association Conference, February 1999. I thank Nicholas Onuf for his comments on this chapter and my earlier work.

1. OAS Inter-American Convention Against Corruption status, as of May 1, 2000:
   a. OAS states not signing the 1986 Inter-American Convention Against Corruption: Antigua and Barbuda, Barbados, Belize, Dominica, Grenada, St. Kitts and Nevis, St. Lucia, and St. Vincent and the Grenadines. (All located in the Caribbean.)
   b. OAS states signing but not ratifying the Convention: Brazil, Canada, Guatemala, Guyana, Haiti, Jamaica, Suriname, and the United States.
   c. OAS states signing and ratifying the Convention: Argentina, the Bahamas, Bolivia, Chile, Colombia, Costa Rica, Dominican Republic, Ecuador, El Salvador, Honduras, Mexico, Nicaragua, Panama, Paraguay, Peru, Trinidad and Tobago, Uruguay, and Venezuela.
   d. OAS states signing, ratifying, and complying with the Convention: None.
   Source: OAS (2000).

2. Johnston (1994) develops a comparative theory of corruption based upon the structural explanatory factors of public and private boundaries, elite competition, elite accountability, material resource systems, and mass societal participation. My analysis makes extensive use of these explanatory factors in developing a comprehensive theory of the causes of corruption. My analysis advances Johnston's work by expanding the conceptualization of his explanatory factors and linking them with various agency factors.

3. Onuf's version of constructivism should not be confused with several other competing versions of constructivism (see Adler 1997). In the remainder of this chapter, constructivism refers to the use of the analytic frame initially developed in Onuf (1989).

4. Much of the growing constructivist literature refers only to two categories of rules: regulative and constitutive. In Onuf's constructivism, all rules are deemed to have both regulative and constitutive properties. To Onuf there are only three categories of rules—instruction, directive, and commitment—that govern social action.

5. Cultural relativity is an often-cited problem in corruption studies. The cultural relativity argument offers that what is seen as corruption in one culture may not be seen as corruption in another. Many analysts maintain that the Western concept of corruption cannot be applied to developing states in Asia, Africa, or the Americas. Recently the cultural relativity argument has been discredited as more and more developing states adopt

anticorruption programs grounded in the normative Western concept of corruption. This is particularly true for the Americas where the 1994 Miami Summit of the Americas action plan and the 1996 OAS Inter-American Convention Against Corruption adopted the Western concept of corruption as the desired regional norm. This does not, however, eliminate the problem of societies perceiving corruption quite differently.

6. There have been a variety of methods used to describe different categories of political culture. Greif (1994) uses only the collectivist and individualistic typologies. Elazar (1966, 1970, 1994) employs the typologies of individualistic, moralistic, and traditionalistic. Ellis (1993) expands the typologies to five: individualistic, egalitarian, fatalistic, hierarchical, and hermetic. Heidenheimer (1970) offers four typologies: traditional family-kinship systems, traditional patron-client systems, modern boss-follower systems, and the civic-culture-based systems. The three typologies used in this study are a synthesis of these previous works on political culture and are in consonance with the use of threes in concepts developed within Onuf's constructivist analytic frame.

7. The Transparency International Corruption Perception Index is a compilation of several corruption surveys (a poll of polls). The 1997 index includes seven different surveys, the 1998 index ten different surveys, the 1999 index seventeen different surveys. The surveys included Transparency International's Internet corruption survey, an international Gallup poll, and several surveys by international business research and consulting groups. The index is prepared for Transparency International by a team of researchers led by Dr. Johann Graf Lambsdorff at Goettingen University, Germany. Each state's score relates solely to the results drawn from a number of surveys and reflects the perceptions of a wide variety of respondents who participated in the surveys. The scores range from 0 (totally corrupt) to 10 (no corruption) and indicate only the corruption associated with foreign business transactions in each state. In Table 7.2, the standard deviation (std. dev.) indicates the spread of the different polls around the state's listed score. The smaller the standard deviation, the more confidence that can be placed in the state's score.

8. Onuf (1989) does not provide a discussion on how to build commitment rules. The process for developing commitment rules provided in this chapter was developed after numerous discussions with Dr. Onuf on the subject.

References

Adler, E. 1997. "Seizing the Middle Ground: Constructivism in World Politics." *European Journal of International Relations* 3(3): 319–363.

Almond, Gabriel A., and Verba Sidney. 1963. *The Civic Culture*. Boston: Little, Brown and Company.

Elazar, Daniel J. 1966. *American Federalism: A View from the States*. New York: Thomas Y. Crowell Company.

———. 1970. *Cities of the Prairie: The Metropolitan Frontier and American Politics*. New York: Basic Books, Inc.

———. 1994. *The American Mosaic*. Boulder, CO: Westview Press.

Ellis, Richard J. 1993. *American Political Cultures*. New York: Oxford University Press.

Geddes, Barbara. 1991. "A Game Theoretic Model of Reform in Latin American Democracies." *American Political Science Review* 85(2): 371–392.

———. 1994. *Politician's Dilemma, Building State Capacity in Latin America*. Berkeley: University of California Press.

Gramsci, A. 1971. *Selections from the Prison Notebooks*. New York: International Publishers.

Greif, Avner. 1994. "Cultural Beliefs and the Organization of Society: A Historical and

Theoretical Reflection on Collectivist and Individualist Societies." *Journal of Political Economy* 102(5): 912–950.

Heidenheimer, Arnold J. 1970. "Introduction." In A.J. Heidenheimer, ed., *Political Corruption, Readings in Comparative Analysis*, pp. 3–28. New Brunswick, NJ: Transaction Books.

Huntington, Samuel P. 1968. *Political Order in Changing Societies*. New Haven, CT: Yale University Press.

Johnson, Bryan T., Holmes, Kim R., and Kirkpatrick, Melanie.1999. *1999 Index of Economic Freedom*. Washington, DC: The Heritage Foundation and *Wall Street Journal*.

Johnston, Michael. 1983. "Corruption and Political Culture in America: An Empirical Perspective." *Publius* 13(1): 19–39.

———. 1994 "Comparing Corruption: Conflicts, Standards and Development." Paper presented at the XVI World Congress of the International Political Science Association, Berlin, Germany, August 1994.

———. 1998. "Fighting Systemic Corruption: Social Foundations for Institutional Reform." *European Journal of Development Research* 10(1): 85–104.

Klitgaard, Robert. 1988. *Controlling Corruption*. Berkeley: University of California Press.

Lasswell, H.D. 1950. *Politics: Who Gets What, When, and How*. New York: P. Smith.

Leiken, R.S. 1996. "Controlling the Global Corruption Epidemic." *Foreign Policy* 105 (Winter): 55–73.

Lijphart, Arend. 1990. "Size, Pluralism, and the Westminster Model of Democracy: Implications for the Eastern Caribbean." In J. Heine, ed., *A Revolution Aborted: The Lessons of Grenada*, pp. 321–340. Pittsburgh, PA: University of Pittsburgh Press.

Manzetti, L., and Blake, C.H.. 1996. "Market Reforms and Corruption in Latin America: New Means for Old Ways." *Review of International Political Economy* 3(4): 662–697.

McCann, James A., and Dominguez, Jorge I. 1998. "Mexicans React to Electoral Fraud and Political Corruption: An Assessment of Public Opinion and Voting Behavior." *Electoral Studies* 17(4): 483–503.

Montesquieu, Charles de Secondat. 1989. *The Spirit of the Laws/* Montesquieu 1748. Anne M. Cohler, Basia Carolyn Miller, and Harold Samuel Stone, trans. and eds. Cambridge: Cambridge University Press.

Noonan, John T., Jr. 1984. *Bribes*. Berkeley: University of California Press.

O'Donnell, Guillermo. 1999. "Horizontal Accountability in New Democracies." In A. Schedler, L. Diamond and M.F. Plattner, eds., *The Self- Restraining State, Power and Accountability in New Democracies*, pp. 29–51. Boulder, CO: Lynne Rienner Publishers.

Onuf, Nicholas G. 1989. *World of Our Making: Rules and Rule in Social Theory and International Relations*. Columbia: University of South Carolina Press.

———. 1998. *The Republican Legacy in International Thought*. Cambridge, UK: Cambridge University Press.

Peters, Donald C. 1992. *The Democratic System in the Eastern Caribbean*. New York: Greenwood Press.

Putnam, Robert D. 1993. *Making Democracy Work, Civic Traditions in Modern Italy*. Princeton, NJ: Princeton University Press.

Ricardo, David. 1960. *The Principles of Political Economy and Taxation*. New York: E.P. Dutton.

Rousseau, Jean-Jacques. 1978. *On the Social Contract*. Ed. R.D. Masters. New York: St. Martin's Press.

Salas, Luis, and Rico, Jose Ma. 1993. *Administration of Justice in Latin America*. Miami: Center for the Administration of Justice, Florida International University.

Schedler, Andreas. 1999. "Conceptualizing Accountability." In A. Schedler, L. Diamond and M. Plattner, eds., *The Self-Restraining State, Power and Accountability in New Democracies*, pp. 13–28. Boulder, CO: Lynne Rienner.

Scott, James C. 1972. *Comparative Political Corruption*. Englewood Cliffs, NJ: Prentice Hall.

Shugart, Mathew S., and Mainwaring, Scott. 1997. "Presidentialism and Democracy in Latin America: Rethinking the Terms of the Debate." In M.S. Shugart and S. Mainwaring, eds., *Presidentialism and Democracy in Latin America*, pp. 12–54. Cambridge, UK: Cambridge University Press.

Shumer, S. M. 1979. "Machiavelli: Republican Politics and Its Corruption." *Political Theory* 7(1): 5–34.

Smith, Adam. 1937. *The Wealth of Nations*. New York: Modern Library.

Smith, Dwight C., Jr. 1980. "Paragons, Pariahs, and Pirates: A Spectrum-Based Theory of Enterprise." *Crime and Delinquency* 26(3): 358–386.

Sussman, Leonard R. 1999. *The News of the Century, Press Freedom 1999*. New York: Freedom House.

Theobald, Robin. 1990. *Corruption, Development and Underdevelopment*. Durham, NC: Duke University Press.

Thurlow, Richard. 1995. *The Secret State*. Oxford: Blackwell.

Transparency International. 1997. "1997 Corruption Perception Index." Berlin, Germany: Transparency International.

———. 1998. "1998 Corruption Perceptions Index." Berlin, Germany: Transparency International.

———. 1999. "1999 Bribe Payers Index, 1999 Corruption Perceptions Index." Berlin, Germany: Transparency International.

Weingast, Barry R. 1997. "The Political Foundations of Democracy and the Rule of Law." *American Political Science Review* 91(2): 245–263.

Wilson, Ronald C. 1989. *Ancient Republicanism, Its Struggle for Liberty Against Corruption*. New York: Peter Lang.

8

Making Sense of the Conflict Between Mainland China and Taiwan

Shiping Zheng

The conflict between the People's Republic of China (PRC) and Taiwan has received a great deal of attention. Despite enormous time, energy, and financial and intellectual capital devoted to the topic by scholars and policy analysts in the United States, the PRC, and Taiwan, and despite its significance and danger, the PRC–Taiwan conflict does not loom large in mainstream International Relations (IR) literature. It is not a critical case either for theory building or for hypothesis testing. Indeed, mainstream IR theorists seem to be positively shy of discussing the PRC–Taiwan conflict, even in the context of other conflicts in the world. While the PRC–Taiwan conflict is a popular and contentious issue for the media and think tanks, many analyses and policy papers have yet to make a significant contribution to reducing the tensions in the Taiwan Straits.

The difficulty for mainstream IR theories in dealing with the PRC–Taiwan conflict is first of all a conceptual one: What exactly is the PRC–Taiwan conflict? Is it a continuation of the Chinese civil war of the 1940s, a legacy of the Cold War in Asia, a conflict between two sovereign states, or a conflict over ethnic differences, nationalist symbols, moral values, political systems, economic interests, and international status? Although the PRC–Taiwan conflict may have some or all of these elements, none of them can define the conflict easily.

Neoliberal theories in IR rely on international regimes and cooperation to manage conflict, especially through collective security and arms control. Multilateralism is not likely to be a recipe for resolving the PRC–Taiwan conflict, however. Taiwan is not a member of key international regimes or of organizations where the status of statehood is required. The PRC considers the conflict in the Taiwan Straits as being part of China's internal affairs and it therefore does not welcome the intervention of international regimes or organizations. Should the PRC decide to take military action against Taiwan, the crisis is unlikely to be viewed in the same light as the case of Iraq invading Kuwait or the case of North Korea invading South Korea. Since the PRC is a permanent member of the Security Council, the United Nations (UN) would be unable to initiate any action that might resolve the conflict.

Moreover, more than 160 countries in the world have recognized Beijing as the legitimate government of China and only about 30 countries, mostly small Latin American and Caribbean nations, maintain official diplomatic relations with Taiwan. Facing a full-scale military war by the PRC against Taiwan, many countries would find the situation unfortunate and regrettable but would feel largely helpless. Multilateral diplomacy or UN diplomacy as a framework for conflict resolution in the Taiwan Straits does not seem feasible.

For all intents and purposes, the PRC does not exercise any actual control over Taiwan, nor, of course, does Taiwan have any control over the PRC. Moreover, there is no authority higher than Beijing or Taipei that can somehow force both or either of the two Chinese regimes to act in certain ways. While the United States is a party to the PRC–Taiwan conflict and does have some leverage over Beijing and Taipei, it would be a gross exaggeration to say that the United States can control Beijing or Taipei. Over recent years, there have been several instances in which Washington was caught by surprise by what the government in Beijing or Taipei chose to do, and quite unhappily so.

Nevertheless, relations in the Taiwan Straits are not necessarily in a state of anarchy or chaos. There are rules governing the behavior and practices of all the parties involved in the conflict. After all, an actual war has not broken out in the Taiwan Straits for the more than forty years since 1958, despite rising tensions and a war of words. The concepts and analytical tools suggested by neoliberal theories, however, seem inadequate for exploring and analyzing the rules that have so far prevented a major military conflict from recurring in the Taiwan Straits.

Realist theories rely on force to manage conflict through the balance of power and deterrence. But as some IR scholars realize, while realist theories suggest that to safeguard Taiwan's security it makes sense for Taiwan to upgrade its military hardware and build a credible deterrent against the PRC, the same theories also suggest that because of the "security dilemma," more aggressive moves by Taiwan to balance or deter the PRC's military power may prove to be highly dangerous to Taiwan's security (Acharya 1999). In recent years, facing an increasing military threat from the PRC, government officials and policy analysts in Taiwan have become more susceptible to realist thinking. Some talk about building a missile defense system while others suggest forming a United States–Japan–Taiwan military alliance. There are others again who suggest that Taiwan should consider striking Hong Kong or Shanghai should Taiwan be attacked by the PRC. The pursuit of the realist strategy of the "balance of power," however, is unlikely to enhance Taiwan's security because it is sure to lead to an arms race between the PRC and Taiwan and is likely to pit the PRC against the United States. Should there be an actual military confrontation between the PRC and the United States in the Taiwan Straits, furthermore, Taiwan's security and prosperity would undoubtedly be among the first casualties.

In line with neorealist thinking, some analysts like Susan Shirk and Amitav Acharya have proposed a "concert of powers" approach to managing the security of the Asia-Pacific region. A concert of powers is a type of collective security system. In it, a small group of major powers agrees to work together to regulate relations between the major powers and to prevent conflicts among regional states from provoking wars among these powers (Shirk 1997, 245–70; Acharya 1999). The "concert of powers" in the Asia-Pacific region, as proposed by Shirk and Acharya, is neither as institutionalized nor as comprehensive as the North Atlantic Treaty Organization (NATO), however. It is an ad hoc and issue-specific concert relationship aimed at defusing high-level regional tensions.

Even though a de facto "concert of powers" may be emerging in certain issue areas in the Asian-Pacific region, its feasibility for managing the PRC–Taiwan conflict is questionable. The first key question to ask is whether Taiwan would be invited to join such a concert or whether it would merely be a problem for major powers to manage. The major powers in the Asia-Pacific concert mentioned by Shirk and Acharya are China, Japan, Russia, and the United States, but not Taiwan. If one major party in the conflict were not invited to join the concert, however, could a concert of powers work in managing a PRC–Taiwan conflict? A second key question is whether China would tolerate any intervention of Japan in PRC–Taiwan relations, even though China has to deal with the now institutionalized intervention of the United States in the PRC–Taiwan conflict. Not surprisingly, in discussing the feasibility of an Asia-Pacific concert of powers, Shirk and Acharya say little about PRC–Taiwan tensions themselves.

Both neoliberal and neorealist thinking then face the serious challenge of how accurately to describe PRC–Taiwan tensions or to prescribe sensible recipes for managing conflict there. Meanwhile, studies of the PRC–Taiwan conflict have become as a consequence a hazardous enterprise full of pitfalls. First, many analysts find it difficult to resist the temptation of turning studies of the PRC–Taiwan conflict into the business of "advocacy." There is certainly nothing wrong with advocacy per se. Books and papers of this

206 CONSTRUCTIVISTS AT WORK

nature have an important service to perform. They highlight the issues, stimulate debate, shape public opinion, influence policy makers, and because of these, may ultimately affect actual foreign policies. But if most studies of the PRC–Taiwan conflict are conducted in terms of advocacy, their theoretical significance will be limited. Once the policy debate becomes emotionally charged and extremely partisan, many different voices will be silenced.

A second related pitfall in PRC–Taiwan conflict studies is that scholars are often expected to choose sides; you are either pro-PRC or pro-Taiwan, not neither, and not both. Scholars originally from the PRC are more likely to be seen as pro-PRC, and scholars originally from Taiwan are more likely to be seen as pro-Taiwan. When scholars fall into this trap and become one-sided, any academic or scholarly dialogue becomes difficult. Even bringing scholars from the PRC and Taiwan to the same table in the same room does not guarantee that they will have a productive exchange of views. When scholars speak as if they were the spokespersons of the PRC or Taiwanese government, the best one can hope for from such an "intellectual exercise" is for both sides to "agree to disagree."

Worse still, by engaging in the advocacy business, by choosing sides or by serving as a government spokesperson, we run the serious risk of producing something that is opportunistic, irrelevant, or short-lived. In recent decades, numerous books and policy papers have been published about the PRC–Taiwan conflict. Their cumulative value, however, is very limited. Have they qualitatively improved our understanding of the sources of the PRC–Taiwan conflict and the dynamics of the interactions between Beijing and Taipei, between the United States and the PRC, and between the United States and Taiwan? Have these many analyses and studies actually helped reduce the tensions in the Taiwan Straits? Indeed, most policy-oriented works (books, monographs, and papers) on the PRC–Taiwan conflict have produced only one of two results: (1) their policy recommendations have often been ignored either because they are impossible to implement or because they have little relevance to the actual policies being formulated by the relevant parties, or (2) their policy recommendations essentially repeat what policy makers in the United States, the PRC, or Taiwan have already been doing.

In this chapter, I do not promise that I can avoid all or any of these pitfalls in PRC–Taiwan conflict studies. To the extent that the analytical tools we use predispose us to make these mistakes, however, a change of tool might well help. I suggest that by borrowing some of the concepts from the emerging theory of constructivism in IR, and by making some necessary modifications, we may be able to understand the PRC–Taiwan conflict in a new and different light.[1] We may be able to explore the conflict in ways that the conceptual and analytical tools of neoliberalism and neorealism may prevent.

A Constructivist Perspective

A key constructivist proposition is that human beings are social beings, and, as such, we make the world what it is. In other words, governments, states, interactions between and among states, and the world of international relations can be understood as social constructions or arrangements.[2] The PRC–Taiwan conflict may be viewed as a social arrangement the PRC, Taiwan, and the United States are all actively making. The convenience or appeal of conceptualizing the PRC–Taiwan conflict as a social construction is that we may at the onset avoid the difficult definition questions of whether the PRC and Taiwan are two separate states, or whether the United States is interfering in China's internal affairs by being a major player in the PRC–Taiwan conflict.

A second concept is that of the agent. This can be any active participant in a society or social arrangement. Top leaders in Beijing, Taipei, and Washington can be viewed as agents in the PRC–Taiwan conflict, as can their staffs and advisors and other large collections of people who have become involved in the conflict. For example, at different levels of analysis, in the United States, agents may include the administration (the National Security Council, the State Department, the Pentagon, the CIA, etc.), the Congress, the military, the media, business people, and concerned lobbyists. In the PRC the agents may include the central leaders and their advisors, the top brass in the People's Liberation Army (PLA), the officials in charge of Taiwan affairs, and economic administrators in coastal provinces like Fujian, Guangdong, Shanghai, and Zhejiang. In Taiwan, agents may include the president's advisors, officials in charge of mainland affairs and cross-strait relations, the military, political parties, think tanks, and business communities.

Third, whenever social divisions are salient, people are more likely to invent correspondingly divergent identities. When groups are in competition or conflict, their identities will become more distinct. Constructivist theorists further suggest that political identity is not completely determined by social structural factors. As Paul Kowert points out, agents who act on behalf of large collections of people play an active role in the "fabrication of their own political identities." In forming their identities, agents who act on behalf of different or competing groups invent "self" and "other" or "in-group" and "out-group" categories. Conflict also encourages "causal attribution bias," which refers to the tendency to attribute other people's behavior to their dispositional qualities, rather than to situational or environmental constraints (Kowert 1998, 103–106).

Fourth, constructivist theories suggest that as agents, we make the world what it is, not only by doing what we do but also by saying what we say to each other. Constructivist theories hence highlight the act of speaking: the "speech act." Speaking is doing and "talking is undoubtedly the most important way that we go about making the world what it is" (Onuf 1998, 59). Observers and students of the PRC–Taiwan conflict are often amazed by the sometimes creative and sometimes silly war of words waged between the PRC and Taiwan and by the hypersensitivity attached to titles and names by the relevant parties in Beijing and Taipei. For a long time, Beijing and Taipei have debated the exact meaning of "China." For example, Beijing has insisted that Taiwan is a province of China, as now represented by the PRC, and that no references to Taiwan that may imply "Two Chinas" or "One China, One Taiwan" should be allowed. Taiwan has argued that "one China" is a "divided China," that "one China is a future tense, not a present tense," and that there are de facto "two governments," "two entities," or even "two separate states" of China. Does the ingenious richness of the language used in Beijing's and Taipei's statements enhance their respective collective interest, however Beijing and Taipei define this interest? Does the war of words truly reflect the nature of the PRC–Taiwan conflict? Or, as constructivist theories suggest, is the war of words the way groups of agents in the PRC and Taiwan manipulate language to "construct" the relationship between the two sides of the Taiwan Straits, and to form their distinctive political identities in order to define their collective interests?

Finally, when agents act to form their distinctive identities and to achieve their collective goals (security, prosperity, independence, unification, international status, etc.), they are not totally autonomous. There exist structural constraints and incentives, or rules. Rules help define situations in which agents make choices. While rules may regulate or stabilize social interactions, they may have different effects in distributing benefits among agents. Agents may choose, after weighing the consequences of different choices, to follow or to break any given rule. Those who choose to break an existing rule can expect more or less predictable consequences, although in a complex world, agents may make choices that have unintended consequences that they may then choose to ignore, make good, or turn to their advantage. If rules and the related practices of agents form a stable pattern, they become institutions that constitute an environment within which agents can act with rationality defined by this social context.

The rest of this chapter analyzes how the agents in the PRC–Taiwan conflict act to define their distinctive identities, pursue their collective goals, and, in so doing, choose to follow or break certain rules that govern the conflict.

Identity and Rule in the Cold War Era

In the early 1950s, the two key players in the Chinese civil war, Mao Zedong and Chiang Kai-shek, now separated by the Taiwan Straits but still entangled in conflict, began a new battle to form a new political identity for China. For Mao, the challenge was to convince the people on the mainland to accept and rally behind the newly founded PRC. Mao also needed to present this new political identity to the world in the hope of winning the international recognition of the PRC as the sole legitimate government of China. Neither task proved to be easy. Domestically, the PRC was at best an "imagined community," for the majority of the Chinese people had yet to learn and understand the meaning of the PRC as their new collective political identity. Internationally, the PRC was very much isolated from the West. A seat in the most prestigious club of nation-states in the world, the UN, was beyond Mao's reach.

By the early 1970s, Beijing had successfully established itself as the legitimate government of China, especially by winning a seat in the UN and by winning diplomatic recognition from most other countries in the world. Yet, the de facto exclusion of Taiwan from Beijing's jurisdiction left the PRC's political identity incomplete. From the 1950s to the time Mao died, and indeed even to this day, Mao and his successors were not able to solve the issue of political identity for China. It can be suggested that since 1949, Beijing has been continuously suffering from the same political identity crisis: the existence of the PRC on the mainland and of the Republic of China (ROC) on Taiwan. What is the political identity of China when two separate governments claim China's sovereignty? Or more specifically, can Beijing successfully claim to represent China without being able to exercise its control over Taiwan?

While Beijing has been suffering from the same political identity crisis, Taipei has gone through four political identity crises, each of which has had a somewhat different meaning. For Chiang Kai-shek, loss of the mainland was a devastating blow to his legitimacy as the leader of China. The ROC, which was founded in 1912 and existed for thirty-seven years on the mainland, had now moved to Taiwan. This was where and when the first political identity crisis emerged in Taiwan. How could the ROC claim to represent China when it no longer exercised jurisdiction over the mainland? For those who followed Chiang to Taiwan, the ROC was a lost identity. For the native Taiwanese, the ROC was a vague and alien concept. It was therefore no surprise that Chiang Kai-shek, even after he lost mainland China, chose to promote the identity of a "Big China" as embodied in the ROC. On the one hand, Chiang tried to convince his followers that the ROC was residing in Taiwan only temporarily and was making every preparation for recovering the mainland sometime soon. On the other hand, Chiang ruthlessly imposed the ROC regime upon local Taiwanese people. Chiang's answer to the first identity crisis in post-1949 Taiwan was thus a combination of the myth of a

"Big China," plus a promise to recover the mainland soon, and an authoritarian rule that prohibited the local Taiwanese from advocating full autonomy, let alone independence.

In their efforts to establish their representative political identities, agents in Taipei and Beijing had to denounce and delegitimize each other. Chiang Kai-shek frequently called the regime on the mainland "Mao's bandits" or "Communist bandits" while Mao used similar language to call the regime on Taiwan "Chiang's bandits." The name calling seemed silly and ironic because it appeared to bring no tangible benefits except that both Chiang and Mao, as agents on behalf of their competing groups, had to invent the appropriate categories of "self" and "other" or "in-group" and "out-group." Using words for achieving these collective goals would sound ironic anyway because in Chinese history there is really no clear distinction between officials and bandits. As the old Chinese saying goes, "Officials and bandits are one family" or "Winners become kings and losers become bandits." In the PRC–Taiwan conflict at the moment, however, the difference is that the winner (Mao) in the Chinese civil war was not a total winner because the PRC tried but failed to "liberate" Taiwan. Without Taiwan, the PRC represented an incomplete or divided China at the best. The loser (Chiang) in the Chinese civil war was not a total loser either because the ROC had at least one piece of territory to hold on to.

Acting as agents on behalf of their respective groups, Chiang and Mao were not totally autonomous. The unfolding confrontation between the United States and the Soviet Union compelled Chiang and Mao to conduct their civil war in the context of the Cold War between the two superpowers. More importantly, the outbreak of the Korean War in 1950 brought the United States back not only to the civil war on the Korean Peninsula but also to the civil war between Chiang and Mao. By sending the Seventh Fleet to the Taiwan Straits and signing the Mutual Defense Treaty with Taiwan, the United States became an active player in the PRC–Taiwan conflict. Structural constraints and incentives or rules began to apply to Chiang and Mao. In this respect, two emerging rules as a part of the social structure constrained Chiang and Mao.

Rule 1 meant that Mao's plan to liberate Taiwan was no longer feasible, for this would have inevitably meant a war with the United States, its Navy and Air Force being in the Taiwan Straits. This the PRC was sure to lose. Mao's decision to bomb two offshore islands in 1954 and 1955 and again in 1958 may be interpreted as Mao's attempts to test or break this rule. Constructivist theories, however, would suggest that Mao used these acts also to rally his own people for domestic collective actions or to display his symbolic political identity to Chiang as well as to the Americans. As terrifying as bombing of the two offshore islands appeared to be, the security of Taiwan Island was not in any serious danger. Despite the bombings, however, Mao's China remained an incomplete one, a reality Mao had to learn to live with. By the end of the 1950s, Beijing had by and large given up any hope for taking over Taiwan militarily. It was therefore no surprise that in 1972, Mao told the visiting U.S. president, Richard Nixon, that Taiwan was a small problem and the world was a big problem. In 1976 Mao, who was remembered as the first Chinese leader who was able to unify mainland China since the 1840s, died without fulfilling his ambition of taking over Taiwan.

Rule 2 was established and enforced by the American military presence in Taiwan and by the U.S.–Taiwan Mutual Defense Treaty. It meant that Chiang Kai-shek could no longer hope to return to mainland China, which he had once ruled, and especially not by using military force. Later this rule was extended to include no provocative actions against the mainland. For Chiang, giving up any hope of returning to the mainland was perhaps the most painful price he had to pay for having the protection of the United States.

Beginning in the late 1960s, as the structure of the international system changed from one of bipolarity to one of tripolarity, the strategic triangular relationship among Washington, Moscow, and Beijing offered the PRC new opportunities. Because the PRC needed the United States to counter the threat from the Soviet Union, Beijing sought no major confrontation with the United States over the Taiwan issue. The United States, for the benefit of playing the "China card" against the Soviet Union, was also willing to accommodate Beijing's wishes, sometimes at Taiwan's expense. In the world of tripolarity that lasted until 1989, the tensions in the Taiwan Straits appeared to remain at their lowest point. But from the Taiwanese perspective, it was precisely during this period that Taiwan's international status and legitimacy were severely damaged. In 1971 Taiwan lost its seat in the UN. In 1972 U.S. president Richard Nixon recognized the legitimacy of the PRC by making his trip to the mainland, and in 1979 the PRC and the United States normalized their diplomatic relations, followed by the termination of the U.S.–Taiwan Mutual Defense Treaty and the withdrawal of American military forces from Taiwan.

Some American analysts and former U.S. President Carter (in a recent trip to Taiwan) insist that Taiwan has not been a total loser in the process of normalizing relations between the United States and the PRC. Taiwan's economy took off during this period. Taiwan's security was not threatened. Taiwan was able to make the transition from an authoritarian regime to a functional democracy, and relations between the mainland and Taiwan also improved. Although all these positive changes are true, opposition politicians in Taiwan are quick to point out that they personally paid a heavy price being imprisoned under the emergency situation triggered by President Carter's decision in 1978 to switch diplomatic recognition from Taipei to Beijing. In their view, this decision also delayed Taiwan's democratization process for ten years.

What was most damaging to the regime in Taiwan, following Richard Nixon's trip to Beijing in 1972 and Jimmy Carter's decision to normalize relations with the PRC in 1979, was the loss of identity. The ROC regime on Taiwan now suffered its second political identity crisis: The ROC was no longer considered a legitimate government representing China, either by the UN or by many of Taiwan's longtime supporters. Increasing isolation in the international community in the late 1970s and 1980s forced the ROC regime, now under the control of Chiang Ching-kuo, to concentrate on economic development, and later on political liberalization. But the identity crisis only deepened. Instead of the earlier debate about who represented China, the debate now focused on the identity of Taiwan, and on what China meant for the Taiwanese. Caught between the legacy of the "Big China" myth created by his father, and the rising demand for Taiwanization, Chiang Ching-kuo proved unable to come up with an answer to the second political identity crisis. This crisis, coupled with the momentous social and political changes in Taiwan in the late 1980s and early 1990s, led to a search for a new political identity for Taiwan. This frequently translated into a full-scale war of words and diplomacy between Taipei and Beijing.

Upon reflection, the PRC was not the total winner during this period. The political identity of China pertaining to Taiwan was neither solved nor was it clearly defined in the three communiqués (1972, 1979, and 1982) that Chinese leaders regarded as the guiding principles (highest rules) governing PRC–U.S. relations. By manipulating the language, the agents in both China and the United States (Mao Zedong, Zhou Enlai, Deng Xiaoping, Nixon, Kissinger, Carter, and Reagan) had essentially muddled through the ever-present tension over the issue of Taiwan and the definition of China. Moreover, in the late 1970s, an impatient leadership in Beijing kept pushing for the normalization of Sino-American diplomatic relations by reminding the Carter administration of the pledges that the previous administrations had made. The unintended consequence was rising opposition on Capitol Hill that ultimately led to the passage of the Taiwan Relations Act (TRA). Chinese leaders and policy analysts have by now realized that nothing complicated and even jeopardized PRC–U.S. relations more than the TRA. The normalization of relations between Beijing and Washington was to happen sooner or later. Had PRC leaders been patient for a year or two, President Reagan might have been able to manage the Taiwan lobby and pro-Taiwan members in the Congress more effectively than President Carter had. Even if something like the TRA was unavoidable, a watered-down version would have caused much less trouble for the future relationship. In a rush to win American diplomatic recognition to boost its international status, the PRC paid a heavy price because, while Beijing was able to normalize its diplomatic relations with Washington, the TRA institutionalized the U.S. role in the PRC–Taiwan conflict and permanently involved the U.S. Congress in setting U.S. policy toward Beijing and Taipei.

Independence Movement and Diplomatic War in the 1980s

In the late 1980s, Taiwan experienced a takeoff in political reforms after the economic takeoff in the 1970s. In 1987, the thirty-eight-year-old martial law was finally lifted. The era of the strongman ended with the passing away of Chiang Ching-kuo in 1988. An authoritarian system was being gradually transformed into a constitutional democracy. The process of democratization was intertwined with that of Taiwanization. Indeed, the two processes were two sides of the same coin, reinforcing each other. By the 1980s, native Taiwanese already comprised 85 percent of the population in Taiwan, with mainlanders accounting for less than 15 percent. Native Taiwanese had also become a rising power group within the ruling Kuomintang (KMT), partly due to Chiang Ching-kuo's pragmatic policy of "Taiwanization" of the party leadership from the mid-1970s on. The aging KMT leaders, who originally came to Taiwan in the late 1940s, were being replaced either by their children who had grown up in Taiwan or by native Taiwanese. To this new ruling group and to politicians of the opposition Democratic Progress Party (DPP), the ROC, as a government representing "Big China," looked more like an empty slogan or a myth. Redefining Taiwan's political identity became the central issue in the ongoing political power struggle.

In the 1989 elections, the issue of Taiwanese independence was openly debated for the first time. Slogans of "Long Live Taiwan Independence" were shouted in the Legislative Yuan. In 1990, eleven newly elected DPP members to the National Assembly changed the words of the "Republic of China" to "the people of Taiwan" in their oath to office.[3] The KMT government appeared to stand firm on this issue: independence for Taiwan was not allowed. In 1988 when the opposition groups were legalized, they received a strong message from the KMT government that the issue of independence was not up for discussion. Yet, before long, even the ruling party under Lee Teng-hui began to search for a new political identity that reflected more of the changes in Taiwan than that of the myth of "Big China."

In its policy toward Taiwan, Beijing insisted that reunification could be accomplished only under Deng Xiaoping's formula of "one country, two systems." For a long time, the KMT government had responded to Deng's offer with a policy of "Three No's" (no contact, no compromise, no negotiation). Meanwhile, the KMT government was exploring the "one country, two teams" model of the 1980 Olympic Games and "one country, two seats" model the Asian Bank instituted in 1989. In the early 1990s, however, the policy of "Three No's" was losing effectiveness. In view of the changes in the world, and under pressure at home, the KMT government gradually changed the "Three No's" policy to a policy of "one country, two governments" to counter Beijing's formula for reunification of "one country, two systems."

"One country, two governments" meant that both the governments in Taipei and Beijing were sovereign and independent state governments, and that both claimed to represent China. In his presidential inaugural speech on May 20, 1990, Lee Teng-hui affirmed that "one country, two governments is the political reality."[4] Lee offered his model of reunification, listing three preconditions for negotiation with PRC; namely, Beijing gives up its one-party political system and embraces a free-market economy, renounces the use of force to retake Taiwan, and stops frustrating Taipei's diplomatic overtures.[5] In response to Lee's offer, PRC president Jiang Zemin insisted that any talks with the mainland should proceed in terms of Deng's formula of "one country, two systems."[6] On the one hand, Beijing believed that Lee's proposal signaled a major policy change on the part of Taipei, for Lee made his call directly to the People's Republic of China. On the other hand, Beijing continued to accuse Lee of trying to create "two Chinas." At issue here is the question of "who is central and who is local government?" Deng's formula of "one country, two systems" meant that Beijing was the central government and Taipei was the local government. Once this precondition was accepted, everything else was negotiable. Lee's formula of "one country, two governments" maintained that both governments in Taipei and Beijing were sovereign and equal, and they should coexist.

On this basis two different approaches to negotiation were built. Beijing insisted that "party-to-party" negotiation was more appropriate than "government-to-government" or "state-to-state" negotiation, while the KMT argued that the two parties could not fully represent the Chinese people, and a "government-to-government" approach was more desirable. For Beijing, to recognize Taipei as an equal in the negotiations meant "two Chinas," or "one China, one Taiwan." For Taipei, accepting the status of a local government endangered its own political identity. Therefore, while each did recognize the other as a legitimate participant in any negotiations, Beijing and Taipei had created a new political stalemate. "One country, two systems" was not the same as "one country, two governments."

Meanwhile, the PRC and Taiwan were waging a fierce diplomatic war against each other. In the early 1990s, for example, after Taiwan's "elastic diplomacy"[7] had successfully won over four small countries (Lesotho, the Bahamas, Belize, and Liberia), mainland China fought back by managing to establish diplomatic relations with Taiwan's allies of many years, Saudi Arabia, and later South Korea, South Africa, Indonesia, and Singapore. This led to severe criticism in Taiwan of the policy of "elastic diplomacy" as one of "winning over little friends and losing big friends." Taiwan's "elastic diplomacy" was also criticized by Beijing as an attempt to create "two Chinas" or "one China, one Taiwan," in which Taiwan established commercial offices, upgraded unofficial organizations to consulate-general status, and lured away countries that had already established or restored diplomatic relations with the PRC.

PRC–Taiwan Relations in the Post–Cold War Era

In the post–Cold War years, as the world order is being reconfigured, international institutions/regimes are being challenged and the structure of international relations is being remodeled in multiple ways, with many unintended consequences. In this broad context, the PRC–Taiwan conflict is also being reconstructed, as groups of agents in the PRC and Taiwan respond to domestic and international changes.

By the mid-1990s, leaders and the people in both mainland China and Taiwan had become more ambitious, more self-confident, and more frustrated, too. The economic reforms that began in the late 1970s had transformed mainland China into an economic powerhouse in the Asia-Pacific region and a major player in world politics. Yet, even though Hong Kong and Macao were soon to be taken over by Beijing, the possibility of reunification with Taiwan remained as remote as ever. In an important speech in January 1980, China's new paramount leader Deng Xiaoping listed three major tasks in the 1980s, which included "opposing hegemonism, unification of China and economic modernization." When Deng died in 1997—almost two decades later—the unification of mainland China with Taiwan was no closer than it had been in 1980. Like Mao before him, Deng had to swallow the bitterness of not being able to take over Taiwan in his lifetime. Beijing's newly elevated status in the international community, along with its rising economic and military power and self-confidence, further increased Beijing's frustration with the stalemate in PRC–Taiwan relations. Beijing's political identity crisis pertaining to Taiwan has thus not only continued but also deepened.

Meanwhile, an economically prosperous and politically democratizing

Taiwan is a new Taiwan, but the new Taiwan remains isolated in the international community and therefore becomes even more frustrated as well. The emotions of this large collection of people put tremendous pressure on their agents. Whereas in Taiwan's first and second political identity crisis, pressure on the KMT regime mainly came from mainland China and the international community, in Taiwan's third political identity crisis in the 1990s, the pressure came mainly from Taiwan's frustrated populace. In dealing with the first and second identity crisis, Taiwan was essentially on the defensive. Now Taiwan was on the offensive. In 1992, the Taiwanese government began to work for reentering the UN. Since then, Taiwan has deemphasized the concept of "one China" while promoting a new Taiwanese political identity. Lee Teng-hui, being the first native Taiwanese president, took upon himself the mission of presenting a new Taiwan to the international community. Among Lee's many acts were his speech at Cornell University in 1995 and his "special state-to-state relations" statement in 1999.

Lee's speeches and the DPP's pro-independence movement in Taiwan provoked strong reactions from the PRC, including denunciation by the mainland media and missile tests and military exercises aimed at Taiwan. Beijing showed a clear tendency to attribute Lee's speeches and behaviors to his personal disposition. Quite a number of government officials and policy analysts in PRC believed that Lee had been pursuing Taiwanese independence all along because he simply did not consider himself Chinese. Many even suspect that Lee thought more like a Japanese. Lee's statements, therefore, were viewed as not only anti-PRC, but also as anti-China. Lee and some DPP politicians were the "significantly different other" or "out-group." By the late 1990s, Beijing seemed to have completely given up any plan to negotiate with Lee Teng-hui.

Finding it difficult to understand why Beijing insisted that Taiwan was only a province of China and why Beijing was actively blocking Taiwan's efforts to reenter the UN and other international organizations, Lee and his advisors showed a similar tendency to attribute the behaviors of President Jiang Zemin and other PRC officials to their personal disposition. The most convenient and popular interpretation was that Jiang and the PRC officials were Communist. All too often, the PRC had been referred to as "Communist China" in news reports, commentaries, and even scholarly analyses in Taiwan. The term "Communist China" is, of course, a carefully chosen one designed to characterize the PRC as the "significantly different other" or "out-group." The label "Communist China" also acquired special meaning after the collapse of the communist regimes in the former Soviet Union and Eastern Europe. Even if it may not turn out to be a new "evil empire," the PRC as "Communist China" is meant to be much disliked. So playing the "communist" card, Taipei is working to weaken the PRC's legitimacy and popularity.

Serious scholars and policy analysts, however, have to wonder if mainland China ever was a "communist" country and how much "communism" exists in today's mainland China. Moreover, the PRC's being "communist" did not prevent the United States and other Western liberal democracies from pursuing normal relations and close cooperation with China in the 1970s. Even if we assume that China has not changed a bit since the 1970s, what has changed in the world that should make "communism" a problem in dealing with Beijing? The most likely answer is that the strategic factor (opposing the Soviet Union), a factor that brought China and the West together in the 1970s, all but disappeared in the 1990s, leaving foreign policies hostage to domestic politics and ideological appeals.

It is not difficult to argue that mainland China has changed dramatically since the late 1970s, however. More importantly, China's social, economic, and even political changes have occurred not because the PRC in the 1980s and 1990s moved closer to the principles of "communism," but precisely because the PRC under Deng Xiaoping abandoned Mao Zedong's centrally planned command economy, and his people's communes and economic self-reliance, and moved toward market economy. If some politicians and media pundits in the West do not quite understand this profound transformation because they have not visited mainland China in recent decades, politicians and policy analysts in Taiwan ought to know better. Yet because of "causal attribution bias," leaders and policy analysts in Taiwan view leaders in Beijing as being not only irrational, but also incapable of being rational.

In manipulating the language to form and display their distinctive political identities, while portraying the other side as "out-group," Taiwan and the PRC are sometimes trapped in the world they construct. In responding to the PRC's pressure for reunification, Taiwan often lists "a free and democratic China" as the ultimate precondition for reunification. The ROC under Chiang Kai-shek already claimed to be a free China, the truth of which was obviously questionable. Before the KMT regime made the transition from authoritarianism to a constitutional democracy, a "democratic China" requirement for reunification was ridiculous. In the 1990s, however, Taiwan was in a much more confident position to talk about democracy. But it is precisely here that the trap of a self-constructed world begins. Talking about "a democratic China" as a precondition tends to create the impression that the obstacle to reunification is the PRC's undemocratic system.

Yet it is not difficult to see that by making "a democratic China" a precondition, Taiwan either intends to play the "democracy card" as a delaying tactic or has rejected the idea of reunification with China. It is simply unrealistic to think that if mainland China today were a democracy as understood in the West, the PRC–Taiwan conflict would be easily resolved. For instance, Samuel Huntington, the advocate of "The Clash of Civilizations" theory, has warned that even if China established an electoral democracy defined "as a political system whose most powerful decision makers are selected through relatively fair, honest, periodic elections, in which candidates can freely compete and in which virtually all the adult population is eligible to vote," it is not difficult "to conceive of a democratic China being a China which is highly nationalistic, in which politicians competing for office appeal to Chinese nationalism and find it worth their while, in terms of votes, to do that sort of thing and to denounce the United States."[8] By Huntington's logic, a democratic China might very well cause more trouble for Taiwan.

Even if we do not accept Huntington's hypothesis, it remains the case that democracies do not necessarily have a better record in managing separatist and independence movements. The England–Northern Ireland conflict and the India–Kashmir conflict are just two examples. Indeed, in view of Russia's recent war against Chechnya and Russian President Putin's rising popularity directly associated with the war in Chechnya, it is entirely possible that top leaders in Beijing, if their political careers depend on popular vote, will be under more pressure to take drastic actions against Taiwan. To bet on a fundamental regime change in mainland China for solving the reunification problem is perhaps to fool ourselves and to become blind to new opportunities and initiatives.

Over the years, mainland Chinese officials have frequently reiterated three circumstances under which Beijing would have to use force to take over Taiwan: (1) declaration of independence in Taiwan, (2) involvement of foreign powers in Taiwanese affairs, and (3) internal turmoil in Taiwan. Meanwhile, Beijing has time and again stressed that the use of force against Taiwan would not be aimed at the people in Taiwan, but at the foreign countries (presumably the United States or Japan) suspected of being involved with the Taiwanese independence movement. Constructivists will say that these statements may be better understood in terms of the PRC's efforts to display to the world community Beijing's symbolic sovereignty over Taiwan. Speech acts by Beijing pertaining to the right to use force against Taiwan do not necessarily pose any real threat to Taiwan's security.

In a world constructed by speech acts, however, politicians in Taiwan repeatedly demand that Beijing renounce the use of force against Taiwan, as if Taiwan's security actually hinges upon Beijing's decision to renounce or not to renounce the use of force. Will Beijing's renunciation of the use of force actually enhance Taiwan's security? Or conversely, does the PRC's refusal to renounce the use of force increase the danger to Taiwan's security? As constructivists, we tend to believe that leaders and policy analysts in Taiwan know well that their demands that Beijing renounce the use of force have little to do with Taiwan's security, but a lot to do with Taiwan's attempts to use the world's opinions to force Beijing to give up what the latter considers to be a sovereign right.

Ironically, if Beijing now had jurisdiction over Taiwan, there would be no need to insist on the use of force against Taiwan as a sovereign right of the Chinese government. Beijing does not insist and indeed does not have to insist on the use of force against any of the provinces or regions on the Chinese mainland should they choose to become independent or separated, whether this be Xinjiang, Tibet, Guangdong, Hainan, or Shanghai, for that matter. Furthermore, Beijing's interests may be better served if Beijing decides to renounce the use of force against Taiwan in exchange for Taiwan giving up its claims to independence. Beijing's insistence on the right to use force therefore is aimed at displaying Beijing's symbolic sovereignty over Taiwan and at deterring the Taiwanese independence movement precisely because the leaders in Beijing fully understand that they currently have no more effective leverage over Taiwan.

Changing Rules and Implications

As suggested earlier, in the 1950s and 1960s, two basic rules were established to govern the PRC–Taiwan conflict, largely due to the military intervention of the United States: namely, no provocation by Taiwan against mainland China, and no military takeover of Taiwan by Beijing. Even though these rules were tested from time to time by Chiang Kai-shek and Mao Zedong, they remained unbroken at the end of the 1960s. Beginning in the 1970s, and throughout the 1980s, the old rules were replaced by two new rules. First, there is the rule of "one China," which means that both Beijing and Taipei agree that there is one China and Taiwan is part of China. Second, there is the rule of "no military threat," which means that the issue of reunification shall be resolved by peaceful means. Both of these two rules are embedded in the three communiqués signed by Beijing and Washington and in the TRA. The United States was again actively involved in shaping and enforcing these rules in the Taiwan Straits. In recent years, however, these two new rules governing the PRC–Taiwan conflict have been seriously tested, while agents in Taipei and Beijing have attempted to reconstruct their relationship as they face a fast-changing political, economic, and military landscape in their own societies as well as in the Asia-Pacific region.

"One China" Rule

Until July 1999, even though Taipei quarreled with Beijing numerous times over the definition and precise meaning of "one China," Taiwan had committed itself to the concept of "one China." Taiwan's previous proposals of "one country, two political entities," "one country, two governments," and "unification under a free and democratic China" were just a few examples of this commitment. However, Lee Teng-hui's characterization of PRC–Taiwan relations as "special state-to-state relations" in July 1999 directly challenged the "one China Rule." Immediately after Lee's statement, Beijing angrily demanded that Lee retract his statement, while the Clinton administration subtly urged Lee to reconsider or reinterpret the statement. There should be no question as to what exactly Lee meant by describing the PRC and Taiwan as two separate states. Nor should there be any doubt that Lee said exactly what he meant. Lee and his advisors had carefully thought through the whole issue and made a determination to challenge the "one China" rule.

Lee's "special state-to-state relations" statement has been seen as Lee's attempt to boost his standing in Taiwanese politics, to set the agenda for the next presidential elections in Taiwan, to test the PRC's tolerance, or to rebut the "Three No's" statement President Clinton made in Shanghai in June 1998, in which Clinton announced that the United States does not support one China, one Taiwan; does not support Taiwanese independence; and does not support Taiwan's membership in international organizations where statehood is required. Most importantly, Lee's special "state-to-state relations" statement reflected Taiwan's increasing frustration with the limited space and maneuverability in the international community that the "one China" rule provides. Lee intended to challenge and break this rule and reshape the world's perception of Taiwan accordingly.

Rule breaking has consequences, as other agents involved in the PRC–Taiwan conflict choose to react. Beijing thus canceled the scheduled visit to Taiwan by Mr. Wang Daohan, president of the mainland's Association of the Cross-Strait Relations. The PRC also conducted several rounds of military exercises in the coastal regions facing Taiwan. Warlike talk intensified and rumors of the imminent invasion of Taiwan by the PLA were widely spread in Hong Kong and other Asian cities. Caught by surprise, Washington also expressed disapproval of Lee's challenge to the "one China" rule. After all, the Clinton administration argued, this rule had worked to institutionalize the stability and prosperity in the Taiwan Straits in the recent decades. It was therefore no surprise that officials in Beijing and Washington viewed Lee as a "troublemaker."

There are some who were puzzled by Beijing's strong reaction toward Lee's statement. Did Lee merely describe the reality that the PRC and Taiwan were indeed two de facto separate states? Furthermore, one may wonder what has changed because of Lee's making this statement and what would be restored if Lee retracted it? In other words, from other perspectives (the tangible national interest, the actual balance of power), the statements by Lee and the strong reactions by agents in Beijing could look like much ado about nothing. From the constructivist perspective, however, it is not what has or has not changed by Lee's pronouncements. It is the "one China" rule that Lee intended to break with his speech acts that matters. If Lee could single-handedly reconstruct the PRC–Taiwan relations as he wished, the "one China" rule would be abandoned; Beijing would recognize Taiwan as an equal, sovereign state; the United States would change Clinton's "Three No's" policy; and the international community would identify the PRC as China and Taiwan as Taiwan. Much is at stake, therefore, not because of what Lee's speeches have changed, but because of what Lee's speeches are intended to make.

Some scholars from Taiwan have complained that Lee was not making trouble, but making noises. But as constructivists see it, making noises in this matter is precisely making trouble because speaking is doing. Lee's speeches were aimed at breaking an existing rule governing the Taiwan Straits conflict, a rule Lee believed had become more beneficial to the PRC than to Taiwan. To the extent that the rule breaking changed the distribution of benefits, both Beijing and the Clinton administration had to act to make sure that the rule breaker faced the kind of consequences that would maintain the "one China" rule.

Rule of "No Military Threat"

The rule of "no military threat" in the PRC–Taiwan conflict kept both sides from military confrontation in their otherwise fierce competition for more than thirty years. In 1995–96, Beijing conducted missile tests in the Taiwan Straits following Lee Teng-hui's speech at Cornell University and before the presidential election in Taiwan.[9] Some of the warheads (empty) were said to have flown over the city of Taipei and Kaosiung. In response to Lee Teng-hui's "special state-to-state relations" statement in July 1999, Beijing also conducted several rounds of military exercises aimed at Taiwan. While these acts were intended to reassert Beijing's symbolic sovereignty over Taiwan, and to deter pro-independence politicians in Taiwan, what Beijing did broke a rule that had been established since the end of the bombing of the offshore islands in the late 1960s.

Beijing's missile tests in 1995–96 were believed to have prompted President Clinton to dispatch two U.S. aircraft carrier battle groups to the Taiwan Straits. This was reportedly the largest deployment of U.S. forces in the region since the end of the Vietnam War. It is debatable whether Beijing's missile tests in the Taiwan Straits achieved their intended results. But a larger U.S. military presence in the Taiwan Straits was perhaps not what Beijing had hoped for.[10] What were Beijing's real intentions in breaking the "no military threat" rule? With missile tests and war games, was Beijing really planning to take over Taiwan militarily anytime soon? We tend to argue that Beijing's war games were designed not so much to threaten Taiwan's security as to warn Taiwan of the consequences of pursuing the course of independence. Threats to Taiwan's security, although they surely exist, may not be as serious or imminent as the war of words and military exercises might suggest. If the element of surprise is a necessary ingredient to success in war, then war is most likely when it is least talked about or expected.

Nevertheless, even if what Beijing did in the Taiwan Straits—the missile tests and war games—has not significantly increased any threat toward Taiwan, Beijing's decision to break the rule of "no military threat" will have far-reaching implications. From Beijing's perspective, while a peaceful reunification is still the most desirable goal, military options must now be combined with other means. As some researchers from the U.S. government and policy research institutes suggested in late 1997, "in fact there is little evidence that the PLA is prepared to use military force to resolve the Taiwan issue." "The PLA's objectives with regard to Taiwan should be characterized as comprising a deterrent strategy. Making Chinese military capabilities in the Strait credible is the PLA's goal. China wants to be able to change political behavior on Taiwan or to influence decisionmaking in the United States" (Culver and Pillisbury 1998).

Reconstructing PRC–Taiwan Relations

The election of the DPP's Chen Shui-bian as the new president of Taiwan in March 2000 not only forced the KMT leadership out of office, but also threw Beijing's Taiwan policy into confusion. Due to poor information about Taiwan's electoral politics in general, and about Chen Shui-bian in particular, officials in charge of Beijing's Taiwan affairs had comfortably placed their bets on the KMT candidate Lien Chen. Leaders in Beijing, therefore, were taken by surprise when the actual electoral results came out. The initial official response from Beijing was standard and predictable: The election in Taiwan meant only a change in the local leadership and did not change the fact that Taiwan was part of China. Highly distrustful of Chen because Chen was known to be a strong advocate of Taiwanese independence in the past, mainland officials nevertheless believed that Chen could be no worse than Lee Teng-hui. They were willing to wait and see, at the least for the moment.

The closely watched inaugural speech by Chen, made on May 20, 2000, failed to mention the "one China" principle, thus falling short of what Beijing had demanded. But Chen's declaration of "five no's"—no declaration of independence, no change of official name, no amendment of the constitution to include "state-to-state" language, no referendum to change the status quo regarding independence or unification, and no abolition of Taiwan's National Reunification Council or the National Reunification guidelines—gave Beijing enough reason to continue to "listen to Chen's words and watch his action." Indeed, a number of scholars and policy analysts in China suggested that Chen's declaration of "five no's" had taken away any reason or excuse for the mainland Chinese to use force against Taiwan.[11]

On June 20, 2000, seizing the momentum created by the dramatic summit in Pyongyang between South Korea's Kim Dae Jung and North Korea's Kim Jong Il, Chen sent an invitation to Jiang Zemin to meet with him in any form at any place. "If North and South Korea can, why can't the two sides of the strait?" Chen asked. Again, Chen had upstaged the leaders in Beijing with his gestures, particularly considering that Beijing was believed to have played a key role in facilitating the Korean summit. Beijing responded to Chen's offer by insisting that any negotiation had to be held under the "one China" principle. A PRC Foreign Ministry spokesman told reporters: "This one China principle is the basis and precondition for achieving peaceful renunciation, and on this major matter of right and wrong, we will not give in."[12] Taipei, however, argued that no precondition should be set for negotiations and that "one China" was only a topic to be discussed. Thus the two sides were still locked in a stalemate over the issue of "one China."

If it could alone determine the status of Taiwan, Beijing would be most likely to turn Taiwan into another Hong Kong: a special administrative region of the PRC, but with full autonomy and more international space. On the other hand, if it could alone determine its status, Taipei would like to see itself become more like Singapore: a predominantly Chinese society, with good economic and cultural relations with mainland China, but a fully independent and separate country. Since a "Hong Kong" scenario is unacceptable to the government and people in Taiwan and a "Singapore" scenario is unacceptable to the government and people in mainland China, Taipei and Beijing have to try to find somewhere between these two end points where both sides can meet.

Despite his dizzying gestures and overtures, Chen Shui-bian's mainland China policy is still to be defined and clarified. Riding on the momentum of the Korean summit, Chen could also be trapped by the comparison of the PRC–Taiwan conflict with the Korean one. For one thing, neither North Korea nor South Korea has recognized the other as an independent and sovereign state. For another, leaders and people in both North and South Korea declare that they are "one people." Moreover, South Korea's Kim Dae Jung has opposed a "containment" policy against the North and has declined to participate in the U.S.-led Theater Missile Defense (TMD) system in Asia. Chen may be the first to suggest a comparison between the two Koreas and the mainland and Taiwan, though he may not be the last to regret making such a comparison.

When the hard work of social reconstruction begins, what cross-Strait relations will look like depends on how the agents in Taiwan answer the following three questions: (1) Is the "one China" concept a trap that inevitably limits Taiwan's international space, or is it a "safety valve" that enhances Taiwan's prosperity and security? (2) Will more economic ties and direct communication with the mainland benefit both sides or work against Taiwan's best interest? and (3) Will a policy of "balancing/hedging" (military buildup, weapon upgrading, possible participation in TMD, etc.) work to promote or reduce Taiwan's security?[13]

Beijing's basic position on the issue of Taiwan seems clear: It will never allow formal separation or independence on the part of Taiwan. For current or future leaders in Beijing, to allow Taiwan to become formally separated or independent would be political suicide. Should a formal declaration of independence be announced by Taiwan, any Chinese leader, democratically elected or otherwise, would have no choice but to take military action, even if that meant a major military confrontation with the United States.[14]

Beijing's policy toward Taiwan, however, remains vague and fluid. The key issue for policy makers in Beijing is how the threat of the use of force can be combined with other strategies and, since Taiwan's Chen administration has already announced "five no's," what other words or actions Chen makes would constitute a compelling reason for the actual use of force against Taiwan. While many details remain to be worked out, Beijing seems to be moving to reconstruct a world of PRC–Taiwan relations in which Taipei has to take into account the credibility of a military attack by Beijing, and Washington has to consider the scenario of war with Beijing, should the United States decide to intervene militarily in the Taiwan Straits.[15]

The United States is by no means a bystander in this new adventure of social reconstruction across the Taiwan Straits. On the one hand, it is up to the agents in Washington to decide whether the "one China" rule is outdated and therefore ought to be changed, or whether they will continue to help Beijing preserve the "one China" rule. On the other hand, Washington needs to decide what to do to persuade Beijing to recommit itself to the rule of "no military threat." Future PRC–Taiwan relations will be what the agents in Beijing, Taipei, and Washington construct, with both intended and unintended consequences for themselves and for the Asia-Pacific region.

Notes

1. For some constructivist writings, see Nicholas Onuf (1989, 1998), and Vendulka Kubálková, Nicholas Onuf, and Paul Kowert (1998).
2. This part of the paper draws heavily from Nicholas Onuf, "Constructivism: A User's Manual" (1998) and Paul Kowert, "Agent Versus Structure in the Construction of National Identity" (1998).
3. They were subsequently thrown out of Chung Shan Hall, where the oath of office was being taken, "on the grounds that their oath was invalid." *Far Eastern Economic Review*, March 29, 1990, p. 35.
4. *Central Daily News*, Taiwan, May 22, 1990, p. 1.
5. *Far Eastern Economic Review*, May 31, 1990, p. 10.
6. *Far Eastern Economic Review*, June 21, 1990, p. 14.
7. This policy is also called "pragmatic diplomacy" or "substantive diplomacy."
8. Huntington offered this comment at the Council on Foreign Relations' Policy Impact Panel: "Democracy: Is It for Everyone?" June 1, 1998.
9. For an analysis of the causes and significance of the crisis, see John W. Garver (1997).
10. The missile tests in 1995–96 were also believed by some to have produced another unintended consequence: Beijing's missile tests helped Lee Teng-hui get elected with 54 percent of the popular vote.
11. Interviews in Beijing and Shanghai, June 6–15, 2000.
12. *Washington Post*, June 20, 2000.
13. For a recent analysis of Taiwan's "balancing" policy toward mainland China, see Steven Goldstein (1999).
14. Indeed, a possible military conflict between China and the United States over Taiwan is considered a likely scenario by the newly released Pentagon report to the U.S. Congress. *The Washington Times*, June 23, 2000.
15. Interviews in Beijing and Shanghai, June 6–15, 2000.

References

Acharya, Amitav. 1999. "International Relations Theory and Cross-Strait Relations." Paper presented at the International Forum on Peace and Security in the Taiwan Strait, Taipei, Taiwan, 26–28 July.
Checkel, Jeffrey T. 1998. "The Constructivist Turn in International Relations Theory." *World Politics* 50(January): 324–348.
Culver, John, and Pillisbury, Michael. 1998. "SESSION 5: Defense Policy and Posture II." In Hans Binnendijk, and Ronald N. Montaperto, eds., Institute for National Strategic Studies, National Defense University, http://www.ndu.edu/ndu/inss/boks/china/chinacont.html.
Garver, John W. 1997. *Face Off: China, the United States, and Taiwan's Democratization.* Seattle: University of Washington Press.
Goldstein, Steven. 1999. "Terms of Engagement: Taiwan's Mainland Policy." In Alastair

Iain Johnston and Robert S. Ross, eds., *Engaging China: The Management of an Emerging Power*, pp. 57–86. New York: Routledge.

Kowert, Paul. 1998. "Agent Versus Structure in the Construction of National Identity." In V. Kubálková, N. Onuf, and P. Kowert, eds., *International Relations in a Constructed World*, pp. 101–122. Armonk, NY: M.E. Sharpe.

Kubálková, Vendulka, Onuf, Nicholas, and Kowert, Paul, eds. 1998. *International Relations in a Constructed World*. Armonk, NY: M.E. Sharpe.

Onuf, Nicholas. 1989. *World of Our Making: Rules and Rule of Social Theory and International Relations*. Columbia: University of South Carolina Press.

———. 1998. "Constructivism: A User's Manual." In V. Kubálková, N Onuf, and P. Kowert, eds., *International Relations in a Constructed World*, pp. 58–78. Armonk, NY: M.E. Sharpe.

Shirk, Susan. 1997. "Asia-Pacific Regional Security: Balance of Power or Concert of Powers?" In D.A. Lake and P. Morgan, eds., *Regional Orders: Building Security in a New World*, pp. 245–270. University Park: Pennsylvania State University Press.

Wendt, Alexander. 1992. "Anarchy Is What States Make of It: The Social Construction of Power Politics." *International Organization* 46(Spring): 391–425.

———. 1994. "Collective Identity Formation and the International State." *American Political Science Review* 88(June): 384–396.

9

Identity and Foreign Policy: The Case of Islam in U.S. Foreign Policy

Nizar Messari

The starting point for this chapter is a rejection of the traditional idea that foreign policy builds bridges between preexisting entities called states. Instead I argue that as it is practiced, and by virtue of the fact that it deals with difference, foreign policy constructs national political identity. Foreign policy is then an identity-making tool that erects boundaries between the self and the other, defining in the process what are national interests. This is an idea developed in the poststructuralist/postmodern literature and I draw on R.B.J. Walker, William Connolly, Michael Shapiro, and David Campbell, and their works on ideas, identity, and otherness. However, I diverge from this literature when I define the construction of the other as emanating not only from negative differences and from antagonism, but also from positive approximation. All *others* can be divided into two different groups: allies and enemies. National political identity is produced or reproduced following its contact with allies *and* enemies. By dealing with enemies, identity is reinforced through the specification of what "identity" is not, presenting these differences as a threat to what the self is believed to be. However, I argue that there is also the other side of identity, the making of which is not to be overlooked. By dealing with allies, one's identity is reinforced by affirming the links and characteristics that make that specific other an ally. This is a positive identification of what constitutes the self. Thus, I argue, constructing identity through antagonisms is not a sufficient explanation, although it does provide a solid beginning to the explanation of foreign policy, national identity, and interest building.

This chapter is divided into two sections. I first present a theoretical discussion of foreign policy and of the concept of identity, adopting elements and ideas from the postpositivist school of International Relations (IR). In the model I develop, I argue that the construction of the other comes not only from difference vis-à-vis one's foes but also from the assimilation of "similar" differences, in what is the permanently ongoing construction project of identity.

Second, having developed my own model of identity making, I apply it to the case of the foreign policy of the United States toward political Islam. I emphasize not U.S. hostility toward Islam in general but the case of U.S. policy toward the Bosnian crisis in particular. Bosnia, in my view, represents a case of the positive construction of national identity through the representation of the other as "similar."

My argument is constructivist, but it is different from most of the contributions to this volume. Foreign policy, in my view, is a crucial factor in the permanently ongoing co-constitution of the state and its international environment. Identity is a *relational* concept insofar as it only makes sense to talk about the self when a relationship with the other is present. The constructivist component of this chapter is not as much rule oriented as it is based on a careful analysis of the pronouncements of the states engaged in a particular foreign policy relationship. A fundamental element in my argument is that the practice of "representing" the other in such discourses allows the construction of a specific representation of the self. This means that these representations are *practices of speech*. They are not the "faithful mirror of an already given real world" characteristic of the positivist use of language. They are more than this. In contradiction to the argument Campbell makes in two of his latest works, the line of constructivism I adopt in this chapter endorses the idea of the co-constitution of agents and structures. It rejects giving ontological precedence to either one or the other of these two.[1] The stress on language in my analysis does not mean the imposition of an idealist/materialist dichotomy. It means that practices of speech allow a representation of "the world out there" upon which agents will act in that same "world out there." The opposition Campbell insists on building between his analysis and specific constructivist approaches seems to me artificial. It goes also certainly beyond my concerns here.

In a nutshell, however, I share with mainstream constructivism the view that states' interests are not exogenously given. Like many postmodern and poststructuralist scholars, I see the relational, that is to say, the self and the other components, as playing a role in determining any state's identity and interests. Like rule-oriented constructivists, I consider very seriously language.

Discussing Self and Otherness

The distinction between a secure and peaceful domestic realm and an insecure and threatening international environment is present under many versions in IR. Mainstream IR scholars accept the dichotomy "secure inside"/ "threatening outside" as a given of the "real world out there." They deal with it as a permanent element in international politics. Postpositivist scholars note the same dichotomy but deal with it differently.

R.B.J. Walker, for instance, discusses the issue of opposed sides within and outside national borders. He assumes the idea of a coeval emergence of both inside and outside, and he develops it eloquently, pointing out that the building of the domestic realm would never have occurred without the simultaneous creation of an external realm. Walker sees the exclusivity of the political space inside national borders making of it a realm where universalism is sought. By the same token, the nonexistence of political life outside national borders negates universalism in the international environment, and makes of it a realm of difference, or even differences. The constitution of this opposition between both realms signals the construction of two antagonistic realms, with the outside a negation of the inside, and a threat to it. Concomitantly, this dichotomy creates national entities where citizens feel safe. It promotes states as the only political space possible, and it transforms into a threat whatever comes from outside national borders.[2] It creates a paradox since states with a central and hierarchical structure coexist without the existence of similar centralized and hierarchical structures at the international level. This paradox becomes acute when claims to particular kinds of identity and national citizenship take the lead over claims to universality and a global political community. From paradoxes like these, a danger is born; that is, the absence of an international political community brings an element of danger to all relationships among the members of that international community. In sum, the state can be seen as a *negative* arena where individuals can develop a *positive* sense of freedom. Securing order inside involves defining outside elements, the presence of which could eventually stand in the way of this domestic order. Once again it is a case of identifying the international realm as the origin of all dangers.

Ashley studies the building of dichotomies in IR theory and identifies what he calls the "heroic practice" of creating dichotomies, where the first element is positively presented and the second one negatively deduced. Each side needs the other to exist, even though their relationship is asymmetrical, hence dialectic. The second looks toward the first as a model and tries to emulate it. The first looks at the second as a threat and tries to avoid it. In IR theory, state sovereignty is usually put together dichotomously with international anarchy, securing the privileged first place to "state sovereignty." Compared to the world of danger that international anarchy represents, the state becomes the least of evils, and the only coherent and ordered alternative. Ashley adds that the "heroic practice" is the only one binding the sovereign state and anarchy. A necessary consequence of the absence of central rule in global life is anarchy, order being established solely within national borders because of the existence of central, supreme, and unified powers, that is, hierarchy.[3]

According to Campbell, identity and difference are linked in a relationship of opposition of one to the other. Identity is established in relation to a series of differences, in fact, not only internationally but also domestically. It requires difference in order to exist, and when identity is under pressure, the upholding of identity includes the conversion of difference into otherness. This conversion serves the purpose of securing a specific definition of a secure self. I differ from Campbell, however, when I argue that this conversion implies that there are two attitudes toward that which is different: one assimilates it, while the other transforms it into an other. Assimilation and otherness are two faces of the same issue: dealing with difference. On the domestic stage, difference is maintained as if it were indifferent, that is, as the confirmation of identity only. On the second, international stage, whenever identity is threatened, or has to be otherwise secured, there follows either the transformation of difference into otherness, or the assimilation of difference as a friend. Both reconfirm an embattled identity. Campbell also says that the threatening other is not perceived as being situated exclusively in the outside realm; thus many domestic groups are also presented as if they were outsiders. Indeed, since some domestic groups do not recognize themselves in the terms of the existing definition of national identity, this dispute puts them in conflict with the dominant identity, and transforms them into a threat. They are then treated in a similar manner to the external others: They are alienated and used in the process to construct a coherent national identity.

This complexity of the self/other relationship is explicit in Todorov's assertion of three different axes of otherness. According to him, the first axis is axiological. A value is expressed (such as good/bad, or superior/inferior). The second axis is paraxeological. There the issue is a distancing one or a rapprochement in relation to the other. In these terms, three different attitudes are expected: imposition of the self on the other, submission of the self to the other, or mere indifference. Third, there is the epistemic axis, where the question is one of acknowledging or ignoring the other. Both approaches define the self: the former by emphasizing similarities, the latter by avoiding the discovery that the other exists.[4] All three axes are interconnected, but none of them can be derived from the others. As the value of the self is supposed to be a given, the attitude toward the other is either an impositional one or one of indifference, which in epistemological terms means ignoring it. In the process of imposing the self, the choice is made between distancing the self from the other or approximating it, which translates into either otherness or assimilation respectively.

Connolly seems to agree with Todorov regarding the complex relationship between identity and difference when he asserts that support for a supposedly established identity ipso facto triggers a process of devising strategies to protect identity through the devaluation of difference. "But if one transcends the domestic field of identity through which the other is constituted, one loses the identity and standing needed to communicate with those one sought to inform"(Connolly 1991, 44). When difference is understood in all its complexity, richness, and diversity, it is recognized as another valid self, thus worthy of respect and tolerance. By the same token, the "demonization" of this complex and rich difference becomes an uneasy task, and the use of force more unlikely.

It is by using the antagonistic nature of the relationship between inside and outside, and identity and difference, and by using discourse and "language," that identity is permanently constructed and reconstructed. Once it is stated that all dangers come from outside, that the inside is secure and peaceful, national political speech will imply that the other represents a danger to the self. This relational aspect of identity emphasizes the role of foreign policy in its continuous making and remaking. The assumption here is that the construction of national identity takes place through "alterity." But the process of alienation is not the privilege of the powerful. It is instead a *mutual* process, operated by all parts in order to produce, reproduce, and confirm national identity. For instance, Der Derrian affirms that the genealogy of diplomacy shows that at the origin of the state system, all states emphasized what they considered to be their unique and rather distinguishing identity (Der Derrian 1987, 110–111). The issue was one of urgency, because the newly born state system was still in the process of making its criteria of inclusion and exclusion. In an environment of widespread fragility, mutual estrangement was not only an easy but also a pragmatic way out. The emergence of new and secular sovereigns instead of the centralized and religiously based sovereigns in Europe required the creation of new mediation instruments. Alienation was one of these instruments. The strategies of estrangement were crucial, therefore, in constituting secure national spaces and identities for all Europe's newly created states.

Consequently, different policies apply in different cases. In its relationship with the other, the general status of the self might either be equal or superior to it, provided that the self's moral superiority is never questioned. According to Michael Shapiro,

> any other that is accorded the same status as the self—it is seen as another equally worthy self which happens to reside in a different field of practices—

will be accorded the same prohibitions and restrictions from harm or interference as well as the same entitlements.

However, to the extent that the Other is regarded as something not occupying the same natural/moral space as the self, conduct toward the Other becomes more explosive. (Shapiro 1988, 102)

Accordingly, whereas behavior toward someone different who is perceived as equal is kept within bounds, it is not the case toward the other. No moral restraint is expected in the latter case, and no remorse results from the annihilation of the other. Justifications of annihilation vary from "it was in self-defense" to "it was necessary" to "there existed a serious threat, which now has been eliminated." Violence toward the other is already justified. By justifying the moral superiority of the self, the value of the self is exalted while the value of the other is deflated. The missionary objective of conquest and violence, in order to bring civilization to the other and make it equal to the self, then becomes a natural consequence of a "legitimate cause."

As I stated earlier, the process of identification is rooted in the relationship between identity and difference. But an identity is established in relation to several socially recognized differences. Identity is thus established politically in terms of the differences it seeks to fix. This political dimension seems "primordial" to the definition of both identity and difference. In foreign policy, since making identity through the relationship with the other is a political process, the international realm is ipso facto a political realm. The existence of an international political space is a direct consequence of the relationship with alterity. In this political space, identity and alterity are permanently made and remade, in a never-ending negotiated political process.

Identities are representations negotiated at specific moments and in given spaces. The emergence of selves stems from the articulation of these identities, diversified and contradictory though they may be. Two processes are party to the constitution of these selves: articulation and interpellation. According to Jutta Weldes, the former is a process whereby meaning is produced by establishing chains of connotation among different linguistic elements (Weldes 1996, 284–289). Terms are accepted within a given society and are then articulated to others. This deliberate construction creates a representation of life that is socially constructed and historically contingent, and permanently contested, too. Interpellation, on the other hand, takes place in two steps. In the first one, specific identities are created when social relations are depicted. One of the main characteristics of this stage is that different representations of the world entail different identities. In the second step, concrete individuals come to identify with these identities and with the representations under which they appear. From then on, things start to appear as "normal," as "they should be," and to reflect "the way the world really is."

An identification process creates "us versus them" narratives, in other words, where "us" corresponds to specific selves that transcend time and space.

In sum, the discourse of identity is possible in the mutual relationship between self and other. The mutual process of simultaneous recognition is central to identification, and both parts actively participate in it. The problem with collective identities is the formation process. According to Connolly, collective identity is

> best presented as a constellation of conjunctions joined by links of interdependence and disrupted by obstructions, frictions, and contingencies built into the interdependencies. A collective identity is a set of interlocking elements in strife and tension, a set periodically scrambled, reorganized, blocked and gridlocked by contingencies from within and without. But it tends to represent itself to itself as a relatively harmonious set of parts functioning smoothly together unless irresponsible, evil, sick, or naïve forces—inside or outside its boundaries—disrupt this harmony. (Connolly 1991, 204)

The insistence that the threat to the harmonious identity comes from outside the identity, which does not necessarily mean outside the territorial boundary, is important here since it reasserts the fragility of collective identity and the importance of its relationship with the other. This threat becomes then the primary target of policies of exclusion and negation. It is even more effective if it can be presented as evil, and if its presence within the collective identity can be translated into defects and failings in the latter. Moreover, if this threat is weak enough to be easily subjected to sanctions and punitive measures, and if it is also resilient enough to continuously renew its status as a source of evil, then it represents the perfect target for negating the sovereign.[5]

Identity materializes then in relationship with otherness. The existence of difference allows for the constitution of an apparently harmonious collective identity. Some would argue that this is a somewhat negative take on the constitution of national political identity, and that a more positive analysis is possible. The argument here is that any argument about the constitution of collective identity is indirectly exclusive since it takes difference for granted. To affirm that a national identity is X, Y, or Z means that non-X, non-Y, and/or non-Z are excluded. It is not enough to define what links people within given parameters. It is important to evaluate as well how this positive identification simultaneously excludes many others. Difference is hence intrinsic to identity, and permanently linked to it. Both can be defined only in terms of each other.

When applied to foreign policy, the concepts of alterity and difference produce a different analysis than that which we are used to. In this reading, the role of foreign policy is to transform difference into otherness, building borders in the process between self and other. Not all difference is transformed into otherness, as assimilation is a possible alternative in foreign policy making. Assimilation and otherness are the two facets of foreign policy making, the objective of which is to secure a national political identity. It is a conscious process and foreign policy makers deliberately follow it in order to construct a domestic collective identity. David Campbell is the main exponent of this alternative analysis of foreign policy. He argues that rather than being the external orientation of preexisting entities we call states, foreign policy is a boundary-making political practice, which is essential to produce and reproduce the identity of the state that it is supposed to represent.[6] Foreign policy serves also to contain challenges to the constituted identity of the state. Foreign policy is a discourse of power that is global in scope, but national in its legitimization impetus. It is only one of the multiple discourses of threat, though it has been granted the privilege of representing the most important danger.

In dealing with difference, three alternative forms of relationship are possible: to like or dislike it, to acknowledge or ignore it, and to impose the self on it or to accept its imposition. Regarding the third alternative, another form is possible: *total indifference to difference*. Liking or disliking difference might influence the third alternative in both ways. The same applies to knowing all about difference or ignoring it. This implies that the three levels of relationship between the self and difference are autonomous. In applying this to foreign policy, three attitudes seem to result: assimilating difference (or at least not alienating it), transforming difference into otherness, (and then justifying the use of violence in order to contain its supposed challenge to national identity), and remaining indifferent to difference (while keeping it under control in order to avoid surprising challenges to national identity).

The making of the other through foreign policy shows ways to understand the constitution of the self. The definition of the other, be it external or internal, underlies what kind of self is in the making. "A self constructed with a security-related identity leads to the construction of otherness on the axis of threats or lack of threats to that security, while a self identified as one engaged in 'crisis management'" (Shapiro 1988, 101–102) would represent otherness in terms of compromise and cooperation rather than clashes. The former leads to a politics of containment, whereas the latter leads to policies that reproduce a secure identity. In all cases, otherness is a result of how the self is defined, and how the self reveals itself. Consequently, on a continuum linking on the one hand total identity, and on the other complete difference, the former deserves equal treatment, while the latter is the object of alienation and hostile policies because of its difference.

According to Shapiro,[7] since animals are regarded as radical nonselves, and since the making of "humanity" depends on this representation, it becomes permissible to "slaughter" animals in "slaughter houses." This means that as long as other human beings are not represented as "radical nonselves," they deserve better treatment than animals. But the Nazis of the Second World War considered the Jews total nonselves. The Serbs during Bosnia's genocide considered Muslims total nonselves, too. The Hutus considered the Tutsis total nonselves also. In all three cases, these nonselves were totally outside any moral inhibition, and genocide could be perpetrated because it was then an existing option.

Ashley pioneered this particular conception of foreign policy. According to him, states should be denied any prior status in international terms, because of the coemergence of the state and the international system. It is necessary to understand foreign policy as a performance that imposes an interpretation of the world and therefore of its structure. Ashley suggests that it is legitimate to understand foreign policy as a specific type of interpretive performance whose effects comprehend

> (a) the constitution and empowering of states and other subjects (b) the defining of their socially recognized competencies and (c) the securing of the boundaries that differentiate domestic and international, economic, and political spheres of practice and, with them, the proper domains in which specific subjects may secure recognition and competently act. . . . In short, why not regard foreign policy as a specific kind of boundary producing political performance?[8]

According to Ashley, the upshot of this analysis is two main understandings of foreign policy. The first refers to all types of exclusion, and all practices of differentiation, and constitutes some objects as external in the process of dealing with them. This is the understanding that has constituted identity throughout history, and that distinguishes between self and otherness. The second understanding is not as implicated in the general process of identity making as the first one. Instead, it serves to "*reproduce* the constitution of identity made possible by 'foreign policy' and to *contain* challenges to the identity which results"(Campbell's emphasis, Campbell 1998a, 76). Campbell distinguishes between both readings by naming the first one foreign policy, while calling the second one Foreign Policy. Both understandings are important and inseparable in order to read foreign policy in the making. While identity is not the result of a state's Foreign Policy, the latter's role is important because it protects and reproduces the identity produced by foreign policy. Once we deal with an already constituted national identity, we are in the presence of a political performance that aims at reproducing it, and that contains all challenges to its continuity.

In dealing with the other, there are then two different categories: those who are close to the representation we make of our national identity, and those who are far removed from it. The main difference between the two categories of "different" in Foreign Policy making is that the first one appeals to the ethical responsibility of the self, whereas the second does not. The first category can be assimilated and is the object of active ethical responsibility. The second is the object of permitted violence and containment, and the ethical component is ignored. The first category represents a case to the reproduction of national identity. The second category constitutes a challenge to national identity, a challenge that needs to be contained.

In this context, the relationship with similar others means reproducing the existing identity. The basic two steps still exist: at first, foreign policy constructs an identity, then, Foreign Policy recognizes an other as similar to the constructed identity. The process of "recognition" is crucial: It is a socially constrained political performance in which *representations* of the self and of the other play a central role. Specific elements of identity between self and other are enhanced in order to *reproduce* them through the relationship with the (similar) other. This constructed similarity relies on representations and discourse to be effective since an emphasis needs to be made. The construction of national identity takes place by emphasizing "who this other really is." It relies on speech and language to make representations of the other. Once this representation is made, and once it is implied that "it is similar to us" and that "we ought to defend it," by defending it, the self reproduces those very same emphasized aspects of its own identity. In other words, by considering the defense of the other an ethical obligation, some specific aspects of the identity of the self are reproduced. This is how identity is constructed by dealing with a similar other.

Reproduction through assimilation is an exercise in representation, therefore, one that relies on the language and speech to be made. In speech like this, the silences are as important as what is said. Indeed, by relying on speech, some aspects are emphasized whereas others are not. Silence is maintained on whatever might characterize the representation differently. This game of representation, emphasis, and silence is played when dealing with the similar other and when dealing with the different other. In the case of assimilation, it plays with the positive aspects of the other. It reproduces a specific representation of national identity. The similarities are hence as important as the differences in the process of reproducing national identity.

Next, I apply this theoretical framework to U.S. policy toward activist Islam in general, and during the Bosnian crisis in particular. I show how the national identity of the United States was reproduced through its dealings with Bosnia's Muslims, in a continuous process of making and remaking national identity through foreign policy.

U.S. Policy Toward Islam—The Case of Bosnia

I defined foreign policy as an identity-making political performance in which the relationship with the other plays a central role. Self and other are mutually constitutive of each other. They both constitute and are constituted by their international environment. Demeaning and despising the other, or accepting its subjective and legitimately different narrative, are two radically opposed options. All *selves* deal with otherness to produce, reproduce, and confirm identity, which means that all *others* deal with identity, too. Demeaning or accepting alterity is the definitive form of behavior in constituting self/identity. By accepting it, a process of "assimilation" can be launched. It is to the empirical application of this framework that I now turn.

In the following part of the chapter, I show that since the end of the Cold War, Islam has replaced communism as the *different*. To do so, I show that the "world out there" is not a reality against which a theory should be checked. By interpreting the "world out there," I—as an observer—actively participate in its construction. The words of policy makers are as important as their deeds. Not only what is said is fundamental, but *what is not said* is also crucial. Hence, my task is to bring together policy statements—and silences—in order to make a case for the construction of friends and enemies. I specially focus on the case of friends or allies. Implicit in this is the fact that traditions are built out of nothing, truths are constituted as eternal, and realities are represented in specific ways rather than others to justify one set of policies rather than another.

Many analysts of U.S. foreign policy present Islam as the successor to communism as a threat to the United States in the post–Cold War era (Quandt 1997). This is possibly a valid comparison, to the extent that Islamic activism stands as one of the main threats to the U.S. interests in the Middle East and elsewhere. However, some factors cloud this comparison. First of all, the Cold War was a confrontation between two ideological models. It mobilized two countries at the global level. With Islam, there is not a specific country that embodies the Islamic threat, although Iran tends to be considered a dangerous regime of this sort. Moreover, because the USSR was a nuclear power, it represented a major threat to the existence of the United States, while Islam is far from representing such an overwhelming danger. It can also be said that the Cold War was a confrontation between two states, whereas Islam can simultaneously be a state, a political party, a "terrorist" organization, and so on. Finally, communism became a threat after the end of World War II, whereas Islam has had confrontations with the West since the Crusades in the eleventh century. While U.S. decision makers may not situate their relationship with Islam in this historical perspective, many Muslims certainly do. There is another disturbing element in this comparison. Presenting U.S. behavior toward communism as a model of what may be done with Islam implies that history repeats itself, and that what is valid in a given situation holds as valid in what appears to be similar circumstances elsewhere. Deterrence, containment, the domino theory and other unfortunate Cold War notions might be seen as valid under these circumstances. Besides the differences I have just pointed to, however, there are two additional observations one can make. U.S. policy toward the USSR was not necessarily correct. The mistakes committed then should be avoided now. Even more importantly, a U.S.-centered view pays little attention to the policies and priorities of other states. U.S.-centered narratives, as used to face the USSR, should not be repeated when dealing with Islam.

Intellectual Foundations of U.S. Foreign Policy Toward Islam

U.S. foreign policy toward Islam is intellectually informed by two academic tendencies: neoutilitarianism and orientalism. The former, in the guise of neorealism/neoliberalism, permeates both academia and decision making. One of the main features of neoutilitarianism is that it discards sociohistorical understanding of the other in order to deal with difference, and to rely on game theory–like logic. The focus of academic debate is then whether players seek relative or absolute gains. The rationality of the participants is assumed and never problematized. The players are considered to be anonymous, homogeneous, and interchangeable. Particular cultures, historical backgrounds, and religious beliefs are not deemed plausible explanations of behavior. Players' positions in the game, and their assessment of absolute or relative gains as intervening variables, are the sole basis for explaining their behavior. Islam, or anything else, does not seem to matter; all the players are believed to react the same way when facing similar situations.

Orientalism as the second source of the attitude of the United States toward Islam claims to be derived directly from "the very nature of Islam."[9] Many Western specialists in Islamic studies, like Bernard Lewis, highlight what they see as Islam's inherent expansionism and totalitarianism, Islam's incompatibility with democracy, and the impossibility of separating religion and state in Islam. These arguments are based on presumptions about how Islam *really* is: how different Islam is from the West, and how incompatible Islam is with Western, Judeo-Christian civilization. The problem is that while comparing religions and civilizations is legitimate, comparisons should deal with what is comparable: Theory should be compared with theory, practice with practice.

This applies to the several characteristics that are said to be *inherent* to

Islam. Bernard Lewis, one of the most prestigious orientalists in the United States, argues that it is necessary to understand *Islam's specificity* (Lewis 1993, 135–136). According to him, religion is the single most important identity for any Muslim, rather than nationhood or statehood. He assumes that it is absurd to judge Islam using ideas developed in the Western tradition, like the separation of state and church. His interpretation of Islam, according to Esposito, is of a clash of distinct and mutually exclusive civilizations, one emphasizing Islamic differences, and one that discards rationality and the possibility of compromise when dealing with Islam (Esposito 1992, 179). Esposito observes that denigrating Islam is not a twentieth-century characteristic among Western intellectuals, and cites Renan, Voltaire, and Montesquieu as eminent Europeans who "satanized" Islam (Esposito 1992, 46).

Islamic activism is perceived among U.S. policy makers as an aggressive movement, and one that is anti-Western in general, and anti-American in particular. Compromise with Islam is allegedly difficult if not impossible, and Islam is considered a threat to secular and modernizing movements in Islamic states. Stressing Islamic activism as different has far-reaching policy-relevant consequences. It leads to supporting authoritarian regimes against Islamic movements in many Muslim countries. Such policies, however, are not unprecedented and are a repetition of what occurred during the Cold War in relation to a range of revolutionary movements. Today, authoritarian regimes in Islamic countries are perceived as the last solid defense of modernity against retrogressive Islamic movements perceived to be a throwback to the Middle Ages. According to Anthony Lake, a former National Security Advisor to President Clinton, the dividing line is neither civilizational nor religious:

> No, it runs instead between oppression and responsive government, between isolation and openness, between moderation and extremism. . . . Our foe is oppression and extremism, whether in religious or secular guise. We draw the line against those who seek to advance their agenda through terror, intolerance or coercion. . . . *There should be no doubt (that) Islamic extremism poses a threat to our nation's interest.* (emphasis added)[10]

The line is clearly drawn and the threat clearly stated. It seems as if Islamic oppression is worse than secular oppression. To whom it is worse is another issue. The regime of Iran's Shah is still considered by some U.S. conservatives a symbol of a modernizing state, and the representation of an enlightened despotic regime. By the same token, the Islamic revolution in Iran is still considered a defeat of modernism and of advanced Westernization. Today in Algeria, the military is believed to stand for modernity against a violent and bloody movement based on Islam. Massacres committed by

Islamists are denounced as a sign of barbarism, but the role of the state in these same massacres is seldom questioned in the United States. In sum, the Western representation of Islam is a negative one, which makes that religion look like a threat to the West, its civilization, and its values.

The United States and Islam

In contrast to the allegedly monolithic U.S. policy toward Islamic activism, the United States's official line toward Islam is one of tolerance and respect. It is concerned with promoting typical U.S. traditions that include defending human rights, democracy, and free speech. Officially, the United States maintains a position of apparent neutrality toward domestic matters of Islamic states. The United States seems to adopt a pragmatic position in its dealings with Muslim countries. On the one hand, after Israel, Egypt is the second largest recipient of U.S. foreign aid, and Saudi Arabia, Pakistan, and Turkey are close U.S. allies, the latter being a NATO member. During the Balkan war that resulted from the collapse of former Yugoslavia, the United States sided with Bosnia's Muslims, who were perceived as the main victims of ethnic cleansing and the other dirty events of that war. On the other hand, other Islamic states figure on any short list of what were until recently labeled "rogue states": Iran, Iraq, and Libya are frequently joined by the Sudan and Syria and several movements such as the Hamas and Islamic Jihad. These are considered to represent threats to regional stability in the Middle East, to U.S. interests, and to the interests of U.S. allies. Islamic radicals are believed to be among the main obstacles to the conclusion of two ongoing peace processes: one in the Middle East and the other in the Balkans. According to President Clinton,

> America refuses that our civilizations must collide. We respect Islam . . . But in the Middle East and elsewhere across the world, the United States sees a contest, a contest between the forces that transcend civilization—a contest between tyranny and freedom, terror and security, bigotry and tolerance, isolation and openness. It is the age-old struggle between fear and hope. This is the conflict that grips the Middle East today.[11]

It is not necessary to reaffirm that the United States represents the positive and Islamic activism the negative pole of President Clinton's eloquent dichotomies. From here on, an opposition between two worlds is constructed, clearly stating where the forces of evil and where the forces of good lie. Presenting the "conflict that grips the Middle East" in these terms, the president of the United States imposes sharp distinctions, based on what are perceived to be clear antagonisms in the region. The policy of the United

States is one that seeks actively to "contain those states and organizations which promote or support religious or secular extremism; and help from a community of like-minded Middle Eastern states which share our goals of free markets (and) democratic enlargement."[12] Indeed, the Middle East is the area of largest contact between Islam and the West. In that region, the objectives of the United States are defined by Clinton Administration officials in unequivocal terms. Accordingly,

> The United States has seven major interests in the Middle East:
> - Securing a just, lasting, secure and comprehensive peace between Israel and its Arab neighbors . . .
> - Maintaining (a) deep-seated commitment to Israel's security and well-being;
> - Developing a framework for security in the inherently unstable Gulf region in order to ensure fair commercial access to its petroleum reserves on which we and the major industrial powers are vitally dependent;
> - Checking the proliferation of weapons of mass destruction and the systems to deliver them;
> - Combating terrorism;
> - Ensuring fair access to the region for American business;
> - And promoting more open political and economic systems, and respect for human rights and the rule of law.[13]

In all four items of regional security, Islamic activism seems to be the main obstacle to U.S. interests. The policy of the United States toward the renewed assertiveness of Islamic activism is based on two major principles: "First, we have no one-size-fits-all policy toward Islam. In fact, we don't have a policy pigeonhole called 'political Islam' . . . Islamic political activism becomes a factor for us when it impinges on a specific U.S. foreign policy goal or interest."[14] The United States has made clear that it has no quarrel with Islam as a religion. The United States, however, identifies Islamic activism with disrespect for basic human rights and democracy, with the oppression of minorities, with the rejection of international law, and with a kind of radicalism that excludes the possibility of a dialogue or compromise. The United States sees in Islamic activism a threat to its interests, and to the stability of its allies. Two broader implications follow. On the one hand, what used to happen during the Cold War is occurring again with Islamic countries. Wherever Islamic activism is present, authoritarian regimes are tolerated and sometimes supported as symbols of the *contest* between modernity and barbarism. These regimes can be authoritarian or based on Islamic law, but they remain faithful to their Western alliances. Human rights, elections, and free speech are sacrificed on the altar of saving democracies from nondemocrats. The formula of "one person, one vote, one time," first applied to Algeria in particular, and the weakness of democratic thinking in

Islamic states in general, became the justification for tolerating authoritarian policies to *save democracy and restore it.* The second implication, which is linked to the first one, distinguishes between two Islams. One is radical, uncompromising, and bent on a continuous rejection of the West. The other is Westernized and modern. This Islam may accept international law and seems to be prepared to deal with the West. It does not matter that in some places it is authoritarian, and in other places more religiously based than any rogue state. Its principal asset is that it is not activist, and that it accepts "dealing" with the West. This is an extremely Western and U.S.-centered narrative that disregards the dynamics of local cultures and societies. The other needs to change and become friendlier in order to be accepted and assimilated as a friend or ally by the United States. The full respect of difference is out of question. Alterity, represented in this case by activist Islam, exists only as a derivation of U.S. centered narratives, policies, and ultimately, identities.

The United States in Bosnia, or the Case for Positive Engagement with Islam

Bosnia is the case of the Muslim friend or ally. On Todorov's axiological axis, Bosnia's Muslims are "good" since they were victims of genocide. On the paraxeological axis, Bosnia's Muslims are "assimilable" since they are Westernized Muslims who defend a multiethnic state. On the epistemic axis, Americans know very little about Bosnia and its Muslims, which is an opportunity to *represent* Bosnia in very specific ways.

Once Bosnia's Muslims were identified as potential friends, the politics of reproducing national identity started taking place: traditions were constructed, histories were written, and the representation of a multiethnic, democratic Bosnia—respectful of human rights and ethnic diversity, and the victim of genocide—was put in place. National identity was produced, I argue, by emphasizing the similarities between the United States and the representation *made* of Bosnia's Muslims. Bosnia provided the United States with the opportunity at the same time of enhancing specific aspects of U.S. identity through its similarities with Bosnia, and of helping victims and saving them from aggressors—another crucial aspect in the constitution of a positive representation of America's self.

Three arguments explain U.S. policy in Bosnia and its siding with the Muslims and Croats against the Serbs. The first is that the Muslims and Croats were victims of Serbian aggression, which included the horrifying process of ethnic cleansing, mass rape, and the siege of Sarajevo. The second argument is that Bosnia's Muslims are different from most other Muslims. Finally, there were the silences and "accommodating" representations Bosnia's Islam allowed.

Regarding the first argument, although the Muslim population was clearly the main victim of the conflict, the sympathy and readiness to help of the United States were not immediately forthcoming. During the summer of 1992, media images of Bosnia's suffering and of the treatment of Muslim prisoners of war brought an outpouring of sympathy from Western public opinion. Consistent and credible reports of the ethnic cleansing that took place in the form of mass killings, the massive expulsion of populations from their hometowns, and mass rape were so compelling that European and American officials were moved "to do something about it."[15] Croats and Muslims were the main displaced populations as Muslim towns, including the capital Sarajevo, were shelled and placed under siege. The U.S. State Department's 1993 Annual Report on Human Rights called the Muslim suffering during the beginning of the war a carnage worse than anything seen in Europe since Nazi times.

Consequently, U.S. officials, together with European leaders, pressured the United Nations Security Council (UNSC) to adopt resolutions that clearly identified Muslims as the main victims of the war and to protect them. Such measures included the creation of safe havens where Muslim populations could seek refuge from Serb threats. The same measures also created "No Flight Zones," the objective of which was to limit the Serb threat to Muslim populations. UNSC resolutions also provided escorts to food convoys heading for Muslim towns and for weapons air-dropped into Muslim areas. In sum, a representation of Bosnia's Muslims as victims was constructed mainly through the official statements of the United States, UN resolutions, and other reports. The construction of this representation relied on the U.S. collective memory of the Second World War and on dichotomies (aggressors/victims) as figures of speech. The representation of alterity as the victim of oppression, with the resort to the United States for help, constructed an American identity as *justice maker, an identity of compassion and of tolerance.*

The second construction and the second argument used to justify the United States' engagement in favor of Bosnia's Muslims relied on another dichotomy. This second dichotomy put "nice Muslims" (in Bosnia) face-to-face with "dangerous Muslims" (in many other places). Bosnia's Muslims were represented as different from many other Muslims throughout the world. Prewar Bosnia was represented among the ethnic and religious components of the former Yugoslavia as a place of tolerance and conviviality. From symbolic gestures such as Sarajevo's organization of the 1984 Winter Olympics, to more substantial modes of behavior such as women's role in Bosnian society, Islam in Bosnia became represented as a tolerant and "modern" Islam. It was neither a militant Islam nor an exclusivist and intolerant Islam. A different religious belief did not stop Bosnia's Muslims from seeking the help of the United States or eventual European Union membership. By helping this tolerant component of Islam, the United States reinforced its own representation as one of tolerance and religious freedom. Alterity as not so different reinforced the positive aspects of the self-representation of identity.

The United States also constructed a representation of what Bosnia *is*, and sided with that. This was a representation that relied on many silences. For instance, interethnic conviviality was deteriorating prior to the beginning of the war in the Balkans, and Bosnia's main Muslim leader had voiced sympathy for the idea of creating a pan-Islamic state in which Bosnia would be included.[16] The leaders of the three ethnic communities (Serbs, Croats, and Muslims) were all radicals who openly defended their own ethnic groups rather than the idea of constituting a multiethnic entity.[17] Nevertheless, the United States still *represented Bosnia's Muslims as victims, Westernized, and favoring multiethnicity and democracy.* The Muslim leaders' noncompliance with the Dayton peace accords was never the kind of motive for retaliation that Serb noncompliance was. The United States created a specific representation of Bosnia and perpetuated it. The objective of this representation was to reproduce certain facets of U.S. identity by positively identifying this self with its other. The similarities constructed between the United States and Bosnia's Muslims were part of a process of confirming a *representation* of national identity.

It would be wrong to argue that this model of U.S. foreign policy results exclusively from the actions of the United States. Bosnia's Muslims do indeed seem to be different from many other Muslims, although not *all* other Muslims. It is the interaction between the self and each one of these different others that determines identity. When alterity is represented *positively*, similarities are stressed, and links are established with this welcome other. This is an affirmative process of identity making, one that deals with a not-so-different alterity.

Conclusion

In its foreign policy, the United States relies exclusively on U.S.-centered narratives where alterity is a mere derivation of U.S. identity. The other does not exist per se, but only as a tool in the making of U.S. identity. The United States does not deal with alterity as an equal, which has its own legitimate narrative. Consequently, befriending or demonizing alterity are two faces of the same coin. The objective of this performance is to reproduce a given representation of U.S. identity. The role of foreign policy is to reproduce national identity through the way it deals with alterity.

From this perspective, the U.S. policy toward Islam seeks to reproduce the U.S. identity. Islam is not represented in its complexity. It is only instrumental in the process of reproducing U.S. identity. Bosnia's Islam was represented as a positive Islam in order to reproduce precise aspects of the U.S. identity. If ever the United States apprehends Islam in its full complexity, the U.S. identity will certainly change, but this has not so far been the case.

Foreign policy is a tool, then, in making and constructing national identity, not only through rejection and opposition but also through assimilation and the construction of similarities. Through the use of speech, similarities are found or constructed between the self and the other, and a national identity is constructed by emphasizing these similarities and affirming them as part of that identity.

Notes

1. David Campbell has addressed the issue of constructivism and its differences with his own framework in two of his latest works (Campbell 1998a, 1998b).

2. Walker argues that "relations between states are conventionally understood as the negation of the community presumed to be possible within the sovereign state" (Walker 1993, 171).

3. For more on Ashley's concept of heroic practice, see Ashley (1988, 229–239).

4. Todorov claims that by trying to know the other, its complexities and richness become obvious, which makes alienating it extremely difficult. Simplistic conclusions that the self is superior and thus has the right to conquer in order to bring civilization, disappear. Nuances are introduced, and with them doubts about the claimed superiority of the self. The solution is then to ignore the other in order to be able to conquer it, and impose the self on it. However, Todorov argues that the relationship with alterity can vary in different directions from one level to the other. One can perfectly well know the other, while disliking it and trying hard to assimilate it.

5. The conditions of negation are listed in Connolly (1991, 207).

6. This discussion is central to Campbell's argument (1998a, 75).

7. For more details on Shapiro's views, see Shapiro (1988, 101–102).

8. This view is defended by Ashley (1987, 53).

9. On the issue of Orientalism, see Esposito (1992). See also Lewis (1993), Said (1979, 1981), and Lewis's reply (1993, chapter 6).

10. Former National Security Advisor Anthony Lake's remarks presented at the Washington Institute for Near East Policy, Washington, DC, on May 17, 1994. As quoted in Hibbard and Little, 1997, p. 6.

11. President Clinton before the Jordanian Parliament in 1994.

12. Lake, as quoted in Hibbard and Little.

13. Address of Robert Pelletreau, Assistant Secretary of State for Near Eastern Affairs, before the Foreign Policy Association, New York, November 27, 1995.

14. Address by R. Pelletreau before the Council on Foreign Relations, New York, May 8, 1996.

15. Estimates vary, but it does not seem an exaggeration to say that approximately 25,000 Bosnian women were raped during the first months of the conflict. Several hearings on ethnic cleansing were held at the U.S. Senate and House of Representatives. At

the international level, ethnic cleansing was also the subject of reports and condemnations. See, for instance, U.S. Secretary of State Lawrence Eagleberger's statement at the International Conference on the Former Yugoslavia, Geneva, December 16, 1992.

16. Sabrina Ramet claims that by 1989, the deterioration of interethnic relations was already visible (1996, 243).

17. See Boyd's strong views on this subject (1998).

References

Ashley, Richard. 1987. "Foreign Policy as Political Performance." *International Studies Notes* 13(2): 51–55.

———. 1988. "Untying the Sovereign State: A Double Reading of the Anarchy Problematique." *Millenium: Journal of International Studies* 17(2): 227–262.

Boyd, Charles. 1998. "Making Bosnia Work." *Foreign Affairs* 77(1): 42–55.

Campbell, David. 1998a. *Writing Security: United States Foreign Policy and the Politics of Identity*, rev. ed. Minneapolis: Minnesota University Press.

———. 1998b. *National Deconstruction: Violence, Identity, and Justice in Bosnia.* Minneapolis: Minnesota University Press.

Connolly, William. 1991. *Identity/Difference—Democratic Negotiations of Political Paradox.* Ithaca, NY: Cornell University Press.

Der Derrian, James. 1987. *On Diplomacy—A Genealogy of Western Estrangement.* Oxford: Blackwell.

Esposito, John L. 1992. *The Islamic Threat—Myth or Reality?* New York: Oxford University Press.

Hibbard, Scott W., and David Little. 1997. *Islamic Activism and U.S. Foreign Policy.* Washington, DC: USIP Press.

Lewis, Bernard. 1993. *Islam and the West.* New York: Oxford University Press.

Quandt, William. 1997. "Foreword." In Scott W. Hibbard, and David Little, *Islamic Activism and US Foreign Policy.* Washington, DC: USIP Press.

Ramet, Sabrina P. 1996. *Balkan Babel—The Disintegration of Yugoslavia from the Death of Tito to Ethnic War*, 2d ed. Boulder, CO: Westview Press.

Said, Edward W. 1979. *Orientalism.* New York: Vintage Books.

———. 1981. *Covering Islam.* New York: Pantheon.

Shapiro, Michael J. 1988. *The Politics of Representation—Writing Practices in Biography, Photography, and Policy Analysis.* Madison: University of Wisconsin Press.

Walker, Rob B.J. 1993. *Inside/Outside: International Relations as Political Theory.* Cambridge, UK: Cambridge University Press.

Weldes, Jutta. 1996. "Constructing National Interests." *European Journal of International Relations* 2(3): 275–318.

III
Reflections

III
Reflections

10

Commonsense Constructivism and Foreign Policy: A Critique of Rule-Oriented Constructivism

Ralph Pettman

How instrumental is foreign policy analysis? A rhetorical question, surely, since International Relations (IR), as thought and taught in the United States, shares with American culture at large a penchant for popular mechanics. As a consequence, it is no surprise to find that most American (and American-trained) scholars speak of constructivism and foreign policy as if it were some kind of building site, or some kind of apparatus.

The most instrumental of such scholars are those who exalt the use of the hypothetico-deductive method. Analysts like these routinely cast their research in falsifiable form. They discriminate between dependent and independent variables, and they employ quantitative means to assess cause and effect.

Those constructivists who exalt this approach are typically the most instrumental, too. By accepting on the one hand the socially constructed character of foreign policy, and by reaffirming on the other their commitment to social science in its most rigorous of forms, they are able, they believe, to stay contemporary, while conserving the hyperrationalist agenda of American modernism. This is the way that mainly mainstream scholars have used the concept of "constructivism" to keep postmodernism at bay.

Analysts like these are enjoined to turn at once to the next chapter. They are likely to find it much more congenial.

Those constructivists less extreme in their commitment to social scientism are enjoined to read on, however. This chapter is written from outside the American context. Its author was not schooled in the American tradition. He has never come to see an issue-area like that of foreign policy making as one to be explained in mechanical, utilitarian, can-do terms. What follows is not about whether constructivism works, therefore, but rather how constructivism should be understood.

The basic argument here is about the pursuit of constructivist concerns *in practice*. More specifically, it takes issue with the conservative way, in both its hard-line and soft-line versions (Pettman 2000), the concept of constructivism is used. It also takes issue with more revisionist approaches, however, like those described and explained in the previous chapters. It is much closer to these revisionist approaches (which elsewhere I have called "social theory" constructivism) than it is to the conservative ones, and as such it should prove analytically more congenial to those who are revisionist. It is a critique of both, however, arguing in the process for its own way of studying foreign policy, that is, the "commonsense" way.

Taking Issue with Mainstream Conservatives

Taking issue with the mainstream conservatives means confronting the disciplinary power of the positivists in North American IR (Smith 2000). It also means confronting the way even those who would reject positivist methodologies feel obliged to talk in terms that get them a hearing. Not talking in these terms means risking the most effective of all forms of criticism, namely, calculated indifference. North American scholars of IR of a revisionist bent still have to sound like dedicated rationalists to get read by positivists, and to get taken at least halfway seriously by them. Hence the care exhibited by most of those who would counter positivist hegemony to speak "respectably."

The conservative constructivists' reluctance to acknowledge the pioneering role that Nicholas Onuf played in applying the concept of constructivism to world affairs is highly instructive in this regard. Onuf was the first to analyze the discipline in constructivist terms (Onuf 1989). Because he did not do so in hyperrationalist (positivist) terms, however, his germinal contribution was marginalized. In the major summaries of the development of the concept that were subsequently made by mainstream scholars, for example, his contribution was either ignored altogether or referred to only in passing (Katzenstein, Keohane, and Krasner 1998, 674–675).

Confronting the assumptions upon which the conservative mainstream bases what they say means analyzing the limits the ideology of rationalism sets. This in turn means analyzing the modernist politicocultural project, of which rationalism is the definitive feature.

All rationalists prioritize the use of reason as an end in itself, a commit-

ment that results in reifying language and ultimately instrumentalist explanations. Not all rationalists do so to the same extent, however. The Miami IR
Group's members are not as rationalistic as the positivists, since the latter
stand back at twice-remove from the world to describe and explain it, and
the Miami IR Group does not. Indeed, the Miami IR Group constructivists
overtly oppose hyperrationalist approaches, proclaiming the significance of
trying to understand people's feelings as well. Thus, though Miami IR Group
thinkers stand back from the world to objectify, they also stand close to
subjectify, seeking to benefit not only from the outlook rationalism provides,
but also from the insights more proximal research techniques can confer.

The Revisionist Dilemma

The problems raised by needing to get heard are hardy perennials. Knowing
is a social process, and, as such, knowers make in-groups and out-groups.
Being "in" means sharing the same basic values and ideas, and even then,
acceptance may be denied for other reasons altogether. Being "out," and
wanting to be given serious consideration by those who are "in," means either some form of confrontation (though with insufficient clout, as already
indicated, one may simply be ignored), or it requires more conciliatory initiatives, that is, it requires proposals that do not look like a rejection of the
in-group's basic values and ideas (though even then, it is at the discretion of
the members of the in-group whether they listen or not).

There is no formula for getting a sympathetic hearing from those who
have the most disciplinary power. This is why revolutionists end up railing
from without, hoping for radical change and risking total rejection, while
revisionists end up seeking reforms from within, hoping to have some incre-
mental influence while risking a degree of cooption.

This is a book by revisionists, not revolutionists. As part of a consciously
counterhegemonic attempt to rethink mainstream foreign policy analysis, it wants
to undermine and subvert. It does not, therefore, confront. It has no intention of
failing from the first. That is why most of those who wrote this book use an
analytic language that is sufficiently acceptable to challenge the hegemonic
mainstream from within, not without, redescribing the discipline using rule-
oriented concepts and categories in such a way as to make sense to those who
posit positivism, but not to concede the need to apply positivist techniques.

The Limits Rationalism Sets

There is a more abstract problem than that of disciplinary compliance, however,
and that is to do with the limits rationalism sets. It is to do with the limits mod-

ernist thinking places upon knowing foreign policy, and the sense that an issue area like this one can be known wisely and well only by going beyond them.

There are limits, in other words, to both the moderate form of rationalism (that uses systematic analysis only) and the extreme form of rationalism (that exalts the positivist approach). The point here is not the difference between these two forms, however, notable though this difference may be, but what they have in common.

When manifest in constructivist research, both kinds of rationalism require the same initial mind-move. Both recommend our stepping back mentally from the world, the better to see the patterns apparent in how we behave. Both start by making an objectivizing, individuating, metasocial mind-move. This is, after all, the definitive feature of modernist thought. Which is why both the more moderate and the more extreme forms of constructivism in this regard are modernist in terms of the priority their proponents place upon the use of reason as an end in itself.

The moderate constructivists who wrote this book are not positivists, however. They move mentally no further away from the world than their systematic analyses need. The objectifying they are able to do by standing back to look at foreign policy at one remove only they believe to be enough to make sense of it in terms of a language of rules and rule. Not being positivists, they are keen to listen as well, finding in what people say an important way of discerning what their behavior means. They are able, in this basically nonrationalistic fashion, to combine modernist rationalism with the process of going beyond the limits that rationalism sets.

Conservative constructivists are positivists. As such, they take the modernist mind-move one step further than moderate constructivists do. They see the initial mental step away from the social context in which we are embedded as being insufficient to sustain the kind of scientific thinking they exalt. So they objectify further. This allows them greater mental distance, and use of such research techniques as rational choice theory, game theory, and the hypothetico-deductive method.

Both are defenders of the rationalist faith nonetheless. Both think of rationalism as necessary. Conservative constructivists want to be more than merely systematic. To them, the kind of rationalism that allows only this more limited degree of objectivity is not sufficient. The counter-hegemonic moderates, by contrast, are quite happy with the mental distance systematic analysis requires. They ask for no greater degree of rationalist objectivity than one mental step back allows them. Indeed, they are prepared to use nonrationalist subjectivity to stand close to listen as well. Both step back from the world to talk about it in objectifying ways, however.

Transgressing the Limits Rationalism Sets by Taking Part

It is argued here that going beyond the limits that rationalism sets can be done in a more thoroughgoing fashion than standing close to listen allows. This requires entertaining a third kind of constructivism, however, one that subjectifies as a matter of course *and as radically as possible*. Subjectifying like this requires us to come much closer to our subject. It enjoins us not only to listen to what those who participate say about it (a move the Miami IR Group has no problem making) but also to take part ourselves (a move most of its members do not make).

It is argued here, then, that going beyond the limits rationalism sets means more than ascertaining what those who make or think about foreign policy say they are doing (an injunction rule-oriented constructivists are happy to observe). It also means participating ourselves in the foreign policy practices we want to understand and explain (an injunction only the commonsense constructivists routinely observe). It means finding out what is involved experientially *as well as* analytically, not only from the "horse's mouth," but from living with horses as one of the herd.

Why? Because so much of what we need to know is in other people's heads. It has to do with perceptions and intentions of an individual, communal, or collective kind, and getting knowledge of these things takes more than trying harder to listen. It requires participation as well.

Conservative constructivists get access to people's perceptions and intentions by objectifying. They stand back to observe the patterns human practice makes from a mental distance. In standing back we get only indirect access to what people think and feel, however. We have to infer their perceptions and intentions from what we "see" them doing, and as a result, our inferences may or may not be accurate or fair.

Rule-oriented constructivists also objectify using their own particular categories and concepts in the process, but they are prepared to listen to the speech acts people use as well. In doing so they are better able to ascertain how some people wield power over others. When a repeated pattern is apparent in this regard, Miami IR Group constructivists talk of "rules making rule."

Being prepared to listen means the possibility of being duped. People bluff and lie, for example. And although their lies can be very revealing to the constructivist who discerns them, as rule-oriented constructivists argue themselves, there is a problem in that we may not discern them, or we may lie to ourselves, because of false consciousness perhaps.

Hence the need to take part. Hence the need for a second, more radically subjectifying move, one that invites our personal participation. In taking part we completely lose our objectivity, of course, surrendering ourselves to our impressions of what we see and hear. Hence the need eventually to stand back and objectify again. Hence the need for a rationalist reprise to allow us to ask if what we have found out is at least in some sense true. Unless we take part, however, something that involves considerably more than standing close to listen, we will find the limits rationalism sets still pressing in upon us. Without taking part *as well*, for example, what we conclude may conceal or even distort what makes for foreign policy rules and world political rule. Without using the most proximal and immediate of methodologies possible, our best attempts at foreign policy analysis may still not succeed.

One reason why this is so is because in objectifying we also individuate. We learn to create a sense of ourselves that is separate from the society in which we live. Without this "other" within, in fact, it is not possible to put the world mentally at a distance and to "see," with the eye of the mind as it were, what is going on there. Some such platform is unavoidable if we are to apply an objectifying perspective, this individuated self being the mental place from which we view the exteriorized version of reality that becomes our subject.

This is a very particular kind of self, typical en masse only of modernist, rationalist cultures of the Western kind, like the North American one. Compare, however, those nonmodernist, nonrationalist, non-Western cultures that do not have preconstituted "individuals" in them. These cultures do not stand a putative "self" up against a separate "society." In these cultures, to interpolate "ideas" or "rules" in the way conservative and rule-oriented constructivists do makes no sense at all. The people in these cultures simply do not constitute discrete agents of the modernist kind. They are social/individual beings instead, who think and act in nonmodernist, nondichotomized, nonindividuated ways; both the conservative and revisionist portrayals of such people is misconstrued.

The Japanese, for example, have not (yet) learned en masse to prioritize the modernist sense of self. They do not, as a consequence, fit the modernist constructivist description of agents and social structures, whether conservative (positivist) or revisionist (rule oriented). This does not mean the Japanese do not have states, or a foreign policy. It does suggest, however, that the terms of reference modernists provide are not as universal as they think. In applying modernist terms of reference as if they were universal, that is, we misrepresent the making of foreign policy in a country like Japan. Our understanding of those who make it becomes distorted. To the extent that foreign policy is the result of those involved, therefore, as opposed to being the outcome of some whole-system logic like neorealism, to the extent that we don't appreciate what it means to make a foreign policy as a nonindividuated nonmodernist, our analysis of foreign policy will fail to move beyond the limits that rationalism sets.

The antidote, I would argue, is first to get close to listen to what Japanese policy makers say they are doing, preferably in their own language. This is a move rule-oriented constructivists happily make. The next step, however, is to take part in their foreign policy making processes. This is a step that rule-oriented constructivists, in the main, do *not* take. And where one of them does make it, like Vendulka Kubálková in her study of Gorbachev's "new thinking," she does so only by going beyond the basic strategy that rule-oriented constructivists recommend.

Foreign policy makers are those who construct foreign policy. They do not just inherit it. That is to say, they learn what it means to make their foreign policy, and they act on what they have learned. These lessons become their "common sense" about the subject, and as such, they are an important part of what we need to know if we are to explain world affairs. This kind of "common sense" is not to be had by standing back to look, however. It is to be had by standing close to listen. And it is to be had by taking part as well.

Finding out what foreign policy making involves, in other words, means finding out about the whole milieu in which it is constructed. This is the "common sense" that commonsense constructivism refers to. As such, it does not mean "practical understanding" as opposed to "abstract understanding." It means that understanding held "in common" by those concerned, that is, the awareness of what in this case foreign policy means, as shared by those foreign policy makers whose sense of that meaning can be said to matter the most. This milieu is to be understood, and subsequently explained, in what we might call the anthropological way.

Transgressing the Limits Rationalism Sets by Post-Modernist Means

This said, there is another way of going beyond the limits rationalism sets that has not been discussed so far. This is to eschew the whole process that set these limits in the first place. This is to "go beyond" these limits in a very particular and radical sense. It means questioning the relevance and role of the modernist mind-move itself.

This kind of questioning is characteristic of postmodernism. Indeed, to be consistent, a postmodernist thinker would have to stop thinking, at least in the modernist way. He or she would have to turn to street theater instead, or some other nonanalytic pursuit. Short of that point, however, postmodernist thinkers question the universalist, eternalist, absolutist assumptions that underpin the rationalist perspective, rejecting outright any idea that we are able to step back from the world to look at it from a mental distance.

People are born into a social realm, and if it is a modernist social realm, they are typically taught to pull away from it mentally as they grow up. Having done so, they hold intellectual conversations with each other, creating in the process an abstract metasocial environment separate from the more concrete one they otherwise inhabit as social beings. Having done so they construct metanarratives that they read back upon the world, in foreign policy terms, for example.

The capacity to pull away from our social environment involves a large amount of pushing by those who would teach us how to do so. The lessons we learn in this regard are deemed by postmodernists to be intellectual conceits, however. Ultimately, postmodernists say, pulling away cannot be done, and they say that pulling away must be seen for what it is—an ideological ploy that promotes and protects particular kinds of world affairs and particular kinds of foreign policy. They contest the objective validity of this ideological ploy (or at least, those who approximate postmodernism do, since this is a position that cannot be more than approximated without ceasing to be intellectually accessible).

Postmodernists reject, therefore, not only the attempt to objectify ("highfly") but also any subsequent attempt to subjectify ("deep-dive"), since both of these mind-moves follow from the same (rationalist) mind-ploy. Postmodernists prefer to watch the "play of light on the water" instead. They value difference, pastiche, bricolage, and other such anti-essentialist delights.

In the light of the above let me join the growing queue of constructivist categorizers and argue the case for four fundamental forms of the concept, namely, conservative, rule-oriented, commonsense, and postmodernist.

Conservative constructivists endorse the hyperrationalism that makes positivism possible. Adler (1997) calls this approach modernist. Ruggie (1998) calls it naturalistic. Katzenstein, Keohane, and Krasner (1998) call it conventional or critical. Wendt (1999) calls it scientific. They are all referring to much the same thing.

Rule-oriented constructivists do not endorse hyperrationalism (positivism), but they are still rationalists. To the extent that they get close to listen, however, they are nonrationalists as well. Adler (1997) calls this kind of approach rule-based. Ruggie (1998) calls it neoclassical. Katzenstein, Keohane, and Krasner (1998) largely ignore it.

Commonsense constructivists do not endorse hyperrationalism (positivism) either. They are also still rationalists, in a moderate, rule-oriented kind of way. Like rule-centered constructivists, they get close to listen, too. Unlike rule-centered constructivists, however, they seek to take part. This makes possible a cycle of knowing, as they see it, that initiates an objectifying/subjectifying/objectifying trialectic. It means taking an anthropological turn, so that proximal methodologies of the participative sort can be used as well.

It seeks experiential understanding of a radical kind, urging us to complement the patterns we discern by standing back to look, by standing close to listen *and* taking part (Pettman 2000).

Postmodernist constructivists are neither hyperrationalist (positivist) nor rationalist. They are radically nonrationalist, though they are nonrationalist in a very particular and very modernist way. That is, they turn reason back on itself to mount an epistemological critique of the assumptions upon which the prioritizing of reason as an end in itself are ultimately based (modernism). They do not seek to be nonrationalists by subjectifying, the way commonsense constructivists would when they take part, or rule-oriented constructivists would when they get close and listen. Instead, they reject the objectivist/subjectivist dichotomy altogether, seeing it as symptomatic of a mind-move whose ambitions they do not endorse. Adler (1997), Ruggie (1998), and Katzenstein, Keohane, and Krasner (1998), all talk of such a postmodernist approach.

It is worth noting that those forms of constructivism that use nonrationalist techniques (like the rule-oriented and commonsense ones) are not antirationalist, nor, as it happens, is postmodernist constructivism. In other words, as much as all these forms of constructivism might seem to be antirationalist, they are not. This is an important point, and it has to be made very clearly to minimize misunderstanding.

Antirationalism involves meditation, prayer, and ritual purification. Much as these ways of knowing may be seen to involve the exercise of human judgment, they are nonetheless spiritual techniques. Those they exalt are gurus and saints.

The nonrationalist subjectifying that rule-oriented and commonsense constructivism entail, as well as the turning of reason back on itself that postmodernist constructivism entails, is not spiritual. It is not, therefore, antirational. It is secular, and as such, it is still an integral part of the modernist (rationalist) project.

In the case of commonsense constructivism, for example, we use participant understanding and other such techniques to reverse the objectifying mind-move. These techniques let us subjectify in radical ways. They stop short, however, except where these might be required in the practice of taking part, of endorsing those antimodernist methodologies (like meditation and prayer) that eschew the modernist project altogether. It is certainly arguable that we should not stop short like this, particularly when we appreciate the power and resolve that spiritual techniques can confer. But stopping short is definitely what modernity entails.

In the case of postmodernist constructivism, we use counterrationalist forms of rationalism that are deeply reflexive. Note the use of the term "counterrationalist," not "antirationalist." The distinction between counter-rationalism and antirationalism may seem slim. It may seem to be a distinction without a difference. This is not the case, however. The difference lies in the way postmodernist constructivists do not embrace antimodernist methodologies, such as meditation or prayer. After all, how could they turn reason back on itself if they did not place a priority upon the use of reason in the first place? Postmodernist constructivism is secular, that is, and not spiritual. It is identifiably part of the modernist project, albeit a profoundly heretic part in terms of the fundamental beliefs that make modernity possible.

Like their conservative and rule-oriented confreres, commonsense constructivists find postmodernist constructivism too radical, too, though postmodernists can be said to perform a vital function in questioning the validity of the claims all modernists make. This helps in turn to provide thinking and speaking spaces for those who get put on modernity's margins, and those who must suffer the injustices that modernity creates. The margins modernity makes include so-called "premodernists," but they also include women and environmentalists. From margins like these we can see very clearly the biases modernist rationalism involves, and the very particular version of world affairs (and foreign policy) that it promotes and protects.

The Commonsense Alternative

At which point let me start performing my textual function as "the fool on the hill" as in the famous song by the Beatles. With the "eyes in my head," let me start appraising the preceding chapters in terms of commonsense constructivism, that is, in terms of how well they not only listen to those who make foreign policy, but also how much they reflect time spent by each author making foreign policy for him- or herself.

Those who wrote this text stand back to look at what foreign policy makers intend and mean. They also try and ascertain the intentions of the agents involved by getting close to listen.

Do they stand close to listen *and* take part, however? Are they prepared to countenance the most radically proximal of all research techniques—participation?

In the first chapter (on the split between foreign policy and international politics) we find critical talk about any approach that makes actors appear automatons, that is, mere "stimulus-response machines" responding in a "mechanical way" to outside stimuli. This is good constructivist stuff, by any standards. We make our foreign policies, after all, and though we may not make them as we please, we do make them. They are constructed.

How are we to know how we make them, though? Is it by debating the identity of the state? Is it by determining the general status enjoyed by the intersubjective agreements arrived at between those who represent these fictional agents? Or does it require something more, and something more participatory? Questions like these highlight the basic question as to how best we might know how agents act. Behaving as something other than mere stimulus-response machines means manifesting will and purpose, for example. It means exhibiting intention. It means knowing what action means. How are these intentions, or this sense of consequence, to be ascertained, however? What are we to do, in this regard, to discover how foreign policy makers think and feel?

Conservative constructivists stand back and look. Rule-oriented constructivists do likewise, though in rule-oriented terms they stand close and listen, too. Commonsense constructivists stand back and look, stand close and listen, take part, then stand back and look again. They objectify, subjectify in the most radical way possible, then objectify again. More particularly, they say we should try to participate in the practices involved before presuming to decide rationally what it is we want to know.

In the second chapter, we are told that foreign policy is volitional, since it is a disciplinary space where people make choices. Foreign policy makers perceive what is happening. They decide what world affairs means. They formulate policies and policy implementation programs. It is people that make foreign policy, it is said, albeit not as they please. Again, all good constructivist stuff.

The next part of the argument is about how foreign policy making is viewed differently from positivist/conservative as opposed to social/rule-centered perspectives. It is about the way the revisionist insights from the latter group are likely to be commandeered, encysted, or otherwise rendered comatose by the paradigm police who promote and protect the former.

A radical epistemological difference is noted in the process between those versions of constructivism that are deemed "explanatory" (rationalist) and those that are deemed "constitutive" (reflectivist). This is a distinction that invites much more talk about what our research into the constitutive kinds of constructivism might actually involve. For example, to *understand* foreign policy (which is what constitutive knowing seems to mean), research techniques other than those that merely explain it are presumably required. What are these research techniques, however? This is the question, though the account that follows—of the way conservative constructivists, like Wendt, are rendering rule-oriented constructivism "mainstream"—does not answer it (Wendt 1999).

Commonsense constructivists talk about the distinction between constructivism of the conservative (positivist) kind and the revisionist (nonpositivist) kind. This distinction makes it easier to see how a constructivist like Wendt (conservative) differs from a constructivist of the Miami IR Group sort (revisionist).

Commonsense constructivists also talk about proximal techniques that entail standing close to listen and taking part. This distinction makes it easier in turn to see how most members of the Miami IR Group (who do the former) differ from commonsense constructivists (who try at least to do the latter).

The counterhegemonic critique the Miami IR Group mounts of the hegemonic conservatives, however, while promoting nonrationalist research techniques like listening to speech acts, does not promote taking part. Rule-oriented constructivists do not require our direct participation in the foreign policy making process. They only indirectly enjoin participant understanding, for example, or any of the other radically proximal ploys.

In chapter 3, rule-oriented constructivism is explained to the reader in four easy steps designed to take us along the (rule-oriented) constructivist way, namely, seeing, thinking, talking, and asking questions. In asking questions we clearly need to get close and listen (to hear the answers). There is a fifth step, however, and that is taking part. And there is arguably a sixth step, too, where we stand back to see again, in terms of what we have heard and done.

Talking of seeing, a distinction is drawn between "seeing" in terms of receiving and processing information, as done in the positivist way, and "seeing" in terms of a social and world-making activity, as done in the rule-oriented way. While positivists stand back and look at foreign policy, in other words, there is an alternative that moves us closer to people and how they effect world affairs, and it is the rule-oriented alternative. In thinking about the world in this other way, it is said, we stress the need not just to "see" the foreign policy making process in action, but to get close to hear it and feel it as well. This would seem to be commonsense constructivism in all but name only, and as such, would seem to be a notable advance beyond the usual rule-oriented constructivist agenda.

The text then returns to a discussion of conceptual thinking as a cognitive universal, however, and an explanation of the way our categories are learned. The significance of learning constructivist categories, and particularly rule-oriented constructivist categories, is outlined, and the importance of language to any understanding of social achievement clearly maintained.

The point to note here, however, is that while concepts and categories are essential thinking tools, and we hear lots of language when we listen and participate, concepts and categories and language are not all that goes on when we take part. This is why the commonsense constructivist asks what nonspeech acts involve, and wants to know how the nonlinguistic dimensions to foreign policy impinge *as well*. That is, the realm of the participatory is arguably much larger than talking and questioning are able to entertain, and that's the rub. Participation engages all the senses. The information obtained is often subliminal. That does not make it less relevant, however. As a talking species we prioritize speech, but in doing so we tend to neglect what else is going on. We neglect, for example, the "silent" languages that are so revealing of context and milieu, and that foreign policy analysis also involves. And we fail to understand the speech we hear in its own politicocultural terms, which may well be very different from our own.

If we scratch the surface of key concepts like power, interest, and anarchy, by listening to those who use them, we find rules, as the Miami IR Group maintains. Even under the anarchic circumstances that define world affairs, we do, as a consequence, find rule. This is why sorting and exploring world affairs phenomena using categories like agent, structure, institution, and the like, proves to be so worthwhile.

Scratching the surface can be done in nonrationalistic as well as rationalistic ways, however. It can be done using research strategies of a nonlinguistic sort, though these strategies are highly participatory ones, as commonsense constructivists avow. So when we are told that only theories point the way to appropriate methodologies, a commonsense constructivist would disagree, arguing that nonrationalist methodologies of the participative sort are highly appropriate, regardless of the theory at stake.

Scratching the surface is best done anthropologically, since anthropologists are the ones who know best how people obey a whole host of rules, even when they do not realize it. This is why rule-oriented constructivists are told to act like anthropologists and to look between the lines of the information they get about world affairs in order to find the rules at work. Anthropologists are arguably most notable for the highly participatory techniques they use, however, techniques that commonsense constructivists explicitly recommend.

Anthropologists (and commonsense constructivists, therefore) do not simply look between the lines to find out what lies there, as a conservative constructivist might do. Nor do they only "listen" to those who peddle these lines, to find out how that peddling is done, as rule-oriented constructivists tend to do. They "take part" in what lies behind these lines, in ways that are as wholly engaged as the circumstances will allow.

Taking an anthropological turn means not only taking an interest in the language used to describe the foreign policy making process, therefore. It means learning to speak the language used in the foreign policy making process itself, the better to take part. This is more than doing case studies or doing close readings of exemplary texts, absolutely vital though these may be. It is more than the thick description of emblematic situations, absolutely vital though this may be, too. It is to speak, as much as possible, from one's own personal experience of the specific milieu *as well*. Granted, there may be severe constraints on how much this can be done, particularly when it comes to foreign policy making, which is often a highly protected, even clandestine, process. There is no substitute for participant understanding, however, particularly when it is couched in the larger context of rationalist re-appraisal.

In chapter 4, Nicholas Onuf speaks of policy in rule-oriented terms. We learn about commitments, agreements, gifts, and observers, and pertinent examples are supplied throughout. We are given a detailed account, in short, of how elusive the concept of policy can be, how policy makers bluff and lie, for example, and how their bluffs and lies are speech acts nonetheless. As such, speech acts of every kind are rich material for the astute constructivist, as noted already.

Onuf tells us a great deal about the intricacies of policy interaction. He is also very aware of how duplicitous policy makers can be. As we look more closely at policy statements, he observes, we discover how fictitious they are, how much is not being said, and who is not talking. Indeed, the closer we look at foreign policy of any kind, he concludes, the less we find.

Onuf also knows that much gets said that is very revealing, and that as information moves "up and down the chain of command," keen ears can catch as much as, if not more than, keen eyes can espy. "Directive speech acts intended only for subordinates' ears provide far better evidence of agents' intentions than their strategic interactions are likely to," he says, and it would be extremely hard not to agree.

At which point the case for commonsense constructivism begins to be made. Onuf points towards oaths of office, major speeches, summit oratory, resolutions of public bodies, agreements, and even formal policy statements as being good places to look and listen in this regard. How are the looking and listening best done, however? The next step would seem to be much greater engagement, and much greater participation. This would seem to be the most effective way to implement Onuf's explicit research agenda.

Imagine, for example, how we might find out how a foreign policy making ministry collectively thinks, that is, how it processes and stores information and, therefore, how it "sees" (and remembers) the world. One way would be to highlight the headings used in its central filing systems. If we are talking of Chinese foreign policy, for example, getting access to China's filing systems on the subject would not mean only learning Chinese, however. It would not mean only learning the particular analytic and bureaucratic languages in which these systems are couched. It would require learning the "silent" languages that active participation entails and the culture-specific ways in which everything is thought and said. And though the access required might prove difficult, if not impossible, to get, a more suitable way of applying Onuf's categories is very hard to imagine.

Standing back to look at the Chinese foreign ministry from afar, however cunningly we categorize our doing so, can tell us only a limited amount about the way its rules make rule. For one thing, it tends to promote the sense that the patterns discerned are what is actually going on. This is only an assumption, however. It may well be wrong. Hence the need not only to get close to listen, but to take part as well, something U.S. intelligence agencies are well aware of the need to do. They are aware, that is, not only of the practical significance of speech acts, and of listening to what foreign policy practitioners have to say, but also of the practical significance of active participation.

So much for the more general injunctions about becoming a constructivist. What about the more specific accounts that follow on from these general ones? What about rule-oriented constructivism at work? When rule-oriented constructivists address themselves to case study material, that is, do they do so using proximal techniques? And if they do so, how participative are these techniques?

The categories that rule-oriented constructivists use in each of the cases discussed in this book have proven efficacy as research tools. Here I am more interested in how much each analyst gets close to listen, however, and how intimately each has taken part in what it is he or she wants to know.

Because rule-oriented constructivist categories are so efficacious, we can put on Onuf's spectacles fully expecting to see better analytically. Should we stop there, however? In a sense, this could be said to be where we need to start. It is at this point, a commonsense constructivist would tend to say, that our research should become much more participatory, and that we should get personally involved as much as we can. After that we return, in good anthropological fashion, to a rationalist reprise, so that our primary conclusions can then be reassessed in the light of what has been learned through taking part. The second-order conclusions that such a reprise provides are invariably different from the first-order ones, being informed by all that gets heard and done experientially. They are arguably better conclusions, too, incorporating as they do the results of experiential research. The implications of this for *any* constructivist agenda are arguably profound.

The cycle of knowing intimated above is well illustrated by Vendulka Kubálková's case study on Soviet "new thinking." Kubálková is extremely well qualified to do this particular case study, although her qualifications were hard won and came at the kind of personal cost she would certainly not want anyone else to have to pay. As a refugee from Czechoslovakia in 1968, as a Russian speaker and reader, and as someone trained in both the Anglo-American West and the Soviet-European East, she knows what she is talking about, not only analytically but experientially as well. What is more, she is not afraid to use experiential research techniques, listening to defectors for example, listening hard for changes in nuance in Soviet pronouncements, and continuing to participate, albeit more and more vicariously these days, in the developments affecting the whole region. This is why I would argue that her analysis is a uniquely satisfying one. It does not put her conclusions beyond dispute, but it does represent a rich blend of distal and radically proximal research strategies. It demonstrates the benefits such a blend can bring to foreign policy analysis.

Kubálková seeks to ascertain the "common sense" exhibited by the Soviet foreign policy makers of the late Cold War period, and by Gorbachev in particular. This "common sense" was informed by Marxist thinking in ways poorly appreciated in the West. For example, Kubálková argues that Gorbachev's own "new thinking" was influenced by the neo-Marxist reappraisals done in the 1920s by Antonio Gramsci. The appreciation by Soviet elites of Gramsci's ideas about hegemony and civil society are the key, she claims, to a puzzle that includes the end of the Cold War.

Without having been taught to share this sort of "common sense" herself as she grew up, Kubálková would have been much less likely to understand the Soviet milieu, and why an explanation in neo-Marxist terms of Gorbachev's "new thinking" about foreign policy might well be valid. She clearly exemplifies the superior analytic power a research regime that shuttles between the distal and the radical proximal is able to provide. She demonstrates very clearly, in other words, why commonsense constructivism matters, and matters a great deal.

Kubálková follows her bid to ascertain the "common sense" shared by the Soviet state elite with an analytic reprise that highlights some of Onuf's key categories. Using these categories allows her to explain why Gorbachev failed to reform the Soviet state structure without having it fall over. She places herself under the particular analytic "rule" that these "rules" represent, and given the rest of what she has to say, she has good reason for doing so. This is not my current concern, however.

The great strength of her account lies, in my terms, in her willingness to push the perimeter of rule-oriented constructivism in the direction of its common sense cousin. Seeing Gorbachev as a closet democrat, as she argues, is to misconstrue, indeed, is to actively distort, the policy milieu in which he lived and worked, and his own way of thinking. The common sense he shared with his advisers was not the same as the commonsense shared in Washington. Nor did he share the common sense with Westerners that they thought he did. Because Washington lacked a proper, that is, a participative, appreciation of the difference between these two policy contexts, the extent to which Soviet foreign policy thinking was governed by the nuanced nature of its Marxist environment was largely missed.

This has important implications for Washington policy makers today. The advice it provides is also clear: Do not trust positivists, that is, those who would only stand back to look at world affairs from a mental distance, on the assumption that differences between foreign policy contexts are not obscured by doing so. Much greater trust should be placed instead in those, like the rule-oriented constructivists, who seek to get close and listen to the policy conversations that go on all the time all over the world. Most trust of all, however, should be placed in those, like the commonsense constructivists, who actively seek (as much as possible) to take part in other people's foreign policy processes, before deciding what it is that foreign policy analysis entails.

References

Adler, Emmanuel. 1997. "Seizing the Middle Ground. Constructivism in World Politics." *European Journal of International Relations* 3(3): 319–363.

Katzenstein, Peter, Keohane, Robert, and Krasner, Stephen. 1998. "International Organization and the Study of World Politics." *International Organization* 52(4): 645–685.

Kubálková, Vendulka, Onuf, Nicholas, and Kowert, Paul, eds. 1998. *International Relations in a Constructed World*. Armonk, NY: M.E. Sharpe

Onuf, Nicholas. 1989. *Worlds of Our Making: Rules and Rule in Social Theory and International Relations*. Columbia: University of South Carolina Press.

Pettman, Ralph. 2000. *Commonsense Constructivism, or the Making of World Affairs*. Armonk, NY: M.E. Sharpe.

Ruggie, John. 1998. "What Makes the World Hang Together? Neo-utilitarianism and the Social Constructivist Challenge." *International Organization* 52(4): 855–885.

Smith, Steve. 2000. "The Discipline of International Relations: Still an American Social Science?" *British Journal of Politics and International Relations* 2: 374–402.

Wendt, Alexander. 1999. *Social Theory of International Politics*. Cambridge, UK: Cambridge University Press.

11

Toward a Constructivist Theory
of Foreign Policy

Paul A. Kowert

Postmodernists, critical theorists, and constructivists have not wrought the intellectual apocalypse in social science that some feared. Instead, a middle ground has gradually emerged on which, to be sure, skirmishes about the nature of social science continue (Adler 1997; Checkel 1998). This book is a product of those skirmishes, and seeks for itself a place on that middle ground. That its contributors often comment self-consciously on this effort to situate constructivism with respect to other approaches to international relations, and rule-oriented constructivism with respect to other constructivisms, gives some indication of the significance they attach to scholars' efforts to police or "discipline" what passes for knowledge.[1] Perhaps this conviction, that science (social science, in this case) is an ethical as well as explanatory process, reflects the extent to which constructivists take normativity seriously.[2] This chapter will argue that they are right to do so. The value of constructivist research is increased rather than diminished by efforts to clarify its own normative purpose and the values to which it speaks.

The understandable fear of many observers is that a scholarship of normativity cannot also be a scholarship of standards (other than, perhaps, moral standards). Critical theorists find solace in making moral and scholarly standards synonymous. They share R.B.J. Walker's skepticism that "ethics is somehow separable from politics" or, indeed, from political science (Walker 1993, 79). Many would go even further, contending along with David Campbell that "ethics is indispensable to the very being of [a] subject, because a subject's being is only possible once its *right to be* in relations to the Other is claimed" (Campbell 1993, 92, emphasis in the original). With this assertion, Campbell surpasses those who maintain only that the practice of science is inevitably biased. Campbell's position is that ontology—that is, a science's choice of subject matter—itself incorporates certain perspectives and values.

If so, the sensible conclusion that science cannot judge itself objectively leads postmodernists away from the enterprise of judging and toward an infinite regress of meanings within meanings. Yet most students of international relations still carry out empirical research as though some other standards for argumentation apply. They still adduce evidence, derived ultimately from the human senses, in support of their claims. Rhetoric to the contrary notwithstanding, therefore, epistemology has changed little or not at all since the enlightenment devalued mystical knowledge.

Much that passes for epistemological controversy really consists of debates about ontology on one hand and methodology on the other. Differences in race, class, or gender are said to confer different "ways of knowing" on individuals who occupy different "standpoints."[3] It is more likely that these differences give people with more or less the same epistemological competence insights into different things. As social beings, we use language to present evidence about these things to others (an epistemological commonality). True, what we choose to investigate (ontology) may require different techniques of evidence gathering (measuring, quantifying, reading, or just listening) suitable to a given subject. The prima facie claim that some problems require a specific methodology (participant observation, say, or detailed historical study rather than experimentation or quantitative analysis), however, is proven wrong often enough by clever evidence gatherers that one can afford to remain an agnostic on the matter of methods. This chapter will say little about methodology, then, and nothing more about epistemology. The contribution of constructivism, when it is not addressing issues of metatheory and philosophy of science, is ontological. Specifically, constructivism broadens scholarship in international relations by reconceptualizing normativity. This makes it easier to "see" previously ignored rule-governed behavior in the putatively anarchic domain of international relations and, at the same time, offers new insight into matters of long-standing concern, such as the formation of (national) interests.

Values were never totally absent from international relations scholarship. They give rise, for example, to the distinction between realism and liberalism. Whether it makes more sense to conceive of the world as fundamentally zero-sum or as positive-sum depends on whether one takes relative security or absolute (material) well-being to be the more pressing problem (Grieco 1988). Realism adopts the more pessimistic premise both as a scientific assumption and as an implicit value.[4] If security is the human (and, specifically, national) value most directly threatened by an anarchical system, then it makes sense for scholars to devote their energies to uncovering the limits of conflict rather than the prospects for cooperation. As Campbell (1992) has taken pains to show, neither the state's pursuit of security nor scholars' efforts to understand it are ethically neutral. The very idea of "national security" (which scholars help transmit, after all) serves state interests. Again, ontology serves an ethical purpose. Similarly, neoliberal investigations of the way international regimes reduce transaction costs and thus promote the generation of national wealth serve another normative purpose.[5] Security and prosperity are such obvious and common objectives that it is easy to take them for granted as "neutral" fixtures of human experience. They are not. There is no reason, to extend Patrick Henry's oft-quoted sentiments, that people cannot prefer liberty (or something else) to either life or wealth. Pursuit of the latter values is unremarkable because so many people share them, but not because all people *must* naturally do so.

International relations theory in general—and its contemporary structural variants, neorealism and neoliberalism, in particular—are poorly equipped to explore normativity in international politics. Stephen Walt (himself unquestionably a realist) recently suggested in the pages of *Foreign Policy* that the efforts of constructivism to address the problem of normativity may make it a third "pillar" of scholarship on international politics (Walt 1998).[6] If so, however, it is an unusual one. Although constructivist scholars typically accept the proposition that all scholarship (indeed, all agency) embodies some kind of normative conviction, they are mostly silent about what kind of values constructivism itself might embrace. In this lacuna resides the untested promise of constructivist theory. Realism and liberalism have been successful as theories of international politics not in spite of their normative content but precisely because people do, in fact, care about security and wealth. For constructivism to fulfill its promise, it must engage the problem of normativity not only as metatheory but also in its substantive (theoretical) claims about international politics.

Constructivism and the Value of Identity

If constructivism addresses any substantive problem (other than wealth or security), it is undoubtedly the way people claim for themselves, and confer on others, *identity* as agents. The growth of interest in identity politics has continued unabated since Yosef Lapid and Friedrich Kratochwil (1996) identified its "return" to the field of international relations. One reason for the renewed attention is that identity politics have become simultaneously more interesting and more difficult to explain. Epic contests such as World War II and the Cold War produced a dualist rhetoric that sharply constrained differences of personal ideology and national purpose to well-defined categories.

Yet in the welcome absence of such sweeping conflicts, identity becomes less certain. Distinguishing self from other, on many different social levels, presents a greater challenge after the "end of history."

Fukuyama (1992) was of course almost exactly wrong in his choice of title. History, along with ethnicity and religion, has not ended at all. It has come flooding back into the public consciousness as a potent new source of identity (and of conflict). To a degree, constructivists have taken advantage of the times to proclaim a new focus for scholarship in international relations. Their claim is compelling in a world where inflamed passions lead to bloodshed in the name of neither conquest nor class, but instead simply because of *who* the enemy is: a Muslim, a Serb, a Tutsi, a Hutu, a Catholic, a Protestant, an Arab, or a Jew. Realism and liberalism are not incapable of explaining hatred, but they struggle to account for widespread violence that serves neither Mammon nor the national interest.

Still, interest in the contribution of identity to international politics is not new. Almost half a century ago, Kenneth Boulding (1956) argued for a new science of "images" that were, he felt, central to knowledge of the social and even the material world. A decade later, Erving Goffman's (1969) pithy analysis of strategies for social interaction began with the observation that, "in pursuit of their interests, parties of all kinds must deal with and through individuals, both individuals who appear to help and individuals who appear to hinder." To pursue their interests, he continues, "parties—or rather the persons who manage them—must orient to the capacities which these individuals are seen to have and to the conditions which bear upon their exercise. . . . To orient to these capacities is to come to conclusions, well founded or not, concerning them; and to come to these conclusions is to have assumptions about the fundamental nature of the sorts of persons dealt with" (Goffman 1969, 3). In just a few sentences, Goffman neatly lays out the strategic problem behind ascribing a particular identity ("image," Boulding might have said) to another party. We must live our lives by taking into account what kind of people we are likely to encounter and by acting appropriately when we do. By extension, on a more abstract level, states must also expect and prepare for encounters with different kinds of national "others."

Goffman's is a simple but powerful explanation for the importance of identity.[7] In a world of scarce resources, fleeting opportunities, and impoverished mechanisms of governance (a world of anarchy at the level of international politics), it is vital to know "whom" one might encounter. All states are not the same. It would be extraordinarily wasteful to treat every state as though it posed the same potential threat or offered the same potential opportunities. As evidence for this claim, one might begin with the infrequency of war among democratic polities. Since democratic states are not markedly less conflict-prone in general, the presumed restraint of democratic institutions appears to have less to do with this phenomenon than the image of the other. As Kant posited, whether or not another state is democratic is a powerful indicator of its intentions, and not simply its institutions (Doyle 1983). In the context of contemporary neorealist and neoliberal theory, however, the democratic peace appears more an isolated fact than a logical extension of core postulates. Perhaps this is so because, unlike Kant, neither of these two prominent variants of international relations theory takes normativity seriously.

Because constructivists do take norms seriously, and particularly normative specifications of identity that confer agency on others, they are well situated to provide what the structural theories of international relations cannot: a theory of agency. So much constructivist scholarship has been devoted to answering neorealism's and neoliberalism's implied determinism on matters of agency, however, that constructivism risks becoming associated with the opposite extreme. Whereas evolutionary neorealism (and neoliberalism, for the most part) expect the international system to socialize states and their leaders to be fundamentally and inevitably self-regarding, constructivism has sometimes tended toward an "anything goes" attitude.[8] Those who suggest that "anarchy is what states make of it" are certainly not obliged to say, however, that states can make of it anything whatsoever (Wendt 1992). Out of the conviction that identities matter, efforts to explain what identities are possible should be of central importance to constructivists (Checkel 1998).

Indeed, a theory of identity is of broader importance for the study of international relations. A better understanding of how national leaders conceive of differences among states is a step toward accounting for the formation of national interest—a topic that is generally excluded from rationalist (neorealist and neoliberal) accounts of international politics on the grounds that no one set of interests is more rational than any other. This exclusion leaves neorealism and neoliberalism without a theory of preferences, and thus without a theory of foreign policy (Legro 1996; Wendt 1994; Yee 1997). Little wonder that, as three former editors of *International Organization* recently put it, "the core of the constructivist project is to explicate variations in preferences, available strategies, and the nature of the players across space and time" (Katzenstein, Keohane, and Krasner 1998, 682).

Alexander Wendt's Cultures of National Identity

If belonging and difference are values of central importance as constructivism seeks to explain how identity is conferred on agents, then the success of constructivist scholarship to date is unremarkable. Alexander Wendt (1994, 1999) is almost alone among constructivists in pursuing an explicit theoretical bridge between nation-state identity and structural theories of international relations.[9] This section focuses on Wendt's claims not as a way of situating them with respect to science, rationalism, or other forms of constructivism (see Smith's chapter in this volume), but instead because they constitute the most prominent constructivist account of national identity.

Wendt's efforts, and particularly his recent *Social Theory of International Politics*, have attracted well-deserved attention. He makes a compelling case that identity plays a crucial role in international relations. To do so, he begins with three distinct logics of anarchy, which he terms Hobbesian, Lockean, and Kantian. These three "cultures" (Wendt's term) of international politics are defined by explicit reference to their dominant assumption about the character or "identity" ascribed to other states: enemies (Hobbesian), rivals (Lockean), or friends (Kantian). Cutting across these cultures are three degrees of internalization—it is not quite clear whether Wendt means *acceptance* or *institutionalization*—that express different levels of commitment to a prevailing international culture (Wendt 1999, 246–312).

Most theories of international relations, Wendt (1999, 254) notes, have made a dual progression along these axes. Structural realism combines highly pessimistic, zero-sum assumptions about the structure of international politics with very limited assumptions about internalization ("might makes right"). Structural liberalism may expect rivalry, but it also acknowledges the possibility of cooperation ("enlightened self-interest"). In this view, states are analogous to firms that compete for market share (i.e., for provision of goods to their citizens), but that nevertheless share an interest in "internalizing" a broadly cooperative system (of property rights, international regimes, etc.) to provide public goods on a global scale. Finally, most optimistic is a Kantian perspective that anticipates the elimination of security dilemmas within a "pluralistic security community." Wendt maintains that a Kantian culture, like the others, can be either weakly or strongly internalized. Yet in the same way that protons must come very close to overcome the electromagnetic force that would otherwise cause positively charged particles (and thus the atomic nucleus) to fly apart, so states must come sufficiently close in their mutual understanding to overcome the myriad competitive dilemmas that drive them apart. There is little reason to expect that poorly internalized Kantian cultures will persist for long.

Wendt's three logics of anarchy might seem plausible underpinnings for the judgments leaders make about other states. Yet this reverses the direction of causation in Wendt's argument. After eloquently explaining that nation-state identity can be thought of as endogenous to the international system and that the structural position of state actors is certain to affect the identities they ascribe to other states, Wendt then turns the tables and *assumes* three distinct identities—enemy, rival, and friend—as bases for three different international systems. In chapter 6 of *Social Theory of International Politics*, Wendt makes a strong case that identity, conceived as an image of the "other," casts a long shadow over international politics. When he returns to the problem of identity formation in chapter 7, however, he is no longer able to offer a compelling theory. He submits that processes of both natural and cultural selection may explain the emergence of particular identities. The former argument, unfortunately, is rendered tautological since identity was assumed in chapter 6 to be grounds for the logic of the international system. If the same system is also supposed, in more or less Waltzian fashion, to select the most ecologically "fit" sort of states for survival, then identity has become its own cause. In a world of enemies, Wendt seems to say, it pays to conceive of states as enemies; in a world of friends, friendship may beget new friends. As a theory of identity, these claims are not compelling.[10]

Wendt divides his other process of identity formation, cultural selection, into two subprocesses: imitation and social learning. Imitation proceeds in much the same fashion as natural selection, except that it is cognitive. It anticipates that states will imitate others that they *perceive* as successful. Imitation is Lamarckian rather than Darwinian selection, but it suffers from the same defect of circularity noted above. Social learning is a more promising source of identity, but it remains underspecified. "The basic idea," according to Wendt, "is that identities and their corresponding interests are learned and then reinforced in response to how actors are treated by significant Others" (Wendt 1999, 327). Drawing heavily on symbolic interactionism, Wendt proposes that states will see themselves as reflections or "mirror-images" of how they believe they are seen by other states (see Howard and Callero 1991; McCall and Simmons 1978; Stryker 1980, 1987). This mirror-imaging is highly contextual. In a simplistic version of the argument, it might even seem that states are obliged to react to almost any self- or other-presentation by another state. To narrow the range of plausible interaction, Wendt goes on to propose four additional "master variables"—interdependence, common fate, homogeneity, and self-restraint—that inform self- and other-presentation. Freed by this point of the constraints of parsimony, the broad theme of Wendt's work is that international politics, and the identities of the states that carry it out, can be constituted in many forms. Yet those who wish to understand what forms of nation-state identity are most plausible will have little confidence that specific categories of identity can be deduced from Wendt's structural principles.

A further problem is that Wendt (1999, 250) associates social constructivism with the most internalized, most ideational (most Kantian) forms of international structure. This formulation has the unfortunate effect of letting realists and liberals completely off the hook in matters of social construction, apparently conceding that judgments about matters such as threat or capabilities are primarily material rather than cultural or ideational. This is probably not a position that Wendt himself would agree with, stated so bluntly. Certainly, the other contributors to the present volume would not agree, and this is one reason they variously label his constructivism "soft," "conservative," or "rationalist."[11] The way out of this impasse is to recognize that sociocultural constructions are themselves intrinsic to judgments about threat and capability. Elizabeth Kier (1995, 1997) argues, for example, that even apparently objective matters such as military efficiency—which is "testable," after all, on the battlefield—actually depend heavily on cultural interpretation. Likewise, Lynn Eden (forthcoming) argues that the meanings of weapons themselves are contingent.

Wendt might, therefore, cast the net of constructivist claims against materialism even more widely than he does. Yet breadth is not a notable failing of *Social Theory of International Politics*. What is ultimately disappointing is that it does not deliver a useful theory of national identity. Although it offers an extended justification for the importance of identity categories such as enemy, rival, and friend, it never explains why these identities and not others should obtain in international relations. No one else has done better at the level of grand theory, but other research does suggest some useful avenues for extending Wendt's insights to produce a genuine theory of national identity in (and other identities relevant to) international relations. This is just the sort of contribution that the chapters in Part II of this volume make, each in a slightly different way.

The Limits of National Identity

Constructivists have been more eager to explore the possibilities of difference in national identities than the limits on identity. This is understandable since, as already noted, neorealist and neoliberal theories insist that states are interchangeable—differing in capabilities and resource endowments, perhaps, but not in function or type. To prove that identity matters, constructivists must first show that it is, indeed, variable. Enough work of this sort has now been published that most constructivists regard it as axiomatic that national (and other sociopolitical) identities vary in consequential ways (see, inter alia, Hopf 1999; Klotz 1995; Ringmar 1996). In this volume, additional confirmation comes from Nizar Messari's account of how different U.S. representations of Islam and Islamic states have affected American policies of intervention and containment, and from Shiping Zheng's exploration of how shifting interpretations of Chinese identity intensify the conflict between Taiwan and the Chinese mainland. None of the chapters in

Part II stops, however, with the simple claim that identity matters. The chapters also seek to provide clues about the ways identity is produced and conferred on agents.

The most straightforward explanation is that identity is created in the service of interests. Vendulka Kubálková's analysis of Soviet "new thinking" is at once a subtle and audacious example of this claim. The more typical account of perestroika is that progressive specialists (*mezhdunarodniki*), drawing partly on Western analysis of the Cold War, developed a new understanding of the Soviet Union as a "normal" (rather than revolutionary) country and managed to persuade Gorbachev to accept this alternative construction (Herman 1996; Risse-Kappen 1994).[12] Kubálková finds a very different strategic purpose at work in "new thinking." She interprets "new thinking" as a *repudiation* of Western thought—specifically, of Western state-centric political identities—and as part of a Gramscian effort to seek new legitimacy for the Soviet system.[13] She agrees, in other words, that "new thinking" was revolutionary, but not in the self-congratulatory way that some Sovietologists imply. It was a "rational choice" (Kubálková's term), in response to Soviet weakness, to transcend statist forms of agency and identity.

Erik Ringmar's (1996) recent effort to explain why Sweden entered the Thirty Years War is another sophisticated effort to make a similar point about the constitution of identity in a very different setting. By all (realist) accounts, Sweden had no business fighting a protracted war against Habsburg Catholics on the continent. It had neither the economic base nor the manpower nor, ultimately, the diplomatic connections with other Protestant states. Yet Sweden did go to war in 1630, successfully for a time, but also at great cost. Ringmar's explanation is that Sweden's interest was in being taken seriously as a member of the European family of nations. The war served neither Sweden's bankers nor its generals; it merely served the Swedish. By establishing Sweden as a power that other European states could not ignore, the war helped to create Swedish identity. In this case, as in Soviet "new thinking," a foreign policy démarche directly targets the promotion of new political identities.

The interests that shape identity need not, of course, be specifically national interests. They may be subnational, as when contemporary Russian generals and nationalist politicians link the survival of Russia's identity as a major power to its nuclear arsenal and to taking steps to reverse the decay of its military forces (Garnett 1997). In this volume, Gonzalo Porcel Quero paints a compelling portrait of how the interests of a single individual can shape regime structure and political identity. Franco's "Crusade" employed three successive strategies to legitimize personal rule and, at the same time, Spain's status as an agent competent to form international agreements (symbolized by Spanish membership in the UN, and also by less successful efforts during the Franco era to join NATO and the European Community).

At still another level, identity may be conditioned by collective interests embodied in international organizations. In his study of Inter-American anti-corruption regimes, Michael Collier hints at this process when he notes the impact of recognition in international fora (Summit of the Americas, Organization of American States) on the salience of political corruption as a political issue and, by extension, as a political identity.[14] Frank Schimmelfennig argues, to take another example, that NATO enlargement is less an exercise in rational adaptation to new or changing threats than it is an effort to inculcate Euro-Atlantic or Western values—of legalism, civil-military separation, civil liberties, and so on—in the Czech Republic, Hungary, and Poland. In short, NATO is engaged in "international socialization" to produce new Eastern European political identities (Schimmelfennig 1998/1999). Thomas Risse finds a similar process at work within NATO during the Cold War, not only shaping self-definition (NATO as a *democratic* alliance) but also defining the other as enemy. Threat, he argues, was as much consequence as cause of the North Atlantic Alliance (Risse-Kappen 1995a, especially p. 32). Martha Finnemore (1996) shows that the United Nations, the International Committee of the Red Cross, and the World Bank have also profoundly influenced what it means to be a modern, legitimate nation-state (see also Risse, Ropp, and Sikkink 1999; Risse-Kappen 1995b).

Most of the constructivists cited here have a nuanced view of the relationship between identity and interests. Although they find evidence of agents working self-consciously to promote certain identities (*major power, democratic partner, legitimate authority, law-abiding international citizen,* and so on), they do not take interests for granted. Actors must define these interests, and they may do so by drawing on their sense of self using what Finnemore has called a "logic of appropriateness"—asking, "'What kind of situation is this?' and 'What am I supposed to do now?' rather than, 'How do I get what I want?'" (Finnemore 1996, 29). Recognizing this contingency is important for Finnemore since she intends to contribute directly to a problem noted earlier this essay: the failure of neorealism and neoliberalism to produce a theory of preferences and, thus, a theory of foreign policy. Identity may reflect certain interests, but it takes on a life of its own and thereby shapes interests. No less than Finnemore, the works in Part II are sensitive to this process.

As in Wendt's *Social Theory of International Politics*, however, the potential for circularity is evident. Finnemore (1996, 31) readily admits that she has "no grand theory as to why or under what conditions one type of logic (of appropriateness or of interests) might prevail." Offering no general theory, she cannot be accused of tautology, and neither can the other authors cited here. Yet if a theory of identity is not only valuable but the *central* value constructivists have most often sought to explain, then such indeterminacy offers little succor. These interest-based accounts are often revealing, but they do not lend themselves to a theory of limits on identity that would be helpful, in turn, for explaining interests.

More promising, perhaps, are efforts to uncover practical or discursive limits on identity construction in the patterned interaction of agents. Practical limits (to the extent they exist) are imposed by the world in which international relations takes place. This world may be ontologically dependent on knowing and speaking subjects, but it exists independently from them.[15] It is possible to conceive of limits on global oil reserves, for example, in different ways: as a *constraint* on economic development or, if one lives in Qatar or Saudi Arabia, as an *opportunity* for development. Yet it is not useful—it is scarcely meaningful—to conceive of the planet's oil reserves as *unlimited*; the material world penetrates the social too much for that.

Unfortunately, but understandably, constructivists intent on demonstrating the proposition that the world can be constructed in different ways have been loathe to explore material constraints on its construction. There is nothing inherently "un-constructivist" in believing, however, that some constructions make more sense in a given environment than do others. Frederick Jackson Turner's (1920) classic account of how an open Western frontier shaped American identity is a good example. That Native Americans were not much of an impediment to conceiving of the frontier as "open" shows social construction at work. But the entire discussion of frontier would have made no sense in, say, pre-Meiji Japan.[16] The material state of Japan's economic and military resources after Commodore Perry's arrival in 1853 also had implications for identity. Japan's feudal elite (*daimyō*) could, and did, interpret Japan's position differently, but for both the shogunal government (*bakufu*) and its opponents, it was hard to mistake the lesson taught by Britain's humiliation of China. Japan's elite disagreed on whether the first order of business should be resisting the West or placating it while building up the wherewithal to resist more effectively. None disputed that both development and defense were necessary. And these conditions, in turn, contributed to a sense of Japan as a nation under siege—a form of national identity that continued to influence Japanese foreign policies in the early twentieth century and, to a degree, ever since (Beasley 1987).

Zheng presents another version of the "practical limits" argument in his thoughtful discussion, in this volume, of mainland Chinese and Taiwanese efforts to find a modus vivendi in their mutual presentations of Chinese identity. Two rules, he says, define what is no longer possible: (1) Taiwanese (and more ambiguous American) military preparations rule out a military settlement of the identity dispute by mainland China (PRC), but (2) PRC forces rule out the nationalist (KMT) dream of reasserting authority over the mainland. In this case, the impasse has had a corrosive effect on the singular identity (and the one-China policy flowing directly from it) that both parties long celebrated. It is no accident that Zheng calls Chen Shui-bian's new proclamations about Taiwan's status "dizzying." In this case, practical constraints work against any clear statement of national identity. Conversely, Messari suggests that the lack of American knowledge about Bosnia created opportunities to represent Bosnian Muslims in distinctive ways (as victims) that diverge from the usual American representation of Islamic groups. Here, freedom from certain informational constraints worked *for* the creation of new Muslim identities.

Practical limits are certainly relevant to identity, therefore, but they are not always as "limiting" as they might appear. The material and social worlds "contaminate" each other (Onuf 1989, 40), but rarely in a way that allows one to dominate the other completely. The limits of identity will thus depend not only on what it is possible to do with things, but also on what it is possible to do with words.[17] To the extent that language works in particular ways, moreover, it may be possible to generalize even more effectively about linguistic constraints on identity than about practical constraints.

Consider, first, Jonathan Mercer's (1995) well-known critique of the claim that "anarchy is what states make of it." Drawing on a theory of social psychology (social identity theory [SIT]), he argues that even in a materially permissive world where social constructions might vary widely, the psychologically robust tendency to attribute negative qualities to relatively unknown outgroups will cause people to construct a Hobbesian world very much in keeping with realist assumptions about security dilemmas (see also Chafetz 1995; Kowert 1998). Mercer is usually taken, and may well consider himself, as a critic of constructivist arguments. Yet SIT is a psycholinguistic theory of constraints on the way people construct their social environment. The negative stereotyping of the "other" described by SIT—indeed, the phenomenon of stereotyping in general—is widely explained by psychologists as a way to accommodate cognitive limitations on the brain's ability to process language and complexity (Hogg and Abrams 1988; Tajfel 1981; Turner 1982; Worchel and Austin 1986). Although Mercer may overestimate the extent to which SIT requires particular (negative) representations of the other, his exploration of limits on social construction is instructive. It is entirely compatible with a constructivist perspective. Indeed, Zheng makes use of SIT as well to explain the persistent war of words across the Taiwan Straits that observers might otherwise find perplexing in its intensity.

Mercer and Zheng are not alone in perceiving psycholinguistic limits on identity. An important theme in Ted Hopf's recent collection of essays on Russian foreign policy is that "states find their own identities in others" (Hopf 1999, 11). One contributor, Henrikki Heikka, takes the Lacanian position that specific discursive positions give rise to characteristic desires for identification. Crudely put, Russia finds itself in the position of seeking legitimation from Western authorities privileged by the fall of Soviet communism. One way of doing so, prominent in contemporary Russian discourse according to Heikka, is to emphasize Russia's unique cultural heritage and identity as a way of reclaiming authority.[18] Foreign policy image theorists such as Richard Cottam (1977) and Richard Herrmann (1985, 1986) draw on yet another body of psychological research (balance theory; see Heider 1958) to make a similar argument. Images of national other—as *enemy, ally, imperialist,* (neo-)*colony,* and so on—are wielded to maintain a positive conception of national self. Cottam, Herrmann, and others building on their insights are sensitive to the way language works to produce cognitive balance (although they do not formalize this part of their argument). Finally, Stephen Walker (1987, 1992; also see Le Prestre 1997) has led an effort, using sociological theories of symbolic interaction and social roles, to explain the emergence of images of national other similar to those identified by Cottam and of national self such as those described by Kal Holsti (1970).

In this volume, attention to the way social interaction shapes identity is less overtly psychological (with the partial exception of Zheng's analysis, noted above) and more purely social or linguistic. Messari cites Todorov, for example, to make a case that the social interaction of self and other occurs along three axes defined by *value* (good or bad), *distance* (similarity or difference), and *recognition* (regard or neglect).[19] Speech acts pertaining to identity must flow down these three paths, structuring the image of "other." In general, this structure works against complexity and thus helps to explain both the American projection of U.S. identity concerns (e.g., with democracy) into Bosnia and the tendency to simplify representations of Bosnian Muslims. In short, this structure helps to create the "many silences" on which Messari says identity depends.[20] The argument is sufficiently intriguing that one cannot help but wish for Messari to do even more to link the structure of social interaction to particular representations of identity that flow from it.

Two other chapters in Part II emphasize linguistic rather than social structure. Of all the chapters in this book, Collier and Porcel Quero do the most to link Onuf's three types of speech acts directly to patterns of identity, authority, and policy. Collier relies on content analysis and Transparency International corruption data—further proof that constructivism need not be bound too tightly to a single (interpretive) methodology—to show how differences in political culture privilege characteristic forms of speech that yield distinctive patterns of corruption and, in turn, specific national images.[21] Rule in collectivist cultures, for example, seemingly relies on hegemonic speech acts (instruction rules) that give rise to systemic corruption and a "piratical" national image.[22] Similarly, Porcel Quero shows how Franco moved from one discursive strategy to another to preserve his rule. The world may have "frowned on" Franco's Spain in general, but Franco was twice able to reinvent his regime by presenting it in new ways: currying a measure of U.S. favor by cracking down on dissent and "communism" after World War II (asserting *directive* authority), and then relaxing this pattern of rule in the mid-1960s to seek legitimacy through a new openness (*committing* the regime to a heteronomous society).

Psycholinguistic theorists (Mercer, Heikka, and Zheng in part), image theorists (Cottam and Herrmann), symbolic interactionists (Walker and Messari), and rule-oriented language theorists (Collier and Porcel Quero) all draw attention, then, to the ways social interaction can limit the possibilities of identity. These diverse efforts do not yet add up to a coherent approach, and some are explicitly critical of constructivism. Their cumulative effect is to suggest, however, that theorizing the limits of national identity is not a futile task. If constructivists wish to explain the impact of identity on international politics, then they should not hesitate to push further down the same path. A better understanding of what it is possible to *say* about identity may be the key to understanding what agents *do* in the name of their own and others' identities.

Conclusion

One reason language is so important to constructivist analysis is that speech binds together *is* and *ought*. Speech varies not only in its propositional or locutionary content, but also in its illocutionary force whereby a speaker promises, requests, or describes (see Onuf 1989, especially chap. 2; also Searle 1969). To the extent that a speech act somehow affects one or more recipients (a perlocutionary act), it has normative consequences. Choosing to agree, to disagree, to support, to deny, or simply to ignore are all expressions of this normativity. It is for this reason, and not because scientists might be clumsy in their efforts to avoid bias, that constructivists view understanding (and therefore science) as an intrinsically value-laden enterprise. Negotiating the path between illocution and perlocution is always normative, as Onuf's contribution to this volume explains in more detail.

Rule-oriented constructivism—the sort of constructivism, that is, that views science as fundamentally a linguistic performance—offers up the tools of language as the tools of science. The most important theorists of rule oriented constructivism in international relations, Onuf (1989) and Kratochwil (1989), address the problem of normativity broadly and don't associate normativity specifically with the problem of identity. As metatheory, theirs is a broadly conceived system that seeks to build new foundations for scholarship in the face of postmodern criticism about the ontological status of science. It solves problems that social scientists (and other scholars) care about. When Walt (1998) describes constructivism as a third pillar of scholarship in international relations on a par with realism and liberalism, however, he suggests that it can also solve problems that practitioners of foreign policy care about. So does Ralph Pettman (2000, and in this volume) when he insists on a "commonsense" constructivism that not only studies but also embraces agency.

One should not invest the distinction between scholars and practitioners with too much meaning. Rule-oriented constructivism is at pains to point out that speech is a form of practice (again, "saying is doing"), and scholars help to create the social worlds in which we all live. Yet the work of scholars who make their normative intent clear (and it is not too difficult to perceive normative concerns at play in each of the chapters in Part II of this volume) is a pragmatic reminder of what critical theorists argue at length: Science must ultimately be judged not within a closed normative system of its own devising, but in the open-ended, "contaminated" normative system of efforts to solve human problems. Metatheory is not problem-solving theory.

Whatever their faults, realism and liberalism give rise to problem-solving theories addressing the most basic human needs, satisfaction of material desires and security in the expectation of their future satisfaction. By targeting identity, constructivism addresses a higher-order, but still very real, need— to belong. The need to identify with others, and to be recognized by others, may be less important than survival. Maslow (1954), at least, argued that it was in his famous hierarchy of needs.[23] There is no reason to assume, however, that international politics is motivated by only the most basic human needs. Constructivists have generated considerable evidence that higher-order constructs of political meaning also matter.

They need not, and should not, limit themselves only to the meanings attached to belonging and identity. As argued in the preceding discussion of Wendt's important contributions, constructivism is not restricted to consideration of only the more "ideational" forms of behavior. This said, its special contribution to a field dominated by concern for security and wealth is to point to a third broad category of interests or values. Onuf (1989, ch. 8) earlier described these values as affecting "standing," anticipating the field's present concern with identity.[24]

He also pointed out that "interests are recognizable to us as the reasons we give for our conduct" (Onuf 1989, 277). Interests (of all types) are expressed, in other words, as policies—foreign policies, in the case of national interests. Onuf's "Speaking of Policy," in this volume, understands policies to be statements of those interests. More precisely, policies are declarations of an agent's intentions presumed to be linked to that agent's interests. There, as Onuf skillfully points out, is the rub, for we also have many reasons to presume that these declarations will *not* represent an agent's interests. The harder we look, and the more we appreciate the many uses to which language can be put, the more we might despair of identifying "real policies" that represent "real interests." What Onuf does not say, though, is that this dilemma is yet another reason for students of policy to accord a distinctive role to identity. Identity stands in for interests. It not only serves to populate the world with agents, but it also gives meaning to statements that we call policies. Identity describes the basis for our assumption that an agent's policy statements reveal (or obscure) intentions. We know these things because that is the kind of agent "they" are. And, if we turn out to be mistaken, then we must rethink who "they" are.

Identity is central, therefore, to foreign policy choices. Identity is the medium through which national leaders and ordinary citizens alike translate recognition of similarity and difference (in threat, capability, productivity, acclaim, and so on) into ontological statements about international relations. It is the way they "construct" the world, and specifically the agents, they hope to affect through their foreign policies. Constructivism is ideally positioned to offer a theory of agency and, in so doing, to make a vital contribution to the study of foreign policy. This is its promise. The danger is that, fascinated with language as they are, constructivists will turn away from a broader investigation of values pertinent to international politics and content themselves instead with repeating, in the trendy new vocabulary of identity and normativity, what realists and liberals have already said about the "traditional" values of international relations.

Notes

The author is grateful to Vendulka Kubálková, Nicholas Onuf, and Stephen Walker for helpful discussions that enriched this chapter, and to the Social Science Research Council and the Japan Society for the Promotion of Science for generous financial support of this research in its earlier stages (grant P 97272).

1. See, for example, the chapters by Vendulka Kubálková (the introduction and chapter 1), Ralph Pettman, and Steve Smith.

2. This claim is made most clearly, in this volume, in Onuf, "Speaking of Policy." On the normative properties of speech acts, Onuf also cites Johnson (1993).

3. Christine Sylvester's (1994) *Feminist Theory and International Relations in a Postmodern Era* is an excellent example. This is a profoundly insightful work that draws attention to women's practice in ways international relations theory typically ignores. Sylvester contrasts feminist empiricist epistemology with standpoint epistemology. The

latter avails itself not of other tools for knowing (Sylvester presents "evidence," after all, about feminist peace workers and silk producers) but of a *position* that offers special insight. Some of us, Sylvester finds, are in a position to see things that others cannot or will not see. Yet this is an ontological rather than an epistemological point.

4. Neorealists typically cast their structural theories of international relations in instrumental terms. Earlier realists, such as Morgenthau or even Machiavelli, were more explicit about the values behind their assumptions.

5. The best-known example of this genre is probably Robert Keohane's (1984) *After Hegemony*.

6. Walt claims that "realism remains the most compelling general framework for understanding international relations" (Walt 1998, 31; also see Walt 1991). Another recent work proposing constructivism as a new paradigm for research on international relations is Katzenstein, Keohane, and Krasner (1999).

7. The problem of properly identifying the nature of social interlocutors (individuals, groups, states, or other agents) is very different from another identity problem that, if anything, has received even more attention from social scientists: What confers status as an agent? In the case of corporate agents such as the nation-state, the latter question has provoked much debate.

Identity demarcates a boundary with the expectation of homogeneity within and difference without. Most accounts of national identity emphasize the first of these two functions, unification, in an effort to explain the emergence and success of the nation-state as an institutional form following the Peace of Westphalia. Important studies of the nation-state's internal cohesion and institutional success include: Anderson (1983), Deutsch (1966), Gellner (1983), Nairn (1977), Posen (1993), Spruyt (1994), and Tilly (1975). On the distinction between "internal" and "external" theories of identity, see Kowert (1998/99), and also Wendt's (1999, 224) four-fold typology of identity.

8. On evolutionary dynamics in international relations, see Inoguchi (1994) and Modelski, Poznanski, Farkas, Florini, Hodgson (1996).

9. Discussions of constructivist approaches to identity can be found in Checkel (1998), and Kowert and Legro (1996). Another explicitly structural constructivist theory is developed in Kowert (1997, 2000).

10. Kubálková also uncovers this apparent circularity in her summary of Wendt's explanation for Soviet "new thinking"; see Kubálková, "'New Thinking' and the End of the Cold War," in this volume. Wendt (1999, 342) acknowledges the potential for circularity but considers it "benign." His point, that social processes are often recursive, is fair enough. But this does not make it good theory. If there is a natural feedback loop between national identity and the international system, it is also fair to ask a theory of identity to explain the permissive conditions of this system. Failing to do so, one is left with the system itself as the prime mover of international politics—a Waltzian position that Wendt sets out to criticize.

11. Kubálková contrasts Wendt's "idealism" and "soft" constructivism with rule-oriented constructivism in "Foreign Policy, International Politics, and Constructivism" and "'New Thinking' and the End of the Cold War." Similarly, Pettman labels Wendt a "conservative" constructivist (in "Commonsense Constructivism and Foreign Policy") and Smith compares Wendt's "rationalism" to "reflectivism" (in "Foreign Policy Is What States Make of It").

12. Herman also points out that there were serious divisions among liberal reformers in the Soviet Union, and that "the ideas and identity that gave New Thinking its revolutionary content had historical antecedents going back to the Khrushchev era and the beginnings of de-Stalinization" (1996, 288–289).

13. One might note, in this regard, that the term "perestroika" itself connotes the rehabilitation of an existing structure rather than the adoption of a new one.

14. Collier's chapter in this volume also shows that recognition by international organizations does not always suffice to make an aspect of identity, such as corruption, salient. The limited success of the Inter-American Convention Against Corruption is a case in point.

15. Here, I part company from postmodern and antifoundationalist thinkers, and perhaps from Steve Smith and Ralph Pettman in this volume. Wendt's scientific realism provides one justification for doing so (although Wendt himself claims to be ontologically "post-positivist"; see Wendt 1999, 91). Onuf's formulation, that "the material and the social contaminate each other," speaks directly to this point (Onuf 1989, 40).

16. An account of Japan's spatial relationship with China and its effect on Japanese national identity during the Tokugawa period can be found in Toby (1985). Other discussions of the contribution of physical geography to national identity include Deudney (1996) and Nash (1982).

17. This formulation offers a way around the dualism that often besets studies of identity politics: Either identity is intrinsic to a given agent or else it is constructed and therefore bears no particular connection to an agent. A few examples of this unfortunate opposition include Klugman (1997), Mertz (1994), Sayer (1997), and Tilley (1997).

18. Heikka's (1999) analysis is more subtle than this brief explanation indicates. Heikka considers himself a critic of both neorealism and constructivism. Yet in fact, as with Mercer, his argument is broadly consistent with constructivism (though not, perhaps, with Wendt's version of it). Another Lacanian study of national identity is Rubenstein (1989).

19. See also Todorov (1984).

20. Benedict Anderson (1983) made a similar point in his well-known *Imagined Communities*. Anderson holds that "all profound changes in consciousness, by their very nature, bring with them characteristic amnesias" (1983, 204). Forgetting not only creates the need for identity, but also makes it possible.

21. Another intriguing application of quantitative data, derived from computer simulation, to test constructivist understandings of collective identity is Lustick (2000).

22. Transparency International (TI) data typically rank such states as more corrupt than Collier's other two types, pariah and paragon. One suspects, however, that TI's coding misses the nuance implicit in Collier's approach. What TI classifies as greater or lesser corruption (on a ten-point scale) might also be thought of as different *types* of corruption and authority. Collier's analysis, if not his data, supports this interpretation.

23. Also see Onuf's (1989, 272) discussion of Maslow in *World of Our Making*.

24. Onuf seems to have something beyond the recognition of competent status as an agent of a certain type, what I have called *identity*, in mind when he speaks of *standing*. The latter evidently involves acclaim and admiration (or their opposite, contempt) derived from "global" comparison with others (Onuf 1989, 269–270).

References

Adler, Emanuel. 1997. "Seizing the Middle Ground: Constructivism in World Politics." *European Journal of International Relations* 3(3): 319–363.

Anderson, Benedict. 1983. *Imagined Communities: Reflections on the Origins and Spread of Nationalism*. London: Verso.

Beasley, William G. 1987. *Japanese Imperialism, 1894–1945*. Oxford, UK: Clarendon Press.

Boulding, Kenneth E. 1956. *The Image: Knowledge in Life and Society*. Ann Arbor: University of Michigan.

Campbell, David. 1992. *Writing Security: United States Foreign Policy and the Politics of Identity*. Minneapolis: University of Minnesota Press.

————. 1993. *Politics Without Principle: Sovereignty, Ethics, and the Narratives of the Gulf War.* Boulder, CO: Lynne Rienner.

Chafetz, Glenn. 1995. "The Political Psychology of the Nuclear Nonproliferation Regime." *Journal of Politics* 57(3): 743 775.

Checkel, Jeffrey. 1998. "The Constructivist Turn in International Relations Theory." *World Politics* 50(2): 324–348.

Cottam, Richard. 1977. *Foreign Policy Motivation: A General Theory and a Case Study.* Pittsburgh, PA: University of Pittsburgh Press.

Deudney, Daniel. 1996. "Ground Identity: Nature, Place, and Space in Nationalism." In Yosef Lapid and Friedrich Kratochwil, eds., *The Return of Culture and Identity in IR Theory*, pp. 129 145. Boulder, CO: Lynne Rienner.

Deutsch, Karl. 1966. *Nationalism and Social Communication: An Inquiry into the Foundations of Nationality.* Cambridge, MA: MIT Press.

Doyle, Michael. 1983. "Kant, Liberal Legacies, and Foreign Affairs, Parts I and II." *Philosophy and Public Affairs* 12(3 and 4): 205–235, 323–353.

Eden, Lynn. Forthcoming. *Deconstructing Construction.* Ithaca, NY: Cornell University Press.

Finnemore, Martha. 1996. *National Interests in International Society.* Ithaca, NY: Cornell University Press.

Fukuyama, Francis. 1992. *The End of History and the Last Man.* New York: Free Press.

Garnett, Sherman. 1997. "Russia's Illusory Ambitions." *Foreign Affairs* 76(2): 61–76.

Gellner, Ernst. 1983. *Nations and Nationalism.* Ithaca, NY: Cornell University Press.

Goffman, Erving. 1969. *Strategic Interaction.* Philadelphia: University of Pennsylvania Press.

Grieco, Joseph, 1988. "Anarchy and the Limits of Cooperation: A Realist Critique of the Newest Liberal Institutionalism." *International Organization* 42(3): 483–508.

Heider, Fritz. 1958. *The Psychology of Interpersonal Relations.* New York: Wiley.

Heikka, Henrikki. 1999. "Beyond Neorealism and Constructivism: Desire, Identity, and Russian Foreign Policy." In Ted Hopf, ed., *Understandings of Russian Foreign Policy*, pp. 57–107. University Park: Pennsylvania State University Press.

Herman, Robert G. 1996. "Identity, Norms, and National Security: The Soviet Foreign Policy Revolution and the End of the Cold War." In Peter J. Katzenstein, ed., *The Culture of National Security: Norms and Identity in World Politics*, pp. 271–316. New York: Columbia University Press.

Herrmann, Richard K. 1985. *Perceptions and Behavior in Soviet Foreign Policy.* Pittsburgh: University of Pittsburgh Press.

————. 1986. "The Power of Perceptions in Foreign Policy Decision Making: Do Views of the Soviet Union Determine the Policy Choices of American Leaders?" *American Journal of Political Science* 30(4): 841–875.

Hogg, Michael, and Abrams, Dominic. 1988. *Social Identifications: A Social Psychology of Intergroup Relations and Group Processes.* New York: Routledge.

Holsti, Kal J. 1970. "National Role Conceptions in the Study of Foreign Policy." *International Studies Quarterly* 14(3): 233–309.

Hopf, Ted, ed. 1999. *Understandings of Russian Foreign Policy.* University Park: Pennsylvania State University Press.

Howard, Judith, and Callero, Peter, eds. 1991. *The Self-Society Dynamic.* Cambridge, UK: Cambridge University Press.

Inoguchi, Takashi. 1994. *Sekai Hendo no Mikata* [The standpoint of global change]. Tokyo: Chikuma Shobo.

Johnson, James. 1993. "Is Talk Really Cheap? Prompting Conversation Between Critical Theory and Rational Choice." *American Political Science Review* 87(1): 74–86.

Katzenstein, Peter J., Keohane, Robert O., and Krasner, Stephen D. 1998. "International Organization and the Study of World Politics." *International Organization* 52(4): 645–685.

————, eds. 1999. *Exploration and Contestation in the Study of World Politics.* Boston: MIT Press.

Keohane, Robert. 1984. *After Hegemony: Cooperation and Discord in the World Political Economy.* Princeton, NJ: Princeton University Press.

Kier, Elizabeth. 1995. "Culture and Military Doctrine: France between the Wars." *International Security* 19(4): 65–93.

————. 1997. *Imagining War: French and British Military Doctrine Between the Wars.* Princeton, NJ: Princeton University Press.

Klotz, Audie. 1995. *Norms in International Politics: The Struggle Against Apartheid.* Ithaca, NY: Cornell University Press.

Klugman, David. 1997. "Existentialism and Constructivism: A Bipolar Model of Subjectivity." *Clinical Social Work Journal* 25(3): 297–313.

Kowert, Paul. 1997. "Place, Politics, and International Identity." Paper presented at the Annual Meeting of the American Political Science Association, Washington, DC, 29–31 August .

————. 1998. "Agent Versus Structure in the Construction of National Identity." In Kubálková, Onuf, and Kowert, eds., *International Relations in a Constructed World*, pp. 101–122. Armonk, NY: M.E. Sharpe.

————. 1998/1999. "National Identity: Inside and Out." *Security Studies* 8(2/3): 1–34.

————. 2000. "The Role of Culture and Identity in National Economic Crises." *Ritsumeikan Kokusai Chiiki Kenkyû* [Ritsumeikan Journal of International Relations and Area Studies] 16: 53–70.

Kowert, Paul, and Legro, Jeffrey. 1996. "Norms, Identity, and Their Limits: A Theoretical Reprise." In Peter J. Katzenstein, ed., *The Culture of National Security: Norms and Identity in World Politics*, pp. 451–497. New York: Columbia University Press.

Kratochwil, Friedrich. 1989. *Rules, Norms, and Decisions: On the Conditions of Practical and Legal Reasoning in International Relations and Domestic Affairs.* Cambridge, UK: Cambridge University Press.

Lapid, Yosef, and Kratochwil, Friedrich, eds. 1996. *The Return of Culture and Identity in IR Theory.* Boulder, CO: Lynne Rienner.

Legro, Jeffrey W. 1996. "Culture and Preferences in the International Cooperation Two-Step." *American Political Science Review* 90(1): 118–137.

Le Prestre, Philippe G. 1997. *Role Quests in the Post-Cold War Era: Foreign Policies in Transition.* Montreal: McGill-Queen's University Press.

Lustick, Ian S. 2000. "Agent-based Modelling of Collective Identity: Testing Constructivist Theory." *Journal of Artificial Societies and Social Simulation* 3, http://www.soc.surrey.ac.uk/JASSS/3/1/1.html.

Maslow, Abraham H. 1954. *Motivation and Personality.* New York: Harper and Row.

McCall, George, and Simmons, Jerry. 1978. *Identities and Interactions.* New York: Free Press.

Mercer, Jonathan. 1995. "Anarchy and Identity." *International Organization* 49(2): 229–252.

Mertz, Elizabeth. 1994. "A New Social Constructionism for Sociolegal Studies." *Law and Society Review* 28(5): 1243–1265.

Modelski, George; Poznanski, Kazimierz; Farkas, Andrew; Florini, Ann; Hodgson, Geoffrey; and Gilpin, Robert. 1996. "Special Issue: Evolutionary Paradigms in the Social Sciences." *International Studies Quarterly* 40(3): 315–431.

Nairn, Tom. 1977. *The Break-up of Britain: Crisis and Neonationalism.* London: Verso.

Nash, Roderick. 1982. *Wilderness and the American Mind.* New Haven, CT: Yale University Press.

Onuf, Nicholas G. 1989. *World of Our Making: Rules and Rule in Social Theory and International Relations.* Columbia: University of South Carolina Press.

Pettman, Ralph. 2000. *Commonsense Constructivism, or the Making of World Affairs.* Armonk, NY: M.E. Sharpe.

Posen, Barry. 1993. "Nationalism, the Mass Army, and Military Power." *International Security* 18(2): 80–124.

Ringmar, Erik. 1996. *Identity, Interest, and Action: A Cultural Explanation of Sweden's Intervention in the Thirty Years War.* Cambridge, UK: Cambridge University Press.

Risse, Thomas, Ropp, Stephen C., and Sikkink, Kathryn, eds. 1999. *The Power of Human Rights: International Norms and Domestic Change.* New York: Cambridge University Press.

Risse-Kappen, Thomas. 1994. "Ideas Do Not Float Freely: Transnational Coalitions, Domestic Structures, and the End of the Cold War." *International Organization* 48(2): 185–214.

———. 1995a. *Cooperation Among Democracies: The European Influence on U.S. Foreign Policy.* Princeton, NJ: Princeton University Press.

———. 1995b. *Bringing Transnational Relations Back In: Non-state Actors, Domestic Structures, and International Institutions.* Cambridge, UK: Cambridge University Press.

Rubenstein, Diane. 1989. "Hate Boat, National Identity, and Nuclear Criticism." In James Der Derian and Michael Shapiro, eds., *International/Intertextual Relations: Postmodern Readings of World Politics,* pp. 231–255. Lexington, MA: Lexington Books.

Sayer, Andrew. 1997. "Essentialism, Social Constructivism, and Beyond." *The Sociological Review* 45(3): 453–487.

Schimmelfennig, Frank. 1998/1999. "NATO Enlargement: A Constructivist Explanation." *Security Studies* 8(2/3): 198–234.

Searle, John R. 1969. *Speech Acts: An Essay in the Philosophy of Language.* Cambridge, UK: Cambridge University Press.

Spruyt, Hendrik. 1994. *The Sovereign State and Its Competitors.* Princeton, NJ: Princeton University Press.

Stryker, Sheldon. 1980. *Symbolic Interactionism: A Social Structural Version.* Menlo Park, CA: Benjamin/Cummings.

Stryker, Sheldon. 1987. "Identity Theory: Developments and Extensions." In Krysia Yardley and Terry Honess, eds., *Self and Identity: Psychosocial Perspectives,* pp. 89–103. New York: Wiley.

Sylvester, Christine. 1994. *Feminist Theory and International Relations in a Postmodern Era.* Cambridge, UK: Cambridge University Press.

Tajfel, Henri. 1981. *Human Groups and Social Categories: Studies in Social Psychology.* Cambridge, UK: Cambridge University Press.

Tilley, Virginia. 1997. "The Terms of the Debate: Untangling Language About Ethnicity and Ethnic Movements." *Ethnic and Racial Studies* 20(3): 497–522.

Tilly, Charles. 1975. *The Formation of National States in Western Europe.* Princeton, NJ: Princeton University Press.

Toby, Ronald P. 1985. "Contesting the Centre: International Sources of Japanese Identity." *International History Review* 7(3): 347–363.

Todorov, Tzvetan. 1984. *The Conquest of America: the Question of the Other.* Richard Howard, trans. New York: Harper and Row.

Turner, Frederick Jackson. 1920. *The Frontier in American History.* New York: Holt.

Turner, John. 1982. "Toward a Cognitive Redefinition of the Social Group." In Henri

Tajfel, ed., *Social Identity and Intergroup Relations*, pp. 15–40. Cambridge, UK: Cambridge University Press.

Walker, R.B.J. 1993. *Inside/Outside: International Relations as Political Theory.* Cambridge. UK: Cambridge University Press.

Walker, Stephen. 1992. "Symbolic Interactionism and International Politics: Role Theory's Contribution to International Organization." In Martha Cottam and Chih-yu Shih, eds., *Contending Dramas: A Cognitive Approach to Post-War International Organizational Processes*, pp. 19–38. New York: Praeger.

———, ed. 1987. *Role Theory and Foreign Policy Analysis.* Durham, NC: Duke University Press.

Walt, Stephen M. 1991. "The Renaissance of Security Studies." *International Studies Quarterly* 35(2) 211–239.

———. 1998. "International Relations: One World, Many Theories." *Foreign Policy* 110: 29–32.

Wendt, Alexander. 1992. "Anarchy Is What States Make of It: The Social Construction of Power Politics." *International Organization* 46(2): 391–425.

———. 1994. "Collective Identity Formation and the International State." *American Political Science Review* 88(2): 384–396.

———. 1999. *Social Theory of International Politics.* Cambridge, UK: Cambridge University Press.

Worchel, Stephen, and Austin, William G., eds. 1986. *Psychology of Intergroup Relations.* Chicago: Nelson-Hall.

Yee, Albert S. 1997. "Thick Rationality and the Missing 'Brute Fact': The Limits of Rationalist Incorporations of Norms and Ideas." *Journal of Politics* 59(4): 1001–1039.

About the Editor and Contributors

Vendulka Kubálková is professor of International Studies and interim chair of the Department of International and Comparative Studies, University of Miami. Her books include: (with A.A. Cruickshank) *Marxism-Leninism and Theory of International Relations*, (1980), *International Inequality* (1981), *Marxism and International Relations* (1985, 1989), *Thinking New About Soviet "New Thinking,"* (1989); (co-edited with N. G. Onuf, and P. Kowert), *International Relations in a Constructed World* (Armonk, New York: M.E. Sharpe, 1998). She is working on a book on religions in International Relations entitled *International Political Theology*.

* * *

Michael W. Collier is research director at the Latin American and Caribbean Center at Florida International University. He received his PhD in International Relations from Florida International University. A retired U.S. Coast Guard Officer, he also holds an M.S. in Strategic Intelligence from the Joint Military Intelligence College. His chapter in this book is based on a paper for which he was the co-winner of the 1999 Alexander George Award for best graduate paper in the Foreign Policy Analysis Section, International Studies Association Conference, February 1999.

Paul Kowert is assistant professor of International Relations at Florida International University in Miami, Florida. He is co-editor (with Vendulka Kubálková and Nicholas Onuf) of *International Relations in a Constructed World*, and author of *Groupthink or Deadlock: When Do Leaders Learn from Advisors?* as well as other studies of the foreign policymaking process and the policy consequences of national identity.

Nizar Messari earned his Ph. D. at the University of Miami. He worked as assistant professor in the School of Humanities and Social Sciences in Al Akhawayn University in Ifrane, Morocco, before taking up his current post as assistant professor at Pontificia Universidade Catolica in Rio de Janeiro, Brazil. He has been working and publishing on foreign policy and international security issues over the last two years.

Nicholas Onuf is professor of International Relations at Florida International University. He taught for many years in Washington, DC, before coming to Miami in 1994. His scholarship brings social theory and conceptual history to bear on the study of international relations. He is the author of *World of Our Making* (1989), (with Peter Onuf*) Federal Union, Modern World* (1993), and *The Republican Legacy in International Thought* (1998). He is currently working on two book projects: *Ruling Fictions* and (with James Lewis and Peter Onuf) *Modern World, Federal Union.* With Vendulka Kubalkova, he is convener of the Miami International Relations Group.

Ralph Pettman has been the foundation professor of International Relations at the Victoria University of Wellington since 1994. Before that he was professor of International Relations at Seinan Gakuin University in Fukuoka, Japan. His previous posts include senior appointments at the University of Sydney, the Australian International Development Assistance Bureau, the Australian Human Rights Commission, Princeton University, and the Australian National University. For his work in human rights teaching, he received a UNESCO award. He was also elected an international member of the Governing Council of the International Studies Association. His publications include: *Human Behaviour and World Politics: A Transdisciplinary Introduction* (1975), *Small Power Politics and International Relations in Southeast Asia* (1976), *State and Class: A Sociology of International Affairs* (1976), *Moral Claims in World Affairs* (1979), *Biopolitics and International Values* (1981), *Understanding International Political Economy, with Readings for the Fatigued* (1996), *International Politics: Balance of Power, Balance of Productivity, Balance of Ideologies* (1991), *Commonsense Constructivism, or the Making of World Affairs* (Armonk, New York: M.E. Sharpe, 2000), and *World Politics: Rationalism and Beyond* (2001).

Gonzalo Porcel Quero received an M.A. in International Studies from the University of Miami, where he is currently completing his Ph.D. dissertation entitled "Culture, Identity and History in a Constructed World." He is also the Spanish translator of the book *International Relations in a Constructed*

World [Los relaciones internacionales en un mundo construido] (eds. V. Kubálková, N. Onuf, and P. Kowert. Armonk, NY: M.E. Sharpe, 1998) and the author of several recent publications about the institutions of the European Union.

Steve Smith is pro-vice chancellor and professor of International Politics at the University of Wales, Aberystwyth, UK. He has previously taught at the State University of New York and the University of East Anglia. He is the editor of the Cambridge University Press series, "Studies in International Relations." He has been vice president of the International Studies Association. He is the author/editor of 13 books, including (with Martin Hollis) *Explaining and Understanding International Relations* (1990), (edited with Ken Booth) *International Relations Theory Today* (1995), (edited with Ken Booth and Marysia Zalewski) *International Theory: Positivism and Beyond* (1996), and (edited with John Baylis) *The Globalization of World Politics* (1997, 2001). He is also the author of over 80 papers.

Shiping Zheng is associate professor in the Department of Political Science at the University of Vermont. He has B.A. and M.A. from Fudan University, Shanghai, China, and M.A. and Ph.D. from Yale University. He is the author of *Party vs. State in Post-1949 China: The Institutional Dilemma* (1997). Currently, he is working on a book examining the fundamental interests and controversial issues in U.S.-China relations.

Index

abduction, 68
absolute gain, 32, 42
Acharya, Amitav, 204, 205
action, 38, 66, 79
  social, 22
action-structure, 61–62
actor, 18, 27, 38
Adler, Emmanuel, 9, 10, 40, 41, 43, 45, 256,
  . 257, 266
administration, 69
administrative regimes, 69
Afghanistan, 111, 117
agency, 22, 54, 66
  theory of, 281
agent, 8, 9, 19, 21, 27, 29, 52, 53, 54, 65,
  66, 77, 92, 135, 207, 210, 215, 219,
  224, 225, 262, 275, 279
  defined, 22
agent and structure, 19, 20, 21, 56
  mutually enabling, reproducing, 21
agent-structure problem/debate, 21, 22
  and levels of analysis, 56
agreement, 7, 83–89, 93, 262
Alker, H., and Biersteker, T., 108
alliances, 32
Allison, Graham, 30
Almond and Verba, 177
altercasting, 21
alterity, 231–33, 237, 242–44
anarchy, 8, 26, 34, 65, 84, 229–30
Andropov, Yuri, 113
Anthropology, 261
anticorruption programs, 174–75, 185–86,
  188, 197–200
antifoundationalist, 103
antipositivist, 102
approaches to the FPA, 18
Armero, José Mario, 149
arms control, 203
Ashley, R., 229, 235, 245
assertion, 82–83, 86, 88–90
  conditional, 83, 66

assertive/assertive speech act, 66, 67–69,
  82, 86, 89, 155, 156, 157
Austin, J.L., 64
autarky, 158

balance of interests, 129, 140
balance of power, 123, 126, 129, 140, 204,
  205
Baldwin, D., 32
Banks, Michael, 108
Beasley, William G., 276
behavior, 18, 22, 26
  as a dependent variable, 22
behavioral
  level, 5, 6
  revolution, 17, 106, 112
  sciences, 18, 27
behavioralism, 18, 27, 106
belief, 70
  belief system, 28, 38
Barthes, Roland, 150
Berger and Luckmann, 39
Bergmann, Gustav, 63
Berner and Dahm, 112, 130, 137
Bhaskar, Roy, 40
Bialer, Seweryn, 130
Big China, 209, 210, 212, 213
billiard balls, 26, 28, 32
binaries of Western thought, 20, 21
binarism, 20
binary comparison, 68
bipolar structure, 110, 136
bluffs, 79, 80, 82, 83, 88, 90
Bohr, Niels, 128
Bolsheviks, 134, 138
Bosnia, 235, 237, 242–44
Boulding, Kenneth, 269
Brandt, Willy, 128, 137
Breton Woods institutions, 153
Brezhnev Doctrine, 115, 124, 127, 131,
  140
Brezhnev, Leonid, 113, 128, 140

293